9412/P

D1346249

THE MECHANISMS OF PERCEPTION

THE MECHANISMS
OF PERCEPTION

JEAN PIAGET

Translated by

G. N. Seagrim

LONDON

ROUTLEDGE & KEGAN PAUL

First published in Great Britain 1969
by Routledge & Kegan Paul Ltd
Broadway House, 68–74 Carter Lane
London, E.C.4
Printed in Great Britain
by Richard Clay (The Chaucer Press) Ltd
Bungay, Suffolk
Translated from the French
"Les Mécanismes Perceptifs"
© Presses Universitaires de Gravee 1961
Translation by Gavin Seagrim
© Routledge & Kegan Paul 1969
SBN 7100 64640

CONTENTS

Contents

PART THREE: STRUCTURES OF PERCEPTION
AND OF INTELLIGENCE

AUTHOR'S PREFACE

Translations are generally less good than the original texts: they usually are less clear, less live and sometimes even contain errors. Experience has shown that the translation is always less well understood than the original and that it sometimes gives rise to misinterpretations which then persist. In addition, some distinctions, which appear to the author to be clear in his own tongue, are difficult to render in the second language: for example, the distinction between the terms 'schème' and 'schéma'. In our usage, these terms correspond to quite distinct realities, the one operative (a scheme of action in the sense of instrument of generalisation) and the other figurative (a figural or topographical schema).

However, the present translation of *Mecanismes Perceptifs*, made by my friend Professor Seagrim, seems to me to represent an outstanding exception to the above generalisation: not only is it as live as the original but even improves on a number of points which were somewhat obscure even in French. The translator has completely re-thought the book and has done so as if he were presenting the data and the theory anew. I cannot thank him too much because we have here a very rare example of intellectual decentration which speaks of exceptional qualities and of a most unusual application of what Finnbogason called 'sympathetic intelligence'.

It is most encouraging for me to see this essay appear in English and for it to be submitted to the critical examination of the numerous Anglo-Saxon specialists in perception (of whom Seagrim is himself an excellent representative). I would like to preface the text which you are about to read with the remark that I continue, after many years, to believe in the hypothesis of 'encounters' and of 'couplings'. Fresh studies have been carried out since I wrote this work, in particular one entitled: 'Contribution à l'étude des dévaluations et sous-estimations d'excitants visuels en présentation tachistoscopique brève', by Rémy Droz.[1] Droz, using presentations of as short duration as 1, 2, 3, 4, 8 and 15 ms (and then of 30, 60, 120 ms, etc.), demonstrated that a loss of information occurs at very short exposures, a loss which is distinct from the genuine deformations found at more normal durations of stimulus presentation. One cannot speak of elementary error I (see p. 87) at very brief exposures because, even at these exposures, impressions of absolute size cannot be attained. Nor can the obtained results be attributed to elementary

[1] Droz, R. *Arch. Psychol.*, 40, *Nos.* 159–60, in press.

error *II*, as usually understood, because the errors now obtained are far greater than those usually obtained with optico-geometric illusions. One is forced, therefore, to adopt a composite explanation, one which necessarily incorporates the hypothesis of a density of 'encounters' which, by its very weakness at these brief exposures, establishes the involvement of these primary factors.

TRANSLATOR'S PREFACE

Some terms and phrases used in this book are intended to have special and restricted meanings. Some of these terms, and other less obvious ones, could have been translated in several ways; to assist the reader, the more important are here listed, the English translation being given second:

Cadre: frame of reference
Couplage: coupling
Couplage de différence: difference coupling
Couplage de ressemblance: equivalence coupling
Effet de champ: field effect
Filiation: filiation
Erreur médiane nulle: median zero illusion
Mise en référence: referral
Rencontre: encounter
Transport: transport or transportation.

'Centration' and 'fixation', which are sometimes interchangeable, have always been translated literally, as have 'grandeur apparente' and 'grandeur projective' (see Chapter 4, 3): the terms appear to be interchangeable. 'Seuil d'égalité' (Chapter 2, 5) has been translated as 'threshold for equality': it clearly refers to the 'just-not-noticeable-difference' of English texts on psycho-physics. Contrary to previous practice, 'scheme' has been translated as 'scheme' and not as 'schema': this is in keeping with a distinction which the author wishes to emphasise.

As the author states in his preface, most of the experiments referred to have been published in a series of *Recherches sur le Développement des Perceptions*, in the *Archives de Psychologie*. These *Recherches* have been numbered serially and are referred to in the text by those numbers, Arabic numerals being substituted for the original Roman numerals. A list of these publications has been included at the end of the translation.

A few of the tables and figures have been rearranged, simplified or expanded as seemed appropriate to the translator: this has been done with the author's approval, but in cases of doubt the French edition should be consulted. The original *Recherches* should be consulted for further details.

The Indices were prepared by M. Pierre Dasen. The translator wishes to acknowledge with thanks the assistance he received from many colleagues at Geneva in 1966–7. In particular he wishes to thank Professor Vinh-Bang and Dr. Rémy Droz for assistance over several years, and Dr. Hermine Sinclair and Professor H. Furth for critical reading of parts of the translation. He also wishes to thank Miss Beverley Pankhurst for much assistance in proof reading.

FOREWORD

This work represents an attempt to synthesise studies on the development of perception which I started twenty or so years ago, when the Faculté des Sciences de Genève appointed me to the Chair of Experimental Psychology and Director of the Psychological Laboratory.

Most of the studies to be reported have already appeared in the *Archives de Psychologie* under the general title of *Recherches sur le Développement des Perceptions* (the most recent of which, at the time of writing, is No. 38). There are, however, more than fifteen studies which have not been published and which we shall deal with in the following pages: they are to be published in due course in the *Archives*.

The need for a synthesis made itself felt primarily for practical reasons: it is forbidding to face forty or fifty separate articles, spread throughout a Review, contributed by different authors and presenting a quantity of not always homogeneous detail. A general survey of the results would facilitate their discussion. In providing this we will, of course, concern ourselves only with major issues, relegating matters of detail concerning techniques and statistical tables to the original publications.

However, this synthesis serves a theoretical purpose above all, because the *Recherches* in question were arranged in the interests of a certain point of view of perception as a whole, which I now want to organise, generally to highlight, and to some extent to develop (parts of Chapters VI to VIII in particular, concerning the relations between perception and intelligence, are new).[1]

In concluding this undertaking, my overwhelming feeling is one of gratitude to all those who collaborated in the *Recherches*. It goes without saying that such a varied topic as the development of perception must involve a collective effort. First, I have found an associate of the first order in Marc Lambercier, as much for his exceptional skill as an experimenter as for his knowledge and ever wakeful spirit of criticism. May he find in this work an expression of my profound and warm gratitude. Among my other associates, who should all be thanked individually, I would like to reserve for special mention Albert Morf (who co-operated in several *Recherches*), Vinh-Bang (who devoted his efforts, among other tasks, to the exhausting,

---

[1] In this connection, the reader who is more interested in general ideas than in the detail of experimental findings will no doubt be well advised to start with Part Three. He could then turn to Parts One and Two for the facts which support the theses advanced.

xiii

but extremely fruitful, analysis of eye-movements, and to whom I am also obliged for the illustrations contained in this work), Benjamin Matalon and Suzanne Taponier. I also wish to thank Pierre Greco most warmly for having read a part of the text and for helping me to correct the proofs.

I also owe a debt of gratitude to the Ford Foundation which was willing to support, over a period of years, our studies into the relations between perception and intelligence. There is no doubt that this volume could never have been achieved without that generous assistance. In this connection, the opportunity must be taken also to thank the Rockefeller Foundation which, in making it possible for us to found Le Centre International d'Epistémologie Génétique, also made several particular investigations into perceptual knowledge possible. Finally, it must not be forgotten that the first draft of this work was written at the Institute for Advanced Studies, Princeton, thanks to the breadth of outlook of its Director, Robert Oppenheimer, who is not afraid to associate psychologists with the work of his Division of Mathematical Sciences.

INTRODUCTION

Perception can be studied in many ways, the best established of which is the psycho-physiological. However, studies which we have undertaken in the past, and which we now continue and interpret in the present work, represent an attempt to resolve two general problems to which most specialists in perception (with a few notable exceptions, among them Michotte) have paid little attention.

I. The first of these problems is that of the relation between perception and intelligence. It was brought to our notice in a particularly urgent manner when we were studying the structures of the pre-operational thought of the young child, structures which are obviously more closely related to perceptual configurations than are later appearing operational structures. Two subsidiary problems of importance are involved. The first is whether notions, as is usually supposed, are abstracted from perception or if they merely make use of the products of perception, incorporating them into more complex systems which then correct and complete them with non-perceptual contributions. The second is to establish the analogies and differences which exist between the functioning of perception and that of intelligence, and between the various resulting structures.

The second general problem whose study has always interested us (and it is only an extension of the first), is that of the epistemological status of perception compared with that of other forms of knowledge. Does perception provide a richer, a more adequate or a more 'authentic'[1] source of information about physical objects and events than do more mediate or indirect modes of approach? If it is found that 'objectivity' is a relatively late product, attributable to the constructions of intelligence, the problem will be to understand why perception does not lead unequivocally to the true nature of objects, and to discover the subjective factors of transposition and deformation that obstruct this apparently direct reading of the properties of the external environment.

II. We have, as is our custom, applied the genetic method to the solution of these problems, applying it to perceptual mechanisms this time. A number of classical test-figures (optico-geometric illusions, etc.) and others of more recent origin, some invented by us, were first examined in the light of the evolution with age of responses to them. The approach is not, of course, a new one, and Binet (who

[1] 'Authentic' in the sense of being closer to the sources.

tackled the most diverse topics with an indefatigable curiosity) had already made a distinction between illusions which diminish quantitatively as a function of development and those which increase with age. But developmental studies, apart from the information they provide on the psychology of children and on the comparison between children and adults, appeared to us to have a special importance for the problems just enumerated.

In the realm of perception, as in that of notions and intellectual operations, the genetic method offers the incomparable advantage of providing us with at least some information about the way in which the mechanisms in question are constructed. For example, when a response appears for the first time at a given age (which is rare in perception but frequent in the case of operations), or increases in importance with age, it is generally possible to determine the factors (or some of them) which underlie this appearance or development. Similarly, when a response diminishes in importance with age (for example, the quantitative diminution of those illusions which we call 'primary'), it must be because an antagonistic factor is developing: understanding this factor would probably help us to understand the nature of the illusory factors whose influence is being reduced. But when a response remains substantially the same at all ages (as in the case of some stereoscopic effects), some innate physiological mechanism is probably involved, at least to some extent. In brief, it is already clear that the comparative examination of different forms of development can lead to a first approximate explanation.

III. But the genetic method is richer and more varied than this simple comparison of developmental trends would indicate. In the first place, the effects of learning can be compared with those of development. The interest of doing this lies in the fact that learning is an acquisition which occurs over time and thus, itself, constitutes a form of development. For example, there may be a broad correspondence between illusions which increase or decrease with age and those which increase or decrease with repeated presentations. Another equally important reason for combining studies of development with those of learning, is that learning itself changes with age and thus constitutes one of the characteristics, or even perhaps one of the factors, of development. For example, in some cases, the diminution of primary illusions with practice (which may even proceed to the total elimination of illusion in adults) does not begin before about the age of 7 years.

A second variable, which at first seems to bear no relation at all to development, is the duration of the exposure of the stimulus figure. We have observed, for example, that some illusions pass through a maximum at certain very short tachistoscopic exposures (when centration is restricted to a certain part of the display). This 'temporal maximum' can be studied in many perceptual situations and, with the effects of repetition, represent a true form of genesis in that the illusion involved increases and then decreases as a function of a temporal factor.

Finally, although the optimum exposure time for a given figure (its temporal maximum) varies with age, it may also vary quantitatively in respect of its extent, or even qualitatively in respect of its direction, again as a function of age: it may be a *positive* maximum at one age and a *negative* maximum at another, which suggests that the subject may pay attention to different parts of the figure at different ages.

To be complete, therefore, the genetic method, as applied to perception, must compare the effects of exposure time, of repetition and of age.

IV. Used in the three ways just described, the genetic method may be expected to yield a three-fold return. The first concerns the classification of different perceptual effects; the second relates to contingent explanations which we shall try to find; and the third relates to the two general problems set out at the beginning of this Introduction (under I).

V. Binet classed those optico-geometric illusions which increase with age as 'innate' and those which decrease with age as 'acquired'. We prefer the term 'primary' to 'innate' because responses to these illusions may depend more on factors of equilibrium and of disequilibrium than on heredity as properly understood. We also prefer the term 'secondary' to 'acquired' because increases in illusion with age probably depend on perceptual activities which will differ with the subject's level and which are not productive of illusion. It will also be necessary to distinguish between those illusions which increase continuously with age, or which exhibit a final levelling off, and those which increase up to a certain age and then diminish slightly (which will call for a special explanation). These two or three classes of illusion[1] will, of course, have to be related to other perceptual responses

---

[1] Exhaustively, one could distinguish five possibilities: (1) no evolution with age; (2) effects diminishing continuously to an average level; (3) effects diminishing up to a certain age and then increasing; (4) effects increasing to an average level; (5) effects increasing to a certain age and then decreasing. The three varieties distinguished under V correspond to possibilities (2), (4) and (5). But (1), in the rare cases in which it is observed, corresponds to two quite distinct possibilities: (*a*) responses due to a seemingly inherited physiological structure (for example, stereoscopic estimates depending on convergence and disparity); (*b*) responses (for example, to an optico-geometric illusion) which exhibit average errors which remain relatively constant with age. But (*b*) is only a limited form of (2) because

(and their courses of development), responses which may have to do with other forms of perception (the constancies, etc.) and which may correct rather than produce illusory effects.

VI. The primary optico-geometric illusions have forms of distribution which do not change qualitatively with age. We shall demonstrate this by varying the physical proportions of various classical figures and examining the forms which the distributions of error take at different ages.

For example, to study the Delbœuf illusion (Chapter I, § 11), one chooses two concentric circles, the inner of which (A, invariant) is compared with a third isolated circle (variable) as a function of variations in the diameter of the outer circle (B). If A' is the distance between the circumferences of A and B, the measurements are made over a wide range extending from $A' = A : n$, through $A' = A$, to $A' = nA$. The errors are plotted as a function of the relation of A to A'. Having obtained this distribution for adults, the experiment is repeated at the different ages at which it is possible: from 5 or 6 up to 11 or 12 years.[1] Then, reciprocally, B is held constant and is measured against an isolated circle while A is varied through the same range of relations of $A' > A$, $A' = A$ and $A' < A$. This experiment also is repeated with subjects of different ages and, not unexpectedly, gives quite different results from the first experiment.

Similarly, the over-estimation of the longer side of a rectangle may be studied as a function of variations in the length of the shorter side; or, again, the under-estimation of the long diagonal of a lozenge may be studied when it and the length of the sides of the figure are held constant and the angles are varied, and so on.

With such results to hand, it has been quite easy to demonstrate that the primary illusions exhibit the two characteristics mentioned above: their qualitative forms do not change with age but their quantitative values do.

if subjects are submitted to an experimental repetition (learning or practice) the error diminishes more in adults than in young children. (3) has not been observed in a general form, but certain limited facts which approximate to it have been observed: in the Delbœuf illusion, with some absolute sizes of the inner circle held constant, or with measures taken on an outer circle of constant size, the illusion is found to diminish from 5 to 10–12 years of age and to increase slightly in adults. But in such cases (not general for the different configurations used), it is always possible to question the adequacy of the 'adult' sample (students of psychology are usually employed, whose professional attitudes complicate their responses), or to suggest that certain secondary factors intervened, such as that comparisons at a distance are easier for adults (in the case of larger figures), etc. By this last suggestion, the effects of type (3) would be due to (2) up to a certain age, and to (4) at greater ages.

[1] The absolute (overall) dimensions of the figure could also be varied, but this factor is of less importance and is relative only to the quantitative value of the illusion.

(1) The distribution of errors has the same form at all ages at which experimentation is possible. As a rule the curve exhibits a maximum, which we will call 'spatial' (to distinguish it from the temporal maximum which was discussed under III), which corresponds to certain specific proportions of the figure (for example, $A = 6A'$ or $A = 3B : 4$ in the Delbœuf illusion, measured on A). This maximum is positive in cases of over-estimation. Equally, as a rule, there is a negative spatial maximum when an under-estimation occurs with certain proportions (which is the case with the Delbœuf figure when $A' > A$, the negative maximum being found at about $A' = 1\cdot7A$). Finally, there is also, for certain proportions, a point of zero illusion which marks the passage from over- to under-estimations (for example, for $A' = A$ in the same example). The unchanging nature of the qualitative distribution of errors is established by the fact that at all ages, on the average, the positive spatial maximum, the negative maximum and the point of zero illusion occur respectively for the same objective proportions of the figure.

(2) In contrast to this, the quantitative values of primary illusions vary with age: while corresponding to the same objective proportions of the figure, the value of the positive maximum diminishes more or less regularly with age, being appreciably greater at 5 to 6 years than at adulthood.

In other words, the errors have the same form of distribution but vary metrically with age.

Clearly, two distinct problems are thus posed in regard to the explanation of perceptual processes:

(*a*) The first is to account for the law of the constant form of distribution for a given figure, that is to say, to understand why the positive and negative maxima and the point of zero illusion always occur for given objective proportions of the figure. It will be even more important, of course, to find a common law for all the primary illusions, one which will predict the positions of the maxima for any given simple figure; and, within the realms of possibility, to discover the rationale of such a law.

(*b*) The second problem is to understand why qualitatively identical errors vary quantitatively and why primary errors diminish with age. This, of course, will entail the comparison of developmental curves with those of learning (by repetition) and with those of the duration of the tachistoscopic presentation of the figures (at all ages in both cases).

VII. Secondary illusions raise analogous problems, but in somewhat modified terms. In the first place they are not always qualitatively constant at different ages. For example, the over-estimation of the upper of two verticals, presented one directly above the other, common enough in adults, does not hold for children for certain intervals between the lines; similarly, while adults over-estimate the vertical element in right-angle figures, even with fixation on the horizontal, children of 5 to 7 years do not. In the second place, the increase of secondary illusions with age does not derive from a single mechanism but from multiple perceptual activities which are not themselves productive of illusion or of deformation: they only become so in relation to certain given situations in which primary factors also come into play.[1] The problem will be to account for the various mechanisms of these perceptual activities.

Finally, it will be found that these perceptual activities give rise to several clear-cut phenomena, such as the constancies, the perception of causality, most forms of the perception of velocity, etc. These are usually accompanied by systematic errors, and all share common mechanisms and a tendency to evolve with age. This will raise the general problem of the structure and function of perceptual activities in relation to the structure and function of other sensory-motor activities and, finally, to adaptations which derive from intelligence.

VIII. Having thus identified the specifically perceptual problems to be studied, we must now specify the types of explanation which we shall use for their solution, and, ultimately, for the discussion of the general problem of the relation between perception and intelligence (see I above).

In choosing our methods of interpretation we must bear in mind the uncomfortable position occupied by the psychology of perception in relation to the strictly psycho-physiological approach: for adherents to this approach, the psychology of perception is, on the whole, merely a 'phenomenology' (etymologically, not philosophically speaking) and by its nature not explanatory. The psychology of perception is also at a disadvantage in comparison with the psychology of intelligence which has a greater freedom of choice in its methods of analysis, because of the nature of its subject matter.

As it is true that perceptual mechanisms have their roots in the physiology of the nervous system, and that their higher manifestations, in so far as several levels of perceptual activity can be distinguished, merge into the elementary adaptations of intelligence, our

---

[1] For example, two unequal elements, $A < B$, will elicit a contrast effect (primary factor) if close together. If farther apart, they will produce no effect unless a perceptual act of 'transportation' results in their being brought into relation with one another. In this case, the act of transportation, not in itself deforming, will elicit the primary effect of contrast which could not otherwise occur.

task is to find an explanatory method which will satisfy both neurologists and those psychologists who study the processes of intelligence; or, if one prefers to be realistic rather than ingenuous, an explanatory method which will not be incompatible with the data of physiology (which are known to change with such rapidity) or with formulations of the operational structures of mathematical and logical thought.

Only the use of purely *relational* language and concepts for the analysis of perceptual phenomena can achieve this: in other words, no appeal must be made to entities, faculties or factors beyond the relations themselves and their inter-connections. If this is done, the relations as such will hold good, whatever physiological model may be applied to the perceptual phenomena in question, whereas a psychological entity is always in danger of being overthrown by the discovery of a correct neurological explanation.

The language of relations is easy to apply to all perceptual structures, both in regard to their adaptive aspects (the acquisition of adequate information) and to their deformative aspects (illusion or systematic error).

For example, in comparing a line, A, with another longer line, B, a subject may perceive an inequality $A < B$, which is a relation conveying an adequate piece of information. But he will at the same time over-estimate B and under-estimate A, which we will express as: $A(B) < A$, meaning: 'A appears to be shorter when compared with B than when judged in isolation', or as $B(A) > B$, meaning: 'B compared with A appears to be longer than B in isolation'. These are also relations, but expressed in their deformative aspect. The specific characteristic of most perceptual relations is, in effect, to modify (to 'deform') their own terms. This contrasts with logical relations in which one would have: $A(B) = A$: 'A compared with B remains identical with A in isolation'. The comparison itself, expressed in the parenthesis (B), does not imply an entity, because its mechanism can be translated into pure relations: it can result from an immediate interaction between the elements A and B within the field of vision provided by a single centration, or because of a 'transportation' of one on to the other, which implies that a displacement has occurred between two centrations. But neither the centration nor the transportation, are entities because they are reducible to complexes of relations: centration corresponds to a space whose different regions can dilate or contract in some probabilistic manner yet to be established, and transportation consists in the establishment of relations at a distance in association with centrations.

In short, one can construct a system of notions, definable in the language of pure relations, which will adequately describe and explain perceptual phenomena. These relations will be metric whenever possible and will thus directly co-ordinate the measurements made during the experiments. In other cases they will be spatial, in the sense of topological, or probabilistic. When the phenomena cannot be expressed mathematically at first, use will be made of logical symbols, but without implying, *ipso facto*, that logical factors intervene in perceptual mechanisms: such symbols will only represent mathematical expressions which have not yet been quantified metrically.

A relational method of this sort cannot be objected to on physiological grounds. Nevertheless, the objection will undoubtedly be made that it explains nothing, being purely descriptive. We believe, on the contrary, that it is perfectly capable of fulfilling the two functions of all scientific method: (1) to establish laws (= description); and (2) to deduce them, in so far as they can be deduced, and thus to confer on them a certain degree of necessity (= explanation). In the most advanced experimental science, namely physics, explanation consists, essentially, only in the deduction of laws, not simply by the insertion of particular laws into the more general (which explains nothing), but by constructions based on spatial or probabilistic structures which carry their own logico-mathematical necessity (for example, structures of groups, lattices, etc.).

So, on an infinitely more modest scale, the use of the relational method in the study of perception can lead to the correct formulation of the laws governing the phenomena, and also to the setting up of models capable of imposing a hypothetico-deductive necessity on some of those laws, which really amounts to explaining them. For example, one is on the way to discovering such an explanation when attempting to deduce Weber's law from a probabilistic model: that this law is found in many instances of physiological excitation[1] does not by itself constitute an explanation, but reducing it to a model of the probability of 'encounters' (see Chapter II) is already explanatory.

But even where it becomes explanatory, the relational method should not necessarily conflict with physiological findings. If the psychology of perception does give rise to a system of well-formulated laws, and to a system of explanations based on purely geometric or probabilistic models, there is no obvious reason why a neuro-physiological, and therefore properly causal, analysis should invalidate them if they are adequate: if the models are correct, they will inte-

---

[1] And even in physics, for example during the exposure of a photographic plate in which it results from a correspondence between the arithmetical progression of exposures and the geometrical progression of the probability that the photons projected on to the plate will encounter the particles of silver nitrate of which it is composed.

grate perfectly with the new perspective. For example, if over-estimations of the kind $B(A) > B$ are due to a probabilistic mechanism, this mechanism will not be contradicted by an understanding of the role played by the retina (for instance, by the retinal induction of Motokawa), or by some other source of action. Organismically inclined authors, it is true, regard abstract models as purely intellectual creations of no value, in contrast to thoroughly concrete, and therefore material and materialistically causal, explanations. But they overlook the role of logico-mathematical deductions in physics, and forget, above all, that neuro-physiology is 'concrete' because it is still in its infancy: as it becomes more exact, it will take on a physicomathematical and therefore an increasingly abstract form. When this happens, the geometric or probabilistic models which a sound psychology of perception may have been able to develop will perhaps stand neuro-physiology in good stead as a deductive instrument! Far from being anti-physiological, the relational method constitutes the best preparation for a complete physiology whose elaboration has scarcely begun.

It must be understood that the real difference between a healthy psychology and neuro-physiology does not lie in the presence of mentalistic entities in the one and their rejection by the other: it exists, in our opinion, solely in the fact that neuro-physiology is exclusively *causal* while psychology is based on *implication*. The reason is that the data of neuro-physiology are concerned with physico-chemical states which can be given purely causal explanations, while states of consciousness and mental behaviour cannot be given causal explanations, but constitute only systems of significations or of significant actions which are inter-related by 'implications' in the broad sense of the term. A healthy psychology consists, in this case, in the replacement of the imprecise and incomplete implications of consciousness by logico-mathematical implications which constitute a coherent body of knowledge and which are adequate representations of experience. But there need be no conflict between physico-chemical causality and psychological implication any more than between physical or material experience and the logico-mathematical deductions used to explain it: there is an isomorphism between causality and implication (which is the source of psycho-physiological parallelism), and the future harmony between causal physiology and analyses based on implication should be sought on the basis of the relations now existing between experimental or causal, and mathematical or implicative, physics.

IX. This leads us back, after this necessary methodological detour, to our two central problems (see I) and we will start with the relation between perception and intelligence. We know, of course, that it is not a new problem but one that has been raised in various forms since the beginning of the experimental study of perception. Thus Helmholtz included 'unconscious inference' among perceptual mechanisms, and Hering rejected this, proposing instead purely 'physiological' explanations (as if inferences were incompatible with physiological concomitants or 'parallels', a question to which Pavlov later provided an answer from his own particular point of view). This conflict recurs between the Gratz (Meinong, Benussi) and the Gestalt schools, etc. It is in the context of such problems (and of the pseudoproblems which may be entailed) that the relational method should introduce some rigour. What, in fact, is it to perceive, and how does perceiving differ from the activity of inferring, or does perceiving entail various degrees of inference? If these terms are not devoid of meaning, they must correspond to relational systems whose structures can be described, not by arbitrary decisions, but by the step by step translation of actual behaviour into precise formulae. But, as soon as this is undertaken, it becomes clear that a unique structure cannot be applied to all perceptions and equally clear that all inferences (or conscious or unconscious 'reasoning') cannot be reduced to one and the same structure: on the one hand, one is faced with a whole collection of perceptual structures of increasing complexity (which one may not be able to order linearly in correspondence with chronological stages) and on the other, with a whole gamut of 'pre-inferences' and of inferences proper (which it would be equally dangerous to consider, *a priori*, as forming a unique series). It then becomes a case of determining, with some exactitude, whether a particular perceptual structure entails a particular form of inference or not; if it does, it can be called 'unconscious' if one wishes.

It now becomes possible to re-examine the fundamental problem, raised by Gestalt theory, of the genetic continuity between the structures of perception and those of intelligence. It is well known that Gestalt theory considered the act of intelligence to consist in the re-structuring of a given situation in the direction of a 'better' form, the forms of intelligence obeying the same laws as those of perception. On this basis, intelligence would have to be thought of as a continuation of perception, whose structures would extend to elements lying outside the perceptual field.

This conception has the merit, which we intend to underline heavily, of saving us entirely from the encumbering, but incessantly recurring notion of a faculty of intelligence which is distinct from other cognitive functions. We fully agree with Gestalt theory that intelligence consists only in the set of all cognitive functions whose laws are to be discovered in the forms of equilibrium towards which the system tends when the subject is faced with tasks or problems whose solutions are not provided by an initial perceptual appraisal. We have constantly endeavoured to show that these advanced forms of equilibrium consist of operational structures capable of co-ordinating the set of all transformations, and we maintain that there is an agreement between such a point of view and the thesis defended by one of the founders of Gestalt theory.[1]

Indeed, we find what amounts to an uninterrupted series of intermediate states between the most elementary perceptual structures and the most complex operational structures of intelligence: one of the most remarkable of these intermediate states is the pre-operational representational intelligence of the child. This is constantly dominated by forms of reasoning which are not based on transformations as such, but on configurations which are remarkably analogous to perceptual configurations (for example, the absence of homogeneity between filled and unfilled spaces, the non-equivalence of divided and undivided wholes, etc.).

However, in spite of the existence of such intermediate states and of this continuity, there is a qualitative difference between the truly operational structures of intelligence and initial perceptual structures. Both, it is true, are forms of equilibrium and both consist of structures characterised by laws of totality. But the non-additive and irreversible compositions of perceptual structures are succeeded by additive and reversible structures of operations, and it becomes inadmissible to reduce the superior structures to the inferior and to be satisfied with only the one type of structuring defined by the clear but limiting notion of 'Gestalt'.

The reason why Gestalt theorists neglected these structural contra-distinctions and tried to maintain the paradox of explaining both the deforming effects of perceptual illusions and essentially rational structures, such as those of Euclidean space or of logical reasoning, by the same 'laws of organisation', was that they applied the relational method inadequately. They were right to advance the theory of Form, with its notions of field and of totality, in opposition to the atomistic ideal of the proponents of associationistic psychology, who hoped to give an account of perceptual and conceptual totalities in terms of associations between the ultimate elements or 'sensations' for which they were searching. The theory of Form seemed to imply a systematic relativism, and it led (with some exaggeration) to a comparison being made between the considerable revitalisation it introduced into the study of perception and the revolution realised in physics by the theory of relativity.

On closer scrutiny, however, it can be seen that the Gestalt notion

[1] Wertheimer, M. *Productive Thinking*, New York, 1960, Harper.

of totality stopped half-way to relativism. Gestaltists gradually came to see the theory as providing an explanation in itself, and not simply a descriptive tool, and they neglected the problem of the way in which compositions are achieved. Since then, the search has been restricted to the discovery of the characteristics of totality and not to the discovery of the laws of its construction or composition. The result has been no more than a simple enumeration of its most general characteristics: simplicity, regularity, continuity, symmetry, order, similarity, proximity, the principles of maximum and minimum, etc. The respective roles of each of these general characteristics have, of course, been studied with meticulous and fruitful experimentation, but the dangerous seduction of the idea of totality has led to the acceptance as explanatory of what were no more than good descriptions of the subordination of the parts to the 'whole'. It is not surprising, therefore, that these more general characteristics of 'good form' were so general that they applied universally, both to intelligence and to perception. It is indeed remarkable that Gestalt theorists have not succeeded in attributing any specific characteristic to perceptual structures ('proximity' itself being a general topological characteristic corresponding to 'neighbourhood') and have simply described the 'good forms' of perception in terms of properties which are equally applicable to logico-mathematical 'good forms'.

But atomism and Gestalt, corresponding in the final analysis to two major concepts of wholes, a geneticism without structure or a structuralism without genesis, are not the only modes of interpretation available; we claim that a third possibility exists in the relational method. While the theory of psychological atomism considers the whole to be made up of associations between primary elements, and Gestalt theory conceives of these elements as being differentiated within a totality which is present from the beginning, we propose that the relational method offers the following alternatives. We claim, with Gestalt theorists, that elements are not given from the beginning because they do not exist independently of the relations which unite them; and in place of directly invoking a whole of which the elements are only a reflection, we see the whole as being compounded of these relations. For the notion of a given but unexplained totality, the relational method thus substitutes a striving towards the construction or composition of a whole, not starting with elements but with the relations between them, which is not the same thing. These relations do not reduce to a simple Gestalt, even if they are inter-dependent; an element, or an elementary relation, is in relationship with 'all' the rest and not with the 'whole' as such; for example, if a whole is made up of four elements, such as the sides of a square, each one is in relationship with the other three and not with the four considered as a whole (even if the element in question is also in 'reflexive' relationship with itself), and the whole is only the set of the *n* relations which can exist between the four elements. This in no way excludes the existence of laws of totality which are laws neither of elements nor of elementary relations, but of the composition itself of relations[1] (for example, a group, a lattice, a probabilistic composition, etc.).

If, and only if, such a point of view is adopted, can the factitious antagonism between a geneticism without structure and a structuralism without genesis be overcome: all genesis is based on earlier structures and creates new ones from them; and all structures thus imply an endless regression, a genesis without an 'absolute beginning'. It is only from the standpoint of the composition of relations that one can hope to discover the differences as well as the continuities that exist between the structures of perception and those of intelligence. Both exhibit structures which have their own laws of totality (for example, the number series which exhibits the structure of a 'field', etc.), but the structures are not the same in the two cases, being irreversible in the one and reversible in the other. The relational method will enable us to characterise these structures in detail and to disengage their differences and analogies at one and the same time without constraining us, in advance, to the alternatives of associationism or of Gestalt.

X. This attempt to describe the characteristics of the multiple structures of perception and of intelligence in detail, right through to the operational structures themselves, makes sense only if it prepares the way for the solution of the problem of the filiation between intelligence and perception. This problem is, after all, inseparable from that of the epistemological significance of perception, understood as the problem (by rights independent of all philosophy and capable of remaining on the strictly factual level) of the relationship between the perceiver and the perceived object (whose characteristics can be ascertained by other means, for example by physical measurement).

The problem of filiation can be tackled in two ways, the one general and the other by making an analysis of individual concepts.

When the differences and similarities between the structures of perception and of intelligence have been established, two general possibilities can be examined. The first is that intelligence derives from perception by simple extensions of the latter to more complex situations (at increasing spatio-temporal distances), by an increasing

---

[1] We are, of course using the term 'relation' in the broadest sense of 'liaison' or 'connection', and not in the strict logical sense of relations. In this sense, a class is a liaison, an operation is both a liaison and a source of new liaisons, etc.

mobility in perception, or by the development of reversible operations out of the semi-reversible regulations of perception. The second is that the apparent continuity in the transition is due to the gradual subordination of perceptual structures to a general sensory-motor schematisation which then becomes the true source of the development of intelligence.

This general discussion then requires to be completed by an individual analysis of each area in which a perceptual structure and an operational conceptualisation occur together. For example, perceptions of space, of movement, of velocity, of time, of causality, etc., coexist with and structure the same content as pre-operational and then operational notions. The problem in each case is to decide whether or not the notion derives from the corresponding perception, or, more precisely, what it borrows from, and what it adds to, perception. Such an analysis can only be made genetically (by making a comparison of perceptions and corresponding notions at different stages of development). This exercise sheds considerable light on the earlier more general discussion.

Such step by step comparisons of the evolution of a concept and of corresponding perceptions (for example, projective space and the perception of projective size, the co-ordinates of Euclidean space and perceptual co-ordinates, etc.), always give rise to three supplementary questions. These are: (1) What information do notions obtain from perception? (2) What new elements (co-ordinations or new properties, etc.) do notions add to perception? (3) What corrections, rather than additions, do notions make to the information they obtain from perception?

That all three questions are raised whenever the above comparisons are made, means that it is impossible to compare knowledge on the perceptual plane with knowledge on notional or operational planes without at the same time posing the question of their respective degree, or even form, of objectivity: this in turn comes down to the problem of the epistemological significance of perception,[1] whether we call it that or not.

The study of the filiation between concepts and percepts must therefore be completed with a brief epistemological analysis of perception. The aim of this will be to decide whether or not perception achieves that immediate contact between subject and object that empiricism has always considered to be the fundamental guarantee of

---

[1] An author as little suspect of taking pleasure in epistemology as Henri Pièron, ends his excellent and purely psycho-physical study, *La Sensation, Guide de Vie*, (Paris, 1945, Gallimard), by insisting on the fact that sensations are essentially 'symbols', but symbols whose informative value is very inferior to that of mathematical equations (p. 413).

objectivity: the particular problems to be tackled by a truly genetic analysis are whether that objectivity is built up or whether it is present from the beginning and, if built up, whether the prime instrument of its eventual elaboration (even in the so-called 'perceptual' verification made by the scientist at the end of a laboratory experiment) is an operational or a perceptual structuring.

PART ONE

PRIMARY EFFECTS

No genetic significance will be attributed to the term 'primary' which might imply an origin necessarily anterior to those perceptual activities to be studied in Part Two. The designation refers only to the greater simplicity of the responses involved: at a given genetic level those perceptual effects which occur in one and the same momentary field of centration will be called primary. The criterion is the possibility of obtaining such effects in tachistoscopic presentations of the stimuli, namely under conditions which prevent visual explorations, transportation by means of displacements of fixation, etc. We need not decide at this stage whether these effects (which are also called 'field effects', but with reference only to the simple field of centration and without suggesting analogies with 'fields' in the physical sense of the term) are anterior to all perceptual activity and result from elements simultaneously perceived in a single perceptual field, or whether they constitute the crystallised product or 'sedimentation' of previous perceptual activities. This problem will be discussed at the end of Chapter III. Similarly, the question of whether the number and extent of primary effects increases or diminishes with age may be postponed: at this stage we will merely describe them and attempt to explain them in terms only of the mechanisms of centration.

I PRIMARY ILLUSIONS AND THE LAW OF RELATIVE CENTRATIONS

The illusions referred to as primary correspond to most of the optico-geometric illusions. Among them are: the illusions of rectangles (the over-estimation of the longer side); the T figure (to the extent that it introduces semi-rectangles, the over-estimation of the vertical as such being actually 'secondary'); the over-estimation of a segment of a straight line either when extended by a smaller segment or when inserted between two smaller segments; the Delbœuf illusions (of concentric circles); the illusions of angles (the over-estimation of acute and the under-estimation of obtuse angles, and the illusions of the arms of angles); the illusions of lozenges (the under-estimation of the longer diagonal); the Müller–Lyer illusions; illusions of parallelograms; of curvature, etc., and finally, marking the transition to secondary illusions, the Oppel–Kundt illusion of divided spaces.

The aim of this chapter is to try to reduce all these perceptual illusions, or deformations, to a single law by reducing each of them to certain constant relations which entail an over-estimation of the greater of two compared segments and an under-estimation of the smaller. The explanation of the law itself, and of the principle of these over- and under-estimations, will be reserved for the next chapter.

§ 1. THE STATUS OF THE PROBLEM

The primary illusions have two fundamental characteristics. The first is that their qualitative characteristics (the location of the positive and negative spatial maxima and of the median zero illusion, in relation to the proportions of the figure) do not change with age, while their absolute quantitative values, the extent of illusion, usually diminish, occasionally remain constant, but do not increase with age. The second characteristic, on a par, no doubt, with their qualitative invariance at all ages, is that they occur even in tachistoscopic presentations which are so short as to exclude ocular movements and consequently secondary activities of exploration, transportation, etc. These primary illusions can therefore be considered to result from simple field effects, that is to say from the quasi-simultaneous interaction of elements perceived together in one single field of centration without the involvement of a displacement of fixation.

B 3

They are called 'primary' for this reason, but this in no way prejudges their physiological status. Binet called them 'innate', which involves an unnecessary hypothesis because they could result from general, but still not hereditary, simple equilibrating mechanisms (see Chapter II).

Thus described, the primary illusions constitute the most elementary perceptual phenomena with which we shall be concerned. We can conveniently open our analysis with their examination which immediately raises a major problem: *do the primary illusions (which are classical examples of the deforming nature of events occurring in space perception and yet only involve the simplest and most rational of figural relations) obey a general law which reveals something of the nature of deformations which may be consubstantial with perception?*

Strangely enough, no one, since the first studies of optico-geometric illusions were made over a century ago, has undertaken the task of discovering such a common law. Until the recent studies of Motokawa on retinal induction, investigators have limited themselves to a series of qualitative and disparate explanations. Woodworth, in his excellent text on psychology, challenged psychologists to extract from the illusions some general relations which would lead to predictions. We, while remaining on purely relational territory, have attempted to meet this challenge, not from an ambition to re-examine this repeatedly discussed problem for its own sake, but from an interest in the general problem of perceptual deformation, an interest which has involved us in the search for a law.

Why has so little thought been given to this problem? No doubt psychophysics was too ambitious in wanting to measure sensations directly, as if they constituted the absolute elements out of which perception could be reconstructed by a form of atomic composition. Psychophysics thus ran into the problem of 'systematic errors' of all sorts (spatial, temporal, etc.), which were regarded simply as obstacles standing in the way of those absolute measurements which were considered to be the ideal to be pursued. In time, however, particularly after the formulation of Gestalt theory, error ceased to be regarded as a troublesome obstacle and came to be regarded as a proper object of study. This was not only because of its ubiquitous nature, but because it exhibits that immediate interaction whose equilibrium, in terms of the totality of the field, finds expression in perception. But the theory of form then took a paradoxical course in trying to explain, by the same principle of the whole, both good forms (circles, squares, etc.), in which deformations are precisely minimal, and illusions, which were invoked to illustrate the subordination of the parts to the whole. Deformations were con-

4

sidered from this particular point of view only, which was insufficiently ambitious, and led Gestalt theory to substitute a simple qualitative description for measurement (which does not mean, of course, that Gestaltists have not measured a large number of the effects of deformation, but they have only drawn a justification of the laws of organisation from these measurements and not a mathematical expression of the systematic deformations proper to perceptual structures).[1]

The relational method, on the other hand, demands that the problem of deformation itself should be faced: why, if A is less than B, is B perceived as larger when accompanied by A than when perceived in isolation, which can be expressed as $B(A) > B$? This is the central question. To resolve it, we have taken illusion after illusion, determining for each the distribution of the error, effects of age aside, and have attempted, experimentally and by successive approximations, to express that distribution in an elementary mathematical form which makes exclusive reference to the objective dimensions of the perceived figure.[2] We have thus tried, always empirically, to find the common form of these different expressions and have eventually arrived at the formulation of a law which so far seems to be adequately applicable to the experimental findings. But as the law interests us only in virtue of its explanatory function, which is intended to throw light on perceptual deformations in general, we also sought to arrive at an explanatory model which would account for the deformations. We believe we have found it in terms of the effects of centration, which will be discussed in Chapter II. That is why this expression will be called the 'Law of Relative Centrations', reference being made to it in its explanatory role. But even if the hypothesis proves to be invalid, the general formula will undoubtedly survive because its establishment and its attempted explanation were, in fact, undertaken independently although it was of course hoped that the law would provide an explanation.

This law will not, of course, provide the absolute quantitative values of the errors (values which are not constant but which diminish with age and with practice), any more than does Weber's law which, while stating that the differential threshold is proportional to the magnitude of the elements compared, does not give it an absolute value. However, in so far as the law is verified, it will predict relative values for the qualitative characteristics of the distribution of errors: that is to say, it will predict the general shape of the curves, and will

---

[1] Except, of course, in the case of those phenomena considered to be directly relevant to field theory, such as the figural after-effects of W. Köhler; and except in certain isolated works, such as those of E. Rausch.
[2] See Introduction, VI.

locate the positions of the spatial[1] positive and negative maxima and that of the median zero illusion.

The plan to be followed will have three stages: (*a*) stating the law (§ 2) without attempting to offer any explanatory hypothesis; (*b*) validating it experimentally for all the primary illusions so far analysed (§§ 3 to 13); and (*c*) only then (Chapter II, §§ 2 to 4) attempting to give the law a probabilistic interpretation and to describe the events (effects of centration, temporal maxima, etc.) which may be capable of justifying the interpretation itself (Chapter II, §§ 1 to 6). These three stages should be carefully distinguished when considering the soundness of the arguments.

§ 2. THE GENERAL FORM OF THE LAW OF RELATIVE CENTRATIONS

The special problem to be solved in the establishment of a law, as distinct from the general problem stated in § 1, is to discover the dimensional proportions of a given figure which will produce the maximum positive illusion, etc.

It will be assumed that one dimension of a given figure can be kept constant (for example, the longer side of a rectangle) while the other is varied, and the subjective estimates of the length of the first will be studied as a function of variations in the second. It will be assumed that the constant and variable elements can always be described in terms of lengths, L. These assumptions present no difficulties in the cases of rectangles and of simple line figures such as Oppel's figure, etc. Variations in the Delbœuf figure of concentric circles can also be described quite simply in terms of lengths, in this case the diameters of the circles and the distances separating their circumferences, because, in fact, subjects seem to evaluate these figures in these terms. In the case of angles, however, the problem is to find out how angular sizes are perceptually assessed and it will be found necessary to forget mathematical trigonometry in order to create a perceptual trigonometry which, it will be found, is also based on lengths.

This accepted, the greater length will be labelled L_1 and the lesser L_2. Experimentation has shown that the main objective dimension which determines the subjective variations in illusions is not simply the absolute difference $L_1 - L_2$, but this difference multiplied by L_2 and divided by a product which will be provisionally labelled the surface, or S. This is a function of both L_1 and L_2. This initial proposi-

[1] The 'spatial maximum' of an optico-geometric illusion is defined as the maximum illusion corresponding to certain spatial proportions of the figure, with duration of exposure held constant. The 'temporal maximum' is defined as the maximum illusion corresponding to a certain optimal duration of exposure of the figure, with spatial proportions held constant.

tion indicates that, even if the difference $L_1 - L_2$ plays an essential role in subjective over- and under-estimations, it does so only to the extent that it is related to L_2, which may be expressed as $(L_1 - L_2) L_2$, and to the extent that it is related to the whole field of comparison, S, whence:

$$(1) \qquad \frac{(L_1 - L_2)L_2}{S}$$

But Prop. 1, although corresponding to the most important illusory factor, is not always sufficient by itself. A regulating factor, which does not otherwise play a part in the general cases, when its value is 1, needs to be added when the effects of certain configurations are to be accounted for. This factor comprises the following three elements: (1) the number, n, of separate comparisons between $(L_1 - L_2)$ and L_2, a number which is 1 if L_2 is compared with a single L_1, but which would be 2 if L_1 were a line drawn between two other lines. (2) The maximum length, L_{max}, of the figure: to compare L_1 with a perpendicular L_2, as in the case of a rectangle (in which case $L_{max} = L_1$) is not equivalent to comparing an L_1 with an L_2 which forms an extension of it (in which case $L_{max} = L_1 + L_2$). (3) This maximum length itself should not be thought of as an absolute value because, so far, all values considered have been relative: it is to be understood as part and parcel of the relationship of which the other term is the reference length, L ($L = L_1$ or L_2). The second factor to be considered is therefore:

$$(2) \qquad \frac{nL}{L_{max}}$$

If P is the relative quantitative value of the illusion (P being defined as 'a non-compensated transformation', or as a deformation), the complete expression of the law will be:

$$(3) \qquad P = \frac{(L_1 - L_2)L_2}{S} \times \frac{nL}{L_{max}} = \frac{nL(L_1 - L_2)L_2}{SL_{max}}$$

where P = the deformation (over- or under-estimation) measured against one of the dimensions of the figure held constant at unity. (P is positive if the constant element is L_1, and negative if it is L_2.)

L_1 = the greater of the two lengths compared (for example, the longer side of the rectangle, the height[1] of an acute angle, etc.).

L_2 = the lesser of the two lengths compared.

---

[1] The height of an angle will, for the present purposes, refer to the length of its bisector when this is vertical and when the arms of the angle are equal (both the bisector and the base, which is perpendicular to it, being virtual, not drawn, lines).

L_{max} = the greatest length of the figure (for example, $L_{max} = L_1$ or $L_1 + L_2$, or, if L_1 is inserted between two shorter lengths, $L_{max} = L_1 + 2 L_2$, etc.).

S = the surface of the field of comparison. If L_1 and L_2 are two sides of a rectangle, $S = L_1 L_2$. If the figure is linear, experience shows that the surface to be considered is $(L_{max})^2$, which seems arbitrary. But as will be seen in Chapter II, the surface selected now corresponds (as it does in all cases) to the sum of all possible 'couplings' between the segments of L_1 and those of L_2, for example, $(L_1 + L_2)^2 = L_1{}^2 + L_2{}^2 + 2L_1 L_2$, which is the sum of the couplings when L_1 is related to L_2 and L_2 to L_1. This anticipatory observation indicates that S is not really a surface but the field of comparison between L_1 and L_2.

n = the number of separate comparisons between L_1 and L_2. For example, in the hatched or subdivided line of Oppel–Kundt, L_1 is the total length, L_2 the distance between two hatchings and n the number of segments. In the concentric circles of Delbœuf, L_1 is the diameter of the inner circle, L_2 the width of the band between the two circles and $n = 2$ since L_1 is compared with L_2 to the right and to the left.

L = the given reference length. The presence of L in the law is necessary to ensure that there is an equal number of elements in the numerator and in the denominator (n is only a numerical coefficient). Without this precaution, there would be two lengths in the numerator and three in the denominator. The formula would then express the inverse of a length,[1] and would no longer represent a simple relation between lengths, which is intended.

The proposed law thus expresses a relation between lengths and not an absolute length or the inverse of a length. As a relation, the illusion P is proportional to the lengths involved and thus implies Weber's law.

This formulation of the law of primary illusions is advanced as a hypothesis, and an attempt will be made to verify it by an examination of various kinds of optico-geometric illusions which are found to decrease with age. In each case the formula will be compared with the results of experiments in which the proportions of the figures were varied.

§ 3. ILLUSIONS OF RECTANGLES

Let one side, B, of a rectangle remain constant while the other, A, is varied from the shortest length that can be drawn, through $A = B$

---

[1] In the mathematical sense of the term: if one multiplied the unity by 10 (if, say, $L_1 = 10$ instead of 1) the overall relation P would be reduced to a tenth of its value instead of remaining constant.

and on to $A > B$. In this case B is over-estimated when $B > A$ and under-estimated when $B < A$. It can be seen at once that the median zero illusion will occur when $B = A$, when the figure is a square. It should be noted in passing, however, that we are not proposing, as Gestalt theory does, that the sides of a square appear equal because it is a good figure, but rather that the deformations $B(A) > B$ and $B(A) < B$ compensate each other exactly[1] and thus produce a good figure. In all other figures, the longer side is over-estimated and the shorter under-estimated, which raises two questions concerning the maxima.

Theoretically, the law of relative centrations for a rectangle whose one side varies between $A = 0$, $A = B$ and $A > B$ (B being held constant and equal to 1) results in the following expression:

$$(4) \qquad P = \frac{1B(B - A)A}{AB \times B} = \frac{B - A}{B} \text{ if } B > A$$

where $B = L_1 = L_{max}$ and $A = L_2$.

In this case, the distribution of the positive errors forms a straight line whose maximum is found when $A = 0$.

For negative errors measured on B (if $B < A$), we have:

$$(4b) \qquad P = \frac{1A(A - B)B}{AB \times A} = \frac{A - B}{A} \text{ if } B < A$$

where $A = L_1 = L_{max}$ and $B = L_2$.

The distribution of the negative errors (B remaining constant and equal to 1 while A increases in value) is a rectangular hyperbola in which the errors do not increase indefinitely, as did the positive errors, but tend to flatten off as A is extended.

To verify these hypotheses, the following investigations were carried out in collaboration with Denis-Prinzhorn.[2] It was first necessary to verify the shape of the theoretical curves (rectilinear for positive and hyperbolic for negative errors): to do this, the errors were examined to see if their distributions about arbitrarily chosen points on the positive and negative curves were in fact symmetrical when positive and asymmetrical when negative.

In the first series of trials[3] (the over-estimation of B) two standard rectangles were presented, $I = 6 \times 2.5$ cm and $II = 6 \times 1.5$ cm. The variables consisted of rectangles of side $A = 2$ cm and B varying

---

[1] This is because deformations are still possible when fixation is restricted to one of the sides but these momentary deformations cancel out if $B = A$ objectively.
[2] *Rech.* 16.
[3] See the Appendix for an account of the psycho-physical method employed in the majority of the experiments to be reported.

TABLE 1. *Mean % errors in estimates of the length of the long (L_1) and of the short (L_2) sides of rectangles measured against the standards indicated (n = 31 children and 10 adults)*

	Rech. 16, p. 112			
Age group	5–7 yrs A[I]	5–7 yrs B	9–11 yrs	Adult	Overall
Order	I–IV	IV–I	I–IV	I–IV	Mean
Standard					
I (L_1)	−7·41	−6·98	−6·25	−3·33	−6·0
II (L_1)	9·26	7·82	6·00	2·82	6·4
III (L_2)	−3·61	−5·47	−4·00	−2·62	−3·9
IV (L_2)	6·67	8·44	4·91	4·12	6·0

from 4·5 to 7·5 cm. Subjects were asked to compare the size of the variable side, *B*, with the long sides of the standard rectangles.

In the second series of trials (under-estimation of *A*) the two standard rectangles measured: III = 7·5 × 2 cm and IV = 4·5 × 2 cm. The variable rectangles had side *B* = 6 cm and side *A* varying from 1·6 to 2·4 cm. Here the subject was asked to compare the variable side *A* with the short sides of the standard rectangles. The results are set out in Table 1.

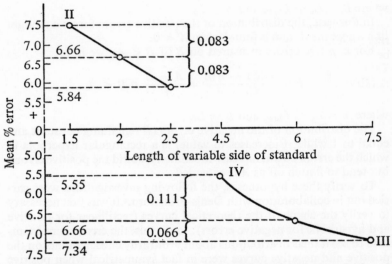

Fig. 1. The distribution of errors for the long and short sides of rectangles, to illustrate respectively their symmetrical and asymmetrical distributions.

The positive and negative signs, contrary to general usage, do not stand for positive and negative errors relative to zero, but to over- and under-estimations of the side in question when compared with the appropriate side of the standard rectangle. The standard itself is

[I] For the age group 5 to 7 the order of presentation was I to IV for group A, and IV to I for group B.

also subject to over-estimation of the long side and under-estimation of the short side, but as the distribution of its dimensions is symmetrical about the dimensions of the variable in question, this distortion is nullified. As can be seen in Table 1 and Fig. 1, the subjective estimates made of the length of the longer side, B in I and II, are symmetrically distributed on either side of the mid-point between the lengths of B in I and in II, the error being of the order of 6 and 6·4%. In contrast, the estimates made on A in III and IV are asymmetrically distributed around the mid-point between the lengths of A in III and in IV. The error in the case of IV is 6%, but is nearly always considerably reduced in III, coinciding with the point of inflection of the curve towards its asymptote.

This first experiment having thus verified the general shape of the curve[1] it then became necessary to see if the positive maximum did in fact occur with the smallest width that could be drawn for the standard rectangle.

To this end a single straight line of 6 cm (which is a very thin rectangle because any drawn line has a thickness) was compared with a line of 6 cm which formed the lower side of a square (the square representing the median zero illusion on the theoretical curve, lying between $B > A$ and $B < A$). The results obtained are set out in Table 2.

TABLE 2. *Comparison of an isolated line with one side of a square* ($n = 25$ *adults*)

Rech. 16, p. 128

Judgement	Line > Side	=	Line < Side
f	21	3	1

A third verification consisted in asking the same twenty-five adults to choose the rectangle which appeared to have the longest side from a series of rectangles measuring 6 cm $\times$ 15, 10, 5, 4, 3, 2, 1 and 0·5 mm, and a straight line 6 cm long and 0·3 mm thick. The results are set out in Table 3.

TABLE 3. *Frequency distribution of judgements of longest rectangle*

Rech. 16, p. 125

Width (mm)	0·3 (filled)	0·5	1	2	3	4	5	10	15
f	6	11	6	1	0	0	1	0	0

It can be seen that the maximum over-estimation coincides very well with the smallest value of L_2, with one reservation: as filled spaces do not have the same perceptual value as empty spaces, the choices were more frequent for 0·5 than for 0·3 mm, whereas, had it been possible to draw a rectangle with lines 0·1 mm thick, with an unfilled space of 0·1 mm between them, it would no doubt have been chosen the most frequently. The thickness of the lines would need to be reduced to measure this illusion accurately but does not affect the

[1] As well as the 'primary' nature of the illusion, in that it diminishes with age.

results in most cases. This variable does need to be considered in this particular case, however, and even more so in that of the Oppel–Kundt illusion, as will be seen in § 13.

The diagonals of the rectangle remain to be discussed. When one of them is represented in the drawing of the figure, they are strongly devalued, which represents a complete contradiction to the preceding illusions[1] (see § 8, Table 11, below). But this reversal of the relations involved when one diagonal is represented derives from an effect which is quite distinct from those of Props. 4 and 4b, one which produces the illusion of angles. It will be discussed in detail in §§ 5 and 8.

§ 4. THE T FIGURE (ALSO KNOWN AS THE 'HORIZONTAL–VERTICAL ILLUSION')

The figure consists of a vertical line erected at the mid-point of a horizontal line of equal length. Two deformations are involved, one being the horizontal–vertical effect and the other the over-estimation of an intersector, which is due to the inequality of the intersector and the two parts of the divided line. The factor of verticality is not of present interest because it involves secondary illusions, in which connection it will be discussed later (Chapter III, § 3). In any case, it plays a predominant role only when the figure is in the form of a set-square or L, but plays only a minor role in other variations. To refer to the T figure as the horizontal–vertical illusion, as is often done, is wrong because the horizontal is usually over-estimated when the figure is in the form of ⊢ because of the influence of the second factor mentioned above.

Only the second factor will be discussed here and it will be referred to as the illusion of semi-rectangles. In its general form, its analysis seems of little interest (at least we have not undertaken it even though something unexpected might well be discovered): no doubt the comparison of a line with a longer line forming a right-angle with it will provoke an attenuated form of the illusion. The novelty of the T figure, however, is that the two lines are of equal length. The variants of this figure used in the present case, all of which involved a right-angle, are shown in Fig. 2.

| 1 | 2 | 3 | 4 | 5 | 6 | 7 | 8 | 9 | 10 | 11 | 12 | 13 | 14 | 15 | 16 |

Fig. 2.

As usual, the problem is to locate the maxima and the zero illusions, if they exist.

[1] Because the over-estimation of the longer side and the under-estimation of the shorter side of a rectangle both entail an implicit over-estimation of the virtual diagonal.

In what follows[1] let A be the divided line (whether horizontal or vertical) and B the intersector. Let A'_1 and A'_2 be the two segments, equal or unequal, of the divided line, whence $A'_1 + A'_2 = A$. Each of these forms a semi-rectangle with B, and will consequently be subject to under-estimation. If P_1 and P_2 represent the effects for A'_1 and A'_2 respectively, then, in calculating the over-estimation of B, we will have the following formula which is derived directly from Prop. 4 (§ 3), when S represents the surface of the whole figure and $A = B = 1$.

$$(5) \qquad P_1 = \frac{(B - A'_1)A'_1 \times B}{AB \times B} = A'_2\, A'_1$$

and

$$P_2 = \frac{(B - A'_2)A'_2 \times B}{AB \times B} = A'_1\, A'_2$$

The values of P_1 and of P_2 are thus always identical for complementary values of A'_1 and A'_2.

In an examination of this effect, conducted with Morf,[2] figures were used in which $A = B = 5$ cm and A'_1 varied from 0 to 50 mm in 5-mm-step intervals. These figures would give the following theoretical values for P, on the basis of Prop. 5 and calculated on the basis of unity (5 mm = $0{\cdot}1$, etc.):

A'_1 (in parenthesis, A'_2) = 0 (50) 5 (45) 10 (40) 15 (35) 20 (30) 25 (25) 30 (20) 35 (15) 40 (10) 45 (5) 50 (0)
$P_1 (= P_2) = 0 \quad 0{\cdot}09 \quad 0{\cdot}16 \quad 0{\cdot}21 \quad 0{\cdot}24 \quad 0{\cdot}25 \quad 0{\cdot}24 \quad 0{\cdot}21 \quad 0{\cdot}16 \quad 0{\cdot}09 \quad 0$

The theoretical maximum occurs when $A'_1 = A'_2 = A/2$ and the curve falls away symmetrically on either side of this point. As these eleven values correspond to configurations 1 to 5 of Fig. 2, the same curves will emerge for configurations 5 to 9, 9 to 13 and for 13 to 16 to 1. On the other hand, if the error is expressed in terms of the vertical (which sometimes plays the role of A and sometimes of B), the theoretical values would sometimes be positive (1 to 5 and 9 to 13) and sometimes negative (6 to 8 and 14 to 16), corresponding to the continuous line in Fig. 3.

Two sets of experimental results, obtained by Morf and independently by Kunnapas,[3] will now be examined. It should be recalled that the error of semi-rectangles forms only one of the two components of the illusion, the other error being that of the over-estimation of the vertical as such, a secondary factor which combines with the first but without, like it, deriving from the law of relative centrations.

In spite of this combination of two factors which are sometimes

[1] Without reference to the notation used in *Rech.* 28.   [2] *Ibid.*
[3] Kunnapas, T. M., *J. Exp. Psychol.*, 1955, **49**, 134–40.

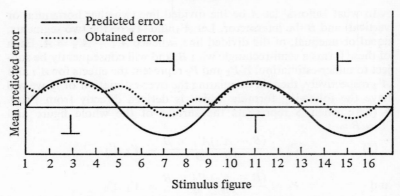

Fig. 3. Comparison of predicted and obtained errors for the T figure.

cumulative and sometimes subtractive, the two groups of results converge to a remarkable degree. They demonstrate the role of the first factor which Kunnapas simply terms the over-estimation of the dividing line (*B*) and which we have just described as the effect of semi-rectangles: (1) the empirical maximum is found when *B* divides *A* into two equal parts; (2) the dividing line is over-estimated even when horizontal, at least in the vicinity of the maximum (other experiments, it is true, have demonstrated the opposite, but in the case of much larger figures, where it is possible to evaluate *A* independently of *B*, and reciprocally, and where the effect of verticality has overwhelmed that of the semi-rectangle); (3) on the other hand, there is conflict with verticality at the extremities of the curve where the effect of the semi-rectangle is minor or negligible and where the effect of verticality is predominant.

(It should be noted that the empirical curve derives from measurements obtained by a method of paired comparisons, in which the subject was asked to choose the figure in which the difference in length between *A* and *B* was greatest. If *A* and *B* are simply compared with a separate figure, as was done by Kunnapas, the curve becomes more rectilinear (more roof-like than dome-like) and like that of the positive part of the illusion of rectangles (Fig. 1); it is as if the subject was influenced by only one of the two semi-rectangles instead of by the whole figure, as in our case where there seems to have been no selective centration.)

§ 5. ILLUSIONS OF ANGLES

One of the most classic of the primary illusions is the over-estimation of acute and the under-estimation of obtuse angles. This illusion is

14

accompanied by an under-estimation of the sides of the first and an over-estimation of the sides of the second. If the perpendicular intersecting the bisector of the angle at its mid-point, to be called the median, is extended to join the arms of the angle (drawn of equal length), an illusion of the median is added, which consists in the median appearing to lie too near to the apex in acute and too far from the apex in obtuse angles.

This complex illusion of angles is in fact a reversed illusion of rectangles in which the shorter side is under-estimated and the longer over-estimated. In the illusion of angles, however, the short side of the virtual rectangles in which both acute and obtuse angles are depicted (see Figs. 5 and 6) is over-estimated. This also applies in the case of a simple rectangle in which the diagonal has been depicted (see Fig. 4).

It will be remembered (Prop. 4) that the principal factor operating in the illusion of rectangles of shorter side A and longer side B, is the difference coupling, or relation, $(B - A)A$. In the case of equilateral angles, the lengths L_1 and L_2 which determine the subject's estimates of the dimensions of the figure are the following (even if only virtual and not actually represented): (1) the height, H, which corresponds to the bisector of the angle, and (2) its median, M (see Fig. 8). This means (and, of course, requires to be verified empirically) that the length of the arm of an angle is judged on the basis of the relation between the height of the figure and the separation of its arms. This separation, however, is not estimated simply as a function of the base line, but of the collection of all the distances between the arms occurring at different points along the bisector, which results in a preferential probability in favour of the average separation, which corresponds to the median, M. But, objectively, the relation between H and M is, $H > M$ for an acute angle, $H = M$ for a right-angle and $H < M$ for an obtuse angle. These two circumstances, of preferential subjective estimation and of objective proportions, lead to the conclusion that the principal factor in the production of the illusion of angles will be the following difference coupling,[1] which corresponds to $(B - A)A$ for rectangles:

(6)   for acute angles, $(H - M)M$;
        for obtuse angles, $(M - H)H$

(it being understood in what follows, and leading up to propositions 9 and 10, that this factor is to be related to $S = HM$ and to $L_{max} =$ the arm, C, of the angle; and that $L = H = 1$).

It turns out, however, contrary to all the usual rules, that H is

---

[1] This reference to the notion of a difference coupling anticipates its systematic description in §§ 2 to 4 of Chapter II.

under- and M over-estimated in acute angles, in which the difference factor is still $(H - M)M$, and conversely in obtuse angles, where the factor is $(M - H)H$. This is why we said that this was a reversed illusion of rectangles.

This reversal must first be explained and its explanation will *ipso facto* provide the relations required for the formulation of the illusion.

The solution to the problem is very simple if based on a factor which is common to both the illusions of obtuse and acute angles and

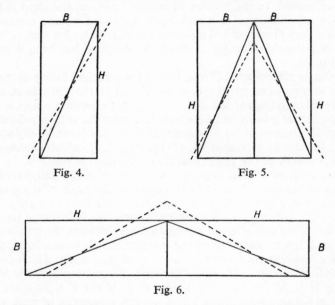

Fig. 4.   Fig. 5.

Fig. 6.

if that factor is related to the illusion of rectangles. The common factor is the tendency (whose existence will be verified shortly) for the perceived inclination of obliques to be exaggerated, as illustrated in Fig. 4.[1] If, therefore, two obliques are juxtaposed in the two symmetries, one will obtain (for the given degree of exaggeration of in-

---

[1] This exaggeration of inclination is defined as a tendency for the diagonal to be perceived as deviating towards 45° (the diagonal of a square). It might be objected that this exaggeration of inclination is itself due to the effect of the angle, and that this precludes its use as a preliminary condition in the production of the illusion of angles. Indeed, when inserted in a reference rectangle (Fig. 4), the oblique forms various angles with the sides, which might be thought to be responsible for the apparent deviations of the oblique. However, it is easy to demonstrate (see *Rech.* 24) that while the over-estimation of some of these angles will reinforce this inclination, the under-estimation of others will exactly counteract this effect.

clination) the over-estimation of acute angles and the under-estimation of obtuse angles, as shown in Figs. 5 and 6.

But, as can be seen in Fig. 4, the oblique in question also constitutes the diagonal of a reference rectangle (a reference constituted by the horizontals and verticals without which a perceptual assessment of the inclination of the line could not be made): if its inclination is exaggerated, the width of the reference rectangle will increase and its height will decrease. Thus the common element in the illusions of acute and obtuse angles becomes, in another context, the under-estimation of the diagonal of a rectangle. It is this which produces the reversal of the usual over-estimation of the longer and the under-estimation of the shorter side of the rectangle.

In short, the reinforcement of the inclination of an oblique (Fig. 4) incorporates both the common element of the two classical illusions of angles (Figs. 5 and 6) and the explanatory principle of the reversal of the illusion of rectangles. It is essential, therefore, before attempting to formulate the illusion of angles, to verify the occurrence of the reinforcement of the inclination of obliques, or, which hypothetically comes to the same thing, of the under-estimation of the diagonals of rectangles. In this connection we have two groups of experimental results, both of which appear to be decisive.

To start with the diagonals of rectangles, it will be seen later (§ 8) that the under-estimation of the long diagonal of parallelograms as a function of variations in the angles of the figures yields a maximum effect when the angles are of 90°, in other words, just when the parallelogram is a rectangle. It follows, therefore, that the illusion will change if one of the diagonals of a rectangle is depicted instead of being virtual. This will be because an under-estimation of the diagonal is consonant only with either an under-estimation of the longer side, whether or not this is accompanied by an over-estimation of the shorter, or with a marked under-estimation of the shorter side, the estimation of the longer side being changed or not. The first of these possibilities (the under-estimation of the longer side) would be realised if the inclination of the under-estimated diagonal to the longer side were increased, and the second (the marked under-estimation of the shorter side) if the inclination of the under-estimated diagonal were reduced. The first of these alternatives is supported by the evidence.

On this point, which is central to the problem of angles, the inclination of obliques was experimentally examined with Morf,[1] by enclosing diagonals either within rectangles or between parallel verticals which intersected the diagonals and thus represented the long sides of rectangles from which the short sides had been omitted.

Let *AF* be a closed rectangle, of 2 × 5 cm, without a diagonal,

[1] *Rech.* 24.

17

BF the same rectangle with a longitudinal median and *CF* the same rectangle with one diagonal. Let *AO*, *BO* and *CO* represent the same figures, but without the short sides. When these three figures were compared two at a time, in an upright position, and in respect of the subjective widths of the figures, the results set out in Table 4 were obtained.

TABLE 4. *Frequency distribution of judgements based on comparisons of the short side of rectangles A (without diagonal), B (with longitudinal median) and C (with diagonal) when drawn open (O, the short side omitted) or closed (F) (n = 40 adults)*

Rech. 24, p. 67–68

A/C comparisons

AF > CF	AF = CF	AF < CF		AO > CO	AO = CO	AO < CO
0	4	36		0	2	38

A/B comparisons

AF > BF	AF = BF	AF < BF		AO > BO	AO = BO	AO < BO
9	16	15		7	12	21

B/C comparisons

BF > CF	BF = CF	BF < CF		BO > CO	BO = CO	BO < CO
7	13	27		1	12	27

It is clear that the width of rectangles with a diagonal (*CF* or *CO*) is over-estimated relative to that of rectangles without a diagonal (*AF* or *AO*) and that this is not just a question of the effect of a divided space (*BF* or *BO*).

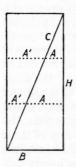

Fig. 7

The facts being thus established, the illusion of angles can be formulated by readopting Prop. 6 and by adding to it the effect of the reinforcement of the inclination of diagonals (Fig. 4), but having first explained and formulated this effect.

The simplest way to explain the effect is to consider it to be an effect of the diagonal of rectangles, or at least an effect of reference rectangles on the basis of which the inclinations of lines are estimated. From this point of view, the inclination has reference to the distances, or virtual lines, shown in dotted form in Fig. 7. Each is composed of the segments *A* and *A'*: when *A* < *A'*, *A'* is over-estimated and *A* under-estimated and the oblique is thus subjectively tilted towards *A*. When *A* > *A'* the inverse applies and the oblique is subjectively tilted towards *A'*. There are thus two tendencies which contribute to an accentuation of its inclination. It might be asked why the same effects do not apply in the vertical direction (the argument having been limited to the horizontal distances *A* and *A'*), which would diminish the inclination rather than increase it. This may happen, but as the number of possible distinct comparisons is less in the vertical than in the horizontal, the latter predominate. At 45°, on the other hand (which would produce an angle of 90° for two

18

diagonals juxtaposed as in Fig. 5), the two kinds of comparison would be equally probable and the resultant, in principle, zero.[1]

This being so, it is easy to formulate the effect of Fig. 7 and then to combine it with Prop. 6 in order to formulate the law of the illusion of angles.

If B is the breadth of the rectangle in Fig. 7, and $B = A + A'$, and if H is its long side (which would become the height of the angle in the juxtaposition of two rectangles, as in Fig. 5), we will have, by the application of the general law (Prop. 3, § 1):

$$(7) \qquad P = \frac{H(A' - A)A}{HB \times C}$$

and

$$P' = \frac{H(A - A')A'}{HB \times C}$$

where $L_1 = A'$ (in P) or A (in P'); $L_2 = A$ or A'; $L_{max} = C$ (the length of the diagonal);[2] $S = HB$ and $nL = H$ because the number of distinct comparisons between A and A' is proportional to H.

If these expressions are now calculated by writing A and A' as fractions of B (for example, 0·1 and 0·9, etc.) the same relative values for a constant H will, of course, always be found for $(A' - A)A$ and for $(A - A')A'$ and only the value of B will change from one rectangle to another. If the collection of the relations $(A' - A)A$ and $(A - A')A'$, whose relative value is a constant function (K) of B, is termed KB, Proposition (7) reduces to:

$$(8) \qquad P = \frac{HBK}{BH \times C} = \frac{K}{C}$$

This expression can now be combined with Prop. 6, but remembering that it concerns only the half (Fig. 4 or 7) rather than the whole figure (Fig. 5 or 6). For acute angles we will then have:

$$(9) \qquad P = \frac{2K(H - M)M}{C^2} \quad \text{if } H > M$$

and for obtuse angles:

$$(10) \qquad P = \frac{2K(M - H)H}{C^2} \quad \text{if } M > H$$

---

[1] The diagonals of a square are not displaced but are nonetheless under-estimated as arms of the two angles of 45° which they form with the sides of the square (see comment II at the conclusion to this §).

[2] The diagonal being the greatest *depicted* length while L_{max} is the long side in a rectangle in which the diagonal is not depicted.

Primary Effects

The surface BH $(= MH$ because $B = M$),[1] need not be introduced again because it is already incorporated (and annulled) in Prop. 8. Calculating from Props. 9 and 10, which give the same results (sign apart) for corresponding acute or obtuse angles, one obtains (for $H = 1$):

	10° (100°)	20° (110°)	30° (120°)	40° (130°)	45° (135°)
$P =$	0·079	0·140	0·183	0·204	0·207
	50° (140°)	60° (150°)	70° (160°)	80° (170°)	90° (180°)
$P =$	0·204	0·183	0·140	0·079	0

As is usually claimed, the theoretical maximum occurs at 45° when positive (over-estimation of acute angles) and at 135° when negative (under-estimation of obtuse angles). The problem is to establish this experimentally without measuring one angle against another which would itself be subject to a systematic error. Two different methods are available and both have produced similar results. The first method is almost direct, and consists in the examination of the under- and over-estimations of the long and short diagonals of lozenges when the angles of the figures are varied: this will be described in the following section (§ 6) on the basis of results obtained by Ghoneim. The second is less direct and consists in the analysis of the illusion of the median of the angle, that is to say, the line joining the mid-points of the two (equal) arms of an angle. In an angle or triangle such as that depicted in Fig. 8, the apparent position of the median is obtained by asking the subject to equate the two segments C_1 and C_2. This position will depend on the two angles, 1 and 2: if angle 1 is acute, segment C_1 will be under-estimated and angle 2, being obtuse, will lead to an over-estimation of C_2. These constitute two cumula-

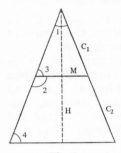

Fig. 8

[1] It is clear that $B = M$ because M (see Fig. 8) $= 2A$ when $A = A'$ (mid-point of Fig. 7) and, at this point, $A + A' = 2A = B$. It is to be noted that $\frac{H}{C} = \sin \alpha$, where α is the angle formed by the side C and the horizontal base (which corresponds to the subjective estimation of its inclination). Moreover, $\frac{M}{C} \left(= \frac{B}{C} \right) = \sin$ β, where β is the complement of α. The expression $\frac{H - M}{C}$ is then the difference between $\sin \alpha$ and $\sin \beta$ and the expressions $\frac{M(H - M)}{C^2}$ and $\frac{H(M - H)}{C^2}$ then correspond to one of these sines multiplied by their difference. Thus one has, again, in terms of sines (relative to the perceptually deformed inclination of the sides C) the general factor of the law, usually expressed in terms of lengths: $(L_1 - L_2)L_2$.

20

tive factors tending to displace the median towards the apex of angle 1. If angle 1 is obtuse, it will produce an over-estimation of C_1, which will displace the median towards the base, but this time in opposition to the effect of angle 2. The effects of angles 3 and 4, being equal and opposite, can be ignored.

The formula for the illusion of the median will then be:

(11) $$P = P_1 + P_2 \text{ if } H > M$$

and $$P = P_1 - P_2 \text{ if } H < M$$

where P_1 and P_2 are the deformations of Prop. 9 or 10 applied to angles 1 and 2.

Calculated on the basis of Props. 9 and 10, the following theoretical values are obtained for the illusion of the median:

	10°	20°	30°	40°	45°	50°	55°	60°	70°	80°
$P =$	0·12	0·22	0·29	0·34	0·36	0·368	0·37	0·366	0·33	0·28
	90°	100°	110°	120°	130°	140°	150°	160°	170°	180°
$P =$	0·20	0·12	0·05	0	−0·04	−0·06	−0·07	−0·06	−0·3	0

The empirical results (Table 5) (obtained with the assistance of Pène) were:[1]

TABLE 5. *Mean error (mm) in judgements of the length of the median of angles*

Rech. 25, Tables 1 and 3

Angle	10°	20°	30°	40°	45°	50°	55°	60°	65°	70°
Adult ($n = 68$)	1·1	1·5	1·6	1·9	1·8	2·03	1·8	2·01	—	1·5
6 to 8 years ($n = 29$)	0·99	1·5	1·8	2·3	2·9	3·0	3·15	3·13	2·9	2·4

Angle	80°	90°	100°	110°	120°	130°	140°	150°	160°
Adult ($n = 68$)	1·3	0·8	0·6	0·15	0·02	−0·3	−0·65	−0·2	0·3
6 to 8 years ($n = 29$)	2·3	1·0	0·2	0·03	−0·3	−1·16	0·98	—	—

The agreement between the experimental results and the theoretical predictions is quite good considering that the illusion of the median is a composite illusion whose calculation is therefore the more approximate: the positive maximum is found at about 55°, the median zero illusion at about 120°, and this is then followed by negative illusions. The measurement of the maximum negative illusion is made somewhat imprecise by the excessive size of the figures involved.

This approximate correspondence between Table 5 and the theoretical values derived from Props. 9, 10 and 11 seems to justify, if confirmed, the sound foundation of Props. 9 and 10 and thus the formulation of the illusion of angles; as already mentioned, a further verification will be examined in respect of the illusion of lozenges.

It may first be recalled, however, that the illusion of angles gives rise to a large number of derived illusions. One of the best known is undoubtedly that of Poggendorf: an oblique bisected by two verticals

[1] *Rech.* 25.

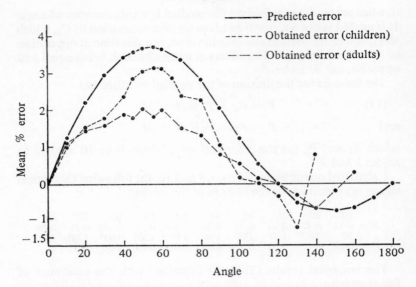

Fig. 9. Comparison of predicted and obtained errors for the median of angles.

separated by an unfilled space seems to consist of two segments which are not in alignment, because, as shown in Fig. 10, the angle α displaces segment 1 to the left and angle β segment 2 to the right. Another well-known illusion is that of Zöllner in which objectively parallel lines are subjectively displaced under the influence of oblique lines forming angles with them.

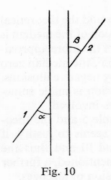

Fig. 10

There is another well-known illusion whose relation to that of angles has not been well established. We have named it the illusion of partially overlapping quadrilaterals and, with Denis-Prinzhorn,[1] have been able to verify that it depends on the influence of the angles α and β (depicted in Fig. 11) added to the over-estimation of the sides *BC* and *EF* of the overlapping squares, under the influence of the segments *AB*, etc. The angle α appears to lead to an under-estimation of its arms *AD* and *BD*, as well as to an over-estimation of its base *AB*, while the side *BC* is over-estimated under the influence of the segment *AB*: the result of the cumulative action of these effects

[1] *Rech.* 21.

and the corresponding effects of angle β, is an under-estimation of the median line to which the quadrilaterals[1] are attached. This interpretation can be verified by modifying the angles α and β: for example, the illusion is accentuated by replacing the squares by upright rectangles, and diminished if the rectangles lie with their long sides along the median line, these changes resulting from alterations in the relevant angles and in the relevant lengths of the segments AB and BC.

This illusion is especially interesting in respect of the changes which occur in its various forms as a function of age. Whereas the simple effects of angles and of rectangles diminish with age, being primary

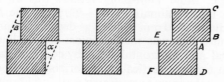

Fig. 11.

(cf. Tables 1 and 5), a secondary factor intervenes in this illusion, one that varies with the figure used. It consists in relating the elements being judged to a reference system. Its importance increases with age and it will be referred to again at a later stage (Chapter III, § 4).

COMMENT I

If this interpretation of the illusion of angles in terms of Props. 7 to 10 is correct, the extent of the illusion should change with changes in the position of the angle and with the equality or inequality of its arms. Figs. 4 to 7 have been drawn in such a way that the sides of the reference rectangles are horizontal and vertical, which means that the bisectors of the inscribed angles are vertical. But if the angles are presented so that their bisectors are not vertical (and the vertical reference rectangles do not stand on one of their sides), or if, above all, the angles are given unequal arms, the illusion should be reduced. This is because the subject could not judge the inclination of the sides of the angles except by referring to vertical parallels and because the calculation based on Fig. 7 (Props. 7 to 8) would be altered by this inequality of the arms. A brief investigation of these two points was carried out by Menillo and the predictions were confirmed. For an equilateral angle of 45° (arms of 10 cm) the mean error was $-7\cdot5\%$ for the length of one of its arms when in the normal position (bisector vertical). It was only $-4\cdot8\%$ when the arm was vertical and

---

[1] The effects of brightness and hue reinforce the effects of the contours and have been analysed in *Rech*. 21, § 4.

the bisector inclined. When judgements were made on one side, held constant in the normal position while the other varied from 1 to 17·5 cm (1, 2, 2·5, 5, 7·5, 10, 12·5, 15 and 17·5 cm), errors of 4·5, 5·1, 7·0, 7·5, 7·9, 7·7, 6·0, 6·0 and 6·3%, respectively, occurred, that is, with a maximum when the arms measured 7·5 and 10 cm (that is, when they were nearly equal).

COMMENT II

We maintained (in footnote 1, p. 19, and in connection with Fig. 7) that the diagonal of a square is under-estimated while its inclination does not change. Mme Vinh-Bang verified this on twenty adults and found an under-estimation of −9·0% in the length of the diagonal of a square of 50 mm which was depicted standing on one of its sides. Measurement was made against simple lines inclined at 45°. The vertical and horizontal sides, by contrast, gave rise, when measured against simple verticals and horizontals, to errors of only 1·7 to 3·4% (when the square was drawn with or without its diagonal). The under-estimation of the depicted diagonal stems, no doubt, from the fact that it forms an angle of 45° with the side of the square: the arms of an angle of 45° being under-estimated, the diagonal is over-estimated. The sides of the square also constitute arms of angles of 45° when this diagonal is drawn in, but as they also form angles of 90° with each other (without deformation of the sides) and as they are also parts of a good form, they tend to resist deformation.

§ 6. ILLUSIONS OF LOZENGES

Another means of verifying the law of the illusion of angles is through the deformations of lozenges, which was undertaken for us by Ghoneim.[1] A lozenge consists in a figure having two pairs of equal and symmetrical angles, one pair acute and the other obtuse. These are the only deforming factors in the figure. This being so, the long diagonal joining the apices of the two acute angles should be under-estimated. This follows, firstly, because the height, H, of the acute angles is under-estimated and because the long diagonal equals $2H$; and, secondly, because the bases of the two acute angles (whose bisectors are the long diagonal, $2H$) are at the same time the heights of the two obtuse angles, and thereby over-estimated. The result is an over-estimation of the short diagonal which reinforces an under-estimation of the long diagonal. The four angles of the lozenge thus co-operate in deforming the figure in the direction of rectangularity. The facts support this, and Ghoneim was able to establish a distribution for the illusion which exhibits two maxima at 45° and 135°.

[1] *Rech.* 37.

It is to be noted that this illusion is produced by two symmetrical angles, and is thus accentuated by comparison with that of a single angle. Consequently the illusion of the two diagonals can be formulated by doubling the numerator in Props. 9 and 10 which, if D_1 equals the long and D_2 the short diagonal, results in:

$$(12) \qquad P = \frac{2K(2H - 2M)2M}{C^2} = \pm \frac{2K(D_1 - D_2)D_2}{C^2}$$

In effect, $2H = D_1$ and $2M = D_2$, and doubling Prop. 10 produces the identical statement, because if $M > H$, then $2M = D_1$ and $2H = D_2$. Furthermore, as this is another case of a reversal of the illusion of rectangles, the sign of P will be negative when the illusion is measured on the long diagonal and positive when measured on the short. The theoretical values calculated on the basis of this proposition will be double those of Props. 9 and 10.

The interest in describing the illusion of lozenges in terms of differences between diagonals is that the same relations between diagonals are found later, in § 7, in the case of parallelograms, but with the term C^2 replaced by a more complex relation between the sides and the surface.

The experimental verifications obtained in support of the above suppositions are presented in Table 6.

TABLE 6. *Mean estimates (% deviations from 50 mm) of the length of the long diagonal (angles 10° to 90°) and of the short diagonal (angles 90° to 170°) of lozenges.*[1] *Figures represent an under-estimation of the long diagonal and an over-estimation of the short diagonal (n = 20 for each age group)*

Rech. 37, Table IX (corrected)

Angle	10°	20°	30°	40°	45°	50°	60°	70°	80°	90°
5 to 6 years	−7·2	−8·8	−10	−10·4	−9·8	−8·8	−7·8	−7·2	−7·0	−7·2
7 to 8 years	−4·8	−6·6	−7·8	−8·2	−9·0	−8·0	−7·2	−7·2	−6·8	−6·4
9 to 10 years	−4·4	−6·0	−7·2	−7·8	−8·2	−6·4	−5·8	−5·8	−5·0	−4·6
11 to 12 years	−3·0	−4·4	−6·0	−7·0	−7·8	−6·4	−5·6	−5·0	−4·8	−4·6
Adult	−4·0	−4·8	−5·6	−6·0	−7·0	−5·4	−5·6	−5·2	−5·0	−4·0

Angle	100°	110°	120°	130°	135°	140°	150°	160°	170°	
5 to 6 years	−7·4	−7·4	−7·2	−7·4	−6·0	−5·4	−5·4	−5·8	−6·2	
7 to 8 years	−5·8	−5·8	−5·8	−5·0	−5·0	−5·4	−5·4	−5·2	−5·2	
9 to 10 years	−5·4	−5·4	−5·0	−4·4	−4·0	−3·8	−4·6	−5·2	−5·8	
11 to 12 years	−5·8	−6·0	−4·8	−4·4	−3·2	−2·8	−3·2	−4·4	−5·0	
Adult	−4·2	−4·0	−3·2	−3·0	−3·2	−1·6	−2·2	−3·4	−3·0	

It can be seen that the negative maximum occurs at 45° for all age groups, except the youngest, which coincides quite well with the maximum over-estimation of acute angles. A minimum under-estimation in the vicinity of 135° or 140° occurs for all ages. But as the measurements involved a comparison between the diagonal, which is a line whose ends are closed, and a simple straight line which is over-

[1] The presentation was made with the diagonal of 50 mm in the vertical position. The order of presentation was ascending. Controls were run with horizontal and oblique presentations and also with descending order of presentation. Under all conditions, the curves remained qualitatively the same.

estimated in so far as it constitutes a very narrow open-ended rect-angle (see § 2), it follows that the position of the abscissa or zero is itself relative to this inevitable error of measurement. But if we take as abscissa for each age the mode, or even the mean, of errors at 10°, 90° and 170°, then all scores falling below this can be considered as genuine negative errors and the others as positive. The minimum under-estimation occurring at 135° to 140° would then in reality be a maximum over-estimation of the short diagonal: for example, if the adult zero is to be located at about −3·5% there would be an approximate under-estimation of the long diagonal of −3·4% at 45° and an over-estimation of +2% of the short diagonal at 140°.

To demonstrate the role played by the angles in the illusion of Table 6, Ghoneim remeasured the long and short diagonals in the same figure but with the apices of the bisected angles omitted. The illusion then decreased, in ten adults, to levels ranging between −0·8 and +4·0% from 20° to 90° and between +0·6 and +2·2% from 100° to 180°, which is equivalent to saying that the illusion was eliminated. The under-estimation of the sides of the lozenge was also measured against the sides of a square and was found to be general (which proves the primacy of acute angles) and to present distributions ana-logous to those of Table 6, with the negative maximum at about 40° or 45°.

§ 7. OVER- AND UNDER-ESTIMATIONS OF CURVATURE

Before proceeding to the discussion of illusions of parallelograms (which, like those of angles, reverse the illusion of rectangles), and then to illusions of trapezia, which in turn lead to the Müller–Lyer illusion, the problem of curvature, which is in some respects related to the illusion of angles, will be examined. It is a problem which we have by no means exhausted, and one which is far more extensive than it seems (including, for example, the illusion of Bourdon, the curvature contrasts of Bühler, etc.). We have limited ourselves to the study, with Vurpillot, of the accentuation of the

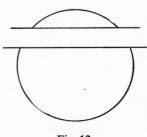

Fig. 12

curvature of some small arcs of circles (which produce a corresponding under-estimation of the chord) and of the over-estimation of the chord in the case of some longer arcs. These two phenomena recall, without in any way being identical with, the under-estimation of obtuse and the over-estimation of acute angles. They merit analysis and independent

26

formulation because they seem to lead to an understanding of most illusions of curvature.

In a circle (Fig. 12) of which a sector is obscured (in the manner of the Poggendorf illusion), the curvature of the lower arc does not seem to coincide exactly with that of the upper arc: its curvature seems to be accentuated. Prompted by the attempted exploration of the illusion of angles (Fig. 7), the following formulation can be applied. If the median of the arc is taken to be the perpendicular bisector, F (Fig. 13), the curvature of the arc can be estimated, at any point, by comparing the distance, A, which separates that point from the chord, Co, with the distance A' which separates the same point from the upper side of the reference rectangle (which is equivalent to the tangent to F). There will be no deformation where the arc intersects the median, but above the median, where $A > A'$, there will be a deformation in the direction of an accentuation of the curvature (as shown in Fig. 13 where the resulting arc is shown in interrupted line); below the median, where $A < A'$, there will be a constriction of the chord, which will be under-estimated.

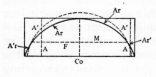

Fig. 13

A two-fold analysis of these effects was undertaken, with the assistance of Vurpillot,[1] measurements being taken on the chord, Co, or on the height, F, as a function of changes in the length of the arc of the circle. Table 7 sets out the results obtained with measurements made on the chord.

TABLE 7. *Mean % error in estimates of the length of the chord of arcs of a circle*
Rech. 27, Table 5

$F\ (= x/32)^2$	1	3	5	8	10	12	16
5 to 6 years ($n = 20$)	1·4	0·8	−6·4	−1·8	−8·4	−2·2	−4·0
7 to 8 years ($n = 30$)	−1·8	−3·6	−2·8	−2·6	−3·8	−4·6	−5·0
9 to 10 years ($n = 20$)	−2·4	−2·6	−3·8	−4·8	−4·0	−6·0	−6·8
Adult ($n = 20$)	−2·4	−3·2	−4·4	−4·8	−5·2	−5·6	−4·8
Overall mean	−1·4	−2·4	−4·2	−3·4	−5·2	−4·6	−5·2
$F\ (= x/32)$	20	22	24	27	29	30	31
5 to 6 years ($n = 20$)	−1·2	1·2	3·8	10·6	17·2	15·8	13·0
7 to 8 years ($n = 30$)	−1·0	0·6	4·4	10·8	13·4	11·0	9·6
9 to 10 years ($n = 20$)	−1·2	0·4	3·2	10·6	13·0	8·6	9·2
Adult ($n = 20$)	−1·6	0·2	3·0	6·6	7·8	6·0	5·2
Overall mean	−1·2	0·6	4·1	9·8	12·9	8·4	9·4

It can be seen that there is a negative error which increases, on the average, until $F = 16$. It then diminishes, passes through a zero

[1] *Rech.* 27.

[2] The letter F represents the 'height' of the arc whose chord, Co, is perceptually evaluated. The values of F (namely 1, 2, 3, ..., 21) have been expressed in thirty-seconds of the diameter of the circle because quarters, eighths and even sixteenths were found to be inadequate: the maximum falls at $F = \frac{29}{32}$ of the diameter of the circle.

illusion at about $F = 21$ or 22, then becomes positive and achieves its maximum at $F = 29$, and finally diminishes again.

An explanation of these facts may be attempted on the analogy of the explanation given for the illusion of angles, by developing the schema sketched out in relation to Fig. 13. Firstly, two sorts of difference coupling could play a part in this case: (1) the relation between A and A'; (2) the relation between the chord and the height of the arc. However, it is suggested that a third possible coupling, not found in the case of angles, may also play a part here. This is the relation between the sector, Ar, of the arc situated above the median and the sector Ar' situated below the median (for example, in the case of the chord, Co_1, of Fig. 14, which coincides with the diameter of the circle, Ar_1, which lies above M, has a value of 2·09 and the combined halves of Ar' a value of only 1·05).[1] But this relation between Ar and Ar' is a function of Co and of F and, in its turn, determines the relations between A and A'. An attempt will therefore be made to apply the general law (Prop. 3, § 2) to this situation, making use of the coupling between Ar and Ar' only, as representative of the two other couplings.

Thus $L_1 = Ar$ and $L_2 = Ar'$ (or the inverse); $L_{max} = Ar + Ar'$ (in which the two halves of Ar' are counted, as they are for Ar in the case of Ar_2); $nL = F$ because the differences between A and A' are a function of F; and $S = CoF$ (the frame of reference). This results in:

$$(13) \quad P = -\frac{F(Ar - Ar')Ar'}{CoF(Ar + Ar')} = -\frac{Ar'(Ar - Ar')}{Co(Ar + Ar')} \quad \text{if } Ar > Ar'$$

that is, until $F = 3/4$ of the diameter ($F = 24$; or until $Co = M_2$ in Fig. 14), and

$$(13b) \quad P = +\frac{F(Ar' - Ar)Ar}{CoF(Ar + Ar')} = \frac{Ar(Ar' - Ar)}{Co(Ar + Ar')} \quad \text{if } Ar' > Ar$$

that is between $F = 24$ and $F = 32$ (= the entire vertical diameter).

The calculation (detailed on page 228 of *Rech.* 27), gives a curve which is remarkably isomorphic with the empirical curve (see Fig. 15), a finding which, we admit, surprised us very much! The theoretical values derived from Props. 13 and 13b are as follows:

$F =$	0·25	0·50	1·0	2·0	4·0	8·0
$P =$	−0·116	−0·118	−0·121	−0·123	−0·131	−0·142
$F =$	12·0	16·0	20·0	22·0	24·0	26·0
$P =$	−0·155	−0·173	−0·116	−0·062	0·0	0·112
$F =$	28·0	29·0	30·0	31·0	31·5	32·0
$P =$	0·169	0·179	0·172	0·139	0·036	0·0

The negative maximum occurs at $F = 16$ and the positive maximum at $F = 29$. The point of zero illusion is theoretically at $F = 24$

[1] In units of radius in $2\pi r$ (2·09 + 1·05 = 3·14 = π if $r = 1$).

whereas it was already present at $F = 21$ in Table 7; however, if the illusion is measured by means of a line representing the chord placed either above the arc or vertically (see Table 4, *Rech.* 27), the median zero illusion occurs at between $F = 23$ and $F = 25$.

By and large, the illusion measured on the height follows the same law (but, of course, with over-estimation of F up to $F = 24$ and then under-estimation). There is one remarkable exception: the under-estimation of the height continues to increase after $F = 29$, finding its maximum at $F = 32$, which implies an under-estimation of the diameter of the complete circle! No doubt the reason is that from $F = 24$ ($= M_2$ in Fig. 14), and above all after $F = 29$, the circular form becomes sufficiently noticeable and 'pregnant' for the evaluation of F to be made as a function of

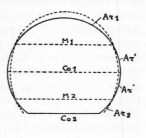

Fig. 14

the vertical and horizontal diameters at one and the same time: in which case the under-estimation of the horizontal diameter ($= Co_1$ in Fig. 12, corresponding to the theoretical negative maximum) carries with it an under-estimation of all the diameters at once. It can be seen, therefore, that not even the 'best' perceptual forms are proof against systematic deformations!

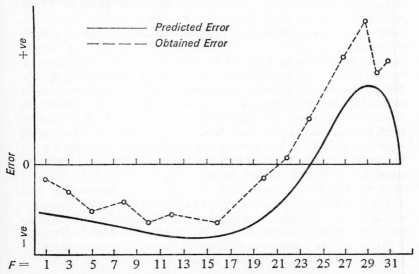

Fig. 15. Comparison of predicted and obtained errors for the judgement of curvature.

§ 8. ILLUSIONS OF PARALLELOGRAMS

While clearly similar to both the lozenge and the rectangle, the parallelogram has neither the four equal sides of the lozenge nor the four equal angles of the rectangle. Nor is it a symmetrical figure in respect of its vertical or horizontal co-ordinates, its transverse or longitudinal medians or its diagonals (unless the figure is folded and one of its halves rotated). If relations of equivalence (simple equality) and of reciprocity (equality by symmetry) possessed by a figure lead to a compensation of deformations, and if inequalities and asymmetries give rise to perceptually uncompensated transformations (deformations), then a greater complexity of perceptual relations can be expected in the case of this figure than has so far been encountered. In fact, it is found that it does give rise to multiple systematic errors (as Sander, and Rausch[1] in particular, have pointed out) which are often very complex (and include some secondary effects which will be analysed later). An example is the well-known illusion to which Sander gave his name.

Although we do not pretend to have exhausted the analysis of this illusion in terms of the general law of primary illusions, it might be of interest to relate its illusory effects to those of lozenges and of rectangles. A start can be made with the under-estimation of the long diagonal, which again reverses the basic principle of the deformation of rectangles (a lengthening of the figure as a result of the over-estimation of its longer side). Sander and Rausch, who were Gestaltists, interpreted this illusion in terms of a tendency for such figures to right themselves (Sander's 'eidotropic' tendency) thus achieving a 'better' because more rectangular form (a tendency which would lead, of course, to an under-estimation of the long diagonal). It could equally well be claimed that the illusory tendencies of lozenges are such as to make these figures more square-like, and that the over- and under-estimation of obtuse and acute angles respectively tends to reduce them to right-angles. But these tendencies, if they exist, themselves require explanation. For this reason the elementary relations have had to be examined first and they simply reveal a tendency for all inequalities to be accentuated. In any case, a rectangle in which no diagonal has been drawn tends to appear less square-like; and although it does exhibit a tendency to appear more square-like when a diagonal is depicted, this is still due to a reinforcement of inequalities (see the explanation given of the reinforcement of inclination, § 5, Fig. 4). The problem of the devaluation of the long diagonal of parallelograms is thus of quite general interest and relates to the

[1] Rausch, E., *Struktur und Metrik figural-optischer Wahrnehmung*, Frankfurt, 1952.

illusion of angles and to all those illusions which were examined in §§ 3 to 5.

In one experimental investigation of this illusion, an attempt was made by Ghoneim,[1] at our request, to compare the long diagonal of parallelograms with those of lozenges. In this, both the diagonal (50 mm) and the angles (the smaller of 45°, which gives the maximum deformation for acute angles and for lozenges) were kept constant, while the four sides and the smaller diagonal of the parallelogram were varied. The sides varied, respectively, from 5 to 45 mm and from 46 to 7·5 mm in ten steps, while the smaller diagonal varied from 32·5 to 21 mm and then to 40 mm. For example, one of the variations considered was a lozenge having sides of 27·5 mm and a small diagonal of 21 mm.

In a second experiment, one diagonal of a parallelogram was compared with one diagonal of a rectangle. This was done with a set of nine parallelograms whose small side (50 mm) and diagonal (100 mm) were kept constant. This diagonal formed the long diagonal of the first five figures (stemming from angles varying from 10° to 75° while the short diagonals varied between 8 and 76 mm) and the short diagonal for the last three figures (stemming from angles of 100°, 110° and 118°, the long diagonal now being of 115, 128 and 140 mm). For example, the sixth variant in the series was a rectangle of 50 × 85 mm. Only one diagonal was depicted in each figure.

A third experiment, to measure the effect of the length of the side, consisted in obtaining measurements of the short diagonal when both diagonals were kept constant (10 and 5 cm), while the lengths of the sides were varied.

In measuring the sides themselves, we thought it would be more interesting to measure the illusions on their median points rather than on the total length of the figures: as each side of a parallelogram is both under-estimated as an arm of an acute angle and over-estimated as an arm of an obtuse angle, the two effects will be opposed; on the other hand, the median point will appear at once too close to the apex of the acute angle and too far from that of the obtuse angle, these two effects being cumulative. Measurements were accordingly taken on the apparent median point of the long side, which was held constant at 9 cm, while in one series (I) the acute angles were varied (from 5° to 60°), while the small side remained constant, and in the other series (II) the angles remained constant while the small side was varied from 2 to 9 cm.

I. Starting with the last experiment (conducted by Dadsetan), the results set out in Table 8 show clearly that the deformation of the

[1] *Rech.* 37.

sides (as measured on the median point) increased as the acute angle became more acute (without exhibiting a maximum at 45°).

TABLE 8. *Mean absolute error (mm) in estimates of the position of the median point of the longer sides of parallelograms as a function of angle. Values represent the combined values for all lengths of the shorter side*

Angle	5°	10°	15°	25°	40°	60°
Upper side						
Series I ($n = 25$ adults)	5·95	4·70	4·42	3·62	3·09	2·00
Series II ($n = 10$)	3·95	3·62	2·44	1·95	1·74	1·07
Mean (upper)	4·90	4·16	3·43	2·78	2·41	1·53
Lower side						
Series I ($n = 25$)	6·81	5·47	4·55	3·96	3·31	2·27
Series II ($n = 7$)	4·07	3·47	3·32	3·04	2·80	1·54
Mean (lower)	5·44	4·47	3·93	3·50	3·05	1·90

When the long side was held constant at 9 cm, and the smaller varied from 2 to 9 cm, the results set out in Table 9 were obtained.

TABLE 9. *Mean absolute error (mm) in estimates of the position of the median point of the longer side of parallelograms as a function of the length of the shorter side. Values represent the combined values for all angles*

Side (cm)	2	3	4	5	6	7	8	9
Upper side								
Series I ($n = 25$ adults)	3·94	4·32	4·24	4·20	4·00	3·30	3·57	3·45
Series II ($n = 10$)	2·21	2·46	2·57	2·12	2·06	1·75	1·36	1·68
Mean (upper)	3·07	3·39	3·40	3·16	3·03	2·52	2·46	2·56
Lower side								
Series I ($n = 25$)	2·74	3·07	3·02	2·81	2·79	2·45	2·34	2·22
Series II ($n = 7$)	3·10	3·53	3·65	3·36	3·28	3·65	2·93	3·10
Mean (lower)	2·92	3·30	3·33	3·08	3·03	3·05	2·63	2·66

It seems possible to reduce these facts to the following formula which accounts both for the increase in the illusion with diminution of the acute angle and for the obtained maximum for a short side of 3 cm ($A = B/3$):

$$(14) \qquad P = -\frac{(D_1 - D_2)\, D_2 \times (B - A)A}{S}$$

where D_1 is the long diagonal, D_2 the short diagonal, B the long side, A the short side and S the surface. Calculated on this formula, the following predicted values emerge.[1]

	2 cm	3 cm	4 cm	5 cm	6 cm	7 cm	8 cm	9 cm
5°	2·17	2·88	2·54	2·00	1·34	0·73	0·26	0·19
10°	1·43	1·44	1·28	1·02	0·70	0·40	0·17	0·18
15°	0·86	0·88	0·83	0·71	0·51	0·31	0·15	0·17
25°	0·50	0·56	0·52	0·45	0·35	0·24	0·13	0·15
40°	0·27	0·33	0·32	0·30	0·29	0·17	0·10	0·13
60°	0·14	0·17	0·18	0·17	0·15	0·13	0·06	0·08

The weakening of the illusion which accompanies the increase of the size of the angle, and the maximum illusion with the small side of 3 cm, are thus catered for.

[1] For the small side of 9 cm the factor $(B-A)\,A$ being equal to 0, only the expression $(D_1 - D_2)D_2/S$ remains.

II. The experiment concerning the deformation of the small diagonal (usually over-estimated) was conducted with the help of Mme Vinh-Bang and produced the results set out in Table 10. The short diagonal was always presented in the vertical position and the diagonals measured 5 and 10 cm.

TABLE 10. *Mean % error in estimates of the length of the shorter diagonal of parallelograms of the dimensions shown (n = 20 adults)*

Sides (mm)	75 × 22	73 × 31	70 × 36	65 × 46	62 × 49	58 × 54	54 × 60	48 × 64	43 × 65
Angles	160°	145°	138°	129°	128°	126°	127°	127°	131°
Mean % error	14·00	13·25	12·05	7·25	7·15	5·85	1·55	2·95	2·60

Prop. 14 gives the following theoretical values which are in approximate agreement with the empirical findings:

Angle =	160°	145°	138°	129°	128°
P =	4·30	2·25	1·67	0·95	0·67
Angle =	126°	127°	129°	131°	
P =	0·21	0·35	1·50	1·67	

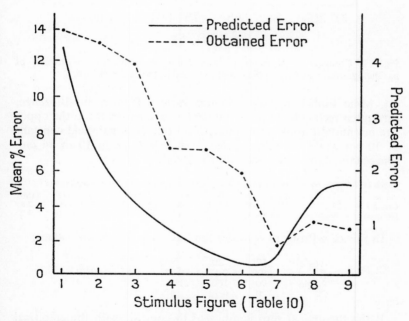

Fig. 16. Comparison of predicted and obtained errors for the illusion of parallelograms of variable sides and angles, with measurement on the short diagonal.

The reversal in the curve from the point 54 × 60 (Table 10) is due to the reversal of the relative values of the sides.

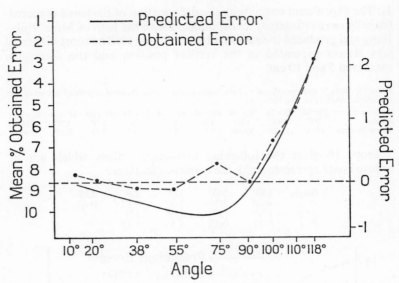

Fig. 17. Comparison of predicted and obtained errors for the illusion of parallelograms measured on diagonals enclosed in the angles shown.

III. Mme Vinh-Bang, using figures varying from a quasi-lozenge, through a rectangle, to non-rectangular parallelograms in the opposite orientation, took measurements on one diagonal, held constant at 10 cm while the other varied from 0·28 through 10 to 14 cm. She obtained the results set out in Table 11.

TABLE 11. *Mean % error in estimates of the length of diagonals enclosed by the angles shown*

Angle	10°	20°	38°	55°	75°	90°	100°	110°	118°
Group I ($n = 20$ adults)	−8·3	−8·5	−8·9	−8·8	−7·7	−8·6	−6·8	−5·1	−2·8
Group II ($n = 20$ adults)[1]	−4·6	−4·7	−5·1	−5·1	−5·3	−5·5	−3·8	−1·9	0·2

In this case Prop. 14 provides the following theoretical values:

Angle =	10°	20°	38°	55°	75°
P =	−0·09	−0·17	−0·32	−0·55	−0·59
Angle =	90°	100°	110°	118°	
P =	0	0·72	1·5	2·4	

If the theoretical zero is adjusted to coincide with the empirical results for the rectangle of 90° (that is to say −8·6% or −5·5%) a theoretical curve results which broadly coincides with the empirical one, but with recovery at 90° and not at 100° as in Table 11 (see Fig. 17).

[1] This second group of subjects was drawn from students of a Technical College and displayed a much weaker illusion.

It may be noted that when the diagonals were no longer vertical but the short sides were horizontal, the maximum was −9·4% at 80° (−8·6% at 90°; −8·8 to −8·9% between 30° and 75°).

IV. When the long diagonals of lozenges (with small angles kept constant at 45°) were compared with the long diagonals of parallelograms of unequal sides (of 5 × 46 mm to 45 × 7·5 mm passing through the dimensions of the lozenge, of 27·5 × 27·5mm), the results set out in Table 12 were obtained by Ghoneim.

TABLE 12. *Mean % error in estimates of the length of the long diagonal of parallelograms of constant angle as a function of the length of one side (n = 10 for each age group)*

Rech. 37, Table XXI (corrected). See also Fig. 24, *Rech.* 37

Side (mm)	5	10	15	20	25	27·5	30	35	40	45
5 to 6 years	−7·7	−9·4	−11·5	−12·3	−13·5	−14·5	−13·9	−10·6	−8·6	−6·9
7 to 8 years	−6·4	−9·1	−10·9	−11·8	−13·2	−14·1	−12·0	−10·4	−8·2	−6·1
9 to 10 years	−6·1	−8·2	−10·6	−11·2	−12·8	−13·3	−11·9	−9·7	−7·3	−5·1
11 to 12 years	−4·5	−7·5	−9·5	−10·6	−11·4	−12·6	10·3	−8·6	−7·0	−4·0
Adult	−2·8	−4·5	−7·2	−7·8	−9·3	−10·0	−8·6	−6·4	−3·5	−2·9

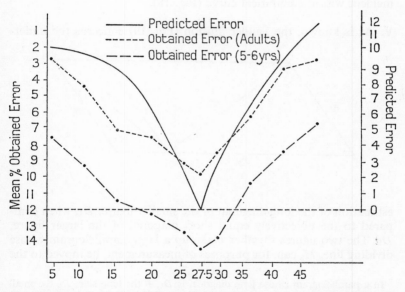

Fig. 18. Comparison of predicted and obtained errors for the illusion of parallelograms with the angle held constant, with measurement on the long diagonal. (See *Rech.* 37. Fig. 24 for further details.)

In this case it can be seen that under-estimation of the long diagonal of a lozenge is greater than that of the long diagonal of other

C   35

parallelograms. This is not the case when a lozenge is compared with parallelograms of different angles. In the present situation, in which the angle remains constant at 45°, it is convenient, in calculating the theoretical values for Table 12, to retain only the factor $(B–A)A$, and to omit that of $(D_1 — D_2)D_2$ which represents the angular variation in Prop. 14.[1] For a constant angle one thus has:

(14b)
$$P = \frac{(B - A)A}{S}$$

which gives

$A =$	5	10	15	20	25	27·5	30	35	40	45 mm
$P =$	9·9	9·5	8·8	6·1	1·9	0	2·8	6·3	9·3	11·3

If the theoretical point of zero illusion is located at the illusion obtained for $A = 27·5$, which can be calculated with the formula for the lozenge, a theoretical curve emerges which is approximately coincident with the empirical curve (Fig. 18).

V. As is known, the Sander illusion (Fig. 19) concerns the under-

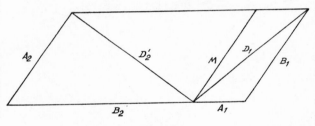

Fig. 19.

estimation of the long diagonal of the smaller figure, D_1, when compared to the objectively equal short diagonal of the larger figure, D_2. The two figures together make up a large parallelogram whose dividing line, M, can, for purposes of measurement, be moved to the

---

[1] In a parallelogram whose long diagonal is D_1, B the long side, D_2 the small diagonal, A the small side, and α the angle formed by A and B, one has:

$$D_1 = A^2 + B^2 + 2AB \cos \alpha$$
$$D_2 = A^2 + B^2 - 2AB \cos \alpha$$

from which it follows that, for a constant angle α, the diagonals and their difference couplings, $(D_1 — D_2)D_2$, are unequivocally determined by the values of A and of B.

right or left (being kept parallel to the shorter sides, A_2 and B_2), until the two diagonals appear to be equal. Vinh-Bang, using Ipsen's[1] technique but without constrained fixation, studied this illusion with groups of ten children aged between 5 and 12 years and with twenty adults. He used 22 variants of the figure, the dividing line being moved while the overall dimensions, 125 × 61 mm and angles of 55° and 125°, were kept constant. The resulting lengths of D_1 and D_2 are shown below and the values of the illusion (supposing those relative lengths to be judged equal) are also shown, having been calculated using Wirth's formula, which was also used by Ipsen: $P = 100 - \dfrac{100 \times u}{xm}$, where $Xu =$ the judged relation between the two diagonals when the subject judges them to be equal (therefore $= 1$) and $Xm =$ the objective relation between the two diagonals:

Figures	I	II	III	IV	V	VI	VII	VIII
D_1	77·5	80	83·5	85·5	86·5	88	89·5	90
D_2	82	80	78	75	73	72·5	71·5	70
P	−6·3	0	6·6	12·3	15·5	17·4	20	21·9

Figures	IX	X	XI	XII									XXII
D_1	92	93	94	95·5	-	-	-	-	-	-	-	-	109
D_2	69	68	67	66	-	-	-	-	-	-	-	-	57·5
P	24·3	26·5	28·7	30·6	-	-	-	-	-	-	-	-	47·4

The results obtained are shown in Table 13:

TABLE 13. *Mean error for the Sander Illusion measured by the Wirth–Ipsen method and with an exposure time of 10 seconds (n = 10 for each group of children, 20 adults)*

Age group	5 yrs	6 yrs	7 yrs	8 yrs	9 yrs	10 yrs	11 yrs	12 yrs	Adult
Mean error (mm)	15·3	21·3	24·6	25·3	24·3	24·5	23·6	24·5	15·1

This distribution of errors raises two problems: (1) why does the mean error fall between 15 and 25 % (around Figure VII and between Figures V and IX); and (2) why does it increase from 5 to 7 years, reach a plateau between 7 and 9 years and then decrease in the adult?

In answer to the first question, Props. 14 and 14b may be applied, but omitting the factor $(D_1 - D_2)D_2$, the angles of the parallelogram in question being constant. If the effects of $(D_1 - D'_2)D'_2$ on the two parallelograms (see Fig. 19) are calculated, it is seen that they are proportional to the surfaces involved in the formula used below. As was done in IV above, we will limit ourselves to the calculation of $P = (B-A)A/S$ and will apply it to the two diagonals D_1 and D'_2 on the assumption that the illusion will be maximal when the under-estimation of D_1 and the over-estimation of D'_2 are approximately equal. This is because if the under-estimation of D_1 is greater than the over-estimation of D'_2, or the converse, the subject will no longer

[1] *Nene. Psychol. Stud.*, 1926.

37

perceive the equality of D_1 and D'_2. The calculation, in values of $(B-A)A/S$ in relation to the lengths[1] of D_1 and D'_2, gives:

Figures	I	II	III	IV	V	VI	VII	VIII
PD_1	10·32	8·13	7·06	6·08	5·67	5·22	4·80	4·44
$PD'_2 =$	5·58	5·62	5·34	5·24	5·19	5·02	4·88	4·77
Diff. =	4·74	2·51	1·72	0·84	0·48	0·20	−0·08	−0·33

Figures	X	XI	XII	XIII	XIV	XV	XVI		
$PD_1 =$	4·02	3·65	3·29	2·93	2·59	2·25	1·91	- - -
$PD'_2 =$	4·58	4·42	4·22	4·01	3·80	3·54	3·29	- - -
Diff. =	−0·56	−0·77	−0·93	−1·08	−1·21	−1·29	−1·38	- - -

It can be seen, therefore, that D_1 and D'_2 are in fact equally deformed in Figure VII of the experimental series, and that differences increase on either side. The values obtained by Vinh-Bang are thus entirely compatible with preceding illusions because the distributions of Table 13 coincide with the predictions made on the assumptions of that compatibility.

As to the question of why the illusion increases between the ages of 5 and 7 years, it is clear that the comparison of the two diagonals, belonging to separate parallelograms, could only be influenced by all the factors involved (sides, etc.) to the extent that the figure is well structured. As a complex figure of nine separate elements is involved, it is to be expected that this structuring would not be achieved immediately but that it would develop with age (in fact, to 7 years). This accounts for the initial increase of the illusion. It then remains stable up to the age when the analytic exploration of the adult gives rise to certain compensations, the two extreme mean errors (15·3% at 5 years and 15·1% at adulthood) being similar but not comparable.

§ 9. OVER-ESTIMATIONS OF THE SHORT SIDE AND UNDER-ESTIMATIONS OF THE LONG SIDE OF TRAPEZIA

A trapezium has two pairs of equal angles, two equal but not parallel sides and two parallel but unequal sides. It is therefore a more complex figure than the parallelogram, lacking the latter's pairs of parallel sides. On the other hand, it is perfectly symmetrical about its

---

[1] Under the form $PD_1 = \dfrac{(B_1 - A_1)A_1}{S_1} D_1$ and $PD'_2 = \dfrac{(B_2-A_2)A_2}{S_2} D'_2$ where B_1, A_1 and S_1 are the sides and surface of the right-hand parallelogram, and B_2, A_2 and S_2 those of the other (see Fig. 19). It is to be noted that the relating of $(B - A)$ A/S to D_1 and to D'_2 does not represent the reintroduction of the factor $(D_1 - D_2)D_2$ but, given that D_1 and D'_2 do not belong to the same parallelogram, is simply a question of calculating the values $(B–A)$ A/S relative to the lengths of the deformed elements, D_1 and D'_2, and not absolutely as would be done if the two diagonals belonged to the same parallelogram.

transverse median (that is, the axis of the vertical co-ordinate if the trapezium is set on one of its parallel sides). Moreover, it incorporates systematic errors that are much simpler than those of the parallelogram.

However, it introduces a new problem, one which will recur in the Müller–Lyer and the Delbœuf illusions. The problem is to explain why the short side is over-estimated and the long side under-estimated when, if this were the only relation involved, the opposite effect should occur? Examples of this inversion already encountered (the enlargement of rectangles under the influence of depicted diagonals, under-estimation of the height of acute angles and their apparent enlargement under the influence of the inclination of their arms, etc.), were all found to be due to effects of inclination (see Fig. 4). The present inversion might also be due to the acute and obtuse angles involved: their respective over- and under-estimation realigns the non-parallel sides and thus changes the relative apparent lengths of the parallel sides. However, this explanation could not be valid for the Müller–Lyer illusion (when drawn without barbs, but merely as parallel but unequal lines (see Fig. 22, No. 3, p. 45, below). It would be even less valid for the concentric circles of Delbœuf when the smaller (inner) circle is over-estimated under the influence of the larger and the larger (outer) circle is under-estimated under the influence of the smaller.

To say that there is assimilation and not contrast in such cases, is to offer only a verbal explanation: our whole concern so far has been to advance beyond such facile distinctions towards a general explanation in terms of the accentuation of inequalities (contrasts), even when the result is a subjective equalisation of some unequal dimensions as a result of an inversion which is itself due to the accentuation of other inequalities (as in the case of inclinations). The problem is to account for this inversion in those illusions (the trapezium, the Müller-Lyer and the Delbœuf illusions) where the effects of angles cannot be invoked because they are not always present.

The perceptual relations involved in the illusion of trapezia are different from those involved in rectangles. The illusion of rectangles derives essentially from the inequality between the long and the short sides, an inequality which does not constitute a genuine part of the figure: it cannot be isolated and perceived as such. In trapezia, however, the difference between the long and the short sides is a virtual line (A' in Fig. 20) which delimits an unfilled but immediately perceptible space, whose extent corresponds to the divergence of the non-parallel sides: A' is a genuine part of the figure (but not, of course, of the geometric operational figure) because the apprehension of obliques always involves reference to verticals and to horizontals.

The novelty lies in the introduction of a virtual line as a factor on an equal footing with real lines. In cases where $A' < A$ (which is not always the case) and $A' < B$ (always the case), A' is devalued by both A and B, with the result that A is over-estimated and B correspondingly devalued. The reversal created by the relation $A < B$ in these cases is due to the under-estimation of their difference under the influence of the two terms of the relation, and not only to the effects of angles. But as the devaluation of the difference can also be expressed in terms of angles (because the difference A' is a function of the

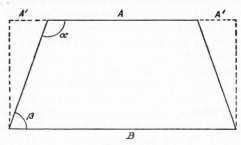

Fig. 20.

angles α and β of Fig. 20), the relation existing between these two interpretations must be examined.

Two experiments involving trapezia were conducted with the help of Deutsch. In the first, we examined the effects on the shorter base (held constant at 60 mm), of variations in the longer (varied between 65 and 500 mm), the height remaining constant at 35 mm. In the second experiment, the effect was measured on the longer base (constant at 60 mm) when variations were made in the shorter (from 5 to 55 mm), with the same constant height of 35 mm. In all cases, measurements were taken against an independent straight line of variable length. The results for adult subjects are set out in Tables 14 and 15.

TABLE 14. *Mean % error in estimates of the length of the shorter (constant) base of a trapezium as a function of variations in the length of the longer base (adult subjects)*

Longer base (mm)	65	70	75	90	100	110	120	130	140	150	160
Mean % error	1·9	3·3	6·0	11·0	11·3	13·9	15·9	16·0	15·2	14·8	10·5

Longer base (mm)	170	180	190	200	210	220	300	350	400	500
Mean % error	10·1	10·3	9·1	8·9	7·5	7·8	8·9	8·3	4·4	5·2

TABLE 15. *Mean % error in estimates of the length of the longer (constant) base of a trapezium as a function of variations in the length of the shorter base*

Shorter base (mm)	5	10	15	20	30	40	50	55
Mean % error	−7·6	−8·3	−8·4	−7·4	−6·8	−5·7	−3·8	−2·2

It can be seen that there is a well-defined maximum positive illusion, in Experiment I, in the region of $B = 120$ to 130 mm, or $B =$

$2A$, and a less well-marked maximum negative illusion, in Experiment II, in the region of $A = 5$ to 20 mm.

I. Without referring to the effects of angles, which will be discussed later, three or five different relations can be considered in accounting for the over-estimation of the short base, A.

(1) That between A and B (see Fig. 20).
(2) That between B and A'; or (2b) between B and $2A'$.
(3) That between A and A'; or (3b) between A and $2A'$.

Note, first, that (1) and (2b) are equivalent because $B - A = 2A'$ and $B - 2A' = A$. It follows from this that if B varies while A remains constant, B should be related to $2A'$ (2b) and not to A' alone (2), because the variations of B and of $2A'$ are concomitant. By contrast, A, held constant, should be related to A' alone, in the form of $2(A - A')$, and not $A - 2A'$, because the variations of A' are independent of A. Therefore only three possible relations remain: (1), (2b) and (3), of which two are equivalent. Furthermore, relations (1) and (2b) cannot apply simultaneously, because if $B = A + 2A'$ and if B devalues A and $2A'$ simultaneously, it must devalue itself. But as A is over-estimated, the relation (2b) is the appropriate one: the devaluation of $2A'$ (a difference between A and B) has the effect of exaggerating A and of devaluing B (but this time indirectly), which conforms to the facts. The principal factor in the over-estimation of A, which will be denoted P_1, can be written as follows:

$$(15) \quad P_1 = \frac{(B - 2A')2A'}{BH} \times \frac{A}{B} = \frac{(B - 2A')2A'}{B^2H} \quad \text{if } A = 1$$

Assigning the value of 1 to A, held constant, and the value of 0·58 to H, the following theoretical values emerge:

$B =$	65	70	75	80	90	100	110	120	130	140	150
$P_1 =$	0·12	0·21	0·27	0·32	0·37	0·41	0·427	**0·431**	0·428	0·422	0·41

$B =$	160	170	180	190	200	210	220	300	350	400	500
$P_1 =$	0·40	0·39	0·38	0·37	0·36	0·34	0·33	0·27	0·24	0·21	0·19

As can be seen, there is a relatively close agreement between theoretical values (which are only relative, not absolute)[1] and the empirical values of Table 14: a maximum in the region of $B = 2A$ (120) and a rapid climb in the curve between 65 and 120, followed by a gradual descent between 120 and 500.

The relation between A and A' (3) passes through a maximum at $B = 90$, zero at $B = 180$ ($A' = A = 60$) and finally increases again.

---

[1] Whence the legality of reducing them to 1 (expressing them in tenths).

41

Either this relationship plays no part, or it is incorporated in the preceding relation[1] (Prop. 15), in which case the maximum would remain at $B = 2A$ (120) and there would be a second rise at about $B = 200$ to 250, which might correspond to certain irregularities in the empirical curves (but, of course, there is no proof that the second relation does interact on an equal footing with the first).

It may be noted at this point that when $B = 2A$ (producing the maximum illusion) the angle formed by the non-parallel sides and the short and long base are respectively 135° and 45° (for the given height). The illusion might then be said simply to derive from the cumulative effects of over-estimated acute and under-estimated obtuse angles. However, these two possible interpretations are not theoretically equivalent because, if the values calculated on the basis of Prop. 15 are recalculated for different heights, the maximum illusion is still found to occur at $B = 2A$, when the angles would no longer be of 45° and of 135°. The problem will therefore be left open and will be resumed when we discuss double trapezia.

II. The devaluation of A' also accounts for the under-estimation of the long base, because the under-estimation of the difference between A and B entails both an under-estimation of B and an over-estimation of A. But since only the short base was varied in Experiment II, it is no longer permissible, within our rules of calculation, to relate B to $2A'$, but only to A', and we thus have:

$$(16) \qquad P_1 = -\frac{(B - A')A'}{BH} \times \frac{2B}{B} = -\frac{2(B - A')A'}{B^2H}$$

whence, for $B = 1$,

$$-\frac{2(B - A')A'}{H}$$

which, with $B = 1$ and $H = 0.58$ ($\frac{35}{60}$ of B), gives:

$A =$	0	5	10	15	20	30	40	45	50	55 mm
$P_1 =$	−0·86	−0·85	−0·83	−0·80	−0·76	−0·64	−0·47	−0·37	−0·27	−0·13

Although the distribution of these theoretical values conforms approximately to that of Table 15, its maximum does not fall at $A = B/4$, as it does in Table 15, but at $A = 0$, that is, when the figure becomes a triangle. It should be noted, in passing, that in a later experiment on double trapezia (see § 10, Table 16) the maximum does occur at $A = 0$. But where a single trapezium is involved and where the figure with $A = 0$ is a single triangle and not a lozenge, it is possible that relation (2), which plays a part in Prop. 16, is not the only

---

[1] In multiplying the numerator by $(A–A')A'$, if $A > A'$, or by $(A'–A)A$ if $A' > A$, but without redividing by B^2H.

one at work but that two other relations identified above may also intervene: relation (3b) (between A and $2A'$ because A and A' co-vary) and relation 1 (between B and A). For $B = 1$, relation (3b) results in:

$$(17) \quad P_2 = -\frac{(A - 2A')2A' \times B}{BH \times B} = -\frac{(A - 2A')2A'}{H} \text{ if } A > 2A'$$

and $\quad \dfrac{(2A' - A)A}{H} \quad$ if $A < 2A'$

This relation does suggest a maximum for $A = 15$ $(= B/4)$ but a zero illusion for $A = 30$ $(B/2)$ and a second maximum for $A = 45$ $(3B/4)$. By contrast, if Props. 16 and 17 are combined (by multiplying their numerators but dividing only once by $H = 0.58$) we find:

$A =$	5	10	15	20	30	40	45	50	55 mm
$P_1 \times P_2 =$	0·59	0·92	1·00	0·84	0·64	0·52	0·46	0·29	0·09

which now produces a single maximum for $A = B/4$, which corresponds to the empirical distribution of Table 15.

For relation (1), we have:

$$(18) \qquad P_3 = \frac{(B - A)A}{BH} \times \frac{B}{B} = \frac{(B - A)A}{H} \text{ if } B = 1$$

which is equivalent to Prop. 15 and, like it, results in a maximum at $A = B/2$. But if this relation is combined with the other two (that is, with 16 and 17) the maximum again occurs at $A = B/4$. It should be noted at this stage that if the empirical maximum of Table 15 did occur at $A = B/4$, it would no longer correspond to an angle of 45°. On the other hand, for $A = 0$, the maximum found for the double trapezia $(H = B/2)$ does correspond to an angle of 45°, but then raises a problem to which we shall return at the end of the next section.

It can thus be seen that while the two illusions of trapezia are adequately explained in terms of the relations between the two base lines and their difference, considered as an element of the figure, this implies that all three relations may intervene simultaneously. If this is so, it is possible either that one of them may carry more weight than the others, that is to say, may impose itself with a greater probability, or that all three may act equally. If one relation does carry more weight, it is most likely to be the relation between B and A' (Props. 15 and 16), because B is the overall length and A' the difference between it and the length of the shorter base. Either way, the prediction agrees well enough with the empirical findings: the clearly accentuated maximum of Table 14 corresponds equally well to Prop. 15 and to its composition with the other factor; and the imprecise maximum of Table 15 is predicted by the composition of Props. 16, 17 and 18. Moreover, as we shall now see, a well-defined maximum illusion is obtained with double trapezia at a point which corresponds to predictions based on Prop. 16.

§ 10. THE MÜLLER–LYER ILLUSION

The famous Müller–Lyer illusion is nothing more than the outcome of a double trapezium effect; the figure with the outward-facing barbs represents two trapezia joined along the shorter of the two parallel sides, and the figure with the inward-facing barbs two trapezia joined along the longer of the two sides, as shown in Fig. 21.

Fig. 21.

This will be established presently by showing that the distribution of errors is the same with the double trapezium as it is with the usual Müller–Lyer configurations. It is strange that of all the many attempted explanations of this illusion none has been offered in terms of an analysis of its elementary component, the trapezium itself.[1]

It might be thought that the [laws of trapezia, established in § 9, would meet the case. However, it is still necessary to verify the explanation offered against variants of the Müller–Lyer figure in which the barbs are included or excluded (that is, with or without the presence of depicted angles). It is also necessary to search for the relation between the proposed schema and the explanation in terms of angles.

The analysis of the figure was accordingly reopened, with the assistance of Müller, in order to complete the results previously obtained[2] and to relate it to the problems of the trapezium. To this end, the forms of the figure depicted in Fig. 22 were studied:

I.1. Double trapezia formed along the shorter base.
I.2. The classical figure with outward-facing barbs.
I.3. The same figure without barbs.
II.1. Double trapezia joined along the longer base.

---

[1] Cf. the explanations of Wundt and of Delbœuf in terms of ocular movements, said to be favoured or inhibited by the outward or inward turning barbs.
[2] *Rech.* 11.

II.2. The classical figure with inward-facing barbs.
II.3. The same figure without barbs.

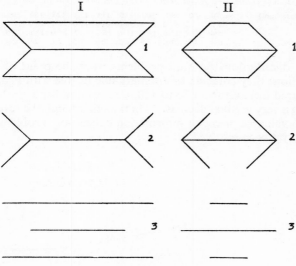

Fig. 22.

To simplify matters, the same symbolism will be employed as was used in § 9 (see Fig. 23): *B* represents the longer base of the trapezium, or its counterpart in forms 2 and 3; *A* the shorter base; and *2A'* the

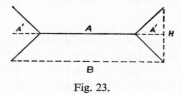

Fig. 23.

difference between the two bases. In all the figures used, *A* measured 60 mm in series I, as did *B* in series II. The height, *H*, was 60 mm (that is, 30 mm in each trapezium and not 35 mm as it was in § 9).

I. The first finding obtained from Experiment I was that Forms I.1, I.2 and I.3 produced the same general distribution of errors with the maximum at the same point but with quantitative differences in the extent of the illusion: the illusion is strongest with the double trapezia (I.1), hardly less so with the classical figure (I.2), and much

45

weaker with the unequal parallels (I.3). These results are set out in Table 16a.

TABLE 16a. *Mean % positive error for the Müller–Lyer figures shown (n = 20 adults for each figure)*

Length of base (mm)	70	80	90	100	110	115	120	125	150	200	250	300
Fig. I.1	4·9	9·2	12·2	15·3	16·0	16·6	17·6	15·7	15·7	11·2	8·8	6·8
Fig. I.2	5·4	10·5	13·8	14·4	11·6	15·5	16·1	15·0	13·8	7·5	5·6	5·3
Fig. I.3	0·9	1·0	1·6	2·9	3·2	2·6	3·5	2·6	2·3	2·6	1·6	1·5

These distributions pose no problems from the point of view of formulation: they coincide to a remarkable degree with Prop. 15 of § 9: a rapid increase from 70 to 110, a maximum for $B = 2A$ (120), and then a very gradual decrease.[1] On the other hand, the results provide two valuable pieces of information concerning problems which have not yet been resolved.

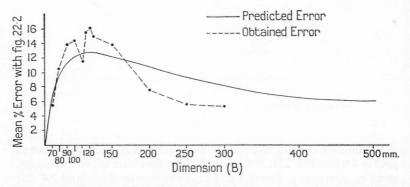

Fig. 24. Comparison of predicted and obtained errors for the classical form of the Müller–Lyer figure.

In the first place, they confirm the identity of the illusions of trapezia and of Müller–Lyer: firstly, the distribution of errors is effectively the same for form I.1 as it is in Table 14 (§ 9: single trapezium), with no appreciable difference in average extent (maxima of 17·6% and 16%); and secondly, this distribution is repeated, in a scarcely weakened form, for the classical figure (II.1), the curve being remarkably similar to that obtained with a single trapezium (Table 14: maxima at 15·9 to 16% and at 16·1% for $B = 120$ mm).

In the second place, a solution to the problem of the respective roles of angles and of the relation $B > 2A'$ can now be proposed: the three figures, I.1, I.2 and I.3, differ markedly in regard to angles but are equivalent in respect of the relations between B and $2A'$.

[1] It is true that H here equals 1 while it was calculated as 0·58 of A in the values given for Prop. 15, but the calculated maximum is still found at $B = 2A$.

(1) When the illusion is at its strongest in form I.1, there are two pairs of depicted angles of 45° and 135° respectively. The angles may play an important role here and add their effects to those of $B > 2A'$. This would explain why this figure provides the strongest illusion.

(2) The classical Form, I.2, has only one deforming angle, of 135°, when the illusion is at its maximum. The barbs themselves include angles, but these are right-angles and do not, therefore, occasion any deformation.

(3) Form I.3, formed of unequal parallels, has no depicted angles. Looking at this figure (with B at its optimum length of 120 mm), one of necessity perceives the virtual angles of 90° formed by the extremities of the longer external lines and those of the shorter inner one, but does not perceive the virtual angles of 45° and 135° corresponding to those of form I.1. This figure produces the weakest illusion.

It is no doubt because the angles contribute to the strength of the illusion that it is strongest with form I.1, slightly weaker with I.2 and very weak with I.3. Caution should still be exercised, however, because the presence of the non-parallel sides of the trapezium in I.1 and of the barbs in I.2 also emphasises the inequality $B > 2A'$. However, the role of the angles, while not denied, is considered to be only a supporting one because it cannot explain either the systematic errors associated with form I.3, weak as they are, or the position of the maximum for this figure, which is still found for $B = 2A$.

Two verifications of the dominance of the effects of the relation $B > 2A'$ over those of the angles were undertaken, as a precaution, with the help of Müller. (1) With the angles of 45° and 135° held constant in form I.1, and with the height constant at 6 cm, A and B were simultaneously varied through $A = 3, 6, 9$ and 12 cm, and $B = 9, 12, 15$ and 18 cm, the difference $B - A = 2A'$ thus remaining constant at 6 cm; (2) with the same angles of 45° and 135° held constant, the length of the non-parallel sides (barbs) was varied. Consequently the length of B (8, 10, 12, 14 and 16 cm), of $2A'$ (2, 4, 6, 8 and 10 cm), and of H (2, 4, 6, 8 and 10 cm) also varied. The length of A remained constant at 6 cm.

The results obtained are set out in Table 16b.

TABLE 16b. *Mean % error in estimates of the length of the shorter base of double trapezia (Müller–Lyer) for the dimensions shown (n = 21 adults)*

	Experiment 1			
A (cm)	3	6	9	12
B (cm)	9	12	15	18
$2A'/B$	6/9	6/12	6/15	6/18
Mean % error	11·3	18·6	12	8·1

		Experiment 2			
A (cm)	8	10	12	14	16
B (cm)	2	4	6	8	10
$2A'/B$	2/8	4/10	6/12	8/14	10/16
Mean % error	15·8	19·5	21·3	19·3	15·8

47

It is thus verified that the error varies considerably as a function of the relation between $2A'$ and B. It more than doubles between $A = 12$ and $A = 6$ in (1), and is still appreciable in (2). In both cases the maximum remains at $2A' = B/2$, as in Table 16. As the angles remained constant, these results seem to prove that the angles play only a secondary role of simple reinforcement.

The genetic evolution of this illusion has been well known since the time of Binet: it decreases in strength with age. *Rech.* 11 provides fresh information in this connection, demonstrating a quite regular diminution of the illusion with age which corresponds to a parallel diminution as a function of repetition (see Chapter III, § 2, Table 56).

II. Forms II.1, II.2 and II.3 provided equally instructive results, which are set out in Table 17.

TABLE 17. *Mean % negative error for the Müller–Lyer figures shown* ($n = 20$ *adults for each figure*)

Length of A (mm)	0	10	20	30	40	50
Fig. II.1	−12·5	−10·3	−9·8	−9·4	−7·0	−4·25
Fig. II.2	—	−6·3	−3·6	−1·6	−0·58	−0·20
Fig. II.3	—	−1·6	−1·3	−1·0	−1·1	−1·5

One interesting fact emerges: in the case of double trapezia, the maximum is found at $A = 0$, when the figure is a lozenge (in fact, a square standing on one corner, because $H = A$). This distribution of errors for II.1 corresponds to the deformation P_1 (Prop. 16, § 9), that is to say, to the devaluation of A' by B. Deformations P_2 and P_3 do not exert any influence here, at least at the maximum when $A = 0$, but the slight difference between the errors for $A = 10$ cm and $A = 20$ cm remind one of the maximum at $A = 15$ mm in Table 15.

There are various indications that angles do play some role in these cases. For example, the relative weakness of the illusion in II.3 suggests their intervention in II.1 and II.2. Similarly, the illusion is much stronger in II.1 than in II.2, a difference which was not found between I.1 and I.2 where the angles are not depicted. However, when the illusion is at its strongest, in II.1, the angles of 45° combine to form an overall angle of 90° and this casts some doubt on the reality of their influence at the very point where the illusion is at its maximum (because an angle of 90° does not exercise a deforming effect). The figures of Table 17 thus confirm the conclusions drawn from the results obtained with forms I. The angles seem to play a reinforcing role but do not exclude the effects of the relations between A' and B, a relation whose major role is indicated by the strong agreement between the distributions obtained with form II.1 and the predictions based on Prop. 16.

The effects of modifying the height of the figures have yet to be

48

discussed, but this need not be done in detail: they can be predicted by introducing the coupling $(H - A')A'$, etc.

§ 11. TWO FORMS OF THE DELBŒUF ILLUSION

The complete Delbœuf figure, shown in Fig. 25, comprises two pairs of concentric circles, the inner circle, A_1, of the first pair being equal in diameter to the outer circle, B_2, of the second pair. Instead of perceiving $A_1 = B_2$, A_1 is over-estimated under the influence of B_1 and

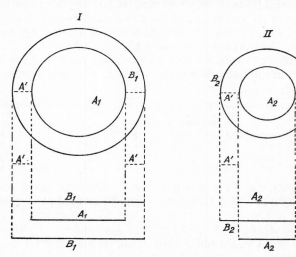

Fig. 25.

B_2 is under-estimated under the influence of A_2. The problem in this illusion, as in those of Müller–Lyer and of trapezia, is to discover whether this is a case of so-called assimilation or whether the illusion is due to an under-estimation of the space between the two concentric circles. The fact that this illusion is isomorphic with the Müller–Lyer illusion when the angular components (barbs) have been removed, shows that we may once more be involved in an effect of inequality between the parts of the figure and the spaces, which are equally figural, which separate them.

The entire Delbœuf figure is complex, and it is convenient, for its analysis, to distinguish between two situations which do not lead to precisely the same relations: (I) that in which the inner circle, A_1, is held constant and the diameter of the outer circle, B_1, and thereby the width of the interval which separates them, A', is varied; (II) that in which the outer circle is held constant and the diameter of the inner

49

circle, and thereby of the interval, is varied. These are the two situations which will be studied in turn without further reference to the complete figure to which the Belgian psychologist gave his name.

I. Situation I was originally studied with Lambercier, Bœsch and von Albertini.[1] Inner circles of various diameters were used ($A_1 = 18$, 24, 30, 36, 72 mm). In each case an outer circle of proportional dimension was varied through a given range of diameters (when $A_1 = 18$ mm, B_1 varied through 19, 20, 22 mm, etc., and where $A_1 = 36$ mm, B_1 varied through 38, 40, 44 mm, etc.). Using these figures, the apparent size of A_1 was measured (as a function of its relation to A', which varied with B_1), on 100 children of 5 to 12 years of age and on thirty adults. The detailed results may be seen in *Rech.* 1, p. 19, and only the overall averages for all ages combined need be given here. These are set out in Table 18 where the values of A' are given as proportions of $A_1 = 1$.

TABLE 18. *Mean % error in estimates of the length of A as a function of variations in A' in Delbœuf Figure I*

Abstracted from *Rech.* 1, p. 19

A'/A	0·02–0·04	0·05–0·08	0·1	0·16	0·2	0·3	0·5
Mean % error	4·1	5·6	9·2	11·7	11·4	8·0	2·3

A'/A	0·8	1	1·5	2	2·5	3	3·5
Mean % error	0·7	−1·0	−2·1	−1·9	−2·0	−0·6	0

These errors can be compared with predictions based on the general law (Prop. 3 of § 2), distinguishing between the two cases $A' < A$ and $A' > A$.

(1) If $A' < A_1$, $L_1 = A$ and $L_2 = A'$; $L_{max} = A + 2A'$; $nL = 2A$ and $S = (A + 2A')^2$. S could equally be taken to be $\pi [0·5 (A + A')]^2$, which gives the same maximum, but, as will be seen later (Chapter II), the sense of S is less that of a geometric surface than that of all the possible couplings, which makes the proposed formula for S, $(A + 2A)^2$, acceptable.

(2) In the negative case, when $A' > A$, $L_1 = A'$ and $L_2 = A$, the other terms will remain unchanged. The law of illusion I will then be:

(19)
$$P = \frac{2A(A - A')A'}{(A + 2A')^2 \times (A + 2A')} = \frac{2A' - 2A'^2}{(A + 2A')^3} \text{ if } A > A' \text{ and } A = 1$$
and

(19b)
$$P = -\frac{2A(A' - A)A}{(A + 2A')^2 \times (A + 2A')} = -\frac{2(A' - A)}{(A + 2A')^3}$$
if $A < A'$ and $A = 1$

[1] *Rech.* 1.

Theoretical values of the illusion (multiplied by 10, because they are relative) are:

$A' =$	0·05	0·1	0·16	0·1666	0·17	0·2	0·3	0·4	0·5	
$P =$	0·7	1·04	1·16	1·178	1·172	1·16	1·0	0·8	0·6	
$A' =$	0·6	0·7	0·8	0·9	1	1·1	1·2	1·3	1·4	
$P =$	0·4	0·3	0·2	0·1	0	−0·06	−0·1	−0·12	−0·14	
$A' =$	1·5	1·6	1·7	1·8	1·9	2	2·5	3	5	10
$P =$	−0·156	−0·162	−0·16435	−0·16437	−0·162	−0·16	−0·138	−0·116	−0·05	−0·02

It can be seen that there is a satisfactory match between the general shape and detail of the empirical and theoretical curves: the

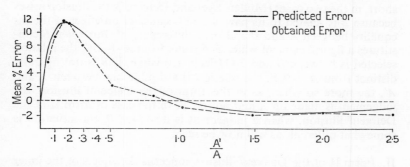

Fig. 26. Comparison of predicted and obtained errors for the Delbœuf figure, form I.

positive error is 6 to 7 times as great as the negative; the positive maximum falls at $A' = A/6$ (hence $A' = 0·166$), that is to say when the radii of the circles A and B are as 3 is to 4; the median zero illusion is at $A' = A$ and the negative maximum lies between $A' = 1·5A$ and $A' = 2A$.

Mean negative illusions were obtained with adults when $A = 18$, 36 and 72 mm, but not, or almost not, when $A = 24$ and 30 mm. However, this negative maximum is somewhat unstable, empirically speaking, because its measurement entails large figures (since $A' > A$). The subject may then no longer experience an illusion because he can isolate A from B. Negative illusions occurred more frequently with children because, in general, they do not see two concentric circles but a solid ring whose contours are formed by the two circles: their global and concrete vision makes for a greater unity between A and B and, especially, between A and A'.

The problem is to know why the deforming relation of this form of the Delbœuf illusion is $2(A - A')A'$ and not $(B - 2A')2A'$, as in the case of the trapezium (Prop. 15) and of the Müller–Lyer illusion (in which, however, the two relations can be combined without changing the maximum). In the present case, $(B - 2A')2A'$ combined with $2(A - A')A'$ would give a maximum at $A' = 0.4A$ and not at $A' = 0.166A$. The explanation is simple: in the case of trapezia (or of the Müller–Lyer figure), the value B corresponds to the longer base, hence to a line separately represented in the drawing and quite distinct from A (the shorter base). In the present case, on the contrary, B is the diameter of the larger circle which contains a smaller circle: the relation which is perceptually obvious is not that which unites B to its parts, $2A'$, but that which unites A to A'. As A is constant, it is necessary to consider $2(A - A')A'$ and not $(A - 2A')2A'$. In short, in the two cases (Müller–Lyer and Delbœuf), the illusion arises because B is related to its part A and because of an effect of the inequality between A and B and their difference, A'. But when B constitutes a figural element which is distinct from $A + 2A'$, the relation selected is between B and $2A'$ (Prop. 15) while, if B is not figurally distinct from $A + 2A'$, the relation is a double one between A and A', the more so when, as in this form of the Delbœuf illusion, the judgement is made on A and not on B. In the case of form II of the Delbœuf illusion, when a judgement is made on B, the situation is somewhat different, as will now be seen.

II. Form II of the Delbœuf illusion concerns the effects of the inner circle on the outer circle ($B2$ in Figure 25, II), A. Experimentally, the outer circle is left constant while the diameter of A is varied and the effects are measured on B. A student of ours, Koshropour, obtained measurements from subjects of various age groups from 6 to 15 years and from twenty adults. Before presenting his results, let us see what becomes of the theoretical formula when an inner variable circle should, according to rule, be related to $2A'$ and not to a single A', as it was when A was held constant (Prop. 19). This would give:

$$(20) \qquad P = \frac{B(A - 2A')2A'}{B^3} \quad \text{if } A > 2A'$$

and

$$(20b) \qquad P = \frac{B(2A' - A)A}{B^3} \quad \text{if } A < 2A'$$

Given that $B = 1$, the following theoretical values result,[1] ignoring the sign for the moment:

$2A' = 0.1$	0.2	0.25	0.3	0.4	0.45	0.5
$P = 0.08$	0.12	**0.125**	0.12	0.08	0.12	0.0
$2A = 0.55$	0.6	0.65	0.7	0.75	0.8	0.9
$P = 0.045$	0.08	0.105	0.12	**0.125**	0.12	0.08

[1] If $2A' = 0.25$ of $B = 1$, then $A' = 0.125$ and $A = 0.75$, hence $A' = A/6$, which is to say that this first maximum coincides with that of Prop. 19.

The first experimental results obtained by Koshropour[1] are presented in Table 19.

TABLE 19. *Mean errors in estimates of the length of B as a function of variations in 2A' in Delbœuf Figure II*

$2A'/B$ (mm)	0·055	0·166	0·277	0·388	0·50	0·611	0·722	0·833	0·944
6 to 7 years ($n = 40$)	−0·46	−0·16	−0·69	0·27	*0·74*	*0·80*	0·46	0·60	0·58
8 to 9 years ($n = 40$)	0·52	0·32	0	0·52	*1·24*	0·80	0·88	1·17	0·55
10 to 12 years ($n = 60$)	0·90	0·47	−0·29	−0·06	*0·96*	0·82	0·29	0·27	0·20
13 to 15 years ($n = 60$)	1·44	0·74	−0·32	0·55	1·24	0·69	0·49	0·38	0·46
Adult ($n = 20$)	0·66	0·83	0	0·55	*1·55*	1·44	1·11	1·11	0·61

A comparison of these results with the theoretical distributions reveals a clear agreement in two respects and a disagreement in a third:

(1) The theoretical maximum at 0·25, on which no sign has yet been conferred, corresponds to an obvious negative maximum in Table 19. This negative maximum (an under-estimation of B) corresponds to the positive maximum of illusion I (over-estimation of A) because if $2A' = 0.25B$, then $A' = 0.166A$ (because, in this case, $A = 0.75$ and $A' = 0.125$).

(2) The median zero illusion of the theoretical values (for $2A' = 0.5$) corresponds to a positive maximum at all ages (except 6 to 7 years): it goes without saying that a positive maximum[2] should be found at this point if the maximum which corresponds to $2A' = 0.25$ is negative.

(3) By contrast, the second negative maximum which could be expected at $2A' = 0.75$ is not found in these first experimental results: there is a slight declivity in the curve, at certain ages, between the positive maximum of 0·5 and the final values, but nothing approaching the theoretical values for 0·25.

Three problems thus remain unanswered: (*a*) that of the sign of the errors; (*b*) that of establishing why the median illusion at 0·5 is positive and not a minimum negative or a zero illusion; (*c*) that of understanding why the theoretical curve, which tallies well with the empirical results for $2A' = 0.25$ and 0·5, does not tally for the value of $2A' = 0.75$. A fourth question may be added: (*d*) why are all these illusions so much weaker than those of form I (Table 18)?

(*a*) P of Prop. 20 was not initially labelled negative. It would have been permissible to do so because, if $2A'$ was devalued by A, or A by $2A'$, B could also have been devalued, but the situation is more complex and very much more interesting. It happens that if circles B_a and B_b, corresponding to $2A' = 0.277$ and to $2A' = 0.50$, are measured against an isolated circle (non-concentric) which we will call B_m, then,

[1] On a circle B of 36 mm diameter. The values of A corresponding to $2A'$ of Table 19 are respectively 34, 30, 26, 22, 18, 14, 10, 6 and 2 mm diameter.
[2] A maximum which could be a minimum negative illusion, situated at 0 or even below it.

ordinarily, for $B_m = 36$ mm and objectively equal to B_a and to B_b, the judgement will be $B_a < B_m$ and $B_b > B_m$. This is because judgements on B_a result, on the average, in a zero or negative error, and judgements on B_b in a maximum positive error. However, when B_a was compared with B_b, directly and without recourse to measuring instruments such as B_m, it was found that of twenty adults, ten (among whom were the most sophisticated subjects, namely ourselves) perceived $B_a > B_b$, eight $B_a = B_b$ and only two $B_a < B_b$! One thus has, for the majority of subjects:

(21) $$B_a < B_m, \ B_b > B_m \text{ and } B_a > B_b$$

Before attempting to explain this intriguing perceptual contradiction we present, in Table 20, the results obtained by Koshropour, for the same twenty adults, of paired comparisons made between all the figures of Table 19.

TABLE 20. *Frequency of judgements of* >, =, < *for each figure of Table 19 when compared with each of the other figures (n = 20 adults who contributed to Table 19)*

$2A'/B$	0·005	0·166	0·277	0·388	0·50	0·611	0·722	0·833	0·944
>	70	70	71	51	35	37	37	34	35
=	54	55	56	64	70	68	69	63	61
<	36	35	33	45	55	55	54	63	64

Comparing these results with those of Table 19, it can be seen that the first four figures, which gave the weakest over-estimations of B when measured against B_m, are here judged to be larger than all the rest, whereas beyond the maximum of Table 19 (at 0·5), the opposite judgement predominates!

The contradiction expressed in Prop. 21 is thus verified and is easily explained. Form II of the Delbœuf illusion is essentially unstable, if Prop. 20 is true, because the under- or over-estimation of the total figure, B, depends simply on those of one of its parts, $2A'$ or A, of which one is over-estimated under the influence of the other: in effect, if $B = A + 2A'$, and if A is over-estimated by the devaluation of $2A'$, or the inverse, the whole figure B can equally well be under- as over-estimated. If B_a (when $2A' = 0·25$ or $0·277$) is compared with an isolated circle, B_m, the conclusion emerges that B_a must appear to be distinct from its concentric circle A: the difference $2A'$, which is devalued by A, thus devalues B_a, and a negative illusion results. On the other hand, if a direct comparison is made between B_a and B_b (both of which contain a concentric circle, A) the concentric circle, contained in B_a now appears to be larger than that contained in B_b. As A_a is exaggerated by $2A'$, and $2A'$ is devalued by A_a, A_a now produces an over-estimation of B_a, being more noticeable than $2A'$.

In summary, the theoretical values of Prop. 20 can be read as either negative or positive because the overall circles are composed of two parts, one of which is over- and the other under-estimated: it thus depends on the context of measurement whether the contributing relations produce a negative or a positive error.

(*b*) But why, in this case, is the median error ($2A' = 0.5$) not zero? The reason is that when the judgement is made on *B*, and not on *A*, the figure made up of concentric circles constitutes a divided space, in the sense of Oppel–Kundt (see § 13). The proof, obtained by Koshropour at our request, may be found in the fact that as the number of smaller circles increases from 1 to 3, circle *B* appears correspondingly larger. From the point of view of Prop. 20, the error for $2A' = 0.5$ does constitute a zero illusion but one whose position is relative to the influence of an additional factor, that of divided spaces. This has the effect of placing the zero illusion at a certain point around which the errors arising from Prop. 20 are distributed, the sign, as we have just seen, being either positive or negative according to the mode of comparison adopted.

(*c*) Let us now turn to what appears to be the most difficult problem of all: why does Prop. 20, which holds for the negative maximum (with measurement on B_m) at $2A' = 0.25$ and for the positive maximum at $2A' = 0.5$, no longer hold for the second negative maximum at $2A' = 0.75$? We wondered whether, in the case of such weak effects, the trouble might not derive from the scale used. Koshropour therefore repeated the experiment with adults, but using step intervals of 2 mm rather than of 4 mm between successive inner circles. We also wondered whether an additional relation, $(B - A)A$, might not be involved (as in the trapezium and the Müller–Lyer illusions) given the fact that, in form II of the Delbœuf illusion, the judgement is made on *B* and not on *A*.

The factor $(B - A)A$ was accordingly incorporated into Prop. 20 in the following forms:

$$(22) \qquad P_{\text{comp}} = \frac{[B(A - 2A')2A'] \times [(B - A)A]}{B^3}$$

and

$$\frac{[B(2A' - A)A] \times [(B - A)A]}{B^3}$$

whose theoretical values are:

$2A'$	= 0.1	0.2	0.25	0.3	0.4	0.5	0.6
P_{comp}	= 0.072	0.192	0.234	**0.252**	0.192	0.0	0.192
$2A'$	= 0.7	0.75	0.8	0.9			
P_{comp}	= **0.252**	0.234	0.192	0.072			

The results obtained are set out in Table 21.

TABLE 21. *Delbœuf Illusion II measured as a function of variations in 2A' when B was constant (36 mm) and A varied in step intervals of 2 mm from 34 to 2 mm*

$2A'/B$	0·055	0·111	0·166	0·222	0·277	0·333	0·388	0·444	0·5
Mean error	1·06	1·46	1·33	1·00	1·00	0·80	−0·40	0·86	1·00
$2A'/B$	0·555	0·611	0·666	0·722	0·777	0·833	0·888	0·944	
Mean error	1·46	0·86	0·40	0·66	−0·53	0·40	0·40	0	

This confirms that there is now a second negative maximum, as clear as the first, and that the empirical curve now approximates more closely to the theoretical one. However, it is difficult to say if the values of Table 21 correspond more closely to Prop. 20 than to Prop. 22, because, if one of the new negative maxima is nearer to 0·3 than to 0·25, the other is even nearer to 0·75 than to 0·7, and the posi-

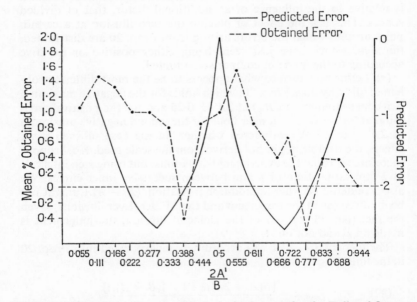

Fig. 27. Comparison of predicted and obtained errors for the Delbœuf figure, Form II.

tive maximum is displaced from 0·5 to 0·55. There thus appears to be a general displacement due to a temporal effect reinforced by the larger number of variables, but not a better agreement with Prop. 22 than with Prop. 20. By contrast, what is found, and this is the main point, is that there are two negative and one positive maxima.

(*d*) Finally, the last question was why form II illusions (Tables 19 and 21) are so much weaker than form I illusions (Table 18). No doubt the argument developed in (*a*) to explain the sometimes positive and sometimes negative sign of the errors can be invoked: the illusion can only be very weak because it is the product of antagonistic components.

We apologise to the reader for dwelling for so long on this interesting illusion, but it seemed worth while because it brought out so clearly both the precautions which needed to be taken in its experimental verification and the difficulties of its theoretical formulation.

§ 12. A LINE OF CONSTANT LENGTH INSERTED BETWEEN TWO VARIABLE LENGTHS AND A LINE OF CONSTANT LENGTH EXTENDED BY A VARIABLE LENGTH

I. The best verification of the sound basis of the interpretation just proposed for the Delbœuf illusion is that the illusion can be represented in a simple linear form by replacing the inner circle by a line, *A*, and the width of the ring formed by this circle and the outer circle, *A'*, by two variable lines between which the first is contained, as shown in Fig. 28. In this case, it is no longer a question of two dis-

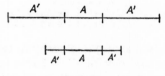

Fig. 28.

tinct figural elements and of an undrawn but perceived difference: *A'* now becomes one of the represented elements, while *B*, incorporating *A*, and corresponding to the larger outer circle of the Delbœuf figure, now represents the whole line, $A + 2A'$, and is no longer perceived as a distinct element. The interest of transforming the Delbœuf circles into a linear figure is that the law remains essentially unchanged, which seems to us to confirm the hypothesis on which our calculations were based: that the principal factor is the difference *A'*, on whose relations with the length *A* the position of the observed maxima depend.

The only difficulty with this linear figure is one of measurement: as the whole line constitutes a divided space, in the sense of an Oppel–Kundt figure (see § 13 below), there will be an over-estimation of *A*, when $A' = A$, relative to an independent comparison line of equal length, which will prevent the measurement of the median zero illusion and of the negative illusions which should follow when $A' > A$.

Primary Effects

Two forms of measurement were therefore adopted, the one in which A was compared with an isolated variable, in order to determine the approximate position of the maximum positive illusion, and the other, of paired comparisons, in which each variable figure was compared with the previous one in the series, ordered as a function of A'. The judgements were made on the segments A, and not on independent comparison lengths.

The first method was applied by Mme Vinh-Bang to twenty adults and gave the results set out in Table 22.

TABLE 22. *Mean % error in estimates of the length of a constant segment ($A = 30$ mm) contained between two variable segments (A')*

A' (mm)	1	2	3	4	5	10	20	30	40	50	60	70
Mean % error	5·3	6·3	9·1	11·4	15·8	12·4	10·8	9·4	7·1	4·3	4·3	4·1

Thus the positive maximum once more occurs in the vicinity of $A' = A/6$, while neither zero nor negative illusions are found for the reason already given. Using the second method, of paired comparisons, with twenty adult subjects, the results set out in Table 23 were obtained.

TABLE 23. *Direct comparisons between successive figures in respect of the length of A as a function of variations in the length of A' (see text for interpretation of values)*

Rech. 4, Table V

A' (mm)	2	5	8	10	17	20	25	30	34	40	50	60	70	80	90	100
$(A_i > A_j) - (A_i \leqslant A_j)$	—	12	9	−4	−1	−3	−6	−2	−6	−7	−9	−13	−8	−6	1	4

These figures signify that: (*a*) a majority of twelve subjects (16 in 20)[1] perceived A associated with $A' = 5$ mm to be longer than A associated with $A' = 2$ mm; (*b*) a majority of nine subjects perceived A associated with $A' = 8$ mm to be longer than A associated with $A' = 5$ mm; (*c*) a minority of four subjects perceived A associated with $A' = 10$ mm to be longer than the preceding figure of A associated with $A' = 8$ mm, and so on. In other words, the segment A increases in length perceptually until $A' = 9$ mm (that is, approximately until $A' = A/6$), then declines until $A' = 80$ mm (when $A' = 1·7A$ approximately), and finally increases again. These comparisons thus confirm the existence of the positive maximum of Table 22, but also indicate the presence of a negative maximum which agrees with that observed and calculated for the Delbœuf figure (§ 11, I). The marked minority of 13 for a comparison of figure $A' = A$ and $A' = 60$ is suggestive of a median zero illusion.

II. It is now appropriate to examine the case of a segment of constant length to which a segment of variable length is added, as shown in

[1] Where an 'equals' judgement was given, one half point was allocated to each category of +ve and −ve response, whence a majority of $−13 = −16\frac{1}{2} + 3\frac{1}{2}$.

Fig. 29. In this case, Props. 19 and 19b, derived for the Delbœuf illusion, no longer apply, but one will have:

$$(23) \qquad P = \frac{A(A - A')A'}{(A + A')^3} \quad \text{if } A > A'$$

and

$$(23b) \qquad P = \frac{A(A' - A)A}{(A + A')^3} \quad \text{if } A < A'$$

If $A = 1$, the theoretical values of the illusion would be:

$A' = 0.05$	0.1	0.2	0.25	0.3	0.4	0.5	0.6	0.7	0.8
$P = 0.40$	0.66	0.92	0.96	0.95	0.87	0.74	0.58	0.42	0.27
$A' = 0.9$	1	1.1	1.2	1.3	1.4	1.5	1.6	1.7	1.8
$P = 0.13$	0	−0.09	−0.15	−0.18	−0.20	−0.21	−0.21	−0.20	−0.16

To verify this theoretical distribution, two forms of measurement were again used, the one consisting in a comparison of successive figures as above, and the other consisting in a comparison of A with an independent line of equal length, while A' varied. Here again, the

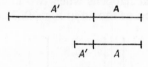

Fig. 29.

inconvenience is that A will be over-estimated, not only in contrast with A' but in so far as it forms part of a divided space $(A + A')$: this will prevent the appearance of negative illusions when $A < A'$.

The first method produced the results set out in Table 24, obtained firstly from fifty adults and then with a further ten practised adults but using a different series of figures selected to see if the maximum positive illusion could be more precisely located (we did not know at the time that the theoretical maximum would be for $A' = A/4$).

TABLE 24. *Direct comparisons between successive figures in respect of the lengths of A (50 mm) as a function of variations in the length of A' (see text for interpretation of values)*

Rech. 4, Tables III and IV

A' (mm): $(A_t > A_j)-(A_t \leqslant A_j)$	2	5	8	10	12.5	17	20	25	30
Group 1 ($n = 50$ adults)	0	25	15	2	0	−8	−9	−5	−8
Group 2 ($n = 10$ adults)	—	—	—	2	5	−6	−3	−5	—
A' (mm): $(A_t > A_j)-(A_t \leqslant A_j)$	35	40	50	60	70	80	90	100	
Group 1 ($n = 50$ adults)	−11	0	−11	−11	−12	3	−1	7	

The positive and negative maxima thus seem to occur in the theoretically predicted regions marked by the transition from positive to negative, at $A' = 12.5$ mm, and from negative to positive, at $A' = 75$ to 100 mm.

The second technique was applied by Mme Vinh-Bang to two groups of twenty and fifteen adult subjects and produced the results set out in Table 25.

TABLE 25. *Mean % errors in estimates of the length of A* (30 mm) *as a function of variations in the length of A'*

A' (mm)	1	2	3	4	5	6	7	8	9
Group 1 (n = 20 adults)	3·2	4·9	5·1	5·3	7·1	—	7·1	—	—
Group 2 (n = 15 adults)	—	—	—	6·4	8·1	9·0	10·2	7·7	8·8

A' (mm)	10	11	12	15	20	30	40	50	70
Group 1 (n = 20 adults)	8·9	—	8·6	7·8	7·6	5·9	5·8	5·3	3·6
Group 2 (n = 15 adults)	9·4	8·2	6·6	—	—	—	—	—	—

Here again, the positive maximum appears to be situated in the predicted region, that is between $A' = A/4$ and $A' = A/3$ (predicted 0·96 for $A' = 0·25$ and 0·95 for $A' = 0·3$). This represents a displacement from the maximum at $A' = A/6$ found when A was inserted between two equal segments (see Table 22).

III. Before passing on to the Oppel–Kundt illusion of divided spaces, which constitutes a generalisation of the present case, it would be interesting to see what happens when two unequal lines are placed parallel to one another, as shown in Fig. 30. The question is whether

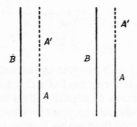

Fig. 30.

there will be a simple devaluation of A by B, as in the case of lines in prolongation (Fig. 29), or whether the experimental results will demand an analysis based on the relation between A and A', where A' is virtual rather than depicted. It will be remembered that this was found to be necessary in the case of the trapezium, the Müller–Lyer and the Delbœuf figures. Theoretically, the second eventuality is to be expected because the figures in fact constitute semi-trapezia if we admit of the virtual non-parallel sides.

This problem was suggested to our student Mansour for study, and his results are clear enough. With B held constant at 7 cm, A varying between 1 and 6 cm by steps of 1 cm, and the distance between A and B being 4 mm, the under- and over-estimations of A were measured against one side of a square placed 9 cm from A. With the figures presented vertically, horizontally and obliquely (at 45°), Mansour obtained the results set out in Table 26.[1]

TABLE 26. *Mean error, % of standard, for variable lengths (A) associated with a constant length (B = 7 cm) (n = 20 subjects 11 to 12 years)*

Mansour (1960) Tables 33, 36 and 39

A (cm)	1	2	3	4	5	6
Vertical	−7	−4	−4	−0·2	1·0	1·6
Horizontal	−9	−5	−4·7	1·0	2·9	2·6
Oblique (45°)	−2·5	−4·4	−2·6	−0·05	1·9	1·5

It can thus be seen that A is not always devalued by B but is progressively over-estimated (with a maximum perhaps at about $A = 5$) once it exceeds the objective value of $A = B/2$. It seems clear that the estimated length of A depends, above all, on its relation with A' and not with B. The theoretical values for these two possibilities may therefore be examined.

The only relations in force in Fig. 30 are those between A and A' and between B and A (identical to those between B and A'), or a combination of both.

The first give:

$$(24) \qquad P_1 = \frac{(A - A')A'}{BH} \times \frac{B}{B} \quad \text{if } A > A'$$

and

$$P_1 = \frac{(A' - A)A}{BH} \times \frac{B}{B} \quad \text{if } A' > A$$

which corresponds in the case in question (for $B = 7$ and $H = 0\cdot4$) to:

$$A = \quad 1 \qquad 1\cdot75 \quad 2 \qquad 3 \qquad 3\cdot5 \quad 4 \qquad 5 \qquad 5\cdot26 \quad 6$$
$$P = -1\cdot78 \quad -2\cdot18 \quad -2\cdot14 \quad -1\cdot07 \quad 0 \qquad 1\cdot07 \quad 2\cdot14 \quad 2\cdot18 \quad 2\cdot78$$

---

[1] It should be noted that these results apply only to the situation in which A is compared with one side of a square or with a figure which differs from A. The figure made up of A and B forms a whole in which A is perceived in relation both to A' and to B. If the variable used were a single line like A, it would be perceptually incorporated into the configuration A, B and V, in which A and V would be linked by the virtual lines joining their extremities. B would then be opposed to $A = V$ and the comparison would be made between B and A and not between A and A'. Mansour employed this technique and obtained the following results, on twenty adult subjects:

$$A = \quad 10 \qquad 20 \qquad 30 \qquad 40 \qquad 50 \qquad 60 \text{ mm}$$
$$\text{Error} = -2\cdot2 \quad -2\cdot75 \quad -3\cdot7 \quad -2\cdot6 \quad -2\cdot0 \quad -1\cdot3$$

It can be seen that these results conform to the predictions of Prop. 25 (sign apart, because A is now under-estimated in comparison with B, not B over-estimated on account of A) rather than of Prop. 24, or 24 and 25 combined, as in the case of the results in Table 26. It is interesting to note the effect of different forms of variable on the outcome of the principal relations involved. See Mansour, M., *Etude Experimentale de l'Interaction de Deux Droites Parallèles et Inégales (Centrations Relatives) de l'Enfant et de l'Adulte*. Thesis No. 11, Institut des Sciences de l'Education, Geneva, 1960.

The second give:

$$(25) \qquad P_2 = \frac{(B - A)A}{BH} \times \frac{B}{B}$$

namely:

$A =$	1	2	3	3·5	4	5·25	6
$P_2 =$	2·14	3·57	4·28	4·37	4·28	3·57	2·14

and the product of the two (leaving BH unchanged):

$A =$	1	2	3	3·5	4	5	6
$P_{comp} =$	−10·7	−2·14	−1·28	0	1·28	2·14	1·07

It is evident that the closest approximation (from a relative, not an absolute point of view) to the empirical data is provided either by Prop. 24 (for the relation between A and A') or by the combined deformations (P_{comp}), which include the relation between A and A'. It can be seen from Table 26 that the distribution for the oblique presentation of the figures has its maxima at $A = 2$ and 5 and not at 1 and 6, which would correspond to the calculation based on Prop. 24.

Other results obtained by Mansour show that if measurements are made on B, results are obtained which are more or less the inverse of the preceding ones: B is generally over-estimated if $A' > A$ and under-estimated if $A' < A$ (because the difference, A', is exaggerated when $A' > A$ and devalued when $A' < A$). Furthermore, if the interval between the parallels is increased, the relation between A and A' remains dominant until the distance approaches 12 mm (for a B of 70 mm), but has hardly any effect between 20 and 28 mm. Finally, if the extremities of A and B are joined to make a semi-trapezium, and if A is progressively displaced until it is symmetrical with B (which creates a complete and isosceles trapezium), all intermediaries between the perceptual properties of Fig. 30 and those of trapezia (§ 9) are found. These results added to those presented in I, re-emphasise the figural role of the difference, A', in trapezoidal, Müller–Lyer and Delbœuf types of configuration.

§ 13. THE OPPEL–KUNDT ILLUSION OF DIVIDED SPACES

The transformation of the Delbœuf illusion just studied indicates that the total length of the figure does not play a major role in the illusion (other than as L_{max} in the denominator of the formula) but that this role devolved upon the relations of inequality between the segments A and A' (or $2A'$). But what happens when A and A' are made equal and increased in number? As has been known since the time of Oppel and of Kundt, a divided line made up in this way is over-estimated in comparison with an undivided line of equal length. But as the segments of the divided line are all equal, it is obvious that no deformation can result from comparisons made between them, as segments or parts of the total figure. But since a compelling over-estimation does occur, it must be that each segment is compared either with the whole itself or with the sum of the other segments

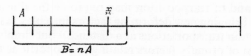

Fig. 31.

$(B - A$ or $nA - A)$. Because of this, we are faced with a new kind of illusion in which the only deforming factor is the relation of the part to the whole itself.[1] It would, therefore, be interesting to see to what extent our general law applies to this case.

It is first necessary to point out that the Oppel–Kundt illusion, unlike the preceding ones, is not entirely primary but incorporates a secondary factor of perceptual activity, in the form of an exploratory activity, which, very interestingly, reinforces rather than diminishes the illusion. In fact, the Oppel–Kundt illusion increases with age, a fact which was not noticed in *Rech.* 17 because we used a method of measurement by superposition, which favoured certain contextual relations. The increase with age has since been brought to light by a fresh study undertaken with Vinh-Bang[2] and by the investigations of Vurpillot. Furthermore, in adults, this illusion either increases or remains stable with practice but seldom decreases, while those of Müller–Lyer and of lozenges clearly decrease with practice.

In purely primary illusions, such as those of trapezia (including the Müller–Lyer illusion), a first glance exaggerates existing inequalities, while a more protracted exploration tends to reduce the illusion. An analysis of the results with the present figure will show, on the contrary, that the illusion is stronger the more the figure is explored: the illusion is less the more global the examination (as it is in children). It will also be shown that the basis of the illusion is the over-estimation of the total length under the influence of each interval, A. A closer exploration of the individual segments thus seems to reinforce

[1] There is no need to distinguish between the whole, B, and the sum of the remaining parts $n - 1(A)$, as this distinction is of theoretical interest only and will be taken up in a later publication. See also Introduction, VIII.
[2] *Rech.* 41.

the multiple $A < B$ relations which combine to exaggerate the total length (this interpretation will be supported in Chapter II, § 2, by analyses made of points of centration actually occurring). This cumulative effect is not corrected by an activity of transposition (which would increase with age): on the contrary, such an activity seems to ensure the perceptual equality of all the segments and has the effect of transferring any illusory effect produced by one to all the others.

These considerations suggest that while perceptual activities of exploration and of transposition may reinforce the illusion, they do not do so by bringing new deforming factors into play (as may be the case with certain transportations at a distance)[1] but simply by favouring the action of primary factors relating to proportions between the parts and the whole. For this reason this illusion, although transitional between primary and secondary illusions, remains in principle primary, and once more derives from the law of relative centrations, as will now be shown.

The illusion was measured on two separate groups of adults, using a horizontal line of 50 mm carrying a varying number of vertical hatchings, one of which was situated at each extremity of the line (two hatchings) and the rest equally spaced about it. The results obtained by Osterreith[2] are set out in Table 27.

TABLE 27. *Mean % error for the Oppel–Kundt Illusion as a function of the number of hatchings*
Rech. 17, Tables 4 and 5

Group I
Hatchings	2	5	10	15	20	30	40	50
Mean % error	1·86	4·58	6·39	6·59	6·31	6·24	4·40	4·02

Group II
Hatchings	2	3	4	5	6	8	10	15	20
Mean % error	0·4	1·6	5·6	6·4	6·2	7·4	8·4	8·2	8·0

The illusion thus seems to increase until about 10 to 15 hatchings have been added, and then to diminish. An attempt will first be made to formulate the illusion and then to explain it.

No choice at all is available in its formulation: as the intervals are equal and the hatchings of the same height, the only remaining factor of inequality which is capable of accounting for the over-estimation is the inequality between each interval and the whole length itself. If, then, $L_1 = B$, $L_2 = A$, $nL = nB$, $n =$ the number of intervals (because B is compared n times with A), $S = B^2$, $L_{max} = B$ and $B = 1$, we will have:

$$(26) \quad P = \frac{nB(B-A)A}{B^2 \times B} = B - A \text{ (because } nA = B)$$

But if the length of A (expressed as a fraction of $B = 1$) passes through values of 1, 0·5, 0·33, 0·25, etc., P will pass through 0, 0·5,

0·666, 0·75, 0·80 . . ., 0·99, . . ., etc., following an indefinite progression having no maximum but being asymptotic. Consequently, a second factor must intervene, one whose relevance is self-evident as soon as it is identified: the thickness of the hatchings should be taken into account because, with their increase in number, the intervals become less and less perceptible.

To verify this, two equal lines (of 50 mm) carrying the same number of hatchings (11 or 21), thick in one case (0·5 mm when there were 11 hatchings and 0·8 to 0·9 mm when there were 21), and thin in the other (0·25 mm when there were 11 hatchings and 0·1 to 0·2 when there were 21), were compared by twenty adults and the results set out in Table 28 were obtained.

TABLE 28. *Distribution of judgements of relative lengths of E (thick hatching) and F' (thin hatching) or 11 and 21 hatchings (n = 20 adults)*

Rech. 17, Table 7

Hatchings	11			21		
	$E > F'$[1]	$E = F'$	$E < F'$	$E > F'$	$E = F'$	$E < F'$
% cases	65	25	10	85	10	5

Incorporating this factor, whose action is thus verified, and if x = the thickness of a hatching and $B = 1$, we will have:

$$(27) \quad P = \frac{nB(B - A)A - (n - 1)x}{B^2 \times B} = B - A - (n - 1)x$$

The following theoretical values result if $x = 0·3$ mm (the thickness of the hatchings in the original figures contributing to Table 27), which becomes $x = 0·006$ when $B = 1$:

Hatchings =	1	2	3	4	5	6	7	8	9
P =	0	0·494	0·654	0·732	0·776	0·803	0·816	0·833	0·840

Hatchings =	10	11	12	13	14	15	20	50	100
P =	0·846	0·849	0·850	0·852	0·850	0·848	0·836	0·686	0·396

It can thus be seen that the theoretical maximum corresponds approximately to the empirical maximum (Table 27) situated between 10 and 15 hatchings.[2]

The implication of this formula is that the whole is over-estimated as a function of its inequality with its parts. By our usual interpretation, and by analogy with what was seen in Form II of the Delbœuf illusion, this could have two meanings: (1) an under-estimation of each A under the influence of B, which would entail an under-estimation of B itself, which is made up of all the A's; (2) an over-estimation

---

[1] $E > F'$ means that the line carrying the thick hatchings was judged to be longer than the line carrying the thin hatchings.

[2] We have ignored the factor of the comparison of the height of the hatchings with the length of B, which would, of course, give rise to other variations on the model of the illusion of rectangles.

of B under the influence of each A which would entail the over-estimation of the A's themselves. As the expression $n(B - A)A$ signifies that each A is related to B and thus exaggerates their difference, both interpretations are logically possible. It is thus interesting to find that they are both perceptually possible too, and it remains to discover why the second (the over-estimation of B) is usually dominant.

In regard to interpretation (1) (the under-estimation of A), it should be noted that negative errors are sometimes found, particularly in children, and that these are too numerous to be attributed to the error of the standard (see Chapter II, § 1). In an attempt to understand this, we asked some practised adult observers to compare any one interval of hatched lines of 9 to 12 cm in length ($A = 12.5$ or 25 mm) with an isolated line of the same length (A) and closed at each end by a similar vertical line. It was found that the isolated line appeared to be longer than any one of the intervals of the hatched line, the intervals being devalued by the whole line, B!

Thus the relation $B > A$ remains perceptually ambiguous: if the instruction is to compare B with variables of comparable length, the attention is concentrated on the whole and this is over-estimated under the influence of the parts, A. But if the attention is directed to one interval, as in our control experiment, this interval may be devalued by the whole which is perceived simultaneously but which does not then play a dominant role.[1]

In brief, in the usual experimental situation, the overall length is nearly always over-estimated because the instruction is to make a judgement on it. It is over-estimated in terms of each relation $(B - A)A$. With the multiplication of the intervals the probability of distinct centrations increases (and thereby the number of encounters, as we shall see in Chapter II) and the reinforcement of the illusion follows by the duplication of the deforming relations $A < B$, whence $n(B - A)A$. Two secondary factors are added to this primary one: (*a*) exploratory activity which reinforces the above process instead of leading to compensations as it does in figures which possess more heterogeneous elements; (*b*) a transposition of equalities ($A = A = A$, etc.) which causes the over-estimation of some of them to generalise to all of them.

The intervention of the primary factors of centration and of encounters was verified in a further tachistoscopic investigation: we found, with Vinh-Bang, and using the same adults and a figure in which the hatched line was extended by a variable unhatched line, an illusion of 6.9% when centration was restricted to the junction of the two lines, of -4.8% when it was restricted to the variable, and of

[1] This situation is similar to that described for Form II of the Delbœuf illusion (§ 11, II).

20·1 % when it was restricted to the hatched line. The question of secondary factors will be taken up in more detail in Chapter III.

§ 14. CONCLUSIONS

In conclusion to this long chapter (which, considering the complexity of the facts, is still very schematic) we claim that one general law (Prop. 3, § 2) is applicable to all the illusions studied, and that a sufficiently encouraging agreement can be seen to exist between the qualitative properties of the experimental and theoretical distributions.

With each category of figure incorporating one or more constituent relations, it was a question of discovering which one or more of these was the dominant one; the law then applied to it either simply or in composite form (in this case without repetitions of the terms S, nL and L_{max}). In passing from one figure to another, an impression may have been created of a sometimes bewildering diversity of component relations, but a retrospective glance indicates that these constitutive relations reduce to six varieties:

(1) Relations of the type $(B - A)A$, or the reciprocal, between a line and a perpendicular which intersects it at one end: rectangles (§ 3) and semi-rectangles (§ 4).

(2) Relations between two intersecting perpendiculars: $(H - M)M$, or the reciprocal, for angles (§ 5), and $(D_1 - D_2)D_2$ for lozenges (§ 6). This concerns a reversal of (1). The relations involved in parallelograms (§ 8) seem to constitute a combination of (2) and of (1).

(3) Relations between parts of an arc $(Ar - Ar')Ar'$, which are characteristic of curvatures (§ 7).

(4) Relations of the sort $(B - 2A')2A'$ or $(B - A')A'$ between a total length and the depicted difference which separates it from a shorter length: trapezia (§ 9) and the Müller–Lyer figure (§ 10).

(5) Relations of the sort $2(A - A')A'$ or $(A - 2A')2A'$ and their reciprocals, between a part length and the difference which separates it from the total length: Delbœuf's figures (§ 11). The illusion of divided lines (§ 12) belongs to this type but under the form $(B - A)A$.

(6) Relations of the sort $n(B - A)A$ between a whole and its parts: divided spaces (§ 13).

It is easy to see the fundamental relation $(L_1 - L_2)L_2$ in this diversity of relations applied to different figures. Thus the same law expressed numerically (Prop. 3 of § 2) can be applied to twenty or more distinct illusions and some satisfaction must be felt, in spite of all the problems of detail that may still be outstanding, at the possibility of reducing such diversity to a single general formula.

An explanation of the law is now required and particularly of the difference coupling, of the form $(L_1 - L_2)L_2$, which constitutes the common element of these six varieties of relation. Its principle, as has been seen repeatedly, is that one of the terms of the relation is exaggerated at the expense of the other: in general this is the larger, except in the case of reversal due to angles (2) or of the common exaggeration of the whole and of its parts (6) and, in part, form II of the Delbœuf illusion (5). This principle thus reduces to the effects of inequality (contrast) with which apparent equalisations (assimilations) are also assimilated. The problem will be to understand this general reinforcement of inequalities.

Before coming to this in the next chapter, attention may once more be drawn to the generality of perceptual deformation: no single figure escapes deformation, not even good forms such as circles and squares (whose diameters and diagonals respectively are under-estimated). We thus begin to see that these good forms do not constitute prototypes of perceptual organisation whose deformations are degenerate derivatives, but that, on the contrary, deformation of inequalities is the rule, equalities and equivalents constituting only limiting cases in which compensations are more or less adequate. Good forms are thus only figures with numerous equivalences, figures in which compensations are more frequent or probable than in the general case. Thus, from the very start, we can see that the perceptual hierarchy obeys laws which are distinct from, and in some respects the inverse of, those laws which govern operational structures.

II EFFECTS OF CENTRATION

Three constructs are required to explain the primary illusions and the general law of which they are an expression:

(a) That of over-estimation, to explain how existing inequalities are perceptually reinforced or, more generally, why one line is over-estimated when compared with another.

(b) That of compensation, to explain why the extent of primary illusions decreases with age or with practice, and more generally, how compensations are made possible.

(c) A probability model which, in terms of (a) and (b) above, is capable of handling the fundamental relation $(L_1 - L_2)L_2$ and other properties of the law.

The three following hypotheses will be advanced:

(a) Reinforcement, which leads to over-estimation, will be said to derive from the effects of centration, that is to say from an over-estimation of that figural element which is centred (or fixated).

(b) Compensation will be said to derive from the co-ordination of centrations, a co-ordination which will be referred to as 'decentration'.

(c) A probability model will be proposed which will account for the effects of centration in terms of the probability of 'elementary encounters' between elements of the perceived figures and elements of the sensory receptors. It will account for the effects of decentration in terms of a probability of couplings, or of the degree of correspondence between elementary encounters occurring on parts of a given figure. The relation $(L_1 - L_2)L_2$ is thus only an expression of the difference couplings between the smaller part of the figure, L_2, and the difference, $(L_1 - L_2)$, between it and the larger part, L_1. Illusions will thus be explained in terms of the distorting effects of deficiencies in difference couplings (when they are incomplete or heterogeneous) relative to the total number of possible couplings.

The course to be followed in the establishment and development of these hypotheses is thus clear. In § 1 the role of centration in the production of over-estimations will be established, and this, together with the function of decentration, will be translated, in §§ 2 and 3, into the probability model of encounters and of couplings. An attempt will then be made in § 4 to explain the law of relative centrations and in § 5 Weber's law in terms of this model. Finally, in § 6, a description will be given of the facts which justify the model, facts which establish the duality of the factors of encounters and of couplings and which reveal their effects at a simpler level than that of the primary illusions so far examined. These facts are drawn principally from an examination of quantitative variations in the illusions as a function of the duration of tachistoscopic presentation; in other words, of the temporal maximum as opposed to the spatial maximum analysed in Chapter I. A discussion of the quantitative variations which occur as a function of repetition or exercise will be deferred to § 2 of Chapter III, in which exploratory activities are discussed.

§ 1. EFFECTS OF CENTRATION

The fundamental point of departure for the explanation of over- and under-estimation is that in visual perception (without necessarily excluding other perceptual modalities), space, as constituted by a collection of objects, is not homogeneous; even in the case of objects of equal size (provided they are not embedded in structures that are so strong as to subjugate them), some are over- and others underestimated as a function of the five following factors: the area of the retina which they stimulate (central or peripheral); the duration of their centration; the temporal order of their centration; the intensity of their centration (attention); and their visual clarity, as a function of illumination, distance from the observer, etc. In other words, tendencies for over- and under-estimation exist which are independent of dimensional inequalities and whose origins are probably of a more general nature. Our hypothesis is that the relatively specific deformations studied in Chapter I can be reduced to the above general causes of deformation.

I. The role of centration makes its first appearance in the error of the standard, first demonstrated by a Japanese psychologist, Akashigi, who did not, however, offer an explanation for it. When it was rediscovered by Lambercier we offered an interpretation of it in terms of the effects of centration.[1]

The principle of the error of the standard is as follows. When two objects (lines or rods, for example), of equal or unequal length, are presented to a subject who is asked: 'Is one longer than the other and, if so, which?' the error in question is observed only if he chooses one of the two as a standard (for example, the one on the left) in terms of which to make his judgement on the other. If one of the two objects is left constantly in place (the standard) while the other is altered in some way, and the subject is asked to make a judgement regarding it

[1] *Rech.* 2, in which Akashigi, of whose work we were not then familiar, is not mentioned. See Akashigi, Y., *Mitt. J. Litt. Fak. Kuysha Univ.*, 1937, **4**, 23–118.

('Is this one, *B*, the variable, longer or shorter than this other one, *A*, the standard, or is it equal to it?'), then one of the two (generally the standard, but it can be the other with children if they neglect the standard, or with adults if the two lines are too close together) is systematically over-estimated just because it plays a privileged role in the comparison.

The facts which led us, with Lambercier, to this notion are extremely simple: we asked our subjects to make a comparison between a vertical standard rod of 10 cm left in one place in view of the subject, with variable rods ranging from 7 to 13 cm placed at 0·03, 0·25, 1, 2 and 3 cm from the standard in the fronto-parallel plane. Under these conditions, with children as with adults, a negative error was found (an under-estimation of the standard) at 0·25 cm (and even at 1 cm with adults), followed by a positive error (an over-estimation of the standard) which increased with the distance between the objects.

The most natural hypothesis was that the subject, being forced constantly to return to the standard in order to make his comparison at greater distances of separation, centred it more frequently, or for a longer time, or more attentively, etc., and by this very fact came to over-estimate it. At smaller distances, on the other hand (smaller for children than for adults), the subject, having both the standard and the variable constantly in view at the same time, and being familiar with the standard which he did not in any case have to lose sight of, preferentially centred the variable and thus over-estimated it.[1]

This interpretation receives support from two sources. (1) If, instead of leaving the standard in place it is removed at the same time as the variable and is then replaced in its original position, but without the subject's knowledge, at the same time as a new variable is presented, then the error disappears altogether or becomes very weak. (2) If, when *A* is the standard and the subject has been making his judgement in respect of the variable, one says to him 'I am not asking you if *B* is bigger than or smaller than *A*, but I am asking you to see if *A* is bigger than or smaller than *B*', it often happens that this reversal in the roles of standard and variable produces an inversion of the error.

In short, the error of the standard, although not yet necessarily having a more general implication, seems at least to demonstrate that the distribution of centrations entails certain over- and under-estimations when comparisons are being made between equal objects.

[1] This is all the more likely because he is able, at these short distances, to combine the standard and the variable into one complete figure while connecting their vertical extremities by a virtual line.

II. A further step was taken when, with Morf,[1] we studied the spatial and temporal effects of centration, this time in more natural situations.

To study the spatial factor, we simply presented the subject with small white discs (1 mm diameter) mounted on small movable black stalks. These stalks, *A*, *B* and *C*, were presented against a black background, with a constant distance of 5 cm between *A* and *B*. The subject was instructed to fixate the space between *A* and *B* and at the same time to place *C* so that, seen peripherally, its distance from *B* appeared equal to that of *B* from *A*. This method of adjustment permitted the experimenter, seated opposite him, to make sure that the subject was fixating on the interval between *A* and *B* and to note, albeit approximately, any ocular movements he actually made.

Subjects were 53 adults, 46 children of 9, and 42 of 7 years of age, of whom we were able to classify respectively 40, 41 and 42 into the three following categories: (1) those maintaining an adequate fixation of the gap between *A* and *B*; (2) those maintaining a fixation of the gap between *A* and *B* but with some eye-movements which passed beyond *B*, but only on one or two occasions; (3) those exhibiting more irregular eye-movements involving several visible excursions beyond *B*.

Category 1 was composed of adults only, while 2 and 3 contained subjects of all ages. The results obtained are set out in Table 29.

TABLE 29. *Mean % error for subjects classified according to adequacy of fixation (figures in parenthesis denote % of n)*

Rech. 20, Table 2

Classification	I	II	III
7 years (*n* = 42)	—	9·4 (31%)	2·8 (69%)
9 years (*n* = 41)	—	7·9 (29%)	3·0 (71%)
Adult (*n* = 40)	11·9 (20%)	7·7 (57·5%)	1·1 (22·5%)

It can be seen that spatial effects of centration occasioned an over-estimation of the interval *A–B* to the extent of over 11% for those adults who followed the instructions, and that this diminished for those subjects who attempted to include the interval *B–C* within their range of vision by indulging in eye-movements in the direction of *B*. The over-estimation almost disappeared in the case of those subjects of Category 3 who occasionally fixated the interval *B–C*. The same tendencies were found with children and, generally speaking, the effect appears to diminish with age.

Temporal effects of centration take two forms. The first is of duration: over-estimations resulting from the centration of an object increase with the duration of the exposure up to a point of stability. The second, well known as the temporal error, concerns the order of

[1] *Rech.* 20.

succession: of two objects exposed for equal but successive or partly overlapping intervals, the one perceived last is over-estimated.

It is simple enough to study the second effect in isolation from the first by equating the times of presentation, but the first cannot be studied entirely in isolation from the second, because, if two objects are exposed for unequal times and in succession, the effect of order is added to that of duration of exposure; if they are presented synchronously, either one must be presented first and both removed together, or they must be presented together and removed successively. In both cases the factor of succession intervenes.

If two objects are presented successively, the two effects will be antagonistic because the object appearing second is perceived for a shorter time. On the other hand, if the two are presented together and are removed in succession, the effects of order and of duration will add, because the object which is removed last is also perceived for a longer time. A comparison of the errors in these two situations should establish the role of duration of exposure because, if effective, the second condition should produce a larger error than the first and the first should produce some error.

The following four experiments were conducted:

Experiment 1. The successive presentation and simultaneous removal of a standard rod of 40 mm and of variable rods, ranging from 34 to 46 mm at 2 mm intervals, for 1·5 and 1 second respectively; and inversely.

Experiment 2. The simultaneous presentation of the standard and the variables with their successive removal, respectively after 1 and 1·5 seconds; and inversely.

Experiment 3. As for Experiment 1 but with durations of 1 and 0·5 second.

Experiment 4. The successive presentation and removal of the standard and the variables with a 0·5-second overlap. Exposure of both for 1 second.

These results are shown in Table 30.

TABLE 30. *Mean % errors as a function of different experimental conditions of centration and o succession. Values represent Experiments A and B where appropriate*

Rech. 20, Table 3. Experiment III of original becomes Experiment IV here and vice versa

Experiment	I (A & B)	II (A & B)	III (A & B)	IV
6 to 8 years (*n* = 31, 31, 10)	0·48	2·29	0·37	
9 to 10 years (*n* = 41, 41, 19)	0·85	1·64	—	2·36
Adult (*n* = 89, 64, 25)	0·35	1·16	1·21	—

It can be seen that the effects of duration and of succession are additive in Experiment 2 where the error is twice as great as in Experiment 1, in which the effects are antagonistic. The error in Experiment 1 is nevertheless neither negative nor zero, although considerably attenuated by the effects of succession. In addition, it appears that there is an optimal time ratio of 1 to 2 for adults (giving rise to the greatest error in Experiment 3) and of 1 to $1\frac{1}{2}$ for children of 6 to 8 years.

The effects of temporal order, already well known in adults, appear also with children of 9 to 10 years, with a value of 2·36% in Experiment 4. A more extended analysis of the types of response to be found was carried out with the same and with longer durations of exposure; the results need not be detailed here, but they revealed that, in adults in particular, there are at least two varieties of response, with intermediate forms, which depend on whether the effects of succession or of duration are stronger.

The effects of centration as a function of the duration of exposure need not be elaborated at this juncture, but will be taken up again in more detail in § 6, when the question of the temporal maximum will be discussed. It is sufficient to note at this stage that the effect of succession, like that of duration, is a product of centration: if the element finally centred is over-estimated in relation to the immediately preceding one, it is because the second centration results in an apparent enlargement which effaces the previous one. The role of duration of exposure, moreover, is self-explanatory: if centration results in a subjective exaggeration of the perceived length, it follows that the effect will increase as a function of time up to a certain limit, after which it will either remain constant or start to decline, ultimately to be effaced by the effects of other centrations.

III. Before examining the decisive advances achieved with the help of the tachistoscope, two groups of earlier studies should be noted, those of Fauville, carried out in 1921 and published in 1947,[1] and those of Hillebrand published in 1928,[2] together with the data recently collected by Rey and Richelle.[3]

Fauville made use of the perimeter. While the subject fixated the centre point at a distance of one metre, a second point was placed on the periphery, and he was asked to halve the distance between the two points with a third movable point. Fauville found the central sector to be over-estimated, in terms of visual angle, with right or left monocular vision, with binocular vision, in normal illumination, and in darkness.

Hillebrand also used a perimeter and obtained measures expressed in terms of *per cent* of over-estimation as a function of eccentricity: she, too, found a marked over-estimation in the central region.

Rey and Richelle provided some fresh data, all of which, with one

---

[1] A. Michotte, *Misc. Psych.*, Louvain, 1947, pp. 323–40.
[2] Hillebrand, Franziska, *Zeitschr. f. Psych.*, 1928, **59**.   [3] *Rech.* 23.

exception, are in agreement with the hypothesis of over-estimation by centration. The exception could be attributed to a conflict between the influence of topography and of attention, which was subsequently verified by Fraisse.[1] They also demonstrated the role of clarity in experiments which controlled centration and which are in particularly direct agreement with the notion of encounters and of couplings which will be advanced in § 2.

In their most interesting experiment, Rey and Richelle presented subjects with two parallel lines, 22 cm long, 1·2 cm thick and 3 cm apart. These were drawn in black ink on a sheet of glass (*B*) 2 mm thick, which was in turn covered by another sheet of glass (*A*) on which nothing was drawn. These two were then placed over three similar sheets of glass, *C*, *D* and *E*. The result was a transparent volume, 1 cm thick. Subjects were instructed to fixate the left-hand line monocularly with the right eye and to state in which plane the right-hand line appeared to lie, relative to the left. Of 35 adult subjects, 23 perceived the non-centred line as more distant, 4 as nearer and 5 were undecided. But, above all, even though the instructions were not phrased to this end, more than half the subjects saw the non-centred line as shorter, none as longer and nine saw it as fluctuating in length. We have here satisfactory confirmation of the effects of centration in depth, which, as will be shown in Chapter IV, § 5, tend to enlarge the centred object and at the same time to bring it nearer.

The experiment which Rey and Richelle found to be equivocal was the following: two lines, whose length could be varied by masking their extremities, were drawn either converging or diverging slightly. The same experiment was carried out with pairs of dots as stimulus objects. They were viewed by the subject either with fixation on the exposed extremity of one of them or with unconstrained viewing, and he was required to say whether they were parallel or not. In unconstrained viewing, a certain length of line is necessary before the subject can perceive a departure from the parallel: the measure of the effect of centration thus becomes the length required to obtain the same result when centration is restricted to the extremity of one of the lines

When the lines were divergent, the results were in support of our hypothesis: the inclination of a line being under-estimated in the periphery, a greater length of line was required for the identification of divergence with centration than with unconstrained viewing. But with converging lines the results were generally unfavourable: a small displacement was more easily perceived in peripheral vision with constrained fixation than with unconstrained viewing.

We have already contended[2] that, with such small separations, the topographical determinants of centration can be compensated for by

[1] *Rech.* 26. [2] *Rech.* 22, Note 1, p. 6.

those of attention: the subject, paying particular attention in peripheral vision to the inclination of the line, at which he is forbidden to look directly, may over-estimate it as a result of a sort of attentional centration which parallels that of the visual fixation of the moment; Fraisse's experiments[1] evidence, in a brilliant way, the possibility of such a division.

On the whole, Rey and Richelle do not attribute the effects of centration directly to the topography of the visual field nor to attention, but rather to the distinctness of central vision and to the absence of such distinctness in the periphery (which, however, fails to account for the case of convergent lines): the hypothesis is that an element is over-estimated to the extent that it is seen distinctly and under-estimated to the extent that it lacks distinctness.

To establish this fact, Rey and Richelle carried out two experiments which were, unfortunately, contaminated with effects of duration of exposure. However, they can still be accepted as being relevant to the issue of under-estimation as a function of lack of visual distinctness in that they are in agreement with other known facts, for instance that a circle presented in dim illumination is perceived to be smaller than one of equal diameter presented in bright illumination. In the first experiment, a black line 52 mm long and 5 mm thick, drawn on a white ground, was exposed in bright illumination for 5 seconds and in dim illumination for 0·4 second. Each condition was repeated twice, in counter-balanced order, for 17 adult subjects who were required to draw a line equal to the stimulus line. The mean lengths of the two reproductions under each condition were: 48·9 and 50·4 mm for the first (5 seconds) and 40·6 and 46·0 mm for the second (0·4 second), differences which are statistically significant. In the second experiment, a line of 52 mm, drawn on a white ground and brightly illuminated, was exposed twice for 2 and twice for 0·2 second. The mean lengths of the reproductions were: 47·4 and 47·2 mm for the exposure of 2 seconds, and 41·1 and 43·6 mm for the exposure of 0·2 second, differences which are statistically significant.

The second experiment confirms what we had already found with Morf concerning the effects of the duration of exposure (but with a method of reproduction whose results are rarely homogeneous with those obtained by the method of paired comparisons that we used). The question of distinctness raises the three following problems which will be discussed at the end of this section. It is necessary to know, firstly, if the variable of distinctness is different from that of the topography of the field, because the central region of the field, corresponding to the fovea, has always been called the 'zone of distinct vision'. The identity of this variable is not established by the

[1] *Rech.* 26.

under-estimation of an element presented under feeble illumination but with otherwise equivalent conditions of centration as applied to the comparison element. This is because fewer receptor cells may be excited in dim illumination and because the different results obtained in foveal and peripheral vision may themselves be due to differences in the density of receptor cells (and specifically to the topographical factor). In the second place, we need to know if this variable is more or less general than the others; and above all, in the third place, we need to understand its mechanisms and to compare them with those of the other variables involved.

IV. After three years of research, Fraisse[1] and his associates Ehrlich and Vurpillot, with the perfection of a more precise tachistoscopic method than that previously used, achieved results which decisively isolated the variables which had hitherto been confounded. Earlier psychophysicists, who did not overlook the effects of centration but who did not recognise their general importance, attributed them to the variable of attention, believing that an element to which attention is paid is thereby over-estimated. We, for our part, always favoured the topographical variable, although reserving a role for a factor of intensity which included attention. The merit of Fraisse's work is to have succeeded in dissociating these two variables in situations in which they were placed in conflict.

Fraisse, Ehrlich and Vurpillot presented subjects with two lines, 20 mm long and 1 mm thick. These lines, which formed a continuation of one another, were demarcated at their junction and at their extremities by transverse lines 3 mm long and 0·33 mm thick. The duration of exposure was approximately 0·1 second and subjects were made to fixate the centre of one of the segments, the other remaining peripheral. A fixated element played the role, turn about, of standard and of variable and was located on the right or on the left. It was found that the element centred was over-estimated to an extent which varied from 3 to 17·6% on the average. Similarly, when fixation was demanded on the extremity of one of the conjoined lines, it was found that the least peripheral of the segments was over-estimated from 8·9 to 17%.

It was found that when the subject did not know on which side of the fixation point the peripheral, or the more peripheral, segment would appear, the effect of centration was almost eliminated. This suggested the hypothesis that, having to scan both sides at once, he dispersed his attention: the 'fixational centration' being dominated by 'attentional centration' under these circumstances, and attention being dispersed, the result was an absence of over-estimation.

[1] *Rech.* 26.

After conducting a series of validating experiments, the authors hit upon the following decisive form. The subject was presented with two out of three possible straight lines separated by an interval which slightly exceeded their length. One line was in the middle and was exposed with one or other of the other two which was located either to its right or to its left. The fixation point was located either on the central line or the subject was simultaneously given two alternative fixation points, which might be referred to as scanning points, situated at positions corresponding to the proximal extremities of the peripheral lines. With the single fixation point, a small over-estimation of 3 % of the central line occurred, but with the double points, there was a strong over-estimation of 17 % of the peripheral lines.

TABLE 31. *Over-estimation of central or peripheral elements as a function of the point of fixation (single or double)*

	Rech. 26, Table 7	
Fixation points	1 ($n = 15$)	2 ($n = 15$)
Central > peripheral (n)	8	0
Range of over-estimation of central element	23 to -10%	-2 to -20%
Mean % over-estimation of central element	3%	-17%

The authors conclude from these results that, in addition to the effects of fixation on centration, which we refer to as topographical effects, there are other effects which will be referred to as attentional centration. These two, usually confounded, can be dissociated and, in this case, that of attention is dominant. Both, however, can be interpreted in terms of the notion of the probability of encounters, to be discussed in § 2, which, Fraisse and his associates say 'provides a complete explanation of all our results. The probability of encounters can just as well be entertained at the level of excitation, with relation to the heterogeneity of the retinal field, as at a central level, determined by the attitude of the subjects' (*loc. cit.*, p. 211). Finally, re-examining the Rey and Richelle hypothesis concerning the role of distinctness, the authors conclude that this law is itself but a particular case of a more general law since 'what we pay attention to is more distinctly perceived' (p. 212).

V. In spite of these important findings of Fraisse and his colleagues, it still had to be established that centration involves more than merely attention. Evidence was also required, and without using the tachistoscopic technique, that a strictly topographical factor, (fixation as such and differences due to foveal and peripheral projection), played the special role attributed to it by Hillebrand and by Fauville. While this role of topography was not denied by Fraisse, it was considered to be secondary, it being unclear whether this simply means that it may be dominated by effects of attention when the two are in conflict, or that it is secondary in the absolute sense of being of minor importance. To some extent Table V on p. 204 of the above study provides an answer to this question, because measurements were made at different distances. But some inconsistencies in the results, and above all the presence of the difficult problem of absolute versus angular sizes, prompted us to re-examine the question as a complement to what we had already done in respect of the classical illusions (see § 6 of this chapter). This would have the additional advantage of permitting us to examine the interesting question of a possible temporal maximum in terms of the duration of exposure.

A. To this end, certain preliminary, and unpublished, investigations were carried out and are now summarised. We started, with Rutschmann, with the same stimuli that were used by Fraisse (the standard of 73 mm and a set of variable lines as above). These were presented at three distances, 60, 120 and 240 cm, representing visual angles of 6° 56', 3° 29' and 1° 45' for the standard. The distances between standard and variables subtended visual angles of 17° 8', 8° 46' and 4° 24' respectively. Twenty-three measurements were taken, the sequence of distances being ascending on eleven occasions and descending on twelve. Presentation was tachistoscopic with an exposure time of 0·08 to 0·09 second.

The results are set out in Table 32.

TABLE 32. *Mean % effects of centration as a function of viewing distance and of the position of the standard. In parenthesis, % error in visual angle*

Rech. 38, Table 4

Viewing distance (cm)	60			120			240		
Position of standard	R	L	$\frac{R+L}{2}$	R	L	$\frac{R+L}{2}$	R	L	$\frac{R+L}{2}$
Ascending order ($n = 11$ adults)	37·0	35·0	36·0 (24·0)	25·3	18·2	21·7 (18·5)	22·8	12·2	17·5 (16·4)
Descending order ($n = 12$ adults)	42·6	34·1	38·3 (26·3)	33·3	27·4	30·3 (26·9)	28·3	30·9	29·6 (27·4)

It can be seen that eccentricity clearly modifies the strength of the effects of centration in that the more peripheral a variable is, the more it is under-estimated. These results, however, call for two qualifications. The first is that an effect of repetition has been added to that of eccentricity. This has a cumulative effect in ascending trials and a subtractive effect in descending trials and thus tends to reduce the overall error. This effect of repetition is interesting in its own right and shows that perceptual activities are already present even at the brief exposure times used: these activities could not involve exploration accompanied by eye-movement, but no doubt ensure a better distribution of encounters (in the sense in which the term will be used in § 2) and lead to a more homogeneous distribution of them between the two objects compared, thus reducing the error.

The effects of repetition are further evidenced in the following tables. The first concerns immediate repetitions and the second delayed repetitions, or retrials, which took place some days, or even weeks, later.

TABLE 33. *Mean % effects of repetition on two trials (n = 16 adults) and on three trials (n = 6 adults). Viewing distance = 60 cm*

Trial	I	II	I	II	III
Standard R	41·3	38·8	36·8	35·2	25·9
Standard L	37·3	32·2	35·4	31·6	26·8
R+L/2	39·3	35·5	36·1	33·4	26·4

The differences are not statistically significant, but there is a rank order correlation for adults of +0·65 and +0·56 for measurements with standard right and left respectively, both of which are significant at the 5% level. Repetition has no effect with children, nor do the correlations differ from zero with them.

TABLE 34. *Mean % effects of 'retrials' at viewing distance of 60 cm*

Rech. 38, Tables 6 and 7

Age group	Adult (n = 13)		5–7 yrs (n = 6)	
Trial	I	II	I	II
Standard R	41·7	38·2	33·1	35·6
Standard L	39·2	35·7	23·2	21·2
R+L/2	40·4	36·9	28·1	28·4

The second qualification to be made in regard to Table 32 is more interesting: while the errors calculated in terms of physical length clearly increase with eccentricity, even when reduced by the effects of repetition in the descending trials, errors calculated in terms of visual angle, while increasing markedly with eccentricity when the effects of repetition are cumulative, either do not increase or actually decrease when this factor is in opposition. The question is then to decide whether the effect of centration, with tachistoscopic presentation of stimuli, can be reduced to the angular geometry of the tangential plane, in which case one would have to admit to the existence of a constant error proportional to the perspective reduction of a peripherally seen line, judgement being made in terms of angles rather than lengths; alternatively, it might be a question of angular expansion, that is to say, a positive angular topographical effect, judgement being made in terms of lengths.

B. It therefore became necessary to change the method and, in place of altering the eccentricity at the same time as the distance from the subject, to keep the latter constant while increasing the distance between the standard and the variable. This was done, in collaboration with Matalon, in a series of investigations in which we also examined the effects of exposure time. Rutschmann had already found that the error was greater (30·5%) at exposures of 0·08 to 0·09 second than at 0·15 second (25·6%). Two experiments were conducted in order to study the effects of practice, one with subjects who repeated the experiment at all exposure times, and the other in which different groups of subjects were used for each exposure time.

The main set of results was obtained with a Gerbrand mirror tachistoscope, with a viewing distance of 55 cm. The stimulus card measured 19 cm square, and the standard, 30 mm long, was drawn at 45 mm from the edge of the card. Some other results obtained with a projection tachistoscope, not strictly comparable in a quantitative sense, are included at the foot of Table 35 as they bear on the problem of the temporal maximum. In their case, the subject was at a viewing distance of 150 cm, the frame measured 50 × 34 cm, the standard, 55 mm long, was drawn at 65 mm from the edge of the frame and was separated from the variables by an interval of 180 mm.

TABLE 35. *Mean % effects of duration as a function of exposure time, of distance between standard and variable and of subjects' experiences*

Rech. 38, Tables 9 to 11

Exposure time (second)	Same subjects (n = 11 adults)					Separate groups (n = 13 adults per group)					
	0·01	0·04	0·10	0·20	0·50	0·01	0·04	0·10	0·20	0·40	0·50
Gerbrand Tach.											
110 mm (*Sepn.*)	26·7	24·0	28·7	12·0	—	30·3	26·2	24·9	12·6	8·7	0·1
55 mm ,,	18·2	21·0	24·7	16·7	—	20·3	19·7	21·8	15·9	5·4	0·2
Projn. Tach.											
180 mm (*Sepn.*)						—	14·0	24·0	6·8	−0·8	—
n =							(11)	(12)	(8)	(7)	

It can be seen that, except at an exposure time of 0·2 second, the error was greater with an interval of 110 mm than with one of 55 mm. The only statistically significant difference, by the Mann–Whitney Test, was in the case of the shortest exposure time (0·01 second), but when the various levels of significance are combined by Stouffer's method, the differences between the two curves become highly significant. The existence of a topographical effect, which we set out to establish, can thus be accepted: the distance between the subject and the stimulus figures was kept constant, and the errors of length correspond to those of visual angle (6° and 12°).

It is interesting to note that in the condition in which subjects served at only one exposure time, the extent of the error decreased as a function of increases in exposure time,[1] while a temporal maximum quite clearly occurs at 0·1 second when subjects served at all exposure times. This temporal maximum occurred at the same exposure time for both interval distances and with both tachistoscopes.

VI. We must now draw our conclusions. While the fact of over-estimation as a result of centration is accepted by all authors who have studied the question, it is nevertheless true that the phenomenon is a

[1] The variation of both curves is monotonic by Jonckheere's Test, *Brit. J. Stat. Psychol.*, 1954, 7, 93–100.

complex one in which at least four or five factors play a part. These are: the topography of the visual field, in terms of differences between central and peripheral vision; attention; the duration of exposure; the order of presentation; and, possibly, distinctness, which we may well consider to represent a fifth factor in so far as it involves only objective stimulus conditions such as illumination or distance from the subject. On the other hand, if this factor is considered in the more general sense preferred by Rey and Richelle, it overlaps with three of the other factors, namely, topography (because the fovea is the zone of distinct vision), attention (as Fraisse noted), and exposure time (which Rey and Richelle included as a variable in their experimental conditions).

It then becomes necessary to decide if these factors are hierarchical. We do not think they are, because their respective dominances are probably relative to the situations involved. Fraisse found attention to be dominant over topography in the situations which he studied; but Ditchburn, in his brilliant studies on stabilised retinal images achieved by means of the neutralisation of eye-movements,[1] showed that if the persistence of one part of the fading figure (for example, one corner of a square) could be attributed to attention, this was only possible within a very narrow visual angle, which speaks in favour of the dominance of the topographical factor. In other situations, attention will be subordinated to distinctness, itself a function of topography and of exploratory eye-movements. The important question is not, then, of the hierarchy, which is no doubt vicarious, but of what these diverse factors have in common.

There is a simple solution to this problem if a probabilistic point of view is adopted, which is the only legitimate point of view with our existing state of knowledge and the complexity of the facts. The topographical factor, to start with, calls for a consideration of the differential density of receptor cells between the fovea and the peripheral retina. This carries the implication of more encounters between foveal than peripheral receptor elements and the parts of the perceived object, whether the latter act directly on the receptors or whether, as Ditchburn and his collaborators have shown, small eye-movements play a part in vision. Attention is a factor of reinforcement and is concerned with directional intensity and, as Fraisse has clearly shown, is consonant with the schema of the probability of encounters. The same argument applies to the duration of stimulation, because, in this case, the probability will be a function of the time of exposure; so, too, for the order of presentation, because here the most recent encounters will have a chance of gaining an advan-

[1] Ditchburn, R. W., and Ginsborg, B. L., *Nature*, 1952, **170**, 36–7; *J. Physiol.*, 1953, **119**, 1–17. Ditchburn, R. W., and Pritchard, R. M., *Nature*, 1956, **177**, 434.

tage over earlier ones. And, finally, it is difficult to conceive of a factor of distinctness, as understood in the sense of optimal objective viewing conditions, as being other than favourable to the number of encounters: with centrations equal, the size and not only the brightness or vividness of the most distinct of two elements is over-estimated. Everything thus points to the construct which we first advanced in 1955[1] and which will now be discussed in detail.

§ 2. THE PROBABILITY MODEL OF ENCOUNTERS AND OF COUPLINGS

This section must be prefaced with an important comment. In attempting to reduce the effects of centration to a probability of encounters, and those of decentration to a system of couplings between these encounters, it is not our aim to make a contribution to the psycho-physiological theory of vision: it would be ingenuous to suppose that anything is explained by replacing the total vision of a line by small fragments of vision applied to its component units. Our aim is simply to explain the law of relative centrations on the basis of the effects of centration, to explain the really extraordinary fact that illusions obey a law which makes reference exclusively to the objective properties of figures. To achieve this, it is necessary to construct a model which relates the component parts of a line, which may be physical points or segments, to the component parts of an act of vision, which may be neural elements, ocular micro-movements, etc. In doing this, the emphasis will be on the laws of composition, as such, of these encounters between component parts of the object and of the observer, and as little recourse as possible will be had to this or to that particular physiological interpretation of the mechanisms involved in the encounters. What we hope to achieve is a model whose basic constructs (encounters and couplings) are of such a general nature that they will fit into any physiological explanation and whose outcome will be a probabilistic explanation of perceptual errors in detail, specifically in the form of the law of relative centrations.

We will consider a line to be divided into an arbitrary number of equal segments and a subject's receptors to consist of a certain number of elementary units which, as we have already said, may equally well be neural units of the retina or of the corresponding cortical area,[2] or nerve impulses, or, again, ocular micro-movements if these

---

[1] *Rech.* 22.
[2] We are thinking, in particular, of those momentary irradiations of electrical activity which accompany perception and which Grey Walter detected with the toposcope.

do play a role in perceptual events. We will then assume that variations in subjective estimates of the length of a line (variations which our experiments have shown to depend on centration in terms of the topography of the field, the duration of exposure, the order of succession and attention) are a function of the probability of encounters between the elements of the line and the elementary units of the receptor system.

The most general meaning possible is intentionally retained for the term 'encounters', without stipulating whether the encountering elements belong to the object and the encountered elements to the subject, or the inverse. In the first alternative, the model would be comparable to the probability of encounters occurring when a photographic plate is exposed, the encountering elements being photons and the encountered elements the particles of silver nitrate of which the plate is composed. But the second alternative cannot be excluded, and may even be the more likely, in view of the studies of Ditchburn and his colleagues[1] who were able to demonstrate that, with stabilised retinal images, the stimulus object ceases to be perceptible. They thus established the essential role played by ocular micro-movements in visual perception,[2] leaving aside the fact that those parts of the figure attended to disappear last. Similarly, Riggs, Armitage and Ratliff[3] recorded the reflections from a corneal mirror during prolonged fixation of a point and demonstrated that minute sweeping movements of the eye occur which increase in amplitude with the duration of fixation. They also reported that a fixated object is perceived to increase in size, up to a certain limit, as fixation is prolonged, thus again confirming the effect of centration and relating it directly to a mechanism of encounters. If ocular micro-movements do play a role, as these studies seem to indicate, it will be necessary to consider encounters to consist of points of interference between the elements of a figure and those micro-movements: for example, all the points of a line intersected by the oscillation of such movements. It thus becomes quite possible, or even probable, that encountering elements belong to the subject himself, or that even the most elementary encounters are the product of a complex interaction in which the subject is not simply passive (which he would in any case cease to be as the couplings multiplied).

---

[1] Ditchburn, R. W., *Optica Acta*, 1951, 171–6; Ditchburn, R. W., and Fender, D. H., *Optica Acta*, 1955, 2, 128–33.

[2] When the stimulus object is a black disc, its border first becomes indistinct, then the image pales and disappears. If it is a square, the angles disappear first, the object appears to become circular and then gradually disappears.

[3] Riggs, L. A., Armitage, J. C., and Ratliff, F., *J. Opt. Soc. Amer.*, 1954, 44, 315–21.

Effects of Centration

I. With this in mind, one of many possible abstract models of encounters will be proposed. The discussion will be restricted for the time being to a single linear stimulus object, and the question of its comparison with other objects and consequently the question of couplings will be left till later. The model will be designed to account for the very concrete fact that a line appears to lengthen as it is centred, up to a limit, and that this growth is exponential.

Consider, first, that encounters are distributed at random along a line, that they constitute only a limited sample of all possible encounters and that an encounter on one point neither increases nor decreases the probability of encounters occurring on immediately neighbouring points. For example, we may suppose that during an initial exposure, say of 0·05 second for convenience, only 500 of 1,000 possible encounters occur. During a second exposure of the same duration, a further 500 encounters will occur, once again at random and on the basis of the same centration or of another involving more or less overlap. Of these 500 new encounters, some will fall on points already encountered but others on points not previously encountered, say to the extent of 250. Added to those previously encountered, this makes a total of 750 points encountered, given that any point encountered twice is only counted once in the tally.[1] A further 500 encounters occur during a third equal exposure, but of these an even smaller number will encounter as yet untouched points (say 125, giving a total of 875), while the majority will make no contribution.

This model is, indeed, very crude, particularly as it does not stipulate zones of unequal probability of encounter on a line as a function

[1] It has sometimes been asked why this need be so. The reason seems mandatory in both possible forms of encounter. In the case where the ocular micro-movements encounter the elements of the line, it is obvious that each segment can count only once: if we imagine that a line has 1,000 segments and that the subject encounters, for example, 500, then 750, then 875, etc., his estimate of the length would be proportional to these numbers and if elements encountered several times counted each time, the line would expand indefinitely. On the other hand, in the case where the receptor elements are encountered by the projection of the line, then similarly each cell, for example, would count only once in a given perceptual event, or the line would once more expand indefinitely. In both cases, the restriction appears to be essential. Moreover, physiologically speaking, it is known that the visual excitation of a receptor is followed by a 'refractory phase'. From the point of view of our abstract model, as each encounter contributes to the dilation or lengthening of the line, the model must be appropriate to the fact to be interpreted: and the fact is that subjectively the line lengthens in an exponential fashion and not indefinitely.

It has also been asked how discontinuous encounters could give rise to the perception of a continuum. In reply to this, one may refer, in the first place, to many situations involving strictly discontinuous segments which are perceived as lines or planes; in the second place, 'points of encounter' can, without difficulty for the model, be translated into the language of continua by the substitution of the term 'zones of dilatation'.

of points of fixation, points which are liable to change with length of the line, etc. But as the intention is to invoke as few hypotheses as possible, it will suffice.

An attempt will now be made to be more specific.

Let us suppose that the line incorporates an arbitrary number, N, of encounterable elements, and that in a period of time t_1, a number, αN, of these is encountered by a number, n, of encountering elements, thus leaving N_1 unencountered elements. Then

$$N_1 = N - \alpha N = N(1 - \alpha)$$

During the period $t_2 (= t_1)$ the same number of elements, n, will encounter a further αN elements. Some of these having already been encountered in t_1, newly encountered elements in t_2 will be αN_1. The sum of elements encountered in t_1 and t_2 is:

$$\alpha N + \alpha N_1$$

and the balance of unencountered elements will be N_2:

$$N_2 = N_1 - \alpha N_1 = N(1 - \alpha)^2$$

and so on.

Stated more precisely, we have:

(a) if N is the number of encounterable elements of L,

(b) and n the number of encountering elements effective in a period of time, t,

(c) then n encountering elements encounter αN encounterable elements. Whence, when n encounters on αN elements have occurred in t_1, the balance of unencountered elements will be N_1, or:

(28) $$N_1 = N - N[1 - (1 - \alpha)] = N(1 - \alpha)$$

After the further n encounters in t_2, N_2 unencountered elements will remain, or:

(29) $$N_2 = N - N[-(1 - \alpha)^2] = N(1 - \alpha)^2$$

and so on,[1] for instance $N_3 = N(1 - \alpha)^3$, $N_4 = N(1 - \alpha)^4$, etc.

---

[1] B. Matalon, who was kind enough to study this chapter, proposes the following proofs for this conclusion:

(1) At each moment t, there are N_t encounterable units.

(2) The probability of an encounterable unit being encountered is α, independently of t. (In other words, the encountering system does not vary with time.)

(3) An element which has been encountered cannot again be encountered.

The following equation can therefore be used to express the number of elements encountered during a unit of time (the duration of one centration):

$$\triangle N_t = -\alpha N_t$$
$$N_{t+1} = N_t (1 - \alpha)$$
$$= N_0 (1 - \alpha)^{t+1}$$

The sum, $\alpha N + \alpha N_1 + \alpha N_2 + \ldots$, of elements encountered after each new set of encounters, n, thus increases exponentially and provides a model of the apparent progressive lengthening, to a limit, of a line during intervals of time t_1; $t_1 + t_2$; etc., corresponding to n, $2n$, $3n$, etc., encounters.

This results in a model obeying a logarithmic law, the arithmetic progression n, $2n$, $3n$, etc., corresponding to the geometric progression $(1 - \alpha)$, $(1 - \alpha)^2$, $(1 - \alpha)^3$, etc. This fundamental characteristic gives expression to the fact that over-estimations due to centration are proportional to the size of the perceived objects. It also points to the relationship of these mechanisms to Weber's law, to be discussed in more detail in § 5 below.

However, Props. 28 and 29 describe only absolute estimations of L, and correspond to what will be referred to as 'elementary error I,' or the error which is due to centration as such on a single object, independently of its dimensional relations with other objects.

II. When two objects ($L_1 = L_2$ in the first instance) are involved, a new factor is added, that of the relation between the encounters on L_1 and those on L_2. There is no particular reason for supposing that, for $L_1 = L_2$, the numbers of encounters in time t will be αN on both objects. On the contrary, very good experimental reasons exist for supposing that the encounters on L_1 and those on L_2 will be different. This could be because one is better centred than the other, one is more peripheral, or one attracts the attention more than the other, is seen before the other, or, again, because the total durations of the respective centrations on them differ.

This possible heterogeneity of encounters, due to unequal densities or frequencies of encounters per unit length of the stimulus objects, is of great theoretical importance: it allows one to proceed from a discussion of the effects of centration on one object (elementary error I) to the effects of centration when two objects are compared, and thus to a discussion of *relative* rather than absolute over-estimations. If elementary error I alone was involved, or if it applied with equal force to all objects, it would be impossible either to demonstrate it or

---

By hypothesis, for some t,
$$N_t = (1 - \alpha)^t N_0$$

Proof by induction:

for $t = 0$
$$N^t = (1 - \alpha)^0 N_0$$
$$= N_0$$
$$N_{t+1} = N_t + \Delta_t$$
$$= N_t - \alpha N_t$$
$$= N_t (1 - \alpha)$$
$$= N_0 (1 - \alpha)^t (1 - \alpha)$$
$$= N_0 (1 - \alpha)^{t+1}$$

for $t \to \alpha$, $\lim N_t = 0$.   Q.E.D.

even to establish its indirect influence on the optico-geometric illusions. But if it applied with unequal force to two compared objects, it would give rise to a new source of error, 'elementary error *II*', which would be amenable to measurement.

The need to distinguish between absolute and relative over-estimations requires the introduction of a hypothetical event in addition to that of encounters, that of coupling, or correspondence between encounters; it then immediately becomes necessary to make a distinction between 'complete' and 'incomplete' couplings. If encounters were homogeneous, or of equal density on all objects, the coupling would, by definition, be complete and neither of the constructs would add anything to that of encounters: effects of centration would be uniformly enlarging or contracting but never deforming. But if encounters are heterogeneous, the heterogeneity must be expressed in terms of correspondences or couplings, and a model has to be found which explains why these couplings may be more or less incomplete. Finally, the eventual achievement of complete coupling raises a new and a specific problem because couplings do not automatically become complete as a result of the generality of encounters.

Theoretically speaking, the matter can be expressed as follows:

(*a*) If encounters on L_1 in time t number αN, and βN on L_2 (when $L_1 = L_2$ or when a part of L_1 is of the same length as L_2), there will be said to be complete coupling between the encounters on L_1 and those on L_2 at a given moment, T, if $\Sigma \alpha N = \Sigma \beta N$, and an incomplete coupling if $\Sigma \alpha N \lessgtr \Sigma \beta N$.

(*b*) Let p_α be the probability (between 0 and 1) that $\Sigma \alpha N$ has a particular value, and p_β the probability that $\Sigma \beta N$ has a particular value at a given moment T.

(*c*) Let $p_{\alpha=\beta}$ represent the probability of a complete coupling, namely, the probability that $\Sigma \alpha N = \Sigma \beta N$ at a given moment, T.

Without entertaining *a priori* hypotheses regarding the degree of independence or dependence between p_α and p_β, it may be conceded that, just because encounters accrue exponentially rather than immediately saturating all encounterable elements or accruing in a linear fashion, the probability is slight that p_α will equal p_β. It is possible that couplings will be equal in the case of a very small number of encounters, near the point of origin of increments in encounters, or in the case of a very detailed scrutiny, at the plateaux of the exponentials. As the increment of encounters, even in the case of a single line, can be likened to some form of random progressive sampling, it follows, *a fortiori*, that when two lines are being compared the probability is slight that the sampling will have the same outcome in both cases: if the points of centration are few in number and unconstrained, and therefore not necessarily situated on the same relative positions on the two lines, the encounters will not necessarily be homogeneous. Even when centration is constrained to a point equidistant between the two lines, the encompassing range of centration need not be equally distributed between them. By hypothesis, one would then have:

(30) $\qquad p_{\alpha=\beta} < p_\alpha$

(30b) $\qquad$ If $p_\alpha > p_\beta$, $\quad$ then $p_{\alpha=\beta} \leqslant p_\beta$;

$\qquad$ and if $p_\beta > p_\alpha$, then $p_{\alpha=\beta} \leqslant p_\alpha$

To justify this hypothesis, a more detailed calculation of the complete and incomplete couplings may be attempted on the basis of Props. 28 and 29. By definition, there will be complete coupling at a given moment, T, when the encounters on L_1 and on L_2 are homogeneous, or of equal density (of equal number per unit length), and there will be incomplete coupling if they are heterogeneous, or of different densities.

Given that $L_1 = L_2$, or that a part of $L_1 = L_2$, we may first calculate the number of encounters already effected on L_1 and on L_2 at times T_0 (on first presentation), T_1 (after an interval, t_1), T_2 (after $t_1 + t_2$), etc. Let R_0, R_1, R_2, etc., represent the encounters already effected on L_1 at times T_0, T_1, etc., and R'_0, R'_1, R'_2, the encounters effected on L_2 at the same points in time. Finally, let N'_2, N'_3, etc., be the as yet unachieved encounters on L_2, to correspond to the N_2, N_3, etc., on L_1 of Props. 28 and 29. We then have, on the basis of Props. 28 and 29:

(31) $\quad R_0 = N - N = 0 \qquad\qquad R'_0 = N - N = 0$

$\qquad R_1 = N - N_2 \qquad\qquad\qquad R'_1 = N - N'_2$

$\qquad R_2 = (N - N_2) - N_3 \qquad R'_2 = (N - N'_2) - N'_3$

$\qquad$ ..., etc. $\qquad\qquad\qquad\qquad$ ..., etc.

This table gives us the difference $R_n - R'_n$ between the encounters already effected on L_1 and on L_2 at the various times T_0, T_1, T_2, etc. The rates of increment of encounters on the two objects can therefore be different, being functions of α and β. Two important consequences follow. The first is that the differences $R_n - R'_n$ will not always have the same value. The second is that complete coupling will not become more or less probable monotonically: its rate of development may exhibit variations. These variations must now be described.

Complete coupling can now be defined more precisely by the number of correspondences 1 to n between the points of encounter on L_1 and those on L_2. It is appropriate to invoke a 1 to n (or one to many) correspondence and not a 1 to 1 (one-to-one and reciprocal) correspondence because the role of the differences emerges, in the law of relative centrations, in the multiplicative form $(L_1 - L_2)L_2$ rather than simply in the form $L_1 - L_2$. If CC represents complete coupling, and CI incomplete coupling, and if $R_n = R$ at the moment T_n, we will then have:

(32) $\qquad CC = R_n{}^2$ if $R_n > R'_n \qquad CC = R'_n{}^2$ if $R' > R$

and

(33) $\qquad CI = R_n{}^2 - R_n(R_n - R'_n)$ if $R_n > R'_n$

Given the existence of an elementary error II, or of a relative and not an absolute over-estimation of the centred element A, and recalling once more that this error is a function of incomplete coupling, CI (complete coupling implies that elementary error I is the same for L_1 and for L_2 and that relative over-estimations are not therefore involved), certain important consequences derive from Props. 31 to 33.

(1) Firstly, the difference $R_n - R'_n$ will initially be zero $(R_0 - R'_0 = 0)$, and consequently a complete coupling is more probable the fewer the encounters. Experimentally, this carries the consequence that relative over-estimations should be attentuated in brief tachistoscopic presentations.

(2) On the other hand, if the value of β differs from that of α, the difference $R_n - R'_n$ will increase more or less rapidly at times T_1, T_2, etc., that is to say, in the accelerated portion of the exponential formulated in Props. 28 and 29. In other words, the probability of complete coupling will diminish during the phase corresponding to the rapid increase of R_n and of R'_n.

(3) By contrast, in proportion as the number of elements as yet unencountered, N_n and N'_n, diminishes and as the rate of achievement of encounters R_n and R'_n decreases (corresponding to the plateaux of the exponential curves, or to the area adjoining the asymptote), the probability of complete coupling will tend to increase, this time in proportion to the increase in the number of encounters.

(3a) Because the two growth functions, R_n and R'_n, are out of phase, their respective values can never coincide while exposure times are of medium duration, or where some systematic reason exists for one of the two objects to be generally more centred or encountered than the other. In spite of this, the probability of a relatively complete coupling is greater during this stable phase than during the growth of R_n and of R'_n.

(3b) But to the extent that a sufficient time is given for the complete exploration of the figure, the total encounters, R_n and R'_n, must in the end be equal if all encounterable elements, N, have been encountered (which implies, because the division of L into N elements is arbitrary, that the encounters on the two objects compared have become homogeneous).

(3c) Furthermore, if L_1 equals L_2, there is a strong probability that the coupling will finally become complete, so long, at least, as the lines have the same orientation, or form parts of a closed figure.

(4) If these conclusions are valid, it follows that a point (2) will be found in the intermediate region of the curves, lying between the initial region (1) and the final region (3) (where the probability of complete coupling is relatively great), where the difference, R_n and R'_n will be maximal and where a maximum value of CI (incomplete coupling) will occur. This point will therefore correspond to the point of maximum relative over-estimation. Tachistoscopic investigations therefore become mandatory and, as will be seen in § 6, generally confirm this formulation.

To summarise, the probabilities of encounters and of couplings on the two figures, L_1 and L_2, may be written as follows:

(*a*) The probability of encounters on L_1, by unit length and during time t, will be:

$$(34a) \qquad 1 - (1 - pL_1)^{nt}$$

where pL_1 is the probability of encounters on L_1 and n the effective number of encounters per unit of time, t.

(*b*) The probability of encounters on L_2, by unit length, will be:

$$(34b) \qquad 1 - (1 - pL_2)^{nt}$$

(*c*) The probability of incomplete coupling between L_1 and L_2 by unit length[1] will be:

$$(35) \qquad P = N_1(1 - pL_1)^{nt} - N_2(1 - pL_2)^{nt}$$

where N_1 and N_2 are the frequencies of encounters on L_1 and on L_2.

We have yet to clarify the distinction between those relatively complete couplings whose probability is great when encounters are few (1 above), and those whose probability once more becomes great when encounters are numerous (3 and 3b above). The initial couplings result from the few encounters occurring at very short exposure times. They constitute 1 to n correspondences between encounters which derive from the subject's centrations only and do not entail any other perceptual activities on his part. By contrast, the final couplings derive from numerous encounters. They consist in a homogenisation of encounters on the two figures and derive from the subject's genuine perceptual activities, such as increasingly systematic explorations of the figures, and, particularly, transportations accompanying ocular movements which relate L_1 to L_2, and reciprocally.

[1] See Fig. 35, p. 128.

It is this distinction between what will be called 'automatic coup-lings' (corresponding to the weak effects of centration when coupling is still almost complete and to the strong effects of centration as it becomes less and less complete) and 'active couplings' (corresponding to a progressive decentration, leading to a gradual co-ordination of centrations) which explains the variation in the probability of complete coupling between T_0 and increasing durations of exposure.

It is the existence of these active couplings, leading to the homo-genisation of encounters, that explains why the primary illusions tend to diminish with age as a function of the development of exploratory activities and of the number of transportations entailed in more extensive and systematic oculo-motor explorations. It is actually very difficult to discover if elementary error I, due only to the increment of encounters on a single figure, diminishes with age or not. This is because the introduction of a yardstick is essential to its measurement and this, *ipso facto*, converts the over-estimation of L into a relative over-estimation, or into a case of elementary error II. On the other hand, tachistoscopic studies give grounds for supposing that, at short exposure times at least, encounters increase more rapidly with age, in the sense that their number increases more rapidly in successive units of time. There is, however, no doubt that elementary error II, of relative over-estimation, diminishes with age and for this reason results in the general weakening of primary illusions. It is this weak-ening which is explained in our model by the increment in active couplings, or of decentration. The same, of course, applies to the weakening of primary illusions as a consequence of repetition or of practice, which will be discussed in § 2 of Chapter III.

It can thus be seen that the model of encounters and of couplings which has just been developed is subject to validation, not only by means of the tachistoscopic studies to be discussed in § 6 but also by means of genetic analyses in general, by the effects of repetition or practice, and, finally, by the examination of differences in effects of practice as a function of age.

The following observations may be added.

The under-estimation of unfilled spaces (or of virtual lines), as opposed to filled spaces (actual lines), lends support to the necessity which we have felt to translate effects of centration into terms of probabilities of encounters, and of complete or incomplete coupling (irrespective of which probability model is adopted). The general nature of this phenomenon is confirmed by some measurements made in our laboratory by Masucco-Costa.[1] Other findings are also confirmatory. It is known, for example, that two equal lines located in the same horizontal plane and separated by an unfilled space

[1] *Masucco-Costa, Mme, Archivio di Psicol. neurol. epsichiatr.*, 1949, **10**, 377–88.

equal to their length, appear to be longer than that space; also that a continuous line, say of 7·5 cm, appears to be longer than the total space occupied by two lines of 2·5 cm separated by an equal unoccupied interval. More important, a continuous line of 6 cm appears to be longer than three discontinuous lines of 1·2 cm separated by two unoccupied intervals of the same length (which is a reversal of the Oppel–Kundt illusion of divided spaces as a result of the intervention of unfilled spaces), as has been described elsewhere.[1]

These results seem to be difficult to explain simply in terms of the retinal areas stimulated. The error of unfilled spaces seems explicable only in terms of a decomposition of the field of centration into a certain number of encounters which are more numerous on actual than on virtual lines. To say that actual lines constitute 'figures' and that intervals constitute 'ground', makes no difference, because if figures have different properties from the ground on which they are situated, it is precisely because more note is taken of them: they are thus more encountered. Even if an observer fixates the centre of the unoccupied interval between two drawn lines, as in the case of two equal lines separated by an equal interval, the depicted lines still appear to be longer, although they are viewed peripherally. This contradiction with the usual effects of centration can only be explained in terms of a heterogeneity of encounters and therefore of incomplete coupling.

§ 3. CENTRATION AND THE ACCENTUATION OF DIMENSIONAL INEQUALITIES

It may be granted that over- and under-estimations result from centration alone, even in the case of lines of equal length and under the various conditions described in § 1. It may also be granted, by hypothesis, that these dimensional deformations are explicable in terms of the model of encounters and of couplings. It then becomes necessary to establish if, and under what conditions, this general fact of over-estimation by centration, and its abstract model of encounters and of couplings, can account for the fundamental event that actual dimensional differences are always perceptually accentuated (except at the level of the threshold, to be examined in § 5). This is the phenomenon in which a line, B, being physically longer than A, appears to be longer when compared with A than when perceived in isolation, which may be expressed as $B(A) > B$.

In a general way, there must be some kinship between the over-estimation by centration and this accentuation of differences: since the optico-geometric illusions are quantitatively, and sometimes qualitatively, modified by changes in the point of centration (a fact

[1] Piaget, J., *Rev. Suisse de Psychol.*, 1952, **11**, 19–25.

mentioned in § 3 of Chapter I in respect of Oppel's figure, and of which further examples will be given in § 6 below), the two kinds of deformation must have something in common. If this is so, it would seem that over-estimations by centration should explain the accentuations of dimensional inequalities, and not the inverse: it is easy to see how the accentuation of dimensional inequalities could be derived from effects of centration, which are of a more general nature, whereas a derivation in the other direction would be scarcely intelligible.

In broad outline, it is immediately comprehensible that over-estimation by centration should lead to a relative over-estimation of the longer of two lines if it is granted that over-estimations are by and large proportional to the length of the line. For example, if two lines, $A = 50$ mm and $B = 60$ mm, are compared and if the co-efficient of over-estimation due to centration which alternates between them is 0·1, the perceived length of A would be 55 mm and of B 66 mm, an apparent difference of 11 instead of 10 mm. This already would offer a partial explanation of the perceptual reinforcement of the existing differences.

But the measuring instrument, M (itself a line if A and B are lines), would also be over-estimated by 10% when centred; and if A, B and M are constantly over-estimated in equal proportions, no illusion would be experienced because, as Poincaré once said, if the dimensions of all the objects in the universe were multiplied by n, we would have no means of detecting it.

The following propositions must therefore be entertained:

(*a*) As a general rule, the coefficient of over-estimation will be proportional to the size of the object perceived (which will stand us in good stead when explaining Weber's law).

(*b*) The co-efficient of over-estimation will nevertheless be subject to momentary variations, particularly according to whether the line is compared with a line shorter than itself, or is perceived in isolation.

The above explanation, given as a first approximation, is insufficient by itself to explain exaggerations of dimensional inequalities, $B(A) > B$ (when $B > A$), because it does not explain why the actual difference in length between A and B has an influence on their perceived lengths when they are perceived together. To resolve this problem, the analysis made in § 2 must be extended and completed.

Three hypotheses suggest themselves on the basis of the model of encounters and couplings, depending on whether a homogeneous (Hypothesis I) or a heterogeneous (Hypotheses II and III) number of encounters is supposed to fall on L_1 and on L_2. It may be stated, in anticipation, that the first hypothesis will be rejected. A final choice will not be made between the second and the third (in spite of a tendency to prefer the third) as it will be shown that calculations based on their respective characteristics lead to equivalent results in so far as difference couplings, $(L_1 - L_2)L_2$, the fundamental relation involved in the law of relative centrations, are concerned.

Hypothesis I states that, on the completion of visual exploration involving several successive or alternating centrations, encounters will be *homogeneously distributed* on $L_2 (= A)$ and on $L_1 (= B > A)$. In other words, their number will be equal by absolute units of length (let us say x encounters per cm on both L_1 and on L_2). In this case, the relative over-estimation of L_1 would not be due to the inequality of encounters on the two lines but only to an asymmetry of coupling. In short, the effects of centration, encounters being equal, would be attributable only to the 'absolute over-estimation' of A $(= L_2)$, $B (= L_1)$ and M, the coefficient of over-estimation being equal for all three: the outcome would vary as a function of the degree to which couplings were in correspondence, which in turn depends on the relative absolute lengths of the lines.

If encounters are homogeneous, couplings will be symmetrical between equal but not between unequal lines. If $B (= M)$ is compared with M, and if there are n encounters on each, there will be 1 to n couplings for each point of encounter on B linked to the n points on M and, reciprocally, 1 to n couplings for each point of encounter on M linked to n points on B, or n^2 couplings. But when B is compared with A, with $B > A$, and if there are n points of encounter on B and n' on A ($n' < n$), the couplings of A would be of the order 1 to n and those of B, 1 to n', which is asymmetrical and involves more connections on A than on B. It could then be conceded that, although A and B give rise to the same absolute over-estimation, or coefficient of over-estimation, there would still be a relative over-estimation of B. This would be because B is linked to A by less couplings than A is to it. Consequently B is likely to be more over-estimated in this situation than when it is compared with M, when there are 1 to n couplings in each direction.

This hypothesis, which we originally preferred[1] has the advantage of implying a general and automatic over-estimation of the greater of two objects. This, however, also leads to its downfall because it has since been discovered by experimentation that illusions are sometimes completely eliminated under repeated presentations of the figures and sometimes considerably reduced at very brief exposures.

Hypotheses II and III retain the above distinction between absolute over-estimation due to the number of encounters and relative

[1] *Rech.* 22.

over-estimation due to couplings or to correspondence between encounters. But they introduce the additional notion that encounters on two unequal lines are *heterogeneous*: by both hypotheses there will be a greater absolute over-estimation of the longer of two lines when the two are seen together. In these terms, relative over-estimation would simply translate this heterogeneity of encounters into correspondences or couplings; it would be an expression of the inequality of the absolute over-estimations. It would be necessary, however, to make a distinction between absolute over-estimations (which alter according to whether B is compared with A or is perceived in isolation) and relative over-estimations ($=$ relation or correspondence between absolute over-estimations or, in other words, couplings between encounters). The relationship between them would, however, be simpler than by Hypothesis I.

The only difference between Hypotheses II and III is that by Hypothesis II encounters would have to be calculated by absolute units of length, while by Hypothesis III they would be calculated by relative units of length (or by fractions of the whole lengths, such as a quarter or a tenth of L_1 and of L_2 respectively, independently of the absolute values of these fractional parts). In other words, the density of encounters would be an 'absolute density' by Hypothesis II (where the 'same density' would mean the same number of encounters by cm or mm) while it would be a 'relative density' by Hypothesis III (where the 'same density' would mean the same number of encounters for a given fraction of L_1 or of L_2). A more detailed examination will now be made of these hypotheses.

By Hypothesis II, L_1 (or B) would be more centred and therefore carry more encounters by absolute unit of length than L_2 when both are perceived together. If perceived in isolation, the encounters and consequent over-estimation would be absolutely less. The relative over-estimation of the longer line would derive from the fact that it would advantageously attract the glance or the attention when presented with a shorter line: this would attract to it a greater absolute density of encounters. In isolation, on the other hand, the absolute density of encounters would be less, perhaps, for example, intermediate between that on B and that on A when the two were seen together.

The apparent inconvenience of this interpretation is that, although the error due to relative over-estimation is no longer considered to be inevitable, as it was by Hypothesis I, it now seems to become too unstable. If the over-estimation of B relative to A is due only to an excess of centrations or of encounters, all that would be needed to eliminate the illusion would be an increasing compensation brought about by prolonged fixation of A. It is for this reason that Hypothesis III is entertained because, if the density of encounters is considered to be relative and no longer absolute, as just described, an exact compensation, or a relative homogeneity of encounters, becomes much less likely and the heterogeneity in favour of L_1 becomes much more stable. However, even by Hypothesis II, the error would not necessarily be unstable if the relative over-estimation of B was due to a greater absolute over-estimation or to an excess of centration or of encounters. Translated into terms of a logarithmic progression (as in § 2), the encounters on L_1 and on L_2 could differ considerably in absolute density at first, (when the figure is first examined in unrestricted vision). The difference could then decrease progressively, while remaining stable, as the two exponentials approached their asymptotes: there is nothing to prevent L_1 from retaining its advantage right to the end. It is also quite likely that a centration on L_2 would be accompanied by an appreciable defection of encounters on to L_1, because, if the lines are perceptually close to one another, they must both be perceived at once and L_2 is the smaller.

Hypothesis II will now be stated formally in order to make its later comparison with Hypothesis III possible in terms of the results of calculations based on it and in terms of the explanation of the difference coupling $(L_1 - L_2)L_2$.

(1) Suppose that two lines of unequal length, $L_1 > L_2$, carry N and N' $(N > N')$ encounterable elements respectively (see Props. 28 and 29, p. 86). The numbers N and N' are estimated in proportion to the absolute lengths of the lines, say n by cm or mm, the number n being arbitrary. Whence we have $N = nL_1$ and $N' = nL_2$.

(2) Hypothesis II states that the apparent length of a line is a function of the number of encounterable elements actually encountered, encounterable elements being understood as segments of equal absolute length. In other words, if $L_1 = xL_2$, their absolute over-estimation will be proportional to their respective lengths (will have the same co-efficient in both cases) if an equal number of encounters (say n per cm or mm) is distributed on identical unit lengths of L_1 and of L_2. This state of affairs will be referred to as an equal absolute density of encounters.

(3) On the other hand, and still in terms of Hypothesis II, if L_1 is perceived in proximity to L_2, it will be absolutely more over-estimated than L_2 if it carries a greater number of encounters by absolute unit length: for example n per cm on L_1 and $n'(<n)$ per cm on L_2. This state of affairs will be referred to as an unequal absolute density of encounters.

(4) In this case, the couplings between L_1 and L_2 would be incomplete and L_1 would *ipso facto* be over-estimated relative to L_2. If n is the number of encounters by unit of absolute length of both L_1, of

length x, and of L_2, of length y, the complete coupling would correspond to $nx \times ny = n^2xy$. But if the densities are unequal, n by unit of absolute length for L_1 and $n'(<n)$ for L_2, the coupling would be incomplete and would have the value of $(nx \times n'y) = (nn'xy) < n^2xy$.

(5) The inequality of densities of encounters, n and n', being a function of the unequal lengths of L_1 and of L_2, the relative over-estimation of L_1 corresponds to the couplings $(L_1 - L_2)L_2$, that is, to the total couplings $(M')L_1L_2$ less the couplings between L_2 and that part of L_1 equal to L_2, whose value is $(n'L_2)^2$, or:

$$(36) \quad [(L_1 - L_2)L_2 = L_1L_2 - L_2^2] \times [(n - n')n' = nn' - n'^2] = (nL_1 - n'L_2)n'L_2 = nn'L_1L_2 - (n'L_2)^2$$

This formula does not, of course, indicate the value of the relative over-estimation of L_1 because this would depend on the value of the absolute over-estimations n and n' (elementary error I) and of their differences (elementary error II). But it indicates that, for a given value of n', if the couplings between two equal lengths are homogeneous, or have the same absolute density (which would give $(n'L_2)^2$ for L_2, or more simply L_2^2 if we consider one encounter per total unit of length), and if the couplings between unequal lengths are heterogeneous, or have unequal absolute densities (which would give $nn'L_1L_2$), then the relative over-estimation of L_1 over L_2 would be of the order of $nn'L_1L_2 - (n'L_2)^2 = (nL_1 - n'L_2)n'L_2$.

It is this heterogeneity of couplings in the case of a simultaneous perception of unequal lengths (a heterogeneity which simply implies, by Hypothesis II, an inequality in the absolute density of encounters on L_1 and on L_2) which would thus explain the relative over-estimation of the greater length and which would then account for the fundamental expression of the law of relative centrations, $(L_1 - L_2)L_2$.

But the above calculations, (1) to (5), are relative only to Hypothesis II, that is, to the supposition that encounters on L_1 and on L_2 are distributed as a function of absolute units of length. It is now necessary to examine the results of the same calculations applied to Hypothesis III, where the distribution is a function of relative units, or of fractions, of the lengths of L_1 and of L_2.

Hypothesis III, which will be stated formally below, retains the distinction between the number of encounters, which is the source of absolute over-estimation, and the correspondence or coupling between those encounters. But in one sense it makes absolute over-estimations relative: the number of encounters would no longer be a function of the number of units of absolute length of the objects centred (which would give, for equal densities, as in Hypothesis I, ten times the number of encounters on a line of 20 cm as on one of

2 cm; and for unequal densities, as in Hypothesis II, more than ten times the number of encounters on the long as on the short line), but would be a function of the relative units of length, or fractions of total length: for instance, n encounters by thirds or tenths of the total lengths of L_1 and of L_2 in the case of equal relative densities. If relative densities mean the number of encounters by relative unit lengths, or fractions of total length, the relative over-estimation of L_1 would be explained, by Hypothesis III, simply in terms of the greater relative density of encounters on L_1 than on L_2, namely n encounters by L_1/f (L_1/f being an arbitrary fraction of L_1) and n' encounters by L_2/f (L_2/f being the same fraction of L_2).

The significance of Hypothesis III is as follows. By Hypothesis II, the estimation of the length of a line is a direct function of the number of encounters on it. This is independent of any global estimate based on visual angle. Should a global estimate based on visual angle intervene, it would automatically engender a number of encounters which would not be simply proportional to the value of the angle, as in the case of absolute judgements when comparisons are not involved, but would increase as a function of increases in the angle, as in relative over-estimations when comparisons are involved. This might be acceptable if the encountering elements were the elementary segments of L and the encountered elements were the units of the receptor organ, for instance the cells of the retina or of the visual cortex. But if the encountering elements belonged to the perceiver and to his active visual exploration, and the encountered elements to the explored line, it would be much more likely that: (1) the length of the object would first be assessed in a global manner, on the basis of visual angle or the amount of the visual field it occupied; and (2) the centrations would then be distributed in detail by fractions of that visual angle (lines of 20 cm are not explored in the same way as lines of 2 cm when both are viewed at normal reading distance). If this were the case, the length of the line would be definitively estimated, by detailed exploration following an anticipatory global estimate, on the basis of centrations or encounters distributed according to the anticipatory estimate, that is to say, by fractions of the visual angle (or of the length of L) and not by absolute units of length. It follows naturally that the longer line, because of a greater relative density of encounters on it, should be relatively over-estimated when the two are perceived simultaneously and close together. Where L_1 (= 20 cm) and L_2 (= 2 cm) are viewed at the same distance, this would simply mean, for example, that, if there are n' encounters per quarter of L_2, there would be $n(>n')$ encounters per quarter of L_1. But if L_1, in isolation, is compared with M (a measuring instrument of the same length), there would be no relative over-estimation because the encounters would be distributed in equal proportions on fractions of equal absolute length.

An additional advantage of this hypothesis is that it accounts directly for what will be referred to in tachistoscopic experiments to be described in § 6 as 'enveloping centrations'. These are centrations which, for a given fixation point, encompass the relationships which generate an illusion, that is, the collection of deforming and deformed elements of a figure. It is remarkable, for instance, that with fixation on the horizontal line of a right-angle, the vertical is over-estimated by adults even at exposure times of 0·02 to 0·1 second. Children over-estimate the horizontal under these conditions, as would be anticipated from a consideration of centration only. It is as though the adult distributed the deforming effects by some sort of activity of attention, even when obliged to fixate the horizontal line. No doubt this is analogous to the distributions of eye-movements in unrestricted viewing when, as recorded by Vinh-Bang (Chapter III, § 3), adults centre mainly on the top of the vertical line and, when fixating the horizontal, do so near to its junction with the vertical. In such cases, and in other similar ones, the density of the effects does not appear to be at all uniform and it is likely that it varies as a function of the length of the lines, or, where they are equal, as a function of their positions relative to the perceptual co-ordinates (which are secondary factors to be described in § 4 of Chapter III).

In brief, and allowing for the general frame of reference provided by visual angles, the advantage of Hypothesis III is that it makes the details of the estimation of length depend directly on the relative density of the partial effects of centration, that is to say on the encounters. Were this not so, one would sooner or later have to make these estimations correspond to distances between encounters and to consider the latter simply as 'local signs', in the sense of nineteenth-century psychology.

This hypothesis can now be formulated in a manner parallel to that adopted for Hypothesis II, making use once more of the general model of encounters and of couplings.

(1) The two unequal lines ($L_1 > L_2$) each entail N encounterable elements (see Props. 28 and 29) which are an arbitrary but equal number of fractional parts of the two lines (for instance, ten tenths or one thousand thousandths).

(2) Hypothesis III states, firstly, that the apparent length of either line, whatever its real length, is a function of the number of encounterable elements actually encountered (this is, of course, provisional upon both lines lying within the bounds of a single initial centration which, in turn, does not preclude subsequent distinct centrations but does exclude transportations at a distance). In other words, if $L_1 =$

xL_2, they will give rise to an equal absolute over-estimation proportional to their respective lengths (of the same coefficient) if an equal number of encounters is distributed on equal fractions of those lengths (for instance, n on each tenth part of each length). This event will be referred to as an 'equal relative density'.

(3) But, by the same hypothesis, if L_1 is compared with L_2, even unintentionally if they are close together, it would be enough for L_1 to carry a relatively greater number of encounters by fractional part for it to be absolutely more over-estimated than L_2, for instance, if there are n encounters on each tenth part of L_1 and $n'(<n)$ on each tenth part of L_2. This will be referred to as an 'unequal relative density'.

(4) This being so, the coupling between L_1 and L_2 would be incomplete and L_1 would be over-estimated relative to L_2. If the number of encounters by equal fractional parts of both lines is n_f throughout the whole of their lengths, a complete coupling would correspond to $n_f{}^2$; if they number n_f on L_1 and $n_f'(<n_f)$ on L_2, the coupling would be incomplete, having a value of $nn_f' < n_f{}^2$.

(5) The relative inequality of density of encounters between n_f and n_f' being thus a function of the unequal lengths of the lines, the relative over-estimation of L_1 will correspond to $(L_1-L_2)L_2$. The relation between $(L_1 - L_2)L_2$ and $n_f n_f'$ based on the system of calculations proper to the hypothesis is:

(*a*) $n_f n_f'$ corresponds to $L_1 L_2$ because n_f is the number of encounters on L_1 and n_f' the number on L_2.

(*b*) $n_f'{}^2$ corresponds to what would be a complete coupling at the rate of n' on L_2, and thus corresponds to $L_2{}^2$.

(*c*) $(L_1 - L_2)L_2$ in turn corresponds to $(n_f - n_f')n_f'$.

One thus has:

$$(37) \qquad n_f n_f' = (n_f - n_f')n_f' + n_f'{}^2$$

whence

$$(38) \qquad (n_f - n_f')n_f' = n_f n_f' - n_f'{}^2$$

which corresponds to $(L_1 - L_2)L_2 = L_1 L_2 - L_2{}^2$ (see Prop. 36, p. 98, under Hypothesis II).

It can be seen that the outcome is the same by both hypotheses, the only difference being the way in which the encounters are calculated. In both cases, incomplete coupling nn' or $n_f n_f'$ is equal to what would be a complete coupling between n' or n_f' on L_2 and the same number of encounters on a part of L_1 equal to L_2, plus the difference in the couplings between L_1 and L_2, or the difference coupling $(n - n')n'$ or $(n_f - n_f')n_f'$. This corresponds to $(L_1 - L_2)L_2$, the fundamental relationship of the law of relative centrations, and we are not therefore forced to choose between the two hypotheses in what follows. Nevertheless the following experiment was carried out in order to assess the relative plausibility of Hypotheses I, II and III.

Although the number of encounters taking place on two unequal lines cannot, of course, be measured (the notion of encounters being still hypothetical), it is possible to count the number of spontaneous centrings which occur on each line during a period of unrestricted viewing, by filming eye-movements. Of course, it cannot be assumed that the number of encounters will be proportional to the number of centrations, but if the number of centrations should turn out to be proportional to the length of the lines, it would be difficult to imagine that the encounters should be otherwise, and this would speak in favour of Hypothesis I. If, on the other hand, this proportionality did not exist, it would be interesting to know if, in the case of two lines of x and nx cm respectively, there would be more or less than nx centrations on the second if there were x on the first: without thereby confirming one or other of the hypotheses, the first eventuality would favour Hypothesis II and the second Hypothesis III.

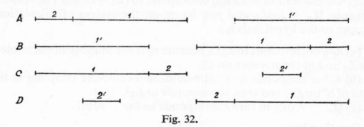

Fig. 32.

Vinh-Bang was kind enough to analyse the cinematographic records of eye-movements made during the inspection of figures A to D of Fig. 32 when the subject was asked to compare the length of the variable, 1 or 2, with that of the standard, 1′ or 2′. The results are shown in Table 36.

TABLE 36. *Distribution of centrations on segments as a function of the figure involved (values in parenthesis represent % of total centrations)*

Figure		A		B		C		D	
On segment 1	(7·5 cm)	4·1	(45)	5·15	(52)	1·10	(16)	0·45	(7)
1′	(7·5 cm)	3·5	(39)	4·0	(40)	—		—	
2	(2·5 cm)	1·1	(12)	0·2	(2)	2·41	(35)	2·55	(42)
2′	(2·5 cm)	—		—		2·25	(33)	2·05	(34)
Between segments		0·4	(4)	0·33	(3)	1·14	(17)	0·4	(7)
Total centrations		9·1		10·00		6·95		6·05	

Some facts of interest emerge. Firstly, centrations on the variable of 7·5 cm were, at most, twice as numerous as those on the variable of

2·5 cm, and not three or more times as numerous (4·1 against 2·41 for *A* and *C*; and 5·15 against 2·55 for *B* and *D*). In the case of the standard, the same relationship holds (3·5 against 2·25 for *A* and *C*; 4·0 against 2·05 for *B* and *D*). These facts favour Hypothesis III rather than I and are particularly unfavourable to Hypothesis II.

However, when segment 1 was being judged, it was centred four times as frequently as the smaller segment, 2, which was not being judged (4·1 against 1·1 in *A* and 5·15 against 0·2 in *B*); but while segment 2 was being judged, it was more centred, but to a lesser extent than above, than the larger segment, 1, which was not being judged (2·41 against 1·10 in *C* and 2·55 against 0·45 in *D*). These two facts are very revealing. They show, firstly, that whereas the over-estimation of 1 in *A* and *B* might appear to be attributable to an excess of centrations, the under-estimation of 2 in *C* and *D* could not be attributed to a lack of centrations. It is therefore essential to distinguish between encounters and centrations and to concede that centrations on 2 could have been sufficiently enveloping (a concept to be discussed in § 6) to distribute more encounters on the non-fixated than on the fixated segment (perhaps as a function of attention, etc.). It also shows that centrations are not exclusively distributed on the segment being judged: when the longer segment is being judged, the smaller does tend to be neglected, but the converse is not true. The following differences between the sums of centrations resulted: 9·1 and 10·0 for *A* and *B*, against 6·95 and 6·05 for *C* and *D* (which include 0·3 and 0·6 centrations beyond the extremities of the lines being judged in *B* and *D* respectively).

In summary, this investigation clearly favours Hypothesis III without absolutely excluding Hypothesis II, because the number of encounters is not necessarily proportional to that of centrations. But whether one chooses Hypothesis II or Hypothesis III, it is still evident that the effects of contrast are due to the same play of encounters and of incomplete couplings as are the effects of centration. This is all that we need at this stage in order to establish the link between the model of § 2 and the explanation of the law of relative centrations which is to follow.

§ 4. AN EXPLANATION OF THE LAW OF RELATIVE CENTRATIONS IN TERMS OF THE MODEL OF ENCOUNTERS AND OF COUPLINGS

We have just stated the reasons for supposing that the over-estimation of the longer of two compared lines is a phenomenon which should be considered to be closely related to over-estimation by centration. Of the three possible hypotheses which could account for this over-estimation by centration, we were led to prefer those (II and III) which point to an absolutely or a relatively greater number of centrations (or at least of partial effects or of encounters) falling on the longer of the two lines.

Moreover, in developing the model of encounters and of couplings (§ 2), we saw, in connection with Props. 32 and 33 (elaborated in subsection 3a, p. 90), that incomplete couplings, sources of relative over-estimations (or of elementary errors *II*), remain incomplete when there is a systematic reason for one of the lines to be more frequently centred or encountered than the other: which is what happens (§ 3) when one of the lines is longer than the other. The analysis of elementary errors *I* and *II* therefore leads on to an explanation of 'composite errors', that is to say, of the primary optico-geometric illusions and of the law of relative centrations in general.

I. Firstly, following on from § 3, it may be conceded that the longer of two lines exhibits an absolutely or a relatively greater density of encounters than the shorter, and that consequently, as a general rule, there will be an incomplete coupling between them. This general factor would then explain the importance, in all the formulae of Chapter I, of the relationship $(L_1 - L_2)L_2$ which we have already referred to as the difference coupling. It will be necessary to confer a more precise meaning on this expression by making use of the theory of couplings (§§ 2 and 3) which was developed for this purpose. This will be done in III.

We are about to pass from an analysis of elementary errors to that of composite errors, to illusions involving a composite figure or a configuration in the ordinary sense of the term, and no longer simply the perception of a single line or the comparison of two lines. To do this, we must first classify the possible forms of coupling, whether complete or incomplete, which could occur in such configurations.

Consider two unequal lines, $L_1 > L_2$, which form part of a figure and which are parallel to one another, or perpendicular (recalling that it was shown in Chapter I, § 4, that when obliques form an angle other than 90° with their reference, the inclination is estimated on the basis of virtual lines which are similarly parallel or perpendicular). Let L_1 be divided into two parts, one equal in length to L_2, labelled L'_2, and the other equal to the difference between L_1 and L_2, and referred to as L_3. Four classes of coupling can be distinguished which involve four classes of 1 to n correspondences which can be calculated separately according to the specific formula for the illusion in question. It is not intended to imply that they necessarily correspond to four distinct modes of comparison on the part of the subject, even if some of these may be possible or even likely.

(1) 'Equivalence' couplings, R, between L_2 and L'_2, which, if complete (if we estimate encounters as proportional to the length of the segment in question), will number $L_2{}^2$.

(2) 'Difference' couplings, D between L_2 and L_3, which, if complete, will number $(L_2 \times L_3)$ or $(L_1 - L_2)L_2$.

(3) 'Reciprocal difference' couplings, D', between the projection of L_2 on to L_1 (namely L'_2) and the projection of L_3 on to L'_3, that is to

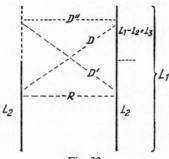

Fig. 33.

say on to a virtual extension of L_2 equal in length to L_3 (see Fig. 33). If complete, they will number $L_2L_3 = (L'_2L'_3) = (L_1 - L_2)L_2$

(4) 'Equivalences between difference' couplings, D'', between L_3 and its projection L'_3. If these exist and are complete, they will number $L_3{}^2 = (L_1 - L_2)^2$.

II. It can be seen that the fundamental expression $(L_1 - L_2)L_2$ corresponds to the most important of these four possible couplings, namely to the difference coupling, D, which is an expression of the perceptual contrast existing between the two lines. The general significance of the law of relative centrations becomes immediately apparent in this case: it simply expresses the relation between the number of difference couplings, $(L_1 - L_2)L_2$, and the number of possible couplings, represented by S. This relation is then itself multiplied by a second relation (which is, in most cases, simply equal to 1) between the number of encounters on the deforming element in question $(= nL)$ and those on the greatest dimension of the figure (L_{max}).

As a result, the general form of the law is (see Prop. 3 of Chapter I, p. 7):

$$P = \frac{(L_1 - L_2)L_2}{S} \times \frac{nL}{L_{max}}$$

Let us re-examine each of these terms to establish its proposed interpretation.

III. From a geometrical point of view, $(L_1 - L_2)L_2 = L_1L_2 - L_2{}^2$. From the point of view of coupling, Hypothesis II of § 3 proposes that line L_1 entails n encounters in all, while line L_2 entails only $n'(< n)$ encounters by unit length, namely $n'L_2$. We do not know if the excess of encounters on L_1 falls on the part $L_1 - L_2$ or is dispersed throughout its length, but this makes no difference to the calculations because they can be set out as follows in both cases:

Couplings: e.g., if $L_2 = 4, L_1 = 7, n' = 50, n = 90$

R	$= (n'L_2)^2$	R	$= (50 \times 4)^2$	$= 40,000$
D	$= (nL_1 - n'L_2)n'L_2$	D	$= (630 - 200)200$	$= 86,000$
D'	$= (nL_1 - n'L_2)n'L_2$	D'	$= (630 - 200)200$	$= 86,000$
D''	$= (nL_1 - n'L_2)^2$	D''	$= (630 - 200)^2$	$= 184,900$

Total $= (nL_1)^2$ $\qquad\qquad (nL_1)^2 = (630)^2 \qquad\qquad = 396,900$

By this hypothesis, the difference coupling, D, is equal to the sum of all possible couplings, $(nL_1)^2$, minus the couplings R, D' and D''.

By Hypothesis III, as encounters are calculated on the basis of equal fractional parts of L_1 and of L_2, one would have n_f encounters on L_1 (say 6 per tenth part of an L_1 of 7 cm, namely 60 in all) and n'_f on L_2 (say 4 per tenth part of an L_2 of 4 cm, namely 40 in all). The couplings would then be:

Couplings: e.g., if $L_2 = 4, L_1 = 7, n' = 40, n = 60$

R	$= n'_f{}^2$	R	$= 1,600$
D	$= (n_f - n'_f)n'_f$	D	$= 800$
D'	$= (n_f - n'_f)n'_f$	D'	$= 800$
D''	$= (n_f - n'_f)^2$	D''	$= 400$

Total $= n_f{}^2$ $\qquad\qquad n_f{}^2 = 3,600$

By Hypothesis III, the difference coupling is again equal to the sum of all possible couplings (here $n_f{}^2$) minus the couplings R, D' and D''. Moreover, this result is analytically necessary, given that one defines the four types of coupling appropriately as a function of the model chosen (II or III). In effect, given that $(A + A')^2 = A^2 + 2AA' + A'^2$, and if the following correspondences are established (if L_1 corresponds to $B = A + A'$, L_2 to A and $L_1 - L_2$ to A'):

$$R = A^2, \quad D = AA', \quad D' = AA' \text{ and } D'' = A'^2$$

then

$$R + 2D + D'' = (A + A')^2$$

IV. The expression S (the denominator of the first fraction in the statement of the law of relative centrations on p. 7) does not really signify a surface (although it happens to correspond to the geometric surface of the figure considered) but rather the collection of possible couplings compatible with the structural relations of the given figure.

106

It is for this reason that, in the preceding hypothetical calculations, the expression S corresponds to $(nL_1)^2$ by Hypothesis II and to $n_f{}^2$ by Hypothesis III.

But it is generally necessary to distinguish between closed figures (or figures perceptually related to virtual rectangular frames of reference) and linear figures (in which L_2 forms an extension of L_1).

In closed figures, the surface, S, equals the sum of equivalence couplings and difference couplings, $R + D$, less couplings D' and D''. The rectangle, for example, has a surface $L_1 \times L_2$ which can be broken up as follows: $L_1L_2 = L_2{}^2 + (L_1 - L_2)L_2$. But $L_2{}^2$ corresponds to couplings R, and $(L_1 - L_2)L_2$ to couplings D. The same applies in the case of angles: the surface is that of the reference rectangle in respect of which the arms of the angle deviate (see Chapter I, § 5; in the case of arcs it is the accentuated curve, see Chapter I, § 7); but the surface of this reference rectangle is, in fact, equal in value to the sum of couplings R and D.

Where L_2 forms a simple continuation of L_1, or where L_1 is included between two shorter lines (as in the Delbœuf and Oppel illusions, etc.), S no longer equals L_1L_2 but $(L_1 + L_2)^2$, etc. In this case, the maximum length, $L_{\max}$, is distinct from L_1, which forms only a part of it. Thus two forms of coupling are involved in the perception of the figure, if we let L_3 be a segment corresponding to $L_1 - L_2$ (see Figs. 33 and 34) and L'_2 the projection of L_2 on to L_1 (see Fig. 34):

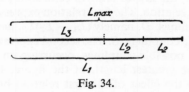

Fig. 34.

(*a*) Couplings of the type $(L_1 + L_2)^2 = L_1{}^2 + 2L_1L_2 + L_2{}^2 = S$. Reference to the definitions of the four classes of coupling, given in I above, shows that $L_1{}^2 (= R)$, $2L_1L_2 (= D$ and $D')$ and $L_2{}^2 (= D'')$ are not couplings between L_1 and L_2 but rather between L_1 and $L_{\max}$, because L_1 is the common part, whence R, between $L_{\max}$ and L_1, and L_2 is their difference. However, if the perception of Fig. 34 does necessitate the relating of $L_{\max}$ to L_1, it is done in terms of the given relations between L_1 and L_2.

(*b*) Couplings between L_1 and L_2, L'_2 being equal to L_2, should be written as $L'_2{}^2 + 2L'_2L_3 + L_3{}^2 = L_1{}^2$, and constitute a sub-set of the couplings listed under (*a*), the total surface of the figure being equal to the whole set (*a*), whence to $L_{\max}{}^2$, and the couplings (*b*) to $L_1{}^2$.

It might be wondered if the couplings described in (a) and (b) do actually play a part in perceptual comparisons; the above analysis might only serve to confer its usual meaning of the set of all possible couplings on the expression S (which is actually calculated as L_{max}^2). Two facts are pertinent in this connection: (1) segmentation of L_1 into $L'_2 + L_3$, as in Fig. 34, occurs when, during comparisons, L_2 is so to speak folded back on to L_1, or L_1 on to L_2; or, more simply, when, during the course of visual exploration, the subject transports one on to the other. (2) Couplings of type (a), do occur either alone, as in the Oppel–Kundt illusion (Chapter I, § 13, Prop. 27), or in conjunction with couplings of type (b), as in the case of the trapezium (Chapter I, § 9).[1]

V. The relation nL/L_{max} expresses the relation between the encounters (or possible couplings) on L and those on L_{max}, which is the longest line in the figure. By Hypothesis III, whereby encounters would be distributed by relative rather than by absolute units of length, this relation enters as an expression of the relation between the lengths themselves. But, even by Hypothesis II, with distribution of encounters by absolute units of length, the relation nL/L_{max} plays a regulatory role in the equation $(L_1 - L_2)L_2$, reinforcing it in some cases, as when $2L_1 > L_{max}$, and restricting it in others.

VI. In conclusion, the law of relative centrations emerges as a twofold probabilistic relation. The first relation expresses the probability of difference couplings, D, namely $(L_1 - L_2)L_2$, having regard to the sum of all possible couplings, S. The second expresses the probability of encounters, or possible couplings, occurring on L, with regard to encounters on the greatest length of the figure. It can thus either reinforce or curb the effect of the first relation but more generally leaves it unchanged when $L_1 = L_{max}$.

Thus conceived, the law suggests a probability of difference couplings as a function of the relational properties of the figure and it is these difference couplings which give rise to elementary errors *II*, or to relative over-estimations. The law thus suggests a greater or lesser probability that these errors will arise as a function of changes in the figure. In particular, it allows one to determine those values of L_1, L_2, L_{max} and S which will give rise to the greatest or to the least relative frequencies of difference couplings, which in turn determine the extent, from maximum (positive or negative) to minimum (zero), of elementary errors *II*. But the law does not confer a value on those errors, any more than it does on elementary errors *I* on whose inter-

[1] But note that in the formulae for the trapezium, the Müller–Lyer illusion, etc., what we here refer to as L_{max} is there designated L_1, and L_1 by L_2, etc.

relationships errors *II* depend. It merely predicts that, if errors *I* and *II* occur, error *II* will fluctuate in value as a function of the structure of the figure and of the transformations of this structure which are relevant to the law. It is for this reason that the agreement between the theoretical and the empirical curves is only qualitative, of shape, and in no sense quantitative, the extent of the illusions varying with age and between individuals.[1] We have, therefore, christened the law 'the law of relative centrations', rather than simply 'of centrations', in order to indicate that, even without knowing the absolute values of the effects of centration on a figure, the relative distributions of the error can be predicted from a knowledge of the relations determined by the structure of the figure.

§ 5. AN INTERPRETATION OF THE THRESHOLD FOR EQUALITY AND THE RELATION OF WEBER'S LAW TO THAT OF RELATIVE CENTRATIONS

All the optico-geometric illusions discussed in Chapter I, the general case of the law of relative centrations, and the case of elementary effects of centration (errors *I* and *II*) discussed in this chapter, have to do only with actions leading either to a subjective reinforcement of objective inequalities (the illusions of Chapter I) or to the introduction of subjective inequalities in the estimation of objectively equal lengths. We have not so far encountered a true case of what traditional studies in perception refer to as 'equalising effects', or 'assimilation', as opposed to 'contrast effects'. Some cases of apparent equalisation have been encountered, one example being that of the two concentric circles of Delbœuf (of which the smaller is over-estimated if $A > A'$, and the greater often under-estimated). A further example of equalisation was between the two bases of the trapezium in which the longer is under- and the shorter over-estimated. But it was concluded that these cases still had to do with effects of contrast, or of accentuation of inequalities, due to the relating of either the longer or the shorter line to the difference between them.[2] The result was either an over-estimation of the shorter or an under-estimation of the longer, in both cases as a consequence of the devaluation of their difference.

---

[1] In the same way Weber's law is confined to stating that the threshold takes on the value of a constant fraction of the perceived dimensions and does not tell us what this fraction is, because it varies with the situation.
[2] We are here referring only to primary effects. The problem of absolute judgements, or of central tendency, is of a different order, being secondary. (See Chapter III, § 6.)

I. But there does seem to be one classical situation in which assimilatory effects occur and which, in contrast to the above cases, is inexplicable in terms of a simple under-estimation of the differences between the two parts of the figure. This is the case of the subliminal difference between two lines ($L_2 < L_1$). In this case, because a subjective equalisation occurs, one must suppose either that there has been an under-estimation of the longer or an over-estimation of the shorter, or that both effects have occurred; and this must occur without any reinforcement of the real inequality, which is imperceptible.

How can this threshold for equality be explained within the system of notions so far employed, and without the introduction of supplementary hypotheses which would endanger the coherence of the models so far advanced? We cannot simply claim that the threshold is a borderline case of the devaluation of differences, a case in which the difference is so under-estimated that it is subjectively eliminated, because we would then be asked how to estimate the point at which under-estimation becomes cancellation. We could not do this on the basis of the law of relative centrations, of course, and it might even be logically impossible, because, by definition, such a point can never be reached.

We may, however, be able to explain the threshold for equality without referring to the law of relative centrations, which has to do exclusively with composite errors (with the relation between elementary error II, $(L_1 - L_2)L_2$, and the terms S and nL/L_{max}). We can fall back instead on elementary errors I and II expressed in terms of the model of encounters and of couplings (as was done in § 2 of this chapter) and applied to the reinforcement of inequalities and to the expression $(L_1 - L_2)L_2$. When we do this, the threshold becomes self-explanatory as a particular case of elementary error II and even as a necessary consequence of the hypotheses which have already been introduced. There is thus no need to introduce supplementary hypotheses to complicate the picture.

In explaining the reinforcement of differences in terms of the model of encounters and of couplings, we have so far only concerned ourselves with perceptible and therefore supraliminal differences. This was not made explicit at the time, because it was unnecessary to do so, but it can now be defined quite easily. An inequality between two simultaneously perceived lines ($L_2 < L_1$), will be said to be supraliminal when the over-estimation of L_2, because of centration on it, preserves the inequality, $L_2 < L_1$, although subjectively diminishing it.

If p is the coefficient of over-estimation of this line (for example, $p = 1 \cdot 1$ or $1 \cdot 2$, etc.), we would have, for a supraliminal inequality:

(39) $$pL_2 < L_1 \text{ and } pL_1 > L_2$$

The reason for the first of these inequalities is that:

(40) $$(pL_2 - L_2) < (L_1 - L_2)$$

For example, if $L_1 = 9$ cm, $L_2 = 7$ cm and if $p = 1\cdot1$, one would have $(pL_2 - L_2) = (7\cdot7 - 7) = 0\cdot7$ cm and $(L_1 - L_2) = (9 - 7) = 2$ cm.

On the other hand, it follows that when the objective differences between L_1 and L_2 are small, centration on L_2 could lead to the following situation which has not yet been considered but which falls within the bounds of possibility for the model:[1]

(41) $$pL_2 \geqslant L_1 \text{ and } pL_1 > L_2$$

The reason for the first of these inequalities, and for its apparent contradiction with the second, is that, effectively, one may easily have:

(42) $$(pL_2 - L_2) \geqslant (L_1 - L_2)$$

For example, if $L_1 = 7\cdot5$ cm and $L_2 = 7$ cm and if $p = 1\cdot1$, one would have: $(pL_2 - L_2) = (7\cdot7 - 7) = 0.7$ cm and $(L_1 - L_2) = (7\cdot5 - 7) = 0\cdot5(<0\cdot7$ cm).

This will be referred to as a case of subliminal differences, which will be defined by saying that the over-estimation of L_2, due to effects of centration on it, no longer preserves the objective inequality of $L_2 < L_1$, even if the effects of centration on L_1 are to reinforce its superiority in length over L_2.

The possibility of the occurrence of subliminal inequalities as defined poses no problems: if the effects of centration result in momentary and alternating over- and under-estimation of the elements according to the distribution of fixations, it follows that these effects of centration could lead to the contradictory judgements exemplified in Prop. 41 when the objective differences are small. This would occur when the coefficient of momentary over-estimation gave rise to subjective differences greater than, and opposite in direction to, the objective ones. The real problem is to show how the subject passes from the contradiction of Prop. 41 to a judgement of equality between L_1 and L_2: can the model of encounters and of couplings, employed so far to explain the reinforcement of inequalities, also explain why an objective difference is subjectively nullified when Props. 41 and 42 hold?

For this to be so, all that we need to assume is that in these cases the distribution of encounters is insufficiently complete, and the correspondence of encounters between the two lines (the coupling)

[1] And which one observes daily in what is known as the interval of uncertainty which is related to, but not identical with, the extent of the threshold.

insufficiently close,[1] for the subject to be able to identify the direction of the inequality, or even its existence. Consequently he may see each line as alternately longer and shorter (even if he does not exhibit the commonly observed phase of contradiction described by Prop. 41).

A certain amount of relevant information is available (some of it derived from analyses of eye-movements).[2] It is known, for instance, that comparisons are more protracted in the region of the threshold: both the number of distinct centrations and exploratory movements on the one object, and the number of transports in both directions between two objects, increase. These increases occur whether the subject at first exhibits the contradiction of Prop. 41 or whether he is at first unable to make a decision. Therefore, if one centration involves a number of encounters, it follows that the number of encounters will be elevated around the threshold. The problem remains of understanding how the same mechanism of coupling which leads to a reinforcement of inequalities in situations represented by Props. 39 and 40, can lead to their cancellation in situations represented by Props. 41 and 42. To find an answer, Hypotheses I to III will have to be re-examined in turn.

According to Hypothesis I, which we have rejected, encounters would be distributed uniformly by absolute units of length. This would entail the disparity between encounters (the number of elements not yet encountered relative to the total number of encounterable elements) remaining in excess of the difference $L_1 - L_2$, even when a large number of encounters was involved. This would result in a priority for resemblance couplings, R, to the exclusion of difference couplings, D.

By Hypothesis II, in which encounters are denser on the longer line but, once more, as a function of absolute units of length, the encounters would be denser alternately on L_1 and on L_2, which would lead to a priority for resemblance couplings and would exclude difference couplings.

By Hypothesis III (in which the lengths are first estimated as a function of visual angle and in which there is then a greater density of encounters on the longer line, but as a function of fractions of its length or of its visual angle), the initial global estimate would not lead to a decision and the greater relative density would then fluctuate between L_1 and L_2. This state of affairs would then be indistinguishable from the alternating greater absolute density of Hypothesis II (the compared objects being nearly equal in length).

---

[1] Where there are still 'elements not yet encountered', $N_2 \ldots, N_n$ (§ 2, I), and where 'elements already encountered', αN, etc., never equal the total number, N, of encounterable elements.

[2] *Rech.* 44.

In all these cases, but more simply by Hypotheses II and III, the apparent equality of L_1 and L_2 in the subliminal zone would derive from the impossibility of establishing difference couplings, D (and couplings D' and D''). This would be so even when the greater frequency of encounters (alternating in relative density between L_1 and L_2 rather than remaining denser on L_1), resulted in an increased number of resemblance couplings, R.

In review, it can be seen that the apparent equality in the region of the threshold does not constitute a type of elementary error (*III*) which is different from absolute (elementary errors *I*) or relative over-estimations (elementary errors *II*). There is only one mechanism involved, that of incomplete coupling, source of relative over-estimations and product of the relation between absolute over-estimations. It leads both to the subjective reinforcement of inequalities when the absolute over-estimations preserve the inequality, $pL_2 < L_1$, and to their subjective suppression when $pL_2 > L_1$. The only difference between the two situations is that, when $pL_2 < L_1$, the coupling is incomplete because of *an excess of difference couplings over resemblance couplings*, and when $pL_2 > L_1$, it is incomplete because *of an excess in the opposite direction*.

II. If this is so, Weber's law is not to be situated at the level of composite errors, which derive from the law of relative centrations, but at that of elementary errors *I* and *II*, which already contain a logarithmic law of growth (error *I*) and a law of proportionality (error *II*).

It is desirable to distinguish between two applications of Weber's law, a distinction which is not usually made. The first is that in which the law is applied to threshold differences, and which corresponds strictly to the situation described above; the second is the so-called application of the law to any differences (with the reservation that the application becomes less strict in proportion to the distance from the threshold): in this case the observed proportionalities no longer derive from elementary errors *I* and *II* but from composite errors and from the law of relative centrations.

Let us first consider Weber's law in its strict sense. This can be written as:

$$(43) \qquad S = k \frac{\Delta L}{L}$$

in which S represents the extent of the threshold and k is a constant.

If it is admitted that the perceived equality of two physically unequal lines derives from alternating absolute over-estimations, as suggested in I, and that the relative over-estimations are cancelled in the region of the threshold, it follows that the encounters will be homogeneous (illusorily so) on the two lines. The proportionality of Weber's law would then stem directly from the fact that the absolute over-estimations are themselves proportional to the lengths of the two lines which are centred alternately (or when centration is on the mid-point between them). This situation has been expressed in Props. 28 and 29.

The argument can be summarised as follows:

(1) Absolute over-estimations (or elementary errors I) are proportional to the lengths of the lines because the estimation of those lengths depends on the fractional parts, α (and their increments $(1 - \alpha)^2$, etc.), of the total number, N, of encounterable elements calculated either in proportion to the lengths (Hypothesis I or II) or by fractions of the lengths (Hypothesis III).

(2) There may be reasons for supposing that the rate of increment of encounters will not be constant either for a given interval of the time during which the encounters are increasing rapidly (tachistoscopic durations, as described in § 6) or when some cause for systematic error exists. In spite of this, however, there is no reason why an approximately constant rate of increment should not occur under some conditions of differential threshold estimation. One such condition would exist when there is no time limit and when we are therefore concerned with the region of stability corresponding to the final plateau of the exponential growth curves.

(3) If our hypotheses are correct, the existence of a threshold is due to the fact that difference couplings are suppressed, to the advantage of resemblance couplings, when the absolute over-estimation of the shorter of two lines increases to the extent that $pL_2 > L_1$ (Props. 41 and 42).

(4) It follows directly that the threshold corresponds to a constant fraction, and that Prop. 43 can be written in the following equivalent form:

(43b) $$S = k\,\frac{pL}{L}$$

where p is the absolute over-estimation of an object under circumstances favourable to Props. 41 and 42.

III. The second application of Weber's law, to any differences, is usually supposed to become less and less precise as the distance from the threshold increases. The problem is to discover if Weber's law is still involved or whether the systematic deformations observed under these conditions could not be explained more simply in terms of relative centrations.

A brief examination of this question was made with the assistance of Rossi.[1] A series of lines measuring 20, 21, 22, 23, 25, 30 and 40 mm was used. The subject was shown a pair of adjacent lines, say A and B, and was asked either to draw, or to select from a second set of lines, a third line, C, such that $C - B = B - A$. Fifteen judgements were elicited from ten subjects for each comparison. The order of presentation was randomised. The results are set out in Table 37.

TABLE 37. *Reproduction or choice of a constant difference between elements of increasing length* (*n: Series I and VI* = 5; *Series II to V* = 10; *see text for interpretation of values*)

Rech. 4, Tables VII and VIII

	Reproduction trials			Choice trials		
	1st 5	1st 10	1st 15	1st 5	1st 10	1st 15
Series I (Diff. = 1 mm)	2·44	2·36	2·36	—	—	—
Series II (2 mm)	2·16	2·18	2·31	1·14	1·32	1·41
Series III (3 mm)	1·90	1·98	2·28	1·17	0·89	1·24
Series IV (5 mm)	1·28	1·64	1·31	0·84	1·00	0·95
Series V (10 mm)	0·97	1·05	0·93	0·70	0·80	0·73
Series VI (20 mm)	0·59	0·69	0·69	—	—	—
Overall mean	1·55	1·65	1·65	0·96	1·00	1·08

The figures given above were arrived at as follows: $x =$ the sum of the drawn or selected differences between B and C for sets of 5, 10 and 15 trials. These are expressed as fractions of the sum of the real differences between A and B. Where the actual difference was 1 mm (series I), the figures given represent $x/5$, $x/10$ and $x/15$. For series II, with an actual difference of 2 mm, they represent $x/10$, $x/20$ and $x/30$, and so on to series VI where, with an actual difference of 20 mm, they represent $x/100$, $x/200$ and $x/300$.

It is immediately apparent that these results, which are reasonably regular for such a crude experiment, are inconsistent with an arithmetical progression, which would have resulted in means fluctuating about the value of 1. It is true that the means of series V (employing the method of reproduction) or of IV (the method of choice) are close to 1, but this is only a case of a median zero error lying between positive errors (> 1), obtained by both methods in preceding series, and negative errors (< 1) in subsequent series. It is probably this non-conformity to an arithmetical progression which is taken to be an application of Weber's law to any differences.

It is also apparent that the obtained errors by no means represent a constant fraction because they progress, at a reasonably regular rate, from a mean value of 2·36 in series I (reproduction) to a mean value of 0·69 in series VI. A similar trend is also found with the method of choice.

Weber's law is being applied inappropriately if this is the sort of changing error meant when it is said that it applies less well at increasing distances from the threshold. In fact, other laws of deformation are involved, laws which exhibit an approximate conservation

[1] *Rech.* 4, p. 32 ff.

of proportionalities. In the case in question, a complex effect is involved in which the following factors play a part: (*a*) an over-estimation of each second length under the influence of the one preceding it (*B* by *A*, *C* by *B*, etc.), which results in an over-estimation of the difference; (*b*) an under-estimation of the difference itself: being considered separately in the role of a length to be reproduced, it is under-estimated under the influence of the lengths involved in each case (*A'* is devalued by both *A* and *B*); (*c*) finally, various secondary effects may intervene to complicate the picture[1] because the reproduction the choice entail and spatio-temporal transports (see Chapter III, §§ 5 to 7).

In summary, the approximate proportionalities observed when judgements are being made on differences which lie beyond the threshold are closer to the proportionality inherent in the law of relative centrations than to the geometrical progression characteristic of the threshold according to Weber's law.

§ 6. EXPERIMENTAL SUPPORT FOR THE MODEL OF ENCOUNTERS AND THE PHENOMENON OF THE TEMPORAL MAXIMUM OF ILLUSIONS

No direct measurement can, of course, be made of the hypothetical encounters and couplings by which we have tried to explain the observed effects of centration. However, the central notion which inspires the model can be subjected to factual testing. This notion, one possible account of which has been given in terms of encounters and of couplings, is that illusions are produced by the dual processes of centration (or encounters and incomplete coupling) and of decentration (or complete coupling) whose effects are opposite. It is proposed that there are, on the one hand, absolute over-estimations. These may differ from object to object (encounters due to centration) and therefore lead to relative over-estimations (or incomplete coupling). On the other hand, there are decentrations, or co-ordinations of centrations, which give rise to a homogenisation of absolute over-estimations (when coupling is complete). It is this duality of opposed tendencies which is subject to experimental examination.

A critical and precise examination of the question can be made by assessing quantitative variations in illusions as a function of the durations of exposure of the figures. The argument is as follows. If the influences of centration alone are involved, directed as they are towards absolute over-estimation, a continuous increment in illusion

[1] And even, perhaps, the effects of central tendency: over-estimation of small and under-estimation of large differences around a neutral point which would be $A/2$ for reproductions V and $A/4$ for choice IV.

116

should occur as a function of increase in exposure time, at least for times extending between the shortest possible exposures (of say, 0·02 second) and the average duration of unrestricted viewing (1 to 3 seconds). On the other hand, if the influences of decentration alone are involved, there should be a gradual decrease in illusion as a function of increased exposure times, with an initial maximum illusion attributable to the impossibility of the occurrence of active comparisons and explorations at the shortest exposure times. Finally, if the two factors are concurrently involved, one would anticipate an increase in the effects of centration (absolute over-estimations and incomplete coupling resulting in relative over-estimations) with increases in exposure time but, at the same time, an increase in the effects of decentration (complete couplings leading to compensations or to the suppression of relative over-estimations). In this case, the most probable result, as we saw in § 2, II, would be an initial increase in illusion followed, after a temporal maximum at some intermediate time of exposure, by a decrease. Even if the maximum were not general, its existence in a sufficient number of different situations (varieties of the illusion obeying the law of relative centrations), would demonstrate the duality of the factors of centration and of decentration as well as the opposite sign of their effects. This would be so because a maximum is a necessary outcome of a situation in which there is a conflict between a factor of reinforcement which is dominant up to a certain point, and a restraining factor which gains the ascendancy thereafter.

Facts collected, first in collaboration with Vinh-Bang[1] and then with Matalon,[2] and later with Ghoneim, Mme Vinh-Bang and Müller on a variety of illusions, seem to be conclusive: a temporal maximum is indeed found in a variety of forms of distribution. One form, I, occurs for the most part when the judgement is made on a variable which lies within, and constitutes a part of, the illusory figure itself. Other forms, II and III, generally occur when the variable is exterior to, or independent of, the illusory figure. Further forms are also found and are all easily explained in terms of the model of encounters and of couplings. In addition, some remarkable changes are found to occur in the distributions as a function of different points of constrained centration.

(1) The illusion first studied tachistoscopically was the Oppel–Kundt illusion (Chapter I, § 13). It was found, first of all, that the illusion varied considerably with changes in the point of centration. The results shown in Table 38 were obtained in collaboration with

[1] *Rech.* 41.
[2] *Rech.* 42. See also Piaget, J., Vinh-Bang, and Matalon, B., *Amer. J. Psychol.*, 1958, **71**, 277–82.

Vinh-Bang, using a cross-hatched line, *A*, of 5 cm with ten vertical cross-hatchings, and a variable line, *B*, which formed a continuation of *A*, and which served as the reference length.

TABLE 38. *Mean % error with the Oppel–Kundt figure as a function of point of centration (n = 20 in each group. Exposure time = 0·1 second)*

	Rech. 41, Table 3					
Centration on	Junction of A & B		Mid-point of B		Mid-point of A	
	Mean	S.D.	Mean	S.D.	Mean	S.D.
5 to 7 years	1·5	6·8	−8·0	5·5	8·8	6·2
Adult	6·9	4·6	−4·8	6·9	20·1	5·1

It can be seen that centration on the cross-hatched line, *A*, produced an increase in the effect described in § 13, Chapter I, from 1·5 to 8·8% for children and from 6·9 to 20·1% for adults. No doubt this is due to a multiplication of encounters achieved on the intervals between the hatchings. Reciprocally, centration on the unhatched line, *B*, led to a negative illusion of −8·0% for children and −4.8% for adults, as a result of a decrease of encounters on *A*.

The results set out in Table 39 were obtained with exposure times shown and centration on the point of junction of *A* with *B*.

TABLE 39. *Mean % error with the Oppel–Kundt figure as a function of exposure time (n = 20 for each group)*

	Rech. 41, Table 4					
Exposure time (second)	0·04	0·1	0·2	0·5	1·0	Unlimited
5 to 7 years	1·0	1·6	4·3	6·0	5·6	5·1
Adult	3·6	6·8	8·2	6·8	6·9	7·2

It is seen that the illusion passed through a maximum value at 0·2 second for the adult, and at 0·5 second for children. The attenuated nature of this maximum is attributable to two circumstances. The first is that the same subjects served at all exposure times (but not always in the same session): because of the absence of practice effects, the maximum generally stands out more clearly when different groups of subjects are used at each exposure time. The second is that the reference and the judged lines here constitute a single *linear* figure which is intermediate between those figures which give rise to form I distributions and those which involve a separation of the reference and judged lengths.

(2) The inverted T figure (Chapter I, § 4), on the other hand, constitutes a good example of a figure giving rise to a form I distribution because the reference length (the horizontal, which varied from 27 to 51 mm against a vertical of 30 mm) constitutes a part of the figure itself. This circumstance favours what we have called enveloping centrations, that is to say, those which bring the deforming elements of the figure, in this case the horizontal and the vertical, into relationship. The results set out in Table 40 were obtained with this figure by

Vinh-Bang and Matalon, using the same subjects at all exposure times.

TABLE 40. *Mean % error with the inverted T figure as a function of exposure time and of point of fixation (separate groups, n = 20 for each group)*

Rech. 42, Table 1

	Fixation on vertical		Fixation on horizontal*	
Time (sec)	5–7 yrs	Adult	5–7 yrs	Adult
0·04	—	28·1	25·0	30·0
0·1	35·5	43·0	26·3	30·5
0·2	39·5	38·5	26·8	32·5
1·0	38·5	32·6	28·1	32·3
Unlimited	32·5	26·1	29·5	28·5

* On one of two points located 10 mm to either side of the point of intersection of the vertical element.

The maxima are more distinct here than they were with the Oppel–Kundt illusion and once again there was disparity between children and adults in respect of the exposure time giving rise to these maxima. Furthermore, it can be seen that switching the centration to the horizontal line not only reduced the illusion, which is to be expected because the vertical is less over-estimated when not centred, but also shifted the adult maximum to somewhere between 0·2 and 1 second. With children, the maximum was shifted into the range of unlimited viewing time, which changes the normal form I of temporal distribution into a new form, which will be referred to as form III. The term form II is reserved for the delayed form of adult maximum which still falls short of the unlimited exposure time. It is immediately apparent that form II is only a weakened derivative of form I, and form III a further weakened derivative of form II. This weakening is no doubt due to the inability of the subject, except with unlimited time, to perceive sufficiently clearly the different relations involved in some figures with certain points of centration (the centration in these cases being insufficiently enveloping).

(3) As was seen in § 4 of Chapter I, the right-angle figure (∟) is a derivative of the T figure. Its temporal maximum was examined

TABLE 41. *Mean % error with the right-angle figure as a function of exposure time and of point of fixation (for n, see original publication. Separate groups)*

Rech. 42, Table 2

Time (sec)	0·02	0·04	0·10	0·20	0·50	1·00	Unlimited
5 to 7 years							
Fixation I*	—	4·0	8·0	3·6	2·6	4·4	5·0
Fixation II	—	−2·4	−2·0	3·2	2·8	2·4	—
Fixation III	—	8·7	6·6	0·2	3·1	7·3	—
Adult							
Fixation I	6·9	7·6	12·4	9·6	7·2	7·0	6·3
Fixation II	4·0	4·2	4·6	2·8	0·6	1·2	1·8
Fixation III	13·6	12·0	6·2	4·2	6·0	6·0	6·0

* Fixation I = mid-point of vertical; II = mid-point of horizontal; III = intersection of perpendiculars to I and II.

by Matalon, both with the same subjects serving at all exposure times and with separate groups for each exposure time. The results obtained with the latter are given above in Table 41 (the results obtained with the other subjects will be discussed later in Chapter III, page 161, Table 66, when the figure is considered in relation to the effect of verticality). These results draw attention to several points which require to be emphasised in regard to the hypothesis of encounters. With fixation on the vertical, the maximum for adults[1] and children occurred at 0·1 second. With centration on the horizontal, on the other hand, children under-estimated the vertical for exposures up to and including 0·1 second (and even with unlimited viewing time in subjects serving throughout, as will be shown in Table 66), while adults exhibited an over-estimation of the vertical from 0·02 second and a rather ill-defined maximum at 0·1 second. This indicates a remarkable capacity for enveloping centration in the adult which would be difficult to explain except by a dispersion of encounters from the fixation point. This dispersion is favoured, no doubt, by the acquired habit (which will be discussed in § 3, Chapter III), of judging the length of verticals from an inspection of their summits. The third fixation point, midway between the mid-points of the vertical and the horizontal lines, gave rise to another interesting phenomenon. With adults, the maximum occurred at the briefest exposure time, as if the subject were noticing nothing but the vertical: this will be identified as a form IV distribution. The same thing happened with children at the shortest exposure time that could be used with them (0·04 second), but with a second maximum at 1 second an analagous tendency is apparent in adults, with a rise in value at 0·5 following the flexion at 0·2 second. It is as if the figure gave rise to two sorts of perception favouring the vertical, the one

TABLE 42. *Mean over-estimation of the long side of a rectangle as a function of exposure time*

Rech. 42, Tables 5 and 6 (corrected)

Time (sec)	0·02	0·04	0·10	0·20	0·50	1·00	Unlimited
5 to 7 years							
Same subjects (n = 19)	—	—	8·6	9·1	10·0	19·1	—
Separate subjects (n = 10–12)	—	17·2	4·5	4·4	26·0	24·4	—
Adults							
Same subjects (n = 28)	—	8·0	7·6	8·6	10·6	10·0	—
Separate subjects (n = 13–21)	2·9	4·2	4·8	5·4	5·4	8·9	5·8

[1] With adults, an error of 17·9% was found for an exposure time of 0·01 second. It is doubtful, however, if this is an effect of the vertical, being quite disproportionate in some subjects: 43·3% of subjects serving at all exposure times exhibited no greater error at 0·01 second than at 0·02 second. It is a question, rather, of the difficulty of perceiving anything except the vertical at very brief exposure times.

because of a neglect of the horizontal and the other because the vertical and horizontal are related. The occurrence of this double maximum will be identified as a form V distribution.

(4) The results shown in Table 42 were obtained with the rectangle (see Chapter I, § 3).

It can be seen that adults exhibited a form II distribution with a maximum at 1 second for separate groups (and no doubt after 0·5 second for subjects serving at all exposure times), while children exhibited a typical form V distribution.

(5) As shown in Table 43, Ghoneim found, with the lozenge and on the basis of measurements of the under-estimation of the long diagonal taken against lines external to the figure itself (as in § 6, Chapter I), that the maximum occurred at the briefest exposures, here 0·2 second. This is typical of form IV, as was seen with adults for the right angle with fixation point II (Table 41, p. 119).

TABLE 43. *Mean % error on the diagonals of the lozenge as a function of exposure time, in ascending order (n = 10 for each group, values in parenthesis represent error in descending order)*

Rech. 37, Tables XXV to XXVII

Age group	5–6 yrs	Adult	
Time (sec)	Long diagonal	Long diagonal	Short diagonal
0·02	—	−10·2 (−8·6)	−13·0
0·04	−14·4	−9·4 (−7·6)	−11·8
0·10	−13·6	−7·6 (−6·8)	−9·0
0·20	−13·6	−6·6 (−5·4)	−7·4
0·50	−13·0	−6·6 (−5·8)	−7·4
1·00	−11·6	−6·0 (−6·0)	−7·4

In order to find out if this form IV distribution was a product of the structure of the figure itself rather than of the use of an external comparison line, or of the shortest exposure time being still too long, it was suggested to Ghoneim that he replicate the experiment (with a group of subjects willing to endure such a perceptual gymnastic), using the illusion of the median[1] and making the shortest exposure time 0·01 second. The results, set out in Table 44, are of great interest.

TABLE 44. *Mean % error on the median of the lozenge as a function of exposure time, for two groups of adults (n = 10 in each group)*

Rech. 37, Tables XXVIII and XXIX

Time (sec)	0·01	0·02	0·04	0·1	0·2	0·5	1
Group I	—	11·4	10·6	10·2	9·6	9·4	8·2
Group II	11·8	12·8	13·4	12·6	12·2	10·4	8·8

It can be seen that the form IV distribution was still present when the comparison line lay within the figure, but that it became a typical form I distribution, with the shifting of the maximum to 0·04 second

---

[1] The median of an angle, it will be remembered, is the perpendicular erected at the mid-point of its bisector. This median is displaced in successive stimulus figures and serves as the variable by which the illusion is measured (see Chapter I, § 5, Table 5).

(in nine out of ten subjects), when the first exposure time was 0·01 second. No doubt this is because the subject, being forced to structure the figure during such a brief exposure while fixating the middle of the figure, only later became aware of the factors responsible for the illusion, later than he did when the first exposure was of 0·02 second, a time which allows of an initially more enveloping centration. It is to be noted that the results are not always the same with an initial exposure time of 0·01 second. This is to be expected because the results will depend on the degree to which the initial centrations are enveloping during the initial structuring of the figure.

In view of Ghoneim's results, a further study of the distribution of the illusion of the vertical in the right-angle figure was undertaken by Matalon. Two groups of adult subjects were used, both serving at all exposure times, one group starting with an exposure time of 0·04 second and the other at 0·01 second. The former showed a very weak maximum (see Table 66, p. 161) at about 0·1 second, as did those subjects belonging to separate groups, as shown in Table 41 above. Those who started with an exposure time of 0·01 second, however, exhibited typical form IV distributions: 17·9 at 0·01, 13·1 at 0·02, 13·7 at 0·04, 12·1 at 0·1, 11·5 at 0·2, 10·3 at 0·5, and 10·6 at 1 second. This is no doubt because subjects see nothing but the vertical when fixating it at an exposure time of 0·01 second, as was suggested in the footnote on p. 120.

(6) The illusion of the minor base of the trapezium (Chapter I, § 9) was re-examined, tachistoscopically, by Mme Vinh-Bang, both with separate and same groups of subjects for each exposure time. The dimensions which previously resulted in the spatial maximum (the minor base = half the major base) were used. The results are set out in Table 45. It can be seen that the distribution is of form IV for sub-

TABLE 45. *Mean % over-estimation of the short base (30 mm) of the trapezium as a function of exposure time and of point of fixation*

	Separate groups		Same subjects
Time (sec)	Fixation short base	Fixation long base	Fixation short base
0·01	41·6	39·0	49·5
0·02	45·9	42·0	46·3
0·04	43·1	37·9	44·0
0·10	34·5	34·2	39·3
0·20	35·3	24·5	34·6
0·50	31·9	24·6	29·6
1·00	—	—	20·6

jects serving at all exposure times and of form I (but with the maximum at 0·02 second and hence verging on form IV) for separate groups.

(7) The Müller–Lyer illusion (Chapter I, § 10) which reduces, it will be remembered, to that of the double trapezium, was studied

tachistoscopically by Müller under the six forms, I. 1–3 and II. 1–3, of Fig. 22 on page 45, to which reference will be made in what follows. For adult subjects, the distribution was of form IV (as it was for separate groups of adult subjects with the trapezium), and of form I for children.

TABLE 46. *Mean % error with Müller–Lyer figures as a function of exposure time and of point of centration (see Fig. 22)*[1]

	Figure I					
Age group	5–7 yrs			Adult		
Centration	I₁	I₂	I₃	I₁	I₂	I₃
Time (sec)						
0·02	—	—	—	60·0 (40·0)	68·3 (32·6)	31·0 (23·0)
0·04	40·0	42·0	15·0	41·6 (40·0)	40·0 (32·0)	21·3 (20·0)
0·10	65·0	62·0	30·0	49·0 (34·3)	62·0 (33·6)	24·3 (10·0)
0·20	38·3	33·3	21·6	40·6 (40·0)	35·0 (39·3)	11·3 (10·3)
0·50	35·3	38·6	20·3	30·0 (33·0)	36·6 (39·3)	11·6 (10·3)
Unlimited	37·3	34·3	14·3	26·0 (23·0)	29·6 (21·6)	5·3 (3·3)
	Figure II					
	II₁	II₂	II₃	II₁	II₂	II₃
0·02	—	—	—	2·0 (−9·0)	0·3 (−9·0)	12·3 (7·6)
0·04	−20·0	−13·3	−8·0	−5·0 (−12·3)	−1·0 (−13·3)	10·0 (15·3)
0·10	−14·0	−15·0	0·0	7·3 (−12·3)	8·0 (−9·6)	16·3 (7·0)
0·20	8·3	3·3	6·0	−6·3 (−8·0)	−6·6 (−11·3)	6·0 (4·3)
0·50	−6·3	−4·6	0·3	1·0 (−0·6)	1·3 (−4·0)	11·1 (7·0)
Unlimited	−6·0	−2·0	3·3	−1·6 (−5·6)	−0·6 (1·0)	1·0 (1·0)

With tachistoscopic presentation, the degree of illusion was once again about the same with figure forms I.1 (double trapezium) and I.2 (the classical Müller–Lyer figure with out-turned barbs) and slightly greater with II.1 (double trapezium) than with II.2 (the classical Müller–Lyer figure with in-turned barbs). The illusion was much weaker with I.3 (unequal parallels) and with unrestricted viewing (Table 16a, p. 46). With II.3, however, this was not found, contrary to the findings with unrestricted viewing (Table 17, p. 48).

The only remaining problem (apart from the need to investigate the effects of starting the series with an exposure time of 0·01 second, with subjects serving at all exposure times) is the number of occasions on which a positive illusion was found with forms II of the figure; it was always negative with unrestricted viewing, (Table 17, p. 48). With centration on the median line of the figure, the mean errors were positive for twelve subjects and negative for six; with centration between the figure and the variable, the mean error was positive for six and negative for twelve subjects. In the first of these two cases, the result was no doubt due to the conflict occasioned by centring on a line which is normally under-estimated. But in the second case, when centration was located between the standard and the variable, the six positive mean errors are less easy to understand unless they

[1] Centrations productive of the values *not* shown in parenthesis were directed on to the median segment of the figure. Those corresponding to the values shown *in* parenthesis were directed, for adults, at a point midway between the centre of the figure and the centre of the measuring variables.

arise from an excess of encounters on the variable because of an insufficient exploration of the figure as a whole.

(8) The Delbœuf illusion has been kept to the last because, when it was studied tachistoscopically by Matalon, it also produced inversions in the sign of the illusion with short exposure times. It also produced some inversions which are instructive in regard to the structuring of the figure which occurs during the form of genetic development that occurs in perception as exposure times increase. The following results were obtained when the smaller of two concentric circles was measured against variable circles lying outside the main figure and with the following fixation points: I, at the centre of the external variable circle; II, half-way between the concentric and the external circle; III, half-way between the circumference of the internal and external concentric circles; and IV, at the centre of the concentric circles. Results are set out in Table 47.

TABLE 47. *Mean % error on the inner circle of the Delbœuf figure as a function of exposure time and of fixation point (separate groups; for n, see original publication)*

Rech. 42, Table 7

Time (sec)	0·02	0·04	0·1	0·2	0·5	1
5 to 7 years					0·5	
Fixation II	—	8·1	15·7	16·7	28·1	12·1
Adult						
Fixation I	—	−17·4	−8·5	−6·5	4·2	8·9
Fixation II	−5·1	−2·7	−5·6	−0·5	2·9	8·8
Fixation III	—	10·9	4·4	3·4	0·7	10·9
Fixation IV	—	16·7	−6·8	2·7	2·5	7·8

The odd fact emerges that children produce a perfectly normal form I distribution, with an obvious maximum at 0·5 second, while adults exhibit what will be called a form VI distribution. With fixation points I and II there is an initial negative illusion; with fixation point III there is an irregular distribution which achieves normal proportions at 1 second only; and with fixation point IV there is an initial positive illusion which is followed immediately by a negative one.

The existence of negative illusions with adult subjects can be explained convincingly by the difficulty of dissociating the two concentric circles at short exposure times in order to compare the inner circle with the independent comparison circle: this effort of dissociation would cause an over-estimation of the inter-space, A', and an under-estimation of the diameter of the inner circle, A. Children, on the other hand, do not 'see' two independent circles but rather a concrete object such as a ring or a bicycle tyre. This tendency to transform a geometrical figure into a significant solid makes it easier for them to perceive the inner circle as an empty space in contrast to the solid ring which encloses it. It remains to be noted that the strong positive illusion exhibited by adults at 0·04 second is unlikely to be of the same type as the positive illusion at 0·5 to 1 second, because they are separated either by a negative illusion or by a clear inflection in the distributions. It is probable, in this case, that the adult perceives some form of single circle outlined with double lines, or some such figure (but not, perhaps, the child's solid object), and that his response therefore approximates to that of the child. This interpretation would also explain, among others, the curious result that no negative illusion is found when the zone A', the inter-space of the concentric circles, is fixated: quite simply, fixation on A' would seem to assist the dissociation of the two concentric circles.[1]

Conclusion. These facts ((1) to (8) above) have been reviewed in some detail, partly because the area is little known, but primarily because the facts seem to provide the best possible confirmation of the hypothesis of encounters and of couplings. On the one hand, given that effects of centration do lead to over-estimations, which was empirically verified and described in § 1 of this chapter, the notion of centration is still much too wide to explain why the various illusions behave so differently with changes either of fixation point or of exposure time. It is therefore necessary to break down the event of centration into elementary actions, or encounters, in order to understand how its effect varies with exposure time and why a single centration may be more or less enveloping. On the other hand, the fact that most of the forms of temporal distribution identified above exhibit a maximum, implies the involvement of two antagonistic factors, one concerned with the growth of encounters and the other with their homogeneity on different parts of the figure, in other words, their correspondences or coupling.

We will start by discussing the generality of this maximum. The typical form I distribution, with a maximum occurring between 0·04 and 0·1 second but not at shorter exposure times, is found in the following illusions: the Oppel–Kundt, the inverted T, the right-angle, the median of the lozenge (when the first exposure time is 0·01 second for subjects serving at all exposure times); and the Müller–Lyer and

---

[1] In addition to the above, Matalon also obtained measures of the illusion with fixation point II, using the same subjects at all exposure times, and with one of three initial exposure times, 0·02, 0·1 and 1·0 second, the last being followed by the inverse order of exposure times. The first two groups produced the same results as the previous separate groups of subjects, except that the negative illusion was a little more pronounced at 0·1 second and at 0·2 second, when the initial exposure is 0·1 second, than when subjects had already experienced exposures of 0·02 and 0·04 second. But for the third group, with exposures in the inverse order, the illusion was still positive at 0·02 second, becoming negative at 0·01 second, but to a lesser extent than for those subjects proceeding in an ascending order of exposure times.

the Delbœuf illusions (for children only). It may therefore be considered to occur with all the forms of illusion studied[1] except the rectangle. Form II also exhibits a maximum, displaced, however, to between 0·2 and 1 second, for the following figures: the inverted T (with fixation on the vertical by children and on the horizontal by adults), the right-angle (with fixation on the horizontal by children) and the rectangle for both adults and children. It is thus only an attenuated variant of form I. Form III (found only with the inverted T and for children fixating the horizontal) does not appear to exhibit a maximum because the illusion continues to increase as a function of time. However, the events occurring during the 'unlimited' inspection time used may in fact be followed by a phase of more attentive exploration and practice (see Chapter III, § 2), which would give rise to a reduced illusion: the decrease in illusion that usually occurs in other figures at exposure times exceeding 0·5 or 1·0 second is, in fact, probably explicable in terms of the onset of eye-movements and of explorations.

Form IV, then, with its maximum at very short exposures, is the only one which presents a problem for the general nature of temporal maxima, and it seems to support the classical notion that the error will be greater the shorter the exposure time. It is found in the following cases: the diagonal of the lozenge; the short base of the trapezium; the Müller–Lyer figure, for adults; and in the comparison of horizontals when subjects serve at all exposure times (see Table 35, p. 81). However, we are of the opinion that this form of distribution does entail a real maximum. For instance, it was sufficient for Ghoneim to start with an exposure time of 0·01 second (with the illusion of the median of the lozenge) for a clear maximum to emerge at 0·04 second (13·4 as against 8·8 at 1 second; see also the results for the trapezium without fixation points). Moreover, we cannot be sure what happens during the first moments when the first exposure is of 0·02 or even 0·01 second (in cases in which a maximum does not appear later). It is likely that the structuring of a figure occurs very rapidly rather than instantaneously, and that it is accompanied by an increase in illusion. If this is an accurate description of events, and it is only a generalisation of Ghoneim's observations, then a maximum illusion obtained at 0·02 second, or even at 0·01second, is a true maximum: it is simply one which is advanced relative to that of form I, and stems from the *pragnanz* of the figure or of that part of it which is measured.

Forms V and VI raise no particular problems. Form V involves two maxima, one precocious and the other delayed. No doubt this is

---

[1] And even in the case of the comparison of two horizontals when using separate groups, see Table 35, page 81.

a combination of forms II and IV brought about, perhaps, by the fact that the perception of the relevant figures is different with short and with long presentation times (for example, in the case of the concentric circles). Form VI, marked by a change in the sign of the illusion, presents no contradiction to the central notion, merely requiring an explanation of the inversion in terms of the model of couplings.

The temporal growth of illusions, with its law of the maximum, thus seems to be the general rule. It only remains to find a reason for the temporal growth and to decide to what extent the facts support the model of encounters and of couplings.

The maximum can be accounted for by reference to Props. 28 to 35 with particular reference to the last, which reads:

$$(35, \text{reptd.}) \quad P = N_1(1 - pL_1)^{nt} - N_2(1 - pL_2)^{nt}$$

and states the probability of incomplete couplings on L_1 and L_2 when the probability of encounters by units of time is $1 - (1 - pL_1)^{nt}$ on L_1, and $1 - (1 - pL_2)^{nt}$ on L_2.

This means that if encounters accrued exponentially on L_1 and on L_2, the coupling would be complete if the rates of increase were identical, or incomplete if they were not. If coupling were incomplete where $P \neq 0$, the result would be a relative over-estimation of one of the objects, or an illusion. All that is required is to arrive at the relative values of P for short, medium and long exposure times, referring to the discussion of Props. 31 to 33.

There will be few encounters at the shortest exposures, and the fewer there are the greater is the probability that coupling will be complete. As the common origin of the growth curves of encounters on L_1 and on L_2 is at zero, there are two possibilities: either the encounters increase much more rapidly on one of the objects than on the other and the couplings rapidly become incomplete (as with distribution of form IV); or the encounters increase at rather similar rates and many encounters would have to occur before an inequality could become apparent. In both cases, couplings would be more complete in the vicinity of the origin.

At exposures which approach unlimited inspection times, the probability of complete coupling tends to increase again, but for a different reason: encounters will increase only slightly when the exposure is sufficiently long and exploratory eye-movements begin. This is illustrated in the plateaux of the exponentials of Fig. 35. As a result, the two curves either fuse again, and coupling is complete (there is no longer an illusion), or they become almost parallel and the coupling is as complete as it can be for a given figure (there is a stable illusion for unrestricted viewing).

It follows that the probability of incomplete coupling is greatest somewhere between the shortest and the longest exposure times because, during this phase, the two growth curves of encounters on L_1 and on L_2 become maximally disparate before once more converging as the encounters fall off. It is for this reason that there is usually a maximum illusion, corresponding to the most incomplete coupling, between the shortest exposure (the point of origin) and unrestricted

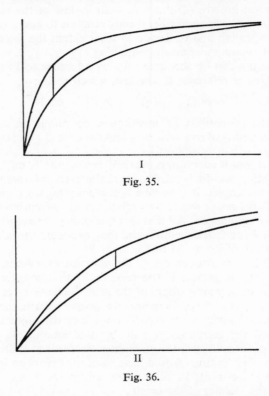

I

Fig. 35.

II

Fig. 36.

viewing: it simply represents the increasing and then decreasing heterogeneity of encounters as they accrue on two objects which are either of different size or in different positions.

It is no exaggeration, therefore, to maintain that the law of the temporal maximum of illusions supports the model of encounters and of couplings because its existence could not be understood except in terms of the existence of the two factors of the number of encounters and of their heterogeneity. If this explanation is accepted, it is easy to account for the six empirically established forms of distribution: they are all reducible to simple varieties of differential growth rates of encounters on L_1 and on L_2. Form I, corresponding to Fig. 35,[1] results from what we will call moderately different growth

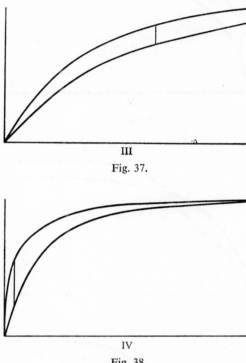

III

Fig. 37.

IV

Fig. 38.

rates; forms II and III (Figs. 36 and 37) also correspond to moderate but more uniform differences when the growth rate itself is slower. In Form IV (Fig. 38), growth rates differ greatly at first (usually when the comparison figure lies outside the figure being judged and when the variable is either favoured in centration or is the only part of the figure to be noticed clearly: for instance, the vertical in the right-angle with an exposure of 0·01 second and with fixation on the vertical, the standard being noticed only later). Form V (Fig. 39) corresponds to a situation in which the growth rate is initially unequal but then tends to become equal (which is a combination of forms III and IV due, no doubt, to two distinct ways of

[1] Figs. 35 to 40 are, of course, only theoretical, being designed to symbolise the various forms of the growth of encounters.

129

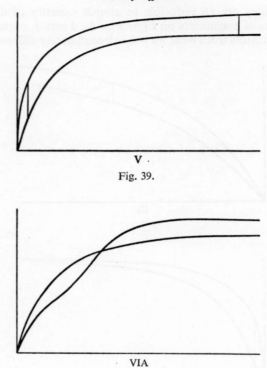

V .

Fig. 39.

VIA

VIB

Fig. 40.

perceiving the figure in terms of changes in the perceived relations between its parts). Finally, form VI, with an initial negative illusion (Fig. 40a), or with an illusion which becomes negative at some time (Fig. 40b, as in the case of the Delbœuf illusion for adults), represents irregularities in growth rates when, for example, it is difficult to dissociate the two concentric circles of the Delbœuf figure.

Thus each of the six forms of temporal distribution of errors can be explained in terms of the one principle of the accession of encounters: the observed progression through a maximum derives from differences in the growth rates of encounters and supports the dual nature of the factors involved, encounters on the one hand and couplings between them on the other.

PART TWO

PERCEPTUAL ACTIVITIES

All the perceptual effects studied in Part One arise in what Gestaltists call 'field effects', the immediate interactions between elements which are simultaneously perceived in a single field of centration. The primary illusions and elementary errors of forms I and II are of this nature because they can all be obtained with restrained fixation and at exposures that are brief enough to exclude any global eye-movements.

The collective term of perceptual activities (collective, because there is a large number of them, all of which do not necessarily relate to the same level of development) will be applied to those perceptual processes which occur when centrations or their effects have to be related across spatial or temporal intervals. These include activities of exploration, of transportation, of spatio-temporal or purely temporal transposition, of referral (to perceptual co-ordinates), of schematisation, etc.

These activities increase in importance and in variety with age. They usually reinforce co-ordinations and reduce primary errors. However, they themselves often lead to new forms of systematic error because they relate previously unrelated elements: these new relations then entail certain deformations which are similar to primary illusions. These new secondary illusions also increase continuously with age,[1] up to a certain age; however they are only indirect products of perceptual activities, deriving from them, so to speak, by repercussion. This indirect derivation does not exclude the effects of those co-ordinating tendencies which are characteristic of perceptual activities in their most general aspects.

Thus defined, the distinction between perceptual activities and primary field effects is only relative, both from a synchronic and from a diachronic point of view, and in no way contradicts a continuous transition between them. Synchronically, it is already obvious that decentration is a form of perceptual activity even if it only operates at very short distances and in immediate temporal successions: complete coupling, which was claimed (in Chapter II, § 2) to result from decentration and to lead to a reduction of relative over-estimations,

---

[1] It is not so much the secondary illusion, as such, which increases with age, but only the activity which establishes the relations. It is these relations, and not the activities, which cause the illusion.

is a product of the perceptual activity of exploration. But it will be recalled that two forms of coupling were distinguished, depending on whether a simple automatic correspondence was involved, expressing the homogeneous or heterogeneous character of encounters (equal or unequal densities), or whether they resulted from true activities of relating and of transportation (when, only they, tend to be complete). These two mark opposite poles of a continuum, not two distinct categories, and it follows that a set of intermediate forms will be found to exist between them. This is a first and sufficient reason for supposing that there is a continuity between primary field effects and the effects of perceptual activities. Similarly, encounters were interpreted either as emissions on the part of the perceived object which are registered by the subject, or as the results of scanning or of elementary explorations on the part of the subject as he tries to assimilate the object. It follows that primary effects of centration will either be relatively distinct from perceptual activities or will actually derive from rather direct or immediate activities which are much more closely related to activities involved in coordination of centrations.

From the diachronic or genetic point of view, a much more general problem arises in connection with this distinction. Even if an approximate division can be drawn between field effects and the effects of perceptual activities at a given age, there is no proof that it will remain stable. The problem is to discover if perception consists, from the first visual or tactilo-kinesthetic recordings of the new-born, of a collection of fully organised field effects which are then progressively elaborated (or even partly eliminated or replaced) by later developing perceptual activities. Gestalt theory paints a genetic picture of this sort, even if the more orthodox adherents of the theory would insist that perceptual activities themselves should be subject to laws of structure similar to those which govern primary effects (because they consider that these laws apply even to the structures of intelligence itself). But it is easy to imagine a total reversal of these positions: activities could exist from the beginning and field effects might be no more than their crystallised or momentarily equilibrated[1] results which extend in scope[2] during the course of development as they are

---

[1] Both a direct and an indirect result: direct, to the extent that initial perceptual activities constitute the cause of the structuring of the figures; indirect, in so far as those structures lead to associations (between L_1 and L_2, etc.) which themselves entail deformations as a result of the simultaneous perception of the associated elements being achieved in a single field of centration. In brief, perceptual activities would provide the structures of field effects and the field (of centration), as such, would be the cause of the deformations.

[2] Even though most of them would diminish from the point of view of the quantitative tally of errors.

progressively laid down by new perceptual activities, on the analogy of well-sedimented alluvia on the borders of the main stream.

This problem (which may, of course, have intermediate solutions) will not be prejudged at this point, but is introduced at the beginning, both to emphasise the relative nature of the distinction which is supposed to exist between primary mechanisms and perceptual activities, and to prepare the way for certain analyses that will be made of perceptual activities. These will contra-indicate the over-simple hypothesis of a direct line of descent from primary mechanisms to perceptual activities and then to elementary or sensory-motor forms of intelligence.

We do not expect to be able to exhaust the immense problem of perceptual activities, but will limit ourselves, in Part Two, to organising our observations under four main headings (the secondary illusions, perceptual constancies, perceptual causality and the perception of movement and of velocity), which will enable us to discuss the question of the relations between perception and intelligence in Part Three.

III PERCEPTUAL ACTIVITIES AND SECONDARY ILLUSIONS

As already stated, perceptual activities give rise to new structures and thereby, in general, to a quantitative diminution of primary illusions. But these activities are, in turn, indirect causes of fresh illusions, in so far as they lead to the relating of hitherto unrelated elements which are separated in space or time. These relations give rise to deformations which are analogous to primary effects but which increase with age, being dependent upon those developing activities, which thus become their indirect causes. In the following chapter, the most important of these activities and the illusions associated with them will be described.

§ 1. EXPLORATORY ACTIVITY, SYNCRETISM OF CHILDISH PERCEPTION AND THE INCREASE WITH AGE OF THE OPPEL–KUNDT ILLUSION

Exploration is undoubtedly the simplest and the most general form of perceptual activity. In the analytical interests of exposition, we started, at the beginning of Chapter II, with effects of a single centration on a line. We then, in connection with couplings and with decentration, introduced the relating of two or more centrations, one on each of two lines. We might now define exploratory activity as an extension of this relating of centrations when their number increases or when they are applied more or less systematically to different parts of the figure. But such a description would be artificial because, of course, the very choice of the first centration on a line, or midway between two lines, is already a function of exploratory activity and could even serve as an index of the level of that activity in the subject: thus a young child fixates at random on a figure, but an adult chooses the point of centration from which he will obtain the maximum amount of information, or number of encounters, with a minimum loss of information (or of elements missed or not encountered by the first glance). Thus exploratory activity, at whatever level, is the activity which directs eye movements and determines pauses or centrations during the examination of a figure.

As such, exploratory activity may vary considerably with age: it may be more or less systematic (one might almost say more or less intelligent, as the subject either allows it, and his attention, to wander passively over the figure, or directs them systematically), more or less automatic or active, and its mean duration for a given figure may vary.

I. The strictly active nature of perceptual activity, and its increase with mental development, is most clearly seen in tactilo-kinesthetic behaviour, in which the extent of centration is much narrower than in vision. For instance, we once studied, with Bärbel Inhelder,[1] the stereognostic perception of children from 3 to 8 years, using familiar objects (scissors, etc.) and cardboard cut-outs which had various topological or Euclidean shapes. We found that younger children simply seized the object without feeling out its contours and that between this passive response and the systematic explorations found at 7 to 8 years, a series of intermediate behaviour patterns could be distinguished which spoke of increasing activity. In such cases, the progress of activity with age is directly observable, simply by watching the subject's hand. In visual explorations, however, it becomes necessary to make use of an analysis of eye-movements and of points of centration, which is always difficult, if the same progress is to be observed. Such an investigation was undertaken with the assistance of Vinh-Bang[2]. To help the later discussion, results will be given here which were obtained from two children of 6 years and from ten adults, who were asked to explore various figures (verticals, horizontals, obliques, etc.).

The first interesting result is the difficulty experienced by children in fixating any given point. Some adults can fixate one point for 2 to 3 seconds with only small[3] micronystagmic movements. Our two younger subjects, however, made small eye-movements (without systematic return to the fixation point) every 0·15 to 0·20 second. Another striking and complementary finding is the difference in time it takes for children and for adults to locate the stimulus figure with their eyes (we here refer to first fixation on the line rather than to aberrant fixations): 0·36 second for children and 0·17 on the average for adults.

The duration of exploration is equally instructive. We have often noticed how quickly some children give their replies in perceptual tests in comparison to the more careful explorations indulged in by adults. But this rule is not absolute, and our two subjects of 6 years took longer to announce their judgements than did adults (possibly because of the reduced nature of our experimental situation: darkroom,

---

[1] Piaget, J., and Inhelder, B., *The Child's Conception of Space*, London, 1956, Routledge and Kegan Paul.
[2] *Rech.* 45.
[3] Up to about 3′ of arc and with a constant return of fixations to the designated point.

film record being taken, etc.). It is therefore all the more interesting to note that the time occupied in centration on the figure was less in their case. The reason is that the adult's centration is well adjusted while many aberrant centrations occurred in the children. These were in addition to adjusted centrations and were distributed as if at random at some distance from the lines. The results are shown in Table 48. It can be seen that the inspection time was longer and the centration time shorter for children, with all figures.[1]

TABLE 48. *Mean time to decision, and mean duration of single centration when comparing two elements in the orientations shown*

Rech. 45, Tables 1 and 9

	Decision time (sec)			Duration (sec)		
	Vert.	Obliq.	Horiz.	Vert.	Obliq.	Horiz.
6 years (*n* = 2)	2·12	2·44	2·19	1·14	1·43	1·31
Adult (*n* = 12)	1·71	1·84	2·15	1·38	1·62	1·75

As the child's gaze is constantly in motion, he achieves a large number of centrations in a short time, but the average time spent on each is also short, as shown in Table 49.

TABLE 49. *Mean number of distinct centrations and their mean durations (sec/100)*

Rech. 45, Tables 1 and 15

Centration on	Verticals		Obliques		Horizontals	
	f	Duration	*f*	Duration	*f*	Duration
6 years (*n* = 2)	7·1	16·05	7·9	18·10	7·6	17·27
Adult (*n* = 12)	5·4	25·67	5·3	30·62	5·2	33·78

It has yet to be shown how the child distributes his numerous centrations, given that he experiences this difficulty in fixating with precision. Analysis reveals that he typically disperses his regard more and more widely around the initial point of fixation. Two sets of data collected by Vinh-Bang are available. Firstly, if the distribution of fixations around the momentarily demanded fixation point (the point, being indicated to the subject by the experimenter, serves as an initial anchor for the analysis of subsequent eye-movements), is circumscribed by the shortest circumference that will include them all, its mean diameter for adults turns out to be 4 mm, independently of time. For children, however, the values shown in Table 50 were obtained.

TABLE 50. *Mean diameter of circles enclosing all eye-movements around the fixation point, as a function of exposure time (n = 2 children aged 6 years)*

Rech. 45, Table 19

Time (sec)	0·5	0·62	1·18	1·25	1·87
Diameter (mm)	4	5	12	14	19

Secondly, if the distribution of points is plotted in projection[2]

[1] One of the young subjects was examined, using a right-angle figure. Time to decision was 2·9 seconds (1·6 for adults) and duration of centration was 1·93 seconds (1·33 for adults). The duration of centration thus represents only 66% of the time to decision in the child, but 80% in the adult.

[2] A projection based on the curved surface used for the screening of the reflections from the subject's eye.

139

(omitting the first two, which are often concerned with finding the figure, and the last, which tends to leave the field), and if a rectangle is drawn to enclose all of them, it is found that the rectangles are longer and wider for children than for adults, which again indicates a greater dispersion in the former, as shown in Table 51.

TABLE 51. *Mean dimensions (mm) of rectangles enclosing all eye-movements associated with the inspection of the figures shown*

Rech. 45, Table 20

Figure	Verticals		Obliques		Horizontals	
	Width	Length	Width	Length	Width	Length
6 years (n = 2)	18·5	50·7	17·3	46·5	26·3	48·3
Adult (n = 12)	10·1	31·6	6·5	28·9	9·9	31·7

These results speak for themselves. Considering the length of the distributions in particular, it can be seen that adult centrations are more enveloping (as had already been suggested by the results of tachistoscopic studies), because only 28·9 to 31·7 mm of a stimulus figure of 55 to 60 mm is covered in making the discrimination. The centrations are also much better aimed, in that their oscillations are from nearly two to three times as restricted in extent as those of children.

But the most important problem is how the subject actually uses his centrations during the act of comparison. As the instruction was to judge whether one line was longer or shorter than the other, the question is whether successive centrations move from one line to the other (which will be referred to as 'transports'), or whether they remain on the same line (which will be referred to, for short, as 'displacement'), no comparison then being made. This is analysed in Table 52.

TABLE 52. *Mean frequency of transports (T) from one line to the other and of displacements (D) on the one line for the figures shown*

Rech. 45, Tables 5 and 7

Figure	Verticals		Obliques		Horizontals	
	T	D	T	D	T	D
6 years (n = 2)	1·60	4·65	1·60	4·40	1·80	5·20
Adult (n = 12)	2·77	2·03	2·97	2·01	2·75	1·42

It can be seen that the ratio of adult to child transports is more than 3 : 2 whereas displacements on one segment alone are more than twice as frequent in children. This, in conjunction with results shown in Tables 50 and 51, does not mean that the child is exploring more than the adult, but only that he finds it difficult to maintain his fixation and is making an effort to re-attain it. The child's comparison itself is much more summary in nature because the mean transports are only 1·66 (not even one in each direction), as compared to 2·83 for the adult (1 in each direction and an extra 1 in 2 as a check).

We have dwelt on this example because it reveals so clearly the difficulty the child experiences in making perceptual explorations, understood in the large sense of a choice of the best points of centration (maximum information and minimum loss) and of an activity directed towards the making of a comparison. The facts seem to indicate that exploration is indeed an activity which develops with age and demands practice, which no doubt itself requires direction. It is even probable that the progress of intelligence in general plays a role in this direction, because to know what must be looked at in an object or configuration for it to be clearly perceived is, in part, a question of intelligence.

II. The poverty of children's exploratory activities can be understood in terms of a general characteristic of the way they perceive, called 'syncretic' by Claparède and 'global' by Decroly. This is not a question of a field effect of the same order as an optico-geometric illusion, or of the primary perception of a good form, but simply the outcome (or better perhaps, the very expression) of an insufficiency of exploratory activity.

Binet[1] has already pointed out that the child's perceptions are not analytical but are restricted to general forms or main outlines. Claparède, telling of his own son who was able to recognise certain pages in a book of songs by their overall patterns before he could read, spoke of the syncretism of the child's perceptions. Decroly stressed the same characteristic and derived from it the famous global method of teaching a child to read (the child is taught to recognise the overall patterns of short phrases first and then to break them down into words and finally into letters).

This global nature of childish perception has sometimes been challenged, and Cramaussel has emphasised the child's perception of minute detail which Meili-Dvoretzki has shown to be very general in responses to the Rorschach test (independently of affective considerations).[2] But Meili-Dvoretzki rightly points out that these minute details are 'in some way correlates of global syncretic perception', and that this is easily demonstrated. The perception of a complex form always goes hand in hand with the perception of some of its elements. If the whole form is well-structured, the synthesis it represents is based on a possible analysis of detail. If, on the other hand, it is ill-structured, or global, the whole is only a correlate of certain isolated and juxtaposed details and it is these that are involved in Cramaussel's and in Meili-Dvoretzki's observations. As a result, the impression is created that the child perceives either a syncretic

[1] Binet, A., *Revue Philos.*, 1890, p. 591.
[2] Dvoretzki, G. M-., *Arch. Psychol.*, 1939, **27**, 233–396.

form, when that is what he reports (having failed to report the various details), or the details without the form (when the latter is too subjective to be described).

Meili-Dvoretzki studied syncretism with ambiguous figures. For instance, one figure might represent a human face with two eyes or a complex object including a pair of scissors, the finger-holes representing the eyes. Adults tend to see one form or the other, while young children seem to see both at once: 'A man and someone has thrown a pair of scissors at his face!' The results obtained are seen in Table 53.

TABLE 53. *Frequency (%) of syncretic responses to ambiguous figures*

After Meili–Dvoretzki (1939)

Age group	3–5 yrs	5–6 yrs	6–7 yrs	7–8 yrs
	80·0	66·6	47·4	36·7

The only explanation that we are aware of concerning syncretism is that suggested by Meili.[1] We cannot adopt it as it stands, but it has the merit of relating the problem to that of the evolution of the factor of proximity (or at best of making a start in this direction). The explanation is based on field effects in which proximity plays a major part in children: if the forms are simple and the structures strong, syncretism dominates; if the forms are complex and the structures weak, minute details dominate, particularly under the influence of proximity, which emphasises minor collections but excludes wider ones.[2] But unless, as Meili-Dvoretzki has insisted, syncretic forms and small details are generally correlated, Meili's explanation is only valid if one accepts, with Gestaltists, the intrinsic and objective character of the 'force' and 'weakness' of a given structure. If these relate only to the subject, the thesis simply reduces to the claim that perception is syncretic when the child perceives the form, and detailed when he does not perceive it (given that we can conclude that he has not perceived it from the fact that he has not reported it). But the problem can and should be turned around: instead of starting with given objective 'forms' (laws of organisation which are independent of development) we should ask *why* the subject structures the contours in different ways according to his level of development. In this case, both syncretism (understood as a lack of both synthesis and analysis) and the dominant factor of proximity (understood as the

[1] Meili, R., *Arch. Psychol.*, 1931, 23, 25–44.
[2] For example, Meili used a Schroff figure in which a line of bowls is represented with one bowl touching the next one. The line formed by the tops of the bowls is thus continuous and parallel to the line formed by their bases. Where the adult sees a line of bowls, relating the right and left edges in spite of their separation, the child sees only the contact made by contiguous sides; he sees a series of curved triangles, the dominant feature of which is the proximity of their sides.

major factor preventing that co-ordination), can be seen to originate in one and the same cause, namely a lack of exploratory activity.

Proximity is not a field effect which exists independently of the subject's activities and whose initial dominance decreases simply because other factors (symmetry, regularity, etc.) then hold it in check. The dominance of the factor of proximity in children simply reflects a narrow field of exploration which is due to a lack of activity. It corresponds to a field which is almost circumscribed by the limits of centration and is denied those extensions which will later be provided by exploratory movements and by transports. If proximity loses its importance with age, it will not be because of an automatic extension of the field of perception but because of some sort of active extension of the field, achieved by exploratory movements and by transports. The reduction of syncretism follows directly from this because the same activities lead to a combined and parallel analysis (exploration) and synthesis (transports, etc.).

III. But exploratory activities do not inevitably give rise to an improvement in perception in the sense, among others, of a diminution of primary errors: exploration itself may become an indirect source of reinforcement of those errors. We know of only one such case in which exploration in the strict sense is involved. This is the Oppel–Kundt illusion of divided spaces which, in contrast to purely primary illusions, increases with practice up to a certain age.

The Oppel–Kundt illusion is primary in its mechanism, and, as we saw in Chapter I, § 13, depends essentially on the number of intervals included between the hatchings of the divided line as well as on the thickness and the length of those hatchings. In terms of encounters, this means that the intervals attract encounters more strongly than the undivided line does and proportionally so as they are better noticed. This is, of course, subject to an optimum because too few intervals produce a weak effect, and too many become indistinguishable.

However, this situation is very different from those involved in other primary illusions in which the error is attenuated by compensations achieved by exploration of the distorting inequalities between the components of the figure. The only relation involved in this illusion is between the part (interval) and the whole, all the parts being equal: the result is that exploration simply leads at first to a better perception of the intervals and thus to a multiplication of encounters and a reinforcement of the error. Only secondarily, and with difficulty, does exploration lead to a partial dissociation of the line itself from its divisions and thus to an accurate comparison between it and the undivided line which is being used as a measuring instrument.

143

This is why children initially exhibit a weak illusion: because of their syncretism, or the inadequacy of their perceptual explorations, they see the figure as a sort of gate or trellis and achieve only a limited number of encounters on the intervals as such. The illusion then increases up to 9 or 12 years, no doubt as a function of increasing exploration and of encounters on the intervals. The illusion finally decreases, probably because of an increasing specialisation in exploration in the form of a capacity to dissociate (to 'analyse' as the Gestaltists say) the line from its divisions. Nevertheless, a considerable illusion remains because this dissociation demands an extended exploration which, in turn, entails a multiplication of encounters on the intervals.

This complex situation is reflected in some distributions of error as a function of age and of practice which were obtained by Vurpillot,[1] who was kind enough to communicate them to us prior to their publication, for which we are most grateful to her. Her research was concerned with the comparison of illusions obtained with geometrical and with meaningful figures. In the case of the Oppel–Kundt illusion, the meaningful figure was a representation of a gate. It was compared with a geometrical figure of the same dimensions, both being measured against an isolated line. The results, which are most instructive from our point of view, are presented in Table 54.

TABLE 54. *Mean % error for geometrical and meaningful forms of the Oppel–Kundt figure as a unction of age (n = 14 for each age group and sex)*

After Vurpillot (1960)

Age group	Male subjects					Female subjects				
	5 yrs	7 yrs	9 yrs	12 yrs	Adult	5 yrs	7 yrs	9 yrs	12 yrs	Adult
Geometrical	8·4	9·9	11·3	12·7	8·4	5·5	6·7	13·8	8·6	8·1
Meaningful	0·5	−3·0	−1·7	0·7	0·6	−3·7	2·3	2·9	3·8	4·0

It can be seen that when the attention was directed to the gate, which makes less demands on exploration than the simple divided line does, the illusion decreased from 8·2 to 2·3 in adults (0·6 in men) and even some negative illusions occurred in children (which can no doubt be explained in terms of the effects of rectangles: the gate, seen globally, and the comparison line, are both seen as rectangles, the second being is much narrower than the first).

It can also be seen that the geometric form of the illusion produced a maximum error at 12 years for boys and at 9 years for girls, an event which cannot be attributed to specific conditions, as will be possible in the case of perceptual co-ordinates etc. (§ 4). Nevertheless, this is the first example of a primary illusion which is reinforced rather than reduced by perceptual activities; it might be better to say

---

[1] Vurpillot, Eliane. Private communication, 1960; this work was subsequently incorporated in: Vurpillot, Eliane, *L'Organisation Perceptive, son Rôle dans l'Evolution des Illusions Optico-géometriques.* Paris, 1963, Vrin.

that it is successively reinforced and then curbed by two different kinds of exploratory activity.

§ 2. COMPENSATORY EFFECTS OF EXPLORATION AND EFFECTS OF PRACTICE OR OF REPETITION

We have just encountered a first example of the reinforcement of an illusion under the influence of a perceptual activity and will meet many more in this chapter. But we have yet to verify our hypotheses (see I and II above) regarding the generally moderating or compensatory effects of exploratory activity when it is applied to figures which incorporate dimensional inequalities.

This can best be done by studying the effects of repetition (or of practice) on the quantitative distributions of primary errors. If this is done as a function of age, it will have the additional advantage of allowing us to establish again the weak nature of exploratory activity in young children and its gradual increase in strength with age.

We have the results of five parallel studies on the effects of repetition available. They concern:

I. The lozenge (Ghoneim).
II. The Müller–Lyer illusion (Noelting).
III. The Oppel–Kundt illusion (Vurpillot), which will allow us to verify what was said in III of § 1 above.
IV. and V. Vertical and right-angle figures (Greco-Fricoteaux) which are partially secondary illusions and which will lead, in § 3, to a more general analysis of the error of the vertical and of those elements of the figure which are situated in the upper half of the visual field.

I and II are two typical primary illusions which decrease with repetition under the influence of exploratory activity.

The under-estimation of the longer diagonal of the lozenge was studied by Ghoneim[1] as a function of practice. His results are presented in Table 55.

TABLE 55. *Mean % error on the long diagonal of the lozenge as a function of practice, method o adjustment (n = 10 for each age group)*

	Rech. 37, Table XXII						
Trials	1	10	20	30	40	1 to 10	31 to 40
5 to 6 years	−27·8	−25·4	−26·4	−25·0	−22·4	−27·8	−22·5
7 to 8 years	−26·0	−23·0	−23·0	−20·0	−17·8	−23·6	−18·0
9 to 10 years	−20·4	−16·8	−14·4	−14·4	−12·2	−18·5	−13·5
11 to 12 years	−21·8	−18·2	−15·0	−12·2	−9·8	−19·7	−11·5
Adult	−17·2	−16·6	−10·2	−8·2	−7·6	−16·0	−7·9

The differences between the means of the first ten and the last ten

[1] *Rech.* 37.

145

settings show that the illusion diminished with an admirable regularity as a function of age and of repetition.[1]

Noelting's results[2] with the Müller–Lyer illusion are very similar, except that the effect of repetition was not apparent before 7 to 8 years (which was also the case with the lozenge, if significance levels obtained with the t-test are adhered to). Noelting's study, which was part of a wider examination of practice effects, was taken much farther and was subjected to a detailed mathematical analysis. Because of its aims, the number of repetitions was not fixed but the largest number was made that the subject could provide without interruption: some children managed fifty or more settings, others less. For this reason only the first twenty settings in the table taken from Noelting's publication are included in Table 56.

TABLE 56. *Mean % error on the Müller–Lyer figure as a function of practice, method of adjustmen Rech.* 40, Table 1

Trials	1–5	6–10	11–15	16–20	1–20
5 years ($n = 19$)	24·7	25·7	24·9	25·6	25·2
6 years ($n = 19$)	25·0	24·5	25·0	23·7	24·6
7 years ($n = 23$)	24·7	23·7	23·3	23·0	23·7
8 years ($n = 24$)	24·2	22·7	21·2	21·1	22·3
9 to 10 years ($n = 20$)	22·8	20·3	19·4	19·1	20·4
Adult ($n = 20$)	17·9	14·8	12·3	11·8	14·2

It can be seen that the illusion decreased both as a function of age and of practice,[3] the decrease with practice increasing with age after the level at which repetition began to have an effect, 5 to 6 years in this case.

These two cases are typical primary illusions all of which, with the exception of the Oppel–Kundt illusion, undoubtedly obey the law of reduction with practice. This reduction must first be explained and it will be found to raise a series of problems closely related to the mechanism of exploration and its relations with the system of encounters and of couplings.

In the first place, it must be noted that if an attempt is made to translate these practice effects (which sometimes even lead to the momentary and complete suppression of the illusion) into the language of learning, a very special form of learning is involved in which external reinforcements cannot play a part. This is because the sub-

[1] 1·23 at 5 to 6 years; 1·31 at 7 to 8 years; 1·36 at 9 to 10 years; 1·70 at 11 to 12 years and 2·02 for adults. The effect of repetition is not significant (t-test) at 5 to 6 years. However, it is difficult to attribute the changes occurring over the forty successive trials (Ghoneim, *ibid.*, Fig. 29) to chance.

[2] *Rech.* 40.

[3] Well known since Judd (1902) studied the question. It has also been studied by Seashore and Lewis (in 1908), Köhler and Fishback and, very recently, by Eysenck and Slater and by Mountpon. But only Noelting has made a genetic study of the effects.

146

ject was not given any knowledge of his results, which excludes the possible intervention of the law of effect in terms of successes and failures. A process of equilibration rather than of learning is therefore involved, or, as we put it elsewhere,[1] a process of learning in the broadest rather than in the strictest sense (learning *sensu stricto* being defined as the adjustment of successive attempts as a function of a comparison of their results with the data of experience). But a process of equilibration consists in progressive compensations, the nature of which will have to be determined in each case, which will lead us back to the effects of successive explorations on the exercise of encounters and of couplings.

If our schema is correct, an optico-geometric illusion has to do with unequal densities of encounters on the elements of the figure, and thereby with their incomplete couplings. It follows that compensations which lead to a diminution of errors must consist in an equalisation of the density of encounters and in the completion of couplings: and it is precisely in such a situation that we may expect to find repeated explorations and improvement with practice.

In the case of the lozenge, the error has to do with the relationship between the longer and the shorter diagonals and with the estimation of the inclination of the sides with reference to the vertical and horizontal frames of reference of the figure (Chapter I, § 6); in the Müller–Lyer figures, it has to do with the relationship between the long base and the difference between it and the short base, which is devalued in relation to the height of the barbs. It goes without saying that the very existence of repeated explorations and of the consequent multiplication of centrations in these cases will give rise to a greater homogeneity (a more uniform density) of encounters on all parts of the figure, and thereby to a more complete coupling, namely to equilibrating compensations. This will be so even if the subject does not pay special attention, in his successive explorations, to those elements of the figure which were neglected in his first centrations.

The process engendered by repeated explorations[2] is thus very similar to that which was described (Chapter II, § 6) as giving rise to the phenomenon of the temporal maximum, or to the evolution of errors as a function of the duration of exposure of the figure. More precisely, it represents an extension of it, a continuation from the point at which the temporal maximum is achieved. For example, consider an extension of Fig. 35 (p. 128), in which the upper exponential represents a growth of the encounters on L_1 and the lower of those

[1] Greco, P., et Piaget, J., *Apprentissage et Connaissance*, Etudes d'Epistémologie Génétique, 7, Paris, 1959, P.U.F.
[2] From 1 to n repetitions after the initial perception with unconstrained vision and for subjects who had not experienced the short exposures.

on L_2, over- and under-estimated respectively: the phase of the reduction of error corresponds to the phases where, in free inspection, convergence of the two exponentials begins to slow down and the two curves reach their plateaux (see Fig. 41). Still separated vertically (which indicates that there are still inequalities in the density of

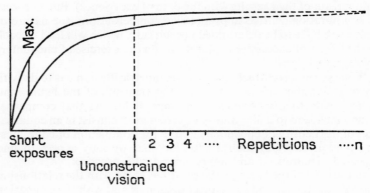

Fig. 41.

encounters), they nevertheless tend progressively to coincide with further explorations, which tendency corresponds with the diminution of errors.

The best proof of the close relationship between the reduction in error and longer presentations or repetitions,[1] is that in many cases (more frequently with children, but still in 5% of cases with adults for the Müller–Lyer figures) the illusion increases somewhat with the first four or five repetitions before it becomes stable (with younger subjects) or decreases, more or less rapidly. This initial increase is only a form of the temporal maximum in those subjects who fail to structure the detail of the figure sufficiently on the first presentation (and this temporal maximum would no doubt have been extended had shorter presentations been used first).

The frequency of this initial increase in illusion in children, coupled with the almost universal absence of its diminution with practice before a certain age, speaks of a lack of exploratory activity. In terms of our present explanation, this no doubt indicates that encounters accrue more slowly in children, with the result that the exponentials will be less steep and that couplings will not continue towards completion beyond certain levels of unequal density (Fig.

[1] This number also, in one sense, represents an increase in the duration of presentation, to the extent of the time occupied by $1, 2 \ldots n$ repetitions.

148

42*A*). With adults the exponentials will be steeper, will attain a higher level, and will tend to converge after a large number of repetitions (Fig. 42*B*).

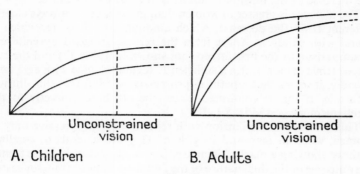

A. Children	B. Adults
Unconstrained vision	Unconstrained vision

Fig. 42.

III. It was seen (§ 1, III) that the Oppel–Kundt illusion, though primary, increases up to a certain age under the influence of exploratory activities which, in its case, do not lead to compensations of dimensional inequalities but rather to an increase in the error as encounters increase. Vurpillot's results, which indicate an increase in this illusion with practice in some cases, are therefore very interesting. They are presented in Table 57.

TABLE 57. *Mean % error on the Oppel–Kundt figure as a function of practice, method of adjustment*[1] *(n = 10 for each age group and sex)*

			After Vurpillot (1960)			
Trials	1–5	16–20	31–35	46–50	1–15	36–50
Male Subjects						
7 years	13·1	8·7	9·7	8·9	12·0	10·1
8 to 9 years	17·5	16·0	14·1	13·4	17·8	13·5
11 years	15·0	14·5	14·9	13·0	15·0	13·1
Adult	10·9	9·0	11·2	10·8	10·2	11·1
Female Subjects						
7 years	11·6	10·8	8·9	7·6	11·5	7·1
8 to 9 years	11·2	9·2	11·2	11·2	10·5	10·3
11 years	9·2	8·4	8·1	8·3	9·4	10·3
Adult	8·6	10·4	14·0	15·2	9·2	14·8

It is to be noted that errors in children are usually greater when the method of adjustment is used[2] because of the addition of errors due to motor inco-ordination. We cannot therefore be sure that the diminution of errors with practice obtained with boys of 7 to 11 years and

[1] We are indebted to Vurpillot for permission to reproduce these results. It will be noticed that the author, no doubt wisely, shows her results for the two sexes separately. Although sex-differences were not detected in our earlier joint studies on curvature, it is possible that the spatial factor, known to be better developed in the male, might have some effect on perceptual estimates.
[2] Compare trials 1 to 5 of Table 57 at different ages with those of Table 54.

with girls of 7 years is not due in part to a reduction of this experimental error, even if it may be explained in terms of perceptual factors alone, as we shall suggest presently. However, we can be sure that the increase in the illusion in adults is not due to this cause.

The increase is greater in women than in men, but is always clearly different from the decrease, which amounts to a halving, which is found with children. Apart from the results provided by children, a comparison of the first fifteen (not shown in Table 57) and the last fifteen trials demonstrates a sufficiently regular change with age[1] and, broadly, it seems that repetition progressively reinforces this illusion with age. If this is confirmed, it can be attributed directly to the mechanism suggested in § 1, III.

This increase in the illusion with repetitions is progressive only in women, while in men and in girls of 11 years it tends to oscillate without showing a marked increase. One might detect in these trends the outcome of the dual nature of the factors of exploration, suggested in § 1: more encounters on the intervals, and a consequent increase in the illusion; a greater dissociation of the line itself from its hatchings, with a consequent decrease in the illusion. The decrease in boys from 7 to 11 years and in girls of 7 years might be thought to be due, if not simply to the method, to the fact that the subject, with repetition, limits his attention more and more to the overall length instead of exploring more and more carefully, which is boring to children (rather like children of 5 years in whom the illusion is weak). This would be equivalent to the active dissociation mentioned above, which similarly reduces the illusion but in this case by an increasing neglect of detail.

IV. To avoid having to come back to the effects of repetition, let us now look at its effect on the comparison of two verticals in extension, a partly secondary illusion which is to be studied later (§ 3). The hypothesis is that practice effects will have the same direction as those of age, namely, that the illusion should increase in both cases unless a compromise is established between the two factors of increased encounters (with polarisation towards the upper ends of the lines) and increased explorations (which lead to a decrease in illusion).

Greco-Fricoteaux obtained the results shown in Table 58a.

This distribution is quite different from those obtained for primary illusions (Tables 55 and 56) and is similar to that obtained for the Oppel–Kundt illusion (Table 57) but with only one case of a regular increase, for subjects aged 9. It is probable that the two antagonistic factors mentioned above are responsible for these irregular trends.

[1] The differences were: 7 years, 1·18 and 1·62; 9 years, 1·24 and 1·01; 11 years, 1·14 and 0·91; adults, 0·91 and 0·62.

150

TABLE 58a. *Mean % error in the comparison of two lines in extension as a function of practice, method of adjustment (standard = 4 cm; n = 10 for each group)*

Trials		1–5	6–10	16–20	26–30	36–40	1–10	11–20	21–30	31–40
5 years	M	2·25	4·50	3·90	1·25	1·05	3·37	3·92	2·45	2·20
	F	−0·80	−0·30	1·00	−0·55	1·90	−0·55	0·92	0·25	1·37
	M+F	0·72	2·10	2·45	0·35	1·47	1·42	2·42	1·35	1·80
7 years	M	0·95	1·35	1·80	0·25	1·30	1·15	1·65	−0·20	1·45
	F	−1·50	−0·50	0·20	1·60	0·50	−1·0	−0·35	1·52	1·05
	M+F	−0·27	0·42	1·00	0·67	0·98	0·07	0·65	0·67	1·25
9 years		−0·25	0·15	0·50	0·95	1·10	−0·05	0·85	1·17	1·25
Adult		1·30	1·35	0·85	2·05	1·45	1·57	1·25	2·37	1·77

It is interesting, if individual results are examined, to notice that between trials 1–5 and 6–10, 45 to 55% of all subjects at all ages exhibited an increase in illusion, 20 to 30% a decrease and that the remainder did not change. This uniform tendency for an initial increase to occur in the illusion at all ages strongly confirms both that the present effects of practice are different from those found in the primary illusions, and the existence of a systematic factor of which we are about to see another example.

V. The right-angle figure also gives rise to a secondary illusion, but in terms of the over-estimation of the vertical in relation to the horizontal, rather than in terms of an occupancy of the upper half of the field. It thus represents a situation which is analogous to the previous one. The results set out in Table 58b were obtained with this figure by Greco-Fricoteaux. The dominant characteristic of these changes with repetition is the initial improvement (1–5

TABLE 58b. *Mean % error on the right-angle figure as a function of age, method of adjustment (vertical = 5 cm; variable = horizontal; n = 10 for each group)*

Trials	1–5	11–15	21–25	31–35
Male Subjects				
5 years	5·2	3·3	4·0	4·2
7 years	5·6	6·0	4·5	5·7
9 years	2·6	1·8	1·3	1·3
Female Subjects				
5 years	7·2	5·0	4·3	4·9
7 years	6·1	5·9	5·9	5·1
9 years	2·9	2·2	0·9	2·2
All Subjects				
5 years	6·2	4·2	4·2	4·6
7 years	5·8	5·9	5·2	5·2
9 years	2·8	2·0	1·1	1·7
Adult	3·4	1·9	2·0	1·8

to 11–15) followed by a plateau (11–15 to 31–35). Apart from minor deviations from this pattern (subjects of 7 years improving between trials 11–15 and 21–25, then exhibiting a plateau, and those of 9 years improving up to 21–25, then, in the case of boys, reaching a plateau and, in the case of girls, reverting to greater errors), no curve shows either a progressive improvement, as in the primary illusions of the lozenge and of Müller–Lyer, or a clear increase in illusion (as in the Oppel–Kundt illusion for adult women). The overall impression

is of an alternating dominance and compensation between two factors. The first of these would, of course, be practice, which tends to produce a progressively homogeneous distribution of encounters on the two parts of the figure and consequently a partial improvement which is usually found only at the start but which sometimes persists (9 years) or appears later (7 years). The second factor would be the over-estimation of verticals. We are about to claim, in § 3, that such a factor does exist, that it is, at least to some extent, resistant to practice effects and that it can often produce an increase in illusion with age. This factor involves a polarisation which emphasises the lengths of verticals by attracting centrations to their upper extremities, thus causing a heterogeneity of encounters (relative to horizontals, which tend to be centred on their mid-points) which is proportional to the degree to which the subject's space is structured by a system of co-ordinates.

§ 3. POLARISED[1] EXPLORATIONS, THE OVER-ESTIMATION OF VERTICALS AND OF ELEMENTS SITUATED IN THE UPPER HALF OF THE FIELD

The illusions just discussed represent a situation, like that of the Oppel–Kundt illusion, which is intermediate between primary and secondary illusions and which will now be analysed in detail. It is more similar to secondary illusions and leads on, with the over-estimation of verticals, to effects of frames of reference and of referral, which are patently secondary in nature.

I. It has been known for a long time that the upper of two elements, presented either in the vertical or in the sagittal plane,[2] is generally over-estimated. For instance, in measuring the outer circle of the Delbœuf figure (Chapter I, § 11, II) Khosropour found an average over-estimation of the comparison circle of 1·13% when it was located above the illusion figure and an under-estimation of 0·44% when located below it (for twenty adult subjects). This means that the upper of two circles is always over-estimated. When two superposed horizontals are used there is little illusion, but when two verticals in extension are used the over-estimation of the upper is usually considerable: we shall be concerned primarily with this case.

The classical explanation invokes an anisotropism of visual space which produces an apparent lengthening of elements lying in the superior sector. But, if this were the case, the error should remain

[1] By definition, leading to unequal densities of centrations as a function of the directions, but not the dimensions, of the elements of this figure.
[2] This means two continuous lines lying in a horizontal plane and extending away from the subject.

constant or decrease with age, which does happen when the interval between the two lines is very small or non-existent, but does not happen when the interval is larger. Moreover, the hypothesis cannot account for the numerous individual differences which exist, nor for the reversal of illusion which often occurs when obliques rather than verticals are compared. Finally, this illusion is very similar to the horizontal–vertical illusion as such (without being identical with it), which suggests that common mechanisms should be looked for.

It might again be possible to reduce this kind of error to effects of centration, but in this case related to polarised explorations or transports. The reasoning is as follows. While all primary illusions have their origins in dimensional inequalities (even the Oppel–Kundt illusion to the extent that it is primary), two vertical lines in extension, whether they are equal or unequal, always give rise to an illusion. If this is due to effects of centration (and of encounters and of couplings) it must be because centrations are heterogeneously distributed because of the positions or orientations of the elements compared and not because of their unequal lengths.[1] One would therefore expect to find polarisations in exploration itself and in transports, polarisations which would dictate the distributions of centrations. It is for this reason that these illusions are either intermediate in form (with the upper segment over-estimated), or frankly secondary (with the vertical, as such, over-estimated).

II. Let us first recall some evidence collected by Morf[2] concerning the over-estimation of superior elements with small intervals between the lines, and by Lambercier[3] with larger intervals.

Using two verticals, one of 4 cm and the other variable, but without either being identifiable to the subject as the standard, and at the separations shown, the results set out in Table 59 were obtained by Morf. It can be seen that the upper element is over-estimated on the average, and increasingly so as the separations increase. The illusion

TABLE 59. *Mean % error in the comparison of verticals in extension as a function of small separations (for n, see original publication. V = vertical and S = sagittal presentation)*

Rech. 30, Tables 1 and 2

Separation	0		10		20		40	80	Prop. Increase 0 to 20		0 to 80
	V	S	V	S	V	S	V	V	V	S	V
5 to 6 years	9·0	7·5	9·5	9·0	12·2	11·7	12·2	12·5	0·35	0·56	0·39
7 to 8 years	8·9	6·5	9·5	9·2	11·7	14·7	12·0	12·2	0·31	1·28	0·37
10 to 11 years	4·2	4·5	6·2	5·5	10·2	10·0	12·0	12·0	1·42	1·22	1·85
Adult	2·0	2·0	3·0	2·0	3·5	4·7	5·7	7·7	0·75	1·37	2·85

[1] It might be thought that this question of position or orientation would also intervene in the case of angles and diagonals of rectangles (Chapter 1, § 5). But it was seen (Fig. 7, p. 18) that there were dimensional inequalities in those cases which cannot be involved in the present figures. See also the beginning of § 4.
[2] *Rech.* 30.   [3] *Rech.* 31.

decreases with age but this decrement is strongly attenuated as the separation increases: in other words, the increase in illusion as a function of separation increases with age. When the figure is presented in the sagittal plane, the results are similar.

It is also interesting to observe, in relation to the over-estimation of verticals as such, that if the intervals of separation of 10 and 20 mm are filled in with a line (so that the comparison is between two verticals separated by a third), the same tendencies are obtained:[1] a relative increase in illusion, at all ages, as the compared lines are more widely separated, and a decreasing diminution of error with age, once again as the intermediate line is lengthened.

Lambercier obtained the results shown in Table 60, using rods attached to vertical screens rather than drawn lines, and with greater separations. The standard was placed alternately in the top and bottom positions, but was not identified for the subject, who was merely asked to say which was longer.

TABLE 60. *Mean % error and frequency distribution of mean judgements in the comparison of verticals in extension at greater separations (L = lower rod as standard; U = upper rod as standard)*

Rech. 31, Table 2

Age group		5–8 yrs ($n = 13$)				Adult ($n = 10$)			
		Mean % error	Direction of error			Mean % error	Direction of error		
			+	−	0		+	−	0
L	20	−0·96	4	6	3	0·87	6	3	1
	80	0·48	5	2	6	2·12	6	1	3
	180	1·42	6	4	3	0	5	3	2
U	20	0·29	7	4	2	1·25	6	2	2
	80	1·44	7	4	2	2·50	6	2	2
	180	1·83	7	3	3	0·38	4	4	2
Overall		0·75	46%	29%	25%	1·18	58%	25%	17%

As might be predicted by extrapolation from the previous results, the average error increases with age: the upper element is judged greater on less than 50% of occasions by children and, even in adults, 25% of the errors are negative and 17% zero. Finally, if the error does increase as a function of separation, this is only so, for adults, at 20 and 80 cm: at 180 cm there is no illusion, as if the elements had become independent.

III. These results in no way support the explanation in terms of an anisotropism of visual space.[2] Given the changes that occur in the illusion with age, and the individual differences that exist, it seems much more likely that the over-estimation of the upper element can be reduced to effects of centration subordinated to an exercise of explorations and of polarised transports.

Such a polarisation is self-evident if one remembers the asymmetry

[1] *Rech.* 30.
[2] Even if this anisotropism exists, and supposing that a meaning can be given to the distinction between perceived space, as containing, and the objects as contained.

of vertical as opposed to the symmetry of horizontal comparisons. If a horizontal comparison is made of two uprights standing on the same base line, or, particularly, of two horizontal lines in extension, the right and left extremities (or the two elements in the case of the two uprights) both point into open spaces (given that there are no accidental asymmetries in the situation: subjectively, certain directional preferences might be present, either congenitally or by acquisition, as, for instance, the habitual direction of reading, but these are particular causes which do not involve a general asymmetry). In vertical comparisons, however, there is an objective asymmetry: the superior element points into an open space while the inferior one is directed towards a closure, the ground. There are also subjective asymmetries: the visual field is less high than it is wide; our eyes and hands are placed side by side and not one above the other; horizontal eye-movements are easier to execute than vertical ones; and finally, we are more accustomed to judging the height of standing objects by referring to the ground and to their summits rather than by referring to the distances between their extremities.

For all these reasons, it may be accepted that a comparison between two horizontals in extension will be made on the basis of centrations directed towards their mid-points, while comparisons made on two verticals in extension will be made on the basis of a comparison between their upper extremities, and consequently with a preponderance of centrations on the interval between their summits: this interval will include the whole of the superior element but will tend to exclude the middle and lower parts of the inferior element. If this schema is correct, as was supposed in *Rech.* 30, it can account for the over-estimation of the upper element at small intervals and the decrease in the illusion with age, that is, with the increase in exploration.

This was no more than a guess when first published in 1956, but has since been amply confirmed by an analysis of eye-movements and of the distribution of centrations. Thanks to an apparatus constructed by Rutschmann, and perfected by Vinh-Bang, it has been possible to study eye-movements made during a comparison of two verticals of 9 cm, separated by 1 cm, when the points shown were aligned with the primary visual axis:

A: the middle of the lower element;
B: the middle of the upper element;
C: the base of the lower element;
D: the summit of the upper element.

Film records taken on ten adults produced the distribution of centrations shown in Table 61, similar records made on two horizontals of 5 cm, viewed centrally and separated by 2 cm, being added for comparison.

TABLE 61a. *Mean % frequency distribution of centrations along and between two vertical lines as a function of the relation of the figure to the primary visual axis (see text. a = top, b = middle, c = bottom of element; I = upper element, II = lower element. Figures in parenthesis denote mean number of centrations. n = 6 adults)*

Rech. 44, Table 1

Positions	A	B	C	D
I $\begin{cases} b \\ a \\ c \end{cases}$	20·2	18·9	20·1	24·0
	16·8	16·2	18·9	16·0
	17·3	24·3	18·2	16·0
I(a+b+c)	54·3 (2·82)	59·5 (3·38)	57·2 (3·03)	56·0 (2·80)
Between I and II	0	0	0·6	0
II $\begin{cases} a \\ b \\ c \end{cases}$	28·8	17·6	27·1	38·0
	13·5	14·9	11·3	6·0
	3·4	8·1	3·8	0
II(a+b+c)	45·7 (2·37)	40·6 (2·31)	42·2 (2·56)	44·0 (2·20)

TABLE 61b. *Comparison of mean % distributions of centrations on vertical lines (for all positions combined) and on horizontal lines (for horizontal presentations, a = left end, b = middle, c = right end; I = left-hand line, II = right-hand line)*

Rech. 44, Tables 1 and 2

	Vertical	Horizontal
I $\begin{cases} a \\ b \\ c \end{cases}$	20·8	9·8
	17·0	12·0
	19·0	24·7
I(a+b+c)	56·8 (3·00)	46·5 (2·40)
Between I and II	0·15	6·9
II $\begin{cases} a \\ b \\ c \end{cases}$	27·9	24·7
	11·4	13·0
	3·8	8·8
II(a+b+c)	43·1 (2·38)	46·5 (2·45)

It can be seen that the upper elements (I) were effectively more centred than the lower ones (II), while the symmetry was perfect in the case of the horizontal lines. The summits (a) of the lines were more centred than the bases (c), except in IB where the primary visual axis bisected the upper element. In particular, the lower extremities of the lower elements, II (c), were centred far less frequently than the lower extremities of the upper elements, I (c), which are situated between the two summits. An analysis of the durations of centrations, of transports, etc., gives the same results: a clear asymmetry with verticals (with a predominance of transports in the upward direction at these small separations, which means more fixations on the upper lines) and a complete symmetry with horizontals when the lines are located centrally in the field of vision.

An explanation in terms of the polarisation of explorations is thus justified at these small separations. The same must apply at greater separations (Table 60) because transports then play a much greater role, if we mean by transports the activity by which the perception of one element is carried over or applied to a second element which is at a sufficient distance to require a second centration.

There are two distinct ways in which transports may intervene in the case of vertical comparisons: (*a*) In passing from the top of the upper element to the top of the lower, or inversely, they reinforce the encounters on the whole length of the upper element while depriving the middle and lower parts of the lower; (*b*) depending on whether there are more transports upwards or downwards, they modify the estimations of length in one of two ways: either by an over-estimation of the transported element during transportation (a tenable hypothesis in regard to horizontals, but very doubtful for verticals); or by a reinforcement of centrations on the point of departure (because of the incipient transportation) or on the point of arrival (because of the stabilisation of centration on the last element perceived).

At small separations (1 cm with verticals of 5 cm), the analysis indicates that 53·3 % of transports took place in an upward direction. This is a small difference but one which was constant in all four positions of the figure, while horizontals attracted transports equally in both directions (50·3 % from left to right). This contradicts the hypothesis that the transported element is over-estimated but favours the notion of a privileged final centration. If this suggestion is generalised to the case of greater separations (hypothetically, because measurements were not taken), one would be led to suppose that the increase in illusion with separation was due to a polarisation of transports, the subject adopting a habit of favouring comparisons in one direction or the other. Such an interpretation would also explain both the increase in illusion with age (polarisation being an acquired habit) and the observed individual differences (a number of negative errors and nine classes of error made up of positive, negative and zero errors with the standard in the top or the bottom position: see Table 5, *Rech*. 31). It would also explain why, with directed comparisons (the standard being always in the same position and judgement being made on the variable, see Table 1, *Rech*. 31), the errors were completely random (but still exhibited an increase with age): in this case the instructions conflicted with preferred polarisations.

IV. The best support for the hypothesis of this polarisation of explorations and of transports comes from the fact that when the comparison is made on obliques set at 45°, the distribution of errors is completely changed: an important number of subjects (often the majority) over-estimate the lower line! The results shown in Table 62 were obtained by Morf, using obliques of 4 cm at separations shown.

As Vinh-Bang had found, when analysing eye-movements on this figure, that four of seven adults over-estimated the upper oblique, we asked Morf to examine the role played by different fixation points on the error, with the figure presented tachistoscopically. The pre-exposure fixation point controlled the experimental fixation point and the results shown in Table 63 were obtained.

TABLE 62. *Mean % error in estimates of the upper of two obliques in extension as a function of separation (V = card in vertical, S = card in sagittal plane)*

Rech. 30, Tables 5 and 6

Age group	5–6 yrs		7–8 yrs		10–11 yrs		Adult	
	V	S	V	S	V	S	V	S
Separation (cm)	(n = 20)	(20)	(20)	(20)	(20)	(20)	(20)	(41)
0	0·5	−1·0	−2·25	−3·5	−8·0	−7·5	−4·5	−3·75
1	−0·25	−0·5	0·5	−1·5	−10·0	−8·75	−8·5	−8·0
2	−1·0	−0·75	−0·5	−0·7	−16·25	−14·75	−15·5	−10·0

It can be seen quite clearly that results are affected by the location of the point of centration, the positive sign in the above table indicating an over-estimation of the upper line. There is, however, a slight asymmetry in the overall means in favour of the upper line, which is rather more over-estimated than the lower line for equivalent centrations.

TABLE 63. *Mean % error in estimates of upper of two obliques in extension, as a function of fixation point, of separation and of exposure time. Stimulus card vertical (I/1 = fixation on top of upper oblique; I/2 = ¾ point upper oblique; I/3 = ½ point upper oblique; II/1 = ½ point lower oblique; II/2 = ¼ point lower oblique; II/3 = bottom lower oblique;*

Rech. 44, Table 19

Separation (cm)	0			1			2			Overall
Exposure (=/100 sec)	2	5	10	2	5	10	2	5	10	Mean
I/1 (n = 12)	2·7	2·3	2·3	2·5	2·5	2·3	2·5	2·5	3·0	2·5
I/2 (n = 16)	1·5	0·7	2·0	2·5	2·5	3·3	2·0	2·3	3·3	2·2
I/3 (n = 16)	−0·5	0·7	0	0·5	0·8	−0·5	0·3	1·0	0·3	0·3
II/1 (n = 12)	0	0·5	0·3	0·3	0·8	0·3	0·3	0·8	0·3	0·4
II/2 (n = 16)	−0·8	−1·0	−2·3	−0·5	−1·3	−3·0	−0·8	−0·8	−2·8	−1·4
II/3 (n = 12)	−1·3	−1·3	−1·5	−1·3	−0·8	−1·3	−1·0	−1·0	−1·8	−1·2

However, whatever the proportions may be, the over-estimation of the lower element in unconstrained vision (Table 62) counters the hypothesis that the error is due to an anisotropism of visual space, or of an asymmetry of the visual field itself. We are here involved (and more clearly than in the case of the verticals) with a polarisation of explorations and of centrations as a function of the orientation of the otherwise equal elements. Why, then, does placing the figure at 45° entirely or partly reverse the polarisations found with verticals?

We advanced the hypothesis in *Rech.* 30 that because an inclined line does not constitute an equilibrated perceptual form, as verticals or horizontals do, the attention or centrations are attracted to its point of attachment, or base, rather than to its upper end. Or, if one prefers it, as an oblique is intermediate between a vertical and a horizontal, the gaze is attracted to the vertex of the angle which it forms with the horizontal or vertical references and therefore to its lower end.

The distribution of centrations assessed by an analysis of eye-movements,[1] set out in Table 64, confirmed this general tendency for

---

[1] *Rech.* 44.

the upper oblique, but there was dominance of centrations towards the middle of the overall figure in respect of the lower line.

TABLE 64. *Mean frequency distribution of centrations on upper oblique (I) and on lower oblique (II) and direction of transports (T) classified according to mean direction of error of estimate (a = upper, b = middle, c = lower segment of element, n = 7 adults)*

Rech. 44, Tables 21 and 22 (corrected)

Location	Ia	Ib	Ic	I (total)	IIa	IIb	IIc	II (total)	Tp I → II	Tp II → I
+ ve error	4·7	17·6	32·3	54·7	31·2	8·7	5·3	45·3	46·7	53·3
− ve error	7·3	8·4	34·7	50·5	29·1	7·6	12·8	49·5	60·5	39·5

It can be seen that the distributions differ markedly from those obtained when verticals were being compared. Subjects having a positive error centred mostly on the upper oblique, mostly towards its lower end, while the lower oblique tended to be centred near its top, because it had to be compared with the upper line. The total number of centrations on either line is less informative in regard to the differences between the positive and negative errors than are the following comparisons: (1) centrations on Ia + Ib compared with those on IIb + IIc (on the upper and middle parts of I compared with the middle and lower parts of II) = 23·3 > 14·0 for subjects having positive errors and 15·7 < 20·4 for subjects having negative errors; (2) transports for positive errors were: upward 53·3%, downward 46·7%; for negative errors they were: upward 39·5%, and downward 60·5%. This again suggests that the over-estimated element is the one towards which the transport is directed.

The results obtained with obliques would seem therefore to be explicable by the same schema that was applied to the case of verticals, but with a partial inversion of the sign which is still consistent with the general sense of the schema. It remains to be noted that comparisons made between verticals situated at different levels but

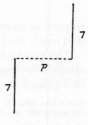

Fig. 43.

with a horizontal separation (and sometimes with a vertical separation in addition; Fig. 43) gave results which are intermediate between the two cases so far studied (verticals and obliques in extension). These results, to be found in Tables 9 (*a*), (*b*) and (*c*) of *Rech.* 30, will be discussed later in § 4, III.

V. If the above facts are to be interpreted in terms of polarisations of centrations, explorations and transports, this kind of systematic error must be directly related to the well—known but so far insufficiently explained over-estimation of verticals. If a vertical is predominantly centred towards its upper end and a horizontal towards its middle, the transport of the one to the other (in both directions), as would occur for instance in a right-angle figure, would entail a greater probability of encounters on the vertical: the passage between the two preferred sectors of the lines favours the vertical as a whole and neglects the free end of the horizontal. We have made many attempts to analyse the right-angle figure from this point of view. We have examined the errors obtained with subjects of all ages and with the figure in its four possible major orientations. We have done this with unconstrained viewing and with tachistoscopic presentations in which the durations of exposure and the fixation points were varied. We have also filmed eye-movements while the figure was being examined: all our findings seem to support the hypothesis of polarisations. However, a more general factor will have to be added to that of polarisation if we are to account for a problem which has not yet been tackled, that there is an increase with age in both this illusion and in that of obliques (see Table 60). This factor is the structuring of perceptual space that occurs with the development of frames of reference and of co-ordinates, a structuring which,

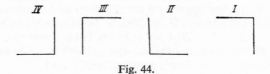

Fig. 44.

in part, determines the polarisations. The facts about to be presented will mark the transition from § 3 to § 4.

The right-angle figure in the four positions shown in Fig. 44 was studied by Morf,[1] and some of the results he obtained are presented in Tables 65a and 65b.

TABLE 65a. *Mean % over-estimation of the vertical in the right-angle figure as a function of figure orientation and of order of presentation (n = 20 adults)*

Rech. 43, Table 7

Orientation Order	I	II	III	IV
II–IV–I–III	7·6	11·2	6·4	11·2
IV–I–III–II	12·4	6·8	12·8	6·8

It can be seen that the vertical was over-estimated in all positions but that the extent of the illusion varied by as much as a factor of two and that the order of presentation had a considerable effect. We saw, in § 2, that the effects of practice were very variable with the figure in position I and when using the method of adjustment. In the present case (but using a different method) the first five presentations in position I yielded an increase from 7·3 to 10·3 for one group of adults and from 8·2 to 11·2 for a second group. With IV, however, the increase was very slight (from 7·8 to 9·4) or almost absent (from 4·4 to 5 or

[1] *Rech.* 43.

4·8 for a second group of subjects). No increase in illusion was noticed before 9 to 10 years.

Using twenty subjects in each age group, and presenting the figures in the order I to IV, we found clear evidence of an increase with age (Table 65b) for I but not for IV (this absence of increase of error with age for IV may be due to an order effect, cf. the values for IV in Table 65a).

TABLE 65b. *Mean % over-estimation of the vertical in the right-angle figure in positions I and IV a function of age (n = 20 for each group)*

Rech. 43, Table 4

Age group	4–5 yrs	6–7 yrs	9–10 yrs	Adult
I	1·9	4·0	9·4	10·6
IV	7·6	7·4	7·4	5·2

In tachistoscopic presentation and using the same subjects for all exposure times, the order being of ascending durations in all cases (cf. Table 41, p. 119) and calculating the error on the vertical, Matalon obtained the results shown in Table 66.

TABLE 66. *Mean % over-estimation of the vertical in the right-angle figure in position I as a function of exposure time and of fixation point (n = 20 for each age group; V = fixation on vertical (variable), H = on horizontal)*

Rech. 42, Table 2

Exposure time (sec)	0·04	0·10	0·20	0·50	1·00	Unlimited
5 to 7 years						
V	5·6	6·2	6·4	3·1	3·6	2·0
H	−2·0	−3·0	−4·0	−7·4	−8·0	−6·0
Adult						
V	6·5	7·9	7·8	7·9	6·8	5·6
H	4·2	2·7	3·0	3·4	2·8	3·2

Three important tendencies emerge. (1) With fixation on the vertical, the adult's error was always greater than the child's (as in Table 65, but to a lesser degree). (2) With fixation on the horizontal, the vertical was under-estimated by children. This was also found for separate groups of subjects (see Table 41 again) up to 0·1 second, but from then on the vertical was over-estimated by these young subjects even with fixation on the horizontal. With the present groups, however, the horizontal was over-estimated at all exposure times. (3) Adults over-estimated the vertical at all exposure times, even when fixating the horizontal, which poses a problem to be dealt with in a moment.

The above findings (Tables 64 to 66) raise three problems. The first is the over-estimation of the vertical. This can probably be resolved in the same way as the problem of the over-estimation of the upper vertical, and as suggested in III above. In this connection, results obtained by Vinh-Bang from an analysis of filmed eye-movements are presented in Table 67.[1]

[1] Illusion I was the strongest and II the weakest for the subjects contributing to this table. Measurements were made during the filming.

TABLE 67. *Mean % frequency distribution of centrations on the two segments of the right-angle figure as a function of figure orientation (n = 12 adults; see Fig. 44, a = top of V and left end of H)*

Rech. 45, Table 27

Orientation	I	II	III	IV	Overall mean
V ⎰a	32·3	12·4	38·3	14·0	24·2
⎱b	19·6	24·8	18·8	19·3	20·6
c	5·1	11·6	6·5	6·0	7·3
V (a+b+c)	57·0	48·8	63·6	39·3	52·2
H ⎰a	7·6	10·1	9·1	20·7	11·9
b	24·7	20·9	17·5	22·0	21·3
⎱c	10·7	20·1	9·7	18·0	14·6
H (a+b+c)	43·0	51·2	36·4	60·7	47·8
Number of centrations	5·85	5·86	5·70	5·55	5·74

It can be seen that these results are concordant with the suggested explanation: either the majority of centrations were on sector *a* of the verticals or on *b* of horizontals (in positions I and III) or on *b* of the vertical and on the parts nearest to the point of fixation on the horizontals (*b* and *c* for positions II, and *a* and *b* for IV). In both cases the most frequent transport followed the vertical rather than a 45° trajectory between it and the horizontal. It follows that if sectors *a* and *b* of the verticals are compared with the equally peripheral parts of horizontals, one obtains:

I	II	III	IV
51·9 v 35·4	37·2 v 31·0	57·1 v 26·6	33·3 v 40·0

Only position IV produces a discordant result, but in this case the transports from horizontal to vertical (which therefore terminate on the vertical) account for 58·3 % of the total, which reverses the relation.

The second problem concerns the variability of the illusion as a function of the figure's position and of the order of presentation. The explanation is no doubt that as the horizontal–vertical illusion results from a polarisation of explorations and of transports, the least change in the direction of the preferred transports will modify the resulting error. As the figure is changed from one position to another, according to the various orders of presentation, the subject may oscillate between momentary prior schemes of transports and brusque changes demanded by the changes in position. In Vinh-Bang's subjects, the maximum error coincided with a transport between *V*a and *H*b and the least error between *V*b and the most proximal part of the horizontal. An alternation between these two procedures, or a per-severation on one, would be sufficient to account for the momentary variations between large and slight errors.

However, this problem of the quantitative variations in the error is of minor interest compared with the third and central problem. This concerns the increase in error with age, or the secondary nature of the illusion of the vertical. We can no longer speak of an increasing polarisation with age, as we did in the case of the upper vertical (cf. II

162

and III), because, in fact, the polarisation is now variable (which is why we had to underline the quantitative instability of the illusion compared with its increasing qualitative stability). We are forced, therefore, to invoke a more general factor than that of polarised explorations and transports, particularly in view of the fact that adults continue to over-estimate the vertical even when fixating the horizontal (Table 66), while only children conform to the rule of over-estimations as a function of the point of centration.

This more general factor selects itself as soon as one tries to find out what perceptual criteria the subject uses when he judges between verticals, horizontals and obliques. His criteria are, of course, relative to the normal direction of his eyes: as everything perpendicular to the sagittal plane is horizontal and everything parallel to that plane is vertical, the inclination of obliques will be assessed with reference to these two orientations. It is likely that young subjects are satisfied with these egocentric criteria, and that the initial polarisations of explorations and of transports do not impose other demands. But as soon as exploratory activities extend beyond the initial limits of syncretism and of the overwhelming importance of proximity for the child (§ 1), certain references will be established, not only to the direction of regard (the sagittal plane), but also to relations between the various objects themselves, and at increasing distances. The vertical and horizontal will now come to be related to these frames of reference in relation to the subject's position and to the direction of his gaze, and no longer only to the internal relations of the figure. As we shall see, it is this activity related to frames of reference, and in general to perceptual co-ordinates, that increases with age. This activity then confers a new perceptual significance on the vertical and horizontal, a significance which is expressed, among other ways, in a better estimation of the inclination of obliques.

It is this progressive structuring of the whole which explains the increase in errors of estimation of the lengths of verticals (Tables 65 and 66) and of obliques (Table 62) with age: as judgements of the directions of verticals and of obliques improve, the lengths of verticals, obliques and horizontals become heterogeneous and lead to different polarisations. This question will now be examined.

§ 4. ACTIVITIES OF REFERRAL: EFFECTS OF FRAMES OF REFERENCE AND THE ESTABLISHMENT OF PERCEPTUAL CO-ORDINATES

We have shown that exploration, the most elementary perceptual activity, generally leads to a reduction in illusion by a process of compensations (§ 2) although it can also reinforce certain errors

(§§ 1 to 3). But we have also claimed (§ 3) that exploration can give rise to privileged polarisations because its direction is variable. These privileged polarisations produce new errors, as in the case of the upper of two verticals and of the horizontal–vertical illusion. Finally, we claimed, these polarisations, which are at first relative to the direction of the subject's regard, can become subordinated secondarily to more 'objective' and general references. It is at this stage that frames of reference have their effects and that perceptual co-ordinates are established. We shall now deal with these.

I. By 'frames of reference' we mean those objective elements which lie outside the perceived figure and have effects on estimates of the directions of elements of the figure but not (or only indirectly) on their dimensions. We shall not refer in this connection to the effects produced by the size of a card on the apparent length of a line drawn on it, except when one of the edges of the card influences the apparent direction of the lines drawn on it. As we have already defined polarised explorations (§ 3) in terms of their relations with directions and not with dimensions, it can be seen that activities of referral will extend exploratory activities whenever the subject is able to overcome the barriers of distance between the figure and its surrounds and thus to relate them.

One possible difficulty must be discussed before we establish that this barrier of distance is overcome only rather late. In the final analysis, direction must be estimated on the basis of dimensions. This is because the perception of one line as being parallel to another, or estimates of the degree to which they diverge, does not depend simply on a global impression of equivalent directions but on estimates of the distances separating several sectors of the lines (even if contradictory judgements may be involved in some cases, such as Luneburg's alley). We saw, for example, that inclinations were judged as a function of dimensional inequalities in the case of angles and of the diagonals of rectangles (Chapter I, § 5). Reciprocally, however, estimations of length have to be made in relation to the relative directions of the elements being judged. But we cannot have it both ways: either the estimation of inclination or of direction is used in making dimensional comparisons (which involve primary illusions when dimensional inequalities are involved, as in the case of angles in which the inclination of the arms is judged on the basis of their apparent separation, and secondary or intermediate illusions when the dimensions are equal, as in § 3); or else dimensional information is used in estimating direction, which would involve effects of frames of reference (secondary effects) which we are about to discuss. This circularity between dimensions and directions is thus ineluctable but is

164

used when drawing fine distinctions between categories of illusion.

II. A striking example of effects of frames of reference in which exploratory activities expand into the activity of relating to external systems of reference is seen in the illusion of partially overlapping quadilaterals (Fig. 11, p. 23). We have already identified the primary mechanism of this illusion, which depends on effects of angles and other over-estimations. But directions are also involved for two reasons: (1) the question posed to the subject involved direction because it involved the judgement of the apparent inclination or horizontality of the median line of the figure and because, to make this easier for children, the figure was drawn within a rectangular frame of 10·8 × 3·2 cm, the whole drawing being on a sheet of paper of 21 × 15 cm; (2) angles α and β of Fig. 11 have to be perceived if they are to influence the direction of the whole median line (because it is one thing to exhibit a strong angle effect, as young subjects do, when the angle is perceived, and quite another to perceive the effect, that is, to discern the inclination). The angles can be perceived only if the directions of all the various parts of the figure in relation one to another, and each in relation to the frame (whether drawn or formed by the edges of the paper), are taken into consideration.

The role played by these effects of direction and of the frame of reference in responses to the thirteen different forms of the figure studied with Denis-Prinzhorn,[1] was such that the evolution of responses with age was not uniform. All three major types of development described in the Introduction (under V) were found to occur. Three classes of figure can be identified. The first consists of Figs. X and XI (see *Rech.* 21) in which the quadrilaterals are not inked in but are only outlined, X being empty and XI filled in in grey but with black contours; the second consists of one figure, IV, in which the squares are inked in in black but in which the figure is not enclosed in the frame of 3·2 × 10·8 cm, the only references being the edges of the card; the third, Figs. I to III, V to IX and XII to XIII, consists of quadrilaterals (squares or rectangles) inked in in black and enclosed in the frame. The evolution with age of the illusion occasioned by these classes of figure is given in Table 68.

The three classes of evolutionary pattern and their relations with the effects of direction and of frames of reference can be identified as follows.

(1) Class I (Figs. X and XI) exhibits a continuous reduction in the illusion with age to the point where it disappears altogether in the adult. The reason is (*Rech.* 21, pp. 308–9) that the squares delineated by lines are much more resistant to distortion than are simple con-

Perceptual Activities

TABLE 68. *Mean proportional error on partially overlapping quadrilaterals as a function of age*

Abstracted from *Rech.* 21, Table 1

Age group Figure	5–7 yrs ($n = 40$)	9–12 yrs ($n = 40$)	Adult ($n = 44$)
X (unfilled)	0·19	0·10	0
XI (grey)	0·38	0·10	0
IV (no frame)	0·50	1·18	1·36
I to III (black)	1·41	1·51	1·44
V, VI and IX[1]	0·86	0·96	0·76
VII and VIII[2]	1·17	1·72	1·67
XII and XIII[3]	0·44	0·92	0·57

tours between black and white which are blurred by brightness differences and by irradiation contrasts. With the help of these rectangular frames, the adult perceives the objective parallelisms and perpendicularities, without any apparent inclinations. Younger subjects, on the other hand, impervious to the effects of the rectangular frames,

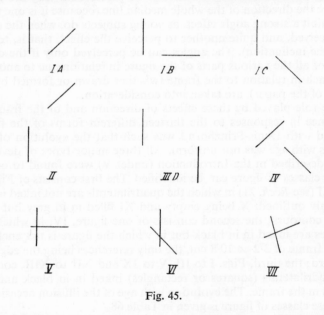

Fig. 45.

perceive slight effects of angles, several subjects perceiving the whole median line to be inclined.

(2) Class II (Fig. IV) produces a continuous increase in the illusion

---

[1] Black squares with overlap in dotted line (V) or continuous line (VI); rectangles with longer side horizontal (XI).

[2] Rectangles arranged along the general median line of the figure.

[3] Grey squares without drawn sides (XII); white squares on black ground with the general median line drawn in white, and without drawn sides (XIII).

166

with age because the absence of the rectangular frame greatly reduces the effect in the very young, while older children (9 to 12 years) and, above all, adults, make more and more reference to the more distant borders of the card.

(3) All the other figures give rise to an increase in illusion from 5–7 to 9–12 years, followed by a decrease. This agrees with what we saw (§ 3, IV) in connection with the evolution of comparisons between obliques (Table 62) and which we are about to see in connection with another example to do with the comparison of an oblique with a vertical. We shall therefore postpone the discussion of this form of illusion until we have examined these new data.

III. Würsten[1] had previously, at our request, compared lines in various orientations with verticals. The extremities of the lines and of the verticals were not joined and the distance between them was varied. The main variants of these figures are shown in Fig. 45, a greater number of separations being used in forms I to IV during the experiment. It is immediately obvious that these experiments concern both the mechanisms of transportation and of perceptual co-ordinates.

Results obtained by Würsten are set out in Table 69a.

TABLE 69a. *Mean error (mm) in estimates of the length of two lines in the orientations shown in Fig. 45. Figures in parenthesis represent mean arithmetic error (n = 20 for each age group)*

Rech. 9, Tables 13 and 15

Age group	5 yrs	6 yrs	7 yrs	8 yrs	9 yrs
Figure					
IC (2 cm)	0·8 (0·8)	0·4 (0·9)	0·2 (0·7)	−0·05 (1·25)	0·3 (0·9)
IC (5 cm)	0·4 (0·7)	0·03 (0·7)	−0·3 (1·2)	−0·5 (1·0)	−0·25 (0·75)
IC (10 cm)	0·7 (0·9)	0·2 (0·8)	−0·4 (0·7)	−0·3 (1·2)	−0·4 (1·1)
IIID (5 cm)	0·2 (0·6)	0·2 (0·6)	0·3 (0·5)	0·3 (0·7)	0·4 (0·7)
IV*	−0·25 (0·6)	−1·3 (1·3)	−1·9 (1·9)	−1·4 (1·7)	−2·15 (2·1)
Overall arithmetic mean	(0·6)	(0·8)	(1·0)	(1·1)	(1·1)

Age group	10 yrs	11 yrs	12 yrs	Adult
Figure				
IC (2 cm)	0·3 (0·8)	0·3 (0·8)	0·1 (0·6)	0·2 (0·5)
IC (5 cm)	−0·5 (0·7)	−0·5 (0·9)	−0·5 (0·8)	−0·1 (0·8)
IC (10 cm)	−0·4 (1·0)	−0·6 (0·9)	−0·7 (1·0)	−0·2 (0·7)
IIID (5 cm)	0·3 (0·5)	0·3 (0·5)	0·2 (0·5)	0·2 (0·5)
IV*	−1·9 (1·9)	−2·2 (2·2)	−1·6 (1·6)	−1·4 (1·4)
Overall arithmetic mean	(1·0)	(1·0)	(0·9)	(0·7)

* Separation varied with the length of lower line.

It can be seen that the separation of the lines had little effect; there was a slight average increase in illusion with an increase in separations from 2 to 5 cm, and then a decrease as the separation increased to 10 cm, as if the elements then became more independent. It was very interesting to note, however, that the *C*-type figures produced much weaker illusions at all distances than did the *A*- and *B*-type figures

[1] *Rech. 9.*

and that, like the *D*-type figures, they exhibited a mixture of over- and under-estimations of the vertical (mainly an under-estimation at 2 and 5 cm separation and an over-estimation at 10 cm). The illusion is slightly stronger with form IV and exhibits an over-estimation of the upper element.

The results obtained for adults with figures II*A* and II*B* (in which the inclination of the oblique shown in II of Fig. 45 was reduced) are shown in Table 69(b).

TABLE 69b. *Mean proportional error for Fig. 45, II, for adults*

Rech. 9, Tables 5 and 6

IIa		IIb	
−1·3	(1·5)	−0·7	(0·9)

The results presented in Tables 69(a) and 69(b) suggest three interesting conclusions concerning the direction and value of the errors and their genetic trends.

(1) That most of the errors found with *C*-type figures were positive (an under-estimation of the vertical) at 2 cm and, at some ages, at 5 and 10 cm also, can be explained as follows: although verticals are usually centred towards their upper and obliques towards their lower ends (as described in § 3), when the oblique is placed below the vertical, as it is in these figures, it is centred successively towards its lower (as usual) and towards its upper end because of the comparison demanded with the upper vertical. This gives rise to its over-estimation.

(2) But as the situation involves conflicts, the mean error can only be small. With type II figures, in which the oblique is the upper element, the error was both negative (for adults, who over-estimate the vertical; Wünsten did not examine children with this figure) and somewhat stronger than with *C* figures, no doubt because centrations tended to be concentrated more on the lower end. With IV, the error was always negative and generally stronger: the two obliques differ in direction and no doubt the upper one was favoured because of the need to give equal consideration to its two extremities.

(3) In spite of the slight extent of the illusion, it still exhibits a genetic change, which was more marked in the results presented in Table 70.[1]

A clear developmental trend can be seen in these results, in the form of an over-estimation of verticals when compared with horizontals or with obliques, this trend being the same as, but clearer than, that of Table 69a. The error (here expressed in mm) increases from − 2·3 % at 5 years to − 9 % at 9 years and then decreases to − 4·6 % for adults.

[1] Preliminary investigations showed that the direction of errors in 1*A* and 1*B* was the same, but somewhat weaker in 1*A*. See *Rech.* 9, Table 6.

Perceptual Activities and Secondary Illusions

TABLE 70. *Mean proportional errors[1] for figures shown (n = 20 for each age group)*

Rech. 9, Table 15

Age group	5 yrs	6 yrs	7 yrs	8 yrs	9 yrs	10 yrs	11 yrs	12 yrs	Adult
IB (2 cm)	−0·9	−1·65	−2·2	−2·45	−2·9	−2·75	−2·3	−2·2	−2·0
IB (5 cm)	−1·25	−2·65	−2·8	−3·2	−4·2	−3·8	−3·3	−3·2	−2·3
IB (10 cm)	−0·8	−2·1	−2·4	−2·4	−3·75	−3·0	−2·7	−2·6	−2·2
V	−0·5	−1·6	−2·0	−1·9	−2·6	−2·5	−2·2	−1·6	−1·1
VI	−0·8	−1·5	−1·55	−1·95	−1·9	−1·8	−1·25	−0·9	−0·7
VII	0·07	0·1	−0·7	−1·1	−0·9	−0·85	−0·7	−0·7	−0·4
Overall mean	−0·7	−1·6	−1·9	−2·2	−2·7	−2·4	−2·1	−1·8	−1·4

The play of centrations and of encounters analysed or proposed to exist, in § 3, cannot alone account for these changes with age. The following explanation would therefore seem to be called for: (1) the lack of perceptual co-ordinates in young subjects facilitates the comparison of the lengths of diverging lines; (2) the development of such co-ordinates then progressively hampers such comparisons, whence the increase in error from 5 to 10 years (the age at which this co-ordinate system is believed to mature); (3) once this system has been constructed, the increasing exercise of transports when changes in direction of elements of the figure are involved once more facilitates the dimensional comparisons involved and results in a reduced error.

It is true that an apparently simpler explanation could be entertained. In an article with Vautrey (see Table 71) Fraisse says, among other things:[2]

For the six-year-old child, Figure A (= 1B of our Fig. 45) seems to be little structured because of the distance between the two segments, and the illusion apparently is weakened consequently. Structuration seems to increase with age. In our opinion, the fact that the two lines do not meet plays a major role. While the Müller–Lyer illusion decreases slightly with age, Triche and Hartmann (1933) found that the illusion, on the contrary, increases with age, when in the figures presented, the extremities only are used as shown here: ⊏ ⊐ ⊏, etc.

But what is meant by 'structuring' a figure? It depends on the relationships involved and, in this particular case, to structure reduces to taking note of the directions as much as of the lengths. But to take note of directions at a distance (and Fraisse is right to emphasise the role of distance) is precisely to construct a system of co-ordinates. Fraisse's interpretations thus come to exactly the same thing as our own and the structuring he invokes simply incorporates a perceptual activity of referral. As for Triche's results, it is not a question of direction, and so of co-ordinates, but simply of relating at a distance, which is the definition of transports, and which necessarily entails an increase of the illusion in question with age.

---

[1] Arithmetic and algebraic means can seldom be distinguished.
[2] Fraisse, P., and Vautrey, P., *Quart. J. Exp. Psychol.*, 1956, **8**, 114–20.

But our account allows of three kinds of verification or points of discussion. (1) First, it must be proved that the supposed perceptual activities (of referral or of the construction of perceptual co-ordinates) do indeed constitute the indirect cause of the observed evolution with age. It will be necessary to show that the trend disappears or changes when the figures are tachistoscopically presented at such short exposures that all referrals and, above all, all transports are excluded. (2) It will then be necessary to give a direct demonstration of the development of activities of referral. (3) Finally, it will be necessary to examine possible causes of the reduction of the illusion (after the age of 9) other than increases in dimensional comparisons when changes in direction are involved.

(1) We are obliged to Fraisse for a tachistoscopic examination of the first point, undertaken for his own information and carried out with Vautrey.[1] This proved to be decisive: without oculo-motor activity, the illusion (measured on IB) remained more or less constant at all ages, the slight increase being attributable simply to encounters (as discussed in § 3). The results obtained by Fraisse and Vautrey are presented in Table 71.

TABLE 71. *Mean error (mm) for the horizontal–vertical illusion (Fig. IB) as a function of age, sex and specialised training*

After Fraisse and Vautrey (1956), Table I

Exposure time	Nature of the groups	6 yrs	(N)	9–10 yrs	(N)	Low educ. level adult	(N)	Arts students	(N)	Science students	(N)
0·2 sec	M	3·5	(7)	4·0	(9)	3·8	(12)	5·1	(11)	4·0	(10)
	F	4·4	(9)	4·6	(9)	4·4	(15)	4·7	(8)	4·1	(10)
	Mean	3·9		4·3		4·1		4·9		4·0	
1 sec	M	3·6	(7)	3·4	(9)	3·7	(12)	4·8	(11)	3·3	(10)
	F	4·0	(9)	4·3	(9)	3·7	(15)	4·5	(8)	3·6	(10)
	Mean	3·8		3·8		3·7		4·6		3·5	
Unlimited time	M	2·5	(10)	3·2	(17)	3·4	(6)	3·0	(11)	3·4	(11)
	F	2·6	(10)	4·3	(20)	4·0	(14)	4·3	(10)	3·7	(12)
	Mean	2·5		3·8		3·7		3·6		3·6	

(2) The supposed development with age of the activity of referral (an activity which is involved in estimates of direction rather than of length), is supported by some evidence collected by Würsten himself and by some provided by Dadsetan, which will be added later.

Accepting the changing dimensional estimates shown in Tables 69a and 70, the problem was to see how children of the same ages performed when asked to judge the inclination of the obliques instead of their lengths. The obliques were kept constant at 135° to the vertical and the comparison was made against a variable series of obliques drawn on separate cards, with a range of 119° to 151° and step intervals of 2°. The problem was simply to judge if the variable and the standard were parallel or not. The results are set out in Table 72.

[1] *Ibid.*

TABLE 72. *Estimates of the inclination of an oblique of* 135° *(Fig. IC; n = 20 for each age group)*

Rech. 9, Tables 20 and 22

Age group	5 yrs	6 yrs	7 yrs	8 yrs	9 yrs	10 yrs	11 yrs	12 yrs	Adult
Threshold (in°)	18·3	16·5	10·4	7·6	5·6	5·6	5·1	3·1	2·3
Mean arithmetic error (in°)	2·2	2·5	1·5	1·2	0·9	1·0	1·1	0·7	0·6
Mean error (in°)	−1·6	−1·2	−0·9	−0·6	−0·2	−0·5	0·2	0·1	0

It can be seen, in contrast to Tables 69 and 70 where the error increased with age, that the error here diminished until about 9 to 10 years, and then became stable.

Würsten also asked his subjects to draw a line (*D*) or to align a rod (*R*) parallel to standards when the standards were vertical (*V*), horizontal (*H*) or inclined (*O*). His results are set out in Table 73.

TABLE 73. *Mean errors of drawings* (*D*) *or of settings* (*R*) *to vertical* (*V*), *oblique* (*O*) *and horizontal* (*H*) *standards. Values represent horizontal error in setting of the top of the subject's line or rod (see Rech. 9, p. 114, Fig. 21),* + = *converging,* − = *diverging. RL and LR represent order in which standard occupied R and L positions. Values in parenthesis represent arithmetic means* (*n* = 20 *for each age group*)

Rech. 9, Tables 25 and 26

	DV	DO (LR)	RV	RO (LR)	RH	RO (RL)
5 to 6 years	0·3 (1·1)	9·1 (9·1)	−1·4 (1·4)	5·9 (5·9)	−1·7 (1·8)	4·3 (5·1)
6 to 7 years	−0·2 (0·8)	7·5 (7·5)	−0·9 (0·9)	4·6 (4·6)	−1·6 (1·8)	3·7 (4·3)
7 to 8 years	0·0 (0·9)	6·3 (6·3)	−1·0 (1·3)	4·5 (4·5)	−1·4 (1·6)	3·1 (4·4)
9 to 10 years	0·3 (0·8)	6·5 (6·5)	−0·8 (0·9)	3·4 (3·4)	−1·1 (1·3)	2·7 (2·9)
Adult	0·0 (0·4)	4·5 (4·5)	−0·3 (0·5)	1·6 (1·6)	−0·5 (0·6)	0·7 (1·3)

It is clear that the development of estimates of direction does not obey the same law as that of length. All the indications are that there is an initial systematic difficulty in estimating orientations (less of course, in the case of verticals and horizontals which are assessed with reference to the line of regard) which is followed by a continuous improvement. The errors from 5 to 8 years (Table 72), and in the case of obliques from 5 to 9–10 years (Table 73), seem to suggest a lack of objective references: the child seems to be content to assimilate his estimates to his own line of regard. But the estimation of the inclination of obliques (Table 72), and the production of equivalent obliques (Table 73), must involve activities of referral, because an inclination cannot be judged, as verticals or horizontals are, by an unconscious reference to the direction of regard. That the child, in fact, tries to do this is suggested by the fact that horizontals and verticals at first give rise to difficulties of evaluation when they are placed in conflict with adjacent frames of reference.

(3) The trends demonstrated in Tables 69 and 70 can be explained as follows: (*a*) at the age of 5 or 6 years, perceptual space is not structured on the basis of objective co-ordinates (or references) but the directions are assessed on the basis of egocentric assimilations to the line of regard. Consequently there is a considerable initial facility in the estimation of lengths irrespective of directions, which are ignored. (*b*) As co-ordinates and objective references develop and assist the

structuring of directions, estimations of length are more and more troubled by considerations of direction; (c) from 9 or 10 years, directions have become structured, or are on the way to becoming so, and the progressive exercise of dimensional transports when changes in orientation are involved once more reduces the errors. However, an objection can be, and has been, raised to this last point.

According to Fraisse, the abundance of geometric (and, above all, of pseudo-geometric) constructions which Würsten detected in older subjects simply indicates that an increasingly operational or metric evaluation is being superimposed on the perception, as such, of length. The decrease in the tally of errors from 9 or 10 years to adulthood would then no longer be a perceptual event but would derive from intelligence itself and would be achieved in a variety of ways. In support of this thesis, Fraisse and Vautrey showed that while the errors decreased towards adulthood in science students, they did not do so in arts students or in uneducated adults (see Table 71).

Had the figures used by Würsten been the only ones to yield this developmental trend, Fraisse's interpretations, the principle of which we of course accept, would have seemed to be adequate. But the same trend recurs in other situations, where the lengths of obliques are being estimated (Table 62), when the constructions are much more difficult to achieve because the obliques form extensions of one another. In particular, this trend is also found in the case of partially overlapping quadrilaterals (Table 68, Figs. I to II, V to IX and XII to XIII). In this case the geometrical construction is easy because the correct response can be made on the basis of a comparison between the two halves of the short sides of the general rectangular shape of the figure, whose mid-points are joined by the longitudinal median on which the quadrilaterals stand. But the reduction in error from 9 to 12 years to adulthood was only of the following order for the three classes of figure: from 1·51 to 1·44 (against 1·41 at 5 to 7 years), from 1·72 to 1·67 (against 1·17 at 5 to 7 years) and from 0·92 to 0·57 (against 0·44 at 5 to 7 years). With the joined squares and recumbent rectangles, it was 0·96 to 0·76 (against 0·86 at 5 to 7 years. See Table 68). If a geometric construction was involved, the adult error would either be annulled or would be much weaker than it was at 5 to 7 years. The fact that this was not so (and this applies equally in the case of the obliques of Table 62) seems to indicate clearly enough that the reduction in error is to be attributed to a perceptual event. The same trend is found with the Oppel–Kundt illusion (Table 54, p. 144) and with projective errors (Table 93 of Chapter IV, p. 216), but does not occur in the case of other secondary illusions (Fig. IV of Table 68, for example). This limited generality also argues against Fraisse's hypothesis.

We readily agree that operational activities, once constituted, can facilitate perceptual activities by orienting them, but they do not substitute for them. Our position would become untenable, of course, if we claimed (and perhaps we have led this to be understood?) that only one perceptual activity was involved, that the increase in error occurred while that activity was being constructed and that the final decrease in error occurred after it had been constructed and while it was being exercised or perfected. We are proposing, on the contrary, the intervention of two distinct perceptual activities. One is the activity of referral to objective references. It is lacking in young children who therefore make good estimates of size even when changes in direction are involved. As the activity is progressively structured, the error increases because the dimensions of the figure can no longer be estimated independently of the relative directions of its elements. The second activity is that of effecting transports with changes in direction. This activity is also lacking in young children because directions have not yet been sufficiently well organised. It makes its appearance when the first systems of reference and of co-ordinates have been achieved. It is only the exercise of this activity which leads to a reduction in error between the ages of 9 to 10 years and adulthood, whether this exercise is supported by contemporaneous operational activities or not.

IV. Finally, it is necessary to demonstrate that, even in the case of verticals and of horizontals, the activity of relating to objective references progressively takes the place of simple egocentric references to the line of regard and leads, as in the case of obliques, to a marked improvement in estimates of direction. At our request, Dadsetan[1] carried out an investigation in which the subject was asked to judge the orientation of lines. These were drawn near to one side of inclined right-angle triangles or squares which, in turn, were drawn on sheets of card which were large enough to make it unlikely that the subject would automatically refer to their borders as guides. A variety of results was obtained.

Firstly, the error (the median of the range of variation), while of course decreasing progressively with age, remained unchanged qualitatively in the sense that the line judged to be horizontal was always inclined towards the side of the figure with which it formed the greatest angle. This is not due to an illusion of angles (over-estimation of acute angles) but to a form of attraction exercised by the inclination of the nearest side (see Fig. 46), and implies that the line is related to

[1] Dadsetan, P., *Les Systèmes Perceptifs de Références et leurs Relations avec les Coordonnées de l'Espace Représentatif.* Thèse No. 10, Institut des Sciences de l'Education, Genève, 1960.

the nearest side of the figure rather than to the external frame of reference provided by the borders of the card.

Secondly, the ranges of variation, which are the best index of the activity of referral, are shown in Table 74. The results obtained with one only of the figures used are shown. The figure consisted of a horizontal of 4·5 cm drawn inside isosceles right-angle triangles having sides of 6·5, 6·5 and 9·2cm and with the hypotenuse inclined between 10° and 60°.

TABLE 74. *Mean range of settings (degrees) of a line to the horizontal as a function of inclination of the hypotenuse of the triangle in which the line was enclosed (n = 20 for each age group)*

After Dadsetan (1960), Table 9

Age group Inclination	5 yrs	6 yrs	7 yrs	8 yrs	9 yrs	10 yrs	11 yrs	Adult
10°	3·8	4·9	3·6	2·7	2·9	2·5	2·0	1·0
20°	4·2	4·6	4·7	2·8	3·1	2·1	1·5	0·9
30°	3·9	5·2	3·7	3·2	2·9	2·6	1·5	0·5
40°	3·9	5·3	3·5	3·3	3·2	2·6	1·9	0·6
50°	3·3	4·1	3·6	3·1	3·1	2·3	1·9	1·0
60°	3·6	4·9	4·8	2·7	2·9	1·4	1·5	0·6
Overall mean	3·8	4·8	4·0	3·0	3·0	2·2	1·7	0·8

It can be seen that the range of errors for children of 5 and 6 years was three or four times as great as that for adults. The distribution of the mean errors also indicated that three stages mark the change to the adult pattern: between 5 and 6 years there is an increasing

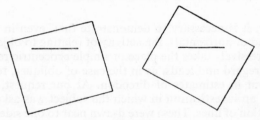

Fig. 46.

relation to the side of the figure; between 7 and 9 years a compromise occurs between relations with the figure and with the external frame of reference; at 10 to 11 years, or adulthood, the external frame of reference dominates.

In tachistoscopic presentation, however, the values shown in Table 75 were obtained.

TABLE 75. *Mean range of settings (degrees) as a function of exposure time (n = 15 for each age group)*

After Dadsetan (1960), Table 36

Inclination	10°		20°		40°	
Exposure (sec)	5 yrs	Adult	5 yrs	Adult	5 yrs	Adult
0·02	6·4	5·0	6·2	4·6	6·6	4·0
0·05	6·1	4·8	6·3	5·0	5·7	3·3
0·10	6·8	4·0	6·1	3·9	6·9	3·7
1·00	6·2	2·6	5·7	2·8	6·2	2·4

174

These results exhibit a greater range than those of Table 74, because of the impossibility of exploration, and an increasing difference between age groups as a function of increasing exposure times.

Another important fact is that when the size of the card on which the figures were drawn was increased, the range of the variation in error did not increase until about the age of 10 years. As soon as the subject began to refer to the external frame of reference, the range of variation increased because of the initial difficulty of this activity.

Table 76 shows the median and the range of errors for judgements made on a line drawn at 45° to the card and adjacent to the upper side of a square set on its corner and tilted through various angles, with step intervals of 2°.

TABLE 76. *Mean range of settings (S) and mean error (ES), in degrees, in matching an isolated line to a standard line drawn at an inclination of 45° and enclosed in a square inclined as shown (n = 20 for each age group)*

After Dadsetan (1960), Tables 52 and 53

Inclination of square	10°		40°		60°	
	S	ES	S	ES	S	ES
5 to 6 years	5·0	−1·8	5·5	−3·3	7·1	−1·6
7 to 8 years	3·2	0·6	4·2	0·6	4·1	−0·4
10 to 11 years	2·4	0·5	2·1	0·6	2·0	0·4
Adult	2·7	0·4	2·6	0·2	2·7	0

Once again there are noticeable differences between the medians and the ranges of error for adults and for children of 5 to 6 years. The differences in range were now less than they were with horizontals, mainly because the adults became far less precise.

But the problem which occupied our attention the most was the relation between the perceptual and the operational responses of children in corresponding situations, for example when they had to anticipate the orientation of the surface of water when the jar containing it was inclined.[1] Dadsetan found an excellent correlation between the two performances (which poses the problem of the filiation between perception and notions which we will take up in Chapter VII), which demonstrates the existence of an increasing reliance on distant references. The child was asked to predict the orientations of the water's surface, under four conditions. Dadsetan obtained the following percentages of correct response, shown by ages and obtained from the same subjects who contributed to the results listed in Table 74.

Age	5	6	7	8	9	10	11
% Success	29	41	46	58	62	71	83

The correlations between these results, obtained in response to

[1] Piaget, J., Inhelder, Bärbel, and Szeminska, Alina, *The Child's Conception of Geometry*, London, 1960, Routledge and Kegan Paul.

operational questions, and the errors shown in Table 74, were not significant at 5, 6 and 9 years, but were highly significant at 7, 8, 10 and 11 years. It thus seems that both in perceptual situations and in situations depending on reasoning, as tested, the subject tends to refer more and more to external references as he grows older. Young children of 5 to 6 years seem for the most part to ignore such distant comparisons while, in 9-year-olds, representational anticipation is ahead of perception.

§ 5. SPATIAL TRANSPORTS AND DIMENSIONAL TRANSPOSITIONS

When two elements of a figure are compared the eyes may move from one point to another on the same element, when we will refer to 'exploratory movements' in the strict sense, or they may move from one point on one element to a point on the other, or reciprocally, when we will refer to 'transports' in the strict sense. The function of exploration is to co-ordinate the centrations made on the one object in order to arrive at a perceptual estimate of its size. The function of transports, on the other hand, is to allow comparisons to be made between two objects (which, by definition, implies a reciprocal transport). In a broad sense, for example when a complex figure is involved or when the figure contains many elements, explorations and transports are constantly and inextricably intermingled. For this reason we have often spoken of transports in connection with explorations, but it is now time to examine the activity of transportation in its own right.

Two forms of transport, and of exploration for that matter, can be distinguished, depending on whether dimensions or directions are involved. That is why the examination of exploration in general (§§ 1 to 3) led on to that of the activity of referral (§ 4), in regard to which we spoke of directional explorations and transports, as well as of dimensional transports with changes in direction. We must now return to simple dimensional transports in order to identify the problems they raise.

We shall refer to 'transpositions' when the transport involves not just a dimension or a direction, but a collection of relations, for example, when a difference between two elements, L_1 and L_2, is compared with a difference between two others, say L_3 and L_4. All spatial transports and transpositions are therefore spatio-temporal because an eye-movement entails a before and an after in time as well as in space. There are, however, some purely temporal transports and transpositions, for example, when figures succeed one another in the same place, and these will be discussed in § 6.

I. Like all perceptual activities, transports and transpositions general-ly lead to a reduction in error, being factors of comparison and there-by of decentration. But the question we would like to tackle now is whether transports as such can also be sources of fresh error: do they lead to over- or under-estimations of the transported element, that is, the one which is carried over in vision to the other with which it is to be compared? We advanced this hypothesis in 1943,[1] but fresh results (particularly records of eye-movements) and improvements in our theoretical model (the introduction of encounters and of couplings) demand that the question be reopened.

In *Rech.* 2, a standard rod of 10 cm was compared with a variable of 7 to 13 cm situated at the various distances from it shown in Table 77. The error was negative at first (25/32 judgements at 3 cm, 132/180 at 25 cm) but then became positive, and continued to increase with the separation of the rods, as can be seen in Table 77.

TABLE 77. *Mean % error in estimates of the length of rods as a function of the separation between standard and variable*

Rech. 2 Table III

Separation (cm)	3	25	100	200	300
5 to 6 years ($n = 15$)	−0·12	−0·30	1·32	2·82	3·17
6 to 7 years ($n = 17$)	−0·15	0·48	1·47	1·90	3·34
Adult ($n = 16$)	0	−1·30	−0·40	0·90	1·30

It may be noted in passing that Tampieri[2] failed to obtain these results with adults: using a standard of 10 cm, he failed to find an under-estimation at small separations and obtained a diminished over-estimation at the greatest separation. On the other hand, he obtained negative errors at all distances with a standard of 50 cm. This seems to us to be equivalent to the under-estimation of an ele-ment of 10 cm at small separations because, if an adult can construct an implicit figure from a variable and a standard of 10 cm when they are separated by 1 cm (by erecting a virtual line between their sum-mits),[3] he would do so *a fortiori* between elements of 50 cm separated by 3 m. On the other hand, Tampieri found a distribution similar to ours when using a standard of 8 cm and small separations (a change from under- to over-estimations), but again with a diminution of over-estimations at greater distances, as if the elements then became inde-pendent.

However, the problem we wish to discuss concerning Table 77 is the following: given that the change in sign of the error with increas-ing separation is due to an error of the standard (Chapter II, § 1), is

[1] *Rech.* 2.
[2] Tampieri, G., *Rivist. di Psicol.*, 1955, **49**, 3–19.
[3] It may be remembered (Chapter I, § 1, I) that it is the ability to construct such figures that explains why the subject neglects the standard, centres on the vari-able, and consequently exhibits a negative error.

the general increase in the mean error that occurs with increasing separation due to transports as such or only to the effects that transports have on the distributions of centration?

If the first possibility is accepted and the changes are due to transports as such, the implication would be that the apparent length of the transported length is changed because of its transportation. This would not exclude supplementary effects of centration. By the second possibility, that transports affect the distributions of centration, the transport as such would not modify the transported element but would produce its effects in one of two ways. Either the element which is about to be transported would be over-estimated, because it therefore receives privileged centration; or the element on to which the first is about to be transported would be over-estimated, being privileged because the direction of transport is towards it and fixation often finally settles on it.

In *Rech.* 2, we opted for the first solution, and accepted the simultaneous intervention of an error of the standard and of a change in apparent size during the course of the transport. However, our present state of knowledge allows us to do without the second of these factors (but, of course, without excluding the possibility of its intervention) and to explain the results of Table 77 in terms of the two following factors only: (1) an error of the standard; (2) privileged centrations arising out of the organisation of transports (there being no need to suppose that a change occurs during the transports themselves).

Analysis of eye-movements reveals the following facts:

(*a*) When a subject compares two elements, eye-movements occur from one to the other and these may or may not be followed by return movements. If we consider each of these movements to represent a transport (that is, in stipulating for them a constant average duration and ignoring possible involuntary movements which were not made in the interests of the comparison), the transports may be said to be either reciprocal or not reciprocal.

(*b*) Generally speaking, elements judged to be equal evoke reciprocal transports and those judged to be unequal do not. For example, two horizontals placed symmetrically around the median plane occasioned a mean of 2·75 transports of which 50·3 % were from left to right and 49·7 % in the other direction (with the error of estimation being 0·2 %). In contrast, verticals in extension gave rise to a mean of 2·79 transports with 55·5 % in the direction of the upper element.

(*c*) In the case of judgements of inequality, and of non-reciprocal transports, it is generally the element towards which the transports are most frequent which is over-estimated. In the case of verticals (Table 61, p. 156) we saw that when the upper element was over-estimated the transports in an upward direction accounted for 55·5% of the total. In the case of obliques in extension (Table 64, p. 159) we saw that transports in an upward direction accounted for 53·3% (and 46·7% downward) of the total when the upper element was over-estimated. But when the lower element was over-estimated, the distributions were 39·5% in an upward and 60·5% in a downward direction. In the case of horizontals placed to the right and left of the median line, and in the case of a right-angle figure, the results were not always concordant, but this was compensated for by the distribution of centrations and above all (which is instructive) by the direction of the centrations immediately preceding the judgement.

It seems that the effects of non-reciprocal transports account for the fact that a non-returning transport gives rise to a final fixation on one of the elements and that this centration thereby favours that element (both in so far as it is centred last and that this last centration tips the balance of transport frequency in that direction). In other words, transports would, in principle, be instruments of compensation in so far as they push active couplings towards completion; but only to the extent that they are reciprocal. When not reciprocal, they give rise to incomplete couplings and to an excess of centrations and of encounters on that element in whose direction they are mostly aimed.

If this is so, the results shown in Table 77 are easily explained. (1) At small separations, when the standard and variable are simultaneously perceived, the variable may be over-estimated for a variety of reasons: the standard, being stable, no longer attracts the attention; the variable is simply more centred, without effects of transport (the error of the standard on the variable); or the standard is more frequently transported on to the variable, which favours the variable. (2) At greater separations, and progressively so, the standard and the variable are no longer simultaneously perceived and the standard is increasingly over-estimated because it has to be referred to repeatedly, as a result of which the dominant transport is in its direction.

It can be seen that this is a simpler explanation than that offered in *Rech.* 2. The effect of transports has been reduced to that of centrations and is assimilated to the error of the standard, which can now be considered under two forms: one due to unequal centrations, and the other to a lack of reciprocity of transports. But this lack of reciprocity is a more general phenomenon (of which the second form of the error of the standard is only a particular case) which gives rise to an inequality of centrations. Consequently everything can be reduced to the schema of encounters and of couplings, transports being simply defined as active couplings.

179

II. Now that the complex play of transports, which are compensatory when reciprocal and deforming when not, has been reduced to that of encounters and of couplings (of which it is only a new extension, following polarised explorations, etc.), it remains to be seen if spatio-temporal transpositions can be treated in the same way.

An experiment[1] was conducted with Lambercier in which children and adults were presented with four rods, $A < B_1 = B_2 < C$, of which the first three were kept constant in length while C varied. Subjects were asked to judge which of the variables, presented in succession, satisfied the equation $B_1 - A = C - B_2$. This is a simple question of the transposition of differences, and was examined as a

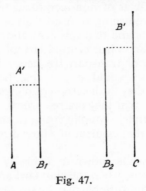

Fig. 47.

function of age, of the distance between B_1 and B_2, and of the absolute value of the difference standard, $B_1 - A$. Orders of presentation were varied, as was the identity of the difference standard (it being either $B_1 - A = A'$ or $C - B_2 = B'$).

The full details of the results may be seen in the original publication and we will limit ourselves here to a presentation of results obtained with the $A - B_1$ differences and the separations shown in Table 78. The order of presentation was that shown in the table and results obtained with standards A' and B' are shown separately.

TABLE 78. *Mean errors (mm) in the transpositions of differences in length*
Rech. 15, Experiments I and IV, Table 1

B—A	2 cm			4 cm			6 cm			2 cm (final)
B_1—B_2	4	50	100	4	50	100	4	50	100	100
Standard A										
6 to 7 years ($n = 12$)	0·3	1·1	1·6	−5·9	−4·0	−3·5	−9·7	−8·8	−7·5	2·1
7 to 8 years ($n = 10$)	−0·5	−0·2	−0·1	−2·4	−1·6	0	−2·5	−2·1	−2·6	1·1
Adult ($n = 14$)	−0·3	0·4	0	2·9	2·6	1·6	5·2	4·2	2·9	0
Standard B										
6 to 7 years ($n = 12$)	−0·3	0	−0·3	−5·8	−5·6	−4·5	−9·3	−9·8	−10·6	2·0
7 to 8 years ($n = 10$)	−0·7	−0·9	−1·5	−3·5	−3·5	−2·5	−5·4	−4·2	−4·3	0·7
Adult ($n = 14$)	−0·7	−1·0	−0·8	−1·2	−0·3	0	−2·5	−3·0	−3·0	0·5

[1] *Rech.* 15.

It can be seen that adults under-estimated[1] the difference B' when A' was the standard, but over-estimated A' when the difference standard was B'. This reversal would be predicted from a consideration of relative centrations because a difference of 2, 4 or 6 cm is not perceptually the same when related to elements of different lengths. This can be expressed as follows:

At 2 cm: $A' = 0\cdot25/A$ and $B' = 0\cdot20/B$.
At 4 cm: $A' = 0\cdot66/A$ and $B' = 0\cdot40/B$.
At 6 cm: $A' = 1\cdot5/A$ and $B' = 0\cdot60/B$.

It can be seen that the difference A' is always relatively greater than the same absolute difference B', which will thus appear shorter. When A' is given and B' has to be selected, a larger B' will be selected, whence the positive error. If B' is the standard and A' has to be selected, a smaller A' will be selected.

The sign of the results obtained with children varied with order. When the order of presentation was 2, 4, 6, and A' had to be chosen, the errors were negative, as with adults. When B' had to be chosen, they were still negative, while adults' errors became positive. When the order was 6, 4, 2, and B' was to be selected, the error for A' was negative and the remainder were positive, etc. These differences from the adult pattern are due to different temporal effects. In the adult, the order of presentation produced a slight temporal contrast effect: small initial differences reinforced the larger ones which followed, while initial large differences reduced the effects of succeeding smaller ones. With children, however, it is as if temporal effects took the form of perseverations: when a start was made with the standard $A' = 2$ cm, the child continued to transpose differences of the same order when A' became 4 or 6 cm, and this resulted in negative errors; starting with a standard of $B' = 2$ cm, the same effect occurred. With an initial standard difference of $A' = 6$ cm, children seemed to perseverate with the greater difference when faced with real differences of 4 and 2 cm, whence their positive errors.

It is true that these temporal errors of children could be explained by the same law of contrast which was applied to the temporal errors of adults, but applied to the variable rather than to the standard differences. But this would only be another way of saying that children neglect new difference standards while perseverating with earlier ones. Further examples of similar temporal reactions in children will be given in § 6.

In conclusion, spatial transpositions, like spatio-temporal trans-

---

[1] A positive error indicates that the difference B' (chosen) is greater than A' (actual). In other words, B' is under-estimated. A negative error indicates that A' (chosen) is smaller than B' (actual) when B' is the standard.

ports, constitute an active coupling at a distance, and the accompanying errors exhibit the general processes of relative centrations. In the particular case, where a difference is given and one equal to it has to be selected, an error of the standard also occurs which, of course, influences the temporal effects above all: when the difference standard is eliminated, for instance leaving B_1 and B_2 equal and constant, and both A and C are simultaneously changed on each trial, the temporal error disappears entirely in children.[1]

§ 6. TEMPORAL TRANSPORTS AND SO-CALLED ABSOLUTE IMPRESSIONS

Transports and transpositions are not only spatio-temporal, relating two or more elements that are more or less separated in space, but may be simply temporal, relating elements which occupy the same position in succession. We have already claimed that transpositions of differences, such as those studied in § 5, are accompanied by effects of succession which we shall refer to as temporal transports or transpositions. This claim must now be studied.

We must first distinguish between temporal effects of centration (a function of the time during which an element is presented or of which element is presented last) and temporal transports. The first are concerned with single elements or, when a comparison between successively presented elements is involved, consist in momentary effects of the second element which partially cancel effects of the first. Temporal transports, like spatial transports, concern the effects that the dimensional estimates made of one element have on the dimensional estimates made of the next. These effects can occur even when there has been no intention of making a comparison, or when a given element is compared with variants of itself or, again, when a given element is compared with successive variables in ascending or descending order of magnitude.

We must also distinguish between two sorts of temporal transports. The first apply to immediate successions and have the effect either of reinforcing dimensional inequalities where they exist (particularly in the case of differences which have an order of succession) or of facilitating explorations where one set of elements is presented several times in succession (we shall not return to this case: the findings reported in § 2 of this chapter are attributable as much to these transports as to exploration). The second apply to successions at increasing temporal intervals and constitute the vehicle of prior perceptual experience: it is these in particular which explain scalar effects, whereby a given element can be classed as either 'large' or 'small' (the

[1] *Rech.* 15, Experiment V, Table 1.

182

so-called impression of absolute size) as a function of the collection of similar elements which have been perceived previously.

I. Let us first examine temporal transports which involve immediate succession. The best-known example is that produced by the psychophysical method of limits with ascending and descending trials, as opposed to the concentric or constant stimulus methods. The different results obtained with ascending and descending orders both attest to the presence of temporal transports and provide an indirect measurement of their effects. An example, obtained in *Rech.* 10, is presented in Table 79. A hatched line of 5 cm (*A*) was measured against a set of non-hatched lines of varying lengths (*B*1 to *B*13 = 4 to 7 cm) and the same measurements were made, for control purposes, with an unhatched line of 5 cm.

TABLE 79. *Mean % error in the comparison of hatched (A) and unhatched (B) lines as a function of the order of presentation*

Rech. 17, Tables 2a and 2b

		Order	Experimental	Control
		Asc.	8·47	—
	5 to 7 years (*n* = 27)	Desc.	8·62	—
		Diff.	0·15	—
Group 1				
		Asc.	3·75	—
	Adult (*n* = 18)	Desc.	9·65	—
		Diff.	5·90	—
		Asc.	2·94	−2·34
	5 to 7 years (*n* = 17)	Desc.	8·74	1·90
		Diff.	5·84	4·24
Group 2				
		Asc.	4·38	0·54
	Adult (*n* = 14)	Desc.	10·20	3·03
		Diff.	5·82	2·50

The results suggest that the variables presented in an ascending order (*B*1 to *B*13) were progressively over-estimated as a result of the contrast set up between successive small elements and succeeding larger ones. In descending order, the variables are under-estimated because the succession is from larger to smaller.

The results presented in Table 79 show that, in the first series of measurements, the temporal transports have much clearer effects on adults than on children. That the effects then increase markedly in children in the second series seems to indicate that the effects of temporal relations increase rapidly with practice.

II. Another example of the differences and similarities between children and adults in respect of temporal transports occurs when absolute judgements are called for.[1] In a piece of research which we have not yet published, conducted with Lambercier, we asked children and adults to classify a series of nine rods, measuring from 5 to 12 cm

[1] Well known since the study of Hollingworth, H. L., *J. Phil.*, 1910, 7, 461–469.

(presented in the order 5, 12, 8, 11, 6, 7, 10, 5, 9, 12), as long or short. We were thus able to calculate the neutral point of the series. We then recommenced the series but this time with a range extending from 6 to 13 cm, then from 7 to 14 cm, 8 to 15 cm and 9 to 16 cm (all in the corresponding order). When this had been done, the first series (5 to 12 cm) was presented again. The sequence was reversed for two new groups of subjects, of 5 to 6 years and adults only. The results are shown in Table 80 in which we also show the arithmetic means, M, the proportional means, $Mp = \sqrt[2]{ah}$, and the geometric means, $M_g = \sqrt[8]{abcdefgh}$.

TABLE 80. *Successive estimates of neutral points (mm) as a function of order of presentation (I–V or V–I). Successive means (see text) shown for comparison*

Series		I	II	III	IV	V	I
	Order						
5 to 6 years	I–V	85·2	90·7	96·0	103·2	108·7	109·4
	V–I	94·6	100·7	106·5	114·3	121·8	—
6 to 7 years	I–V	82·3	87·5	94·8	98·1	104·1	105·8
	V–I	—	—	—	—	—	—
7 to 8 years	I–V	82·5	85·2	90·5	94·5	100·7	98·2
	V–I	—	—	—	—	—	—
Adult	I–V	78·7	82·3	88·7	90·4	92·5	93·2
	V–I	104·7	109·3	113·3	117·5	122·2	—
	M	85	95	105	115	125	85
	Mg	81·8	92·1	102·4	112·6	122·9	81·5
	Mp	77·4	88·2	99·0	109·5	120	77·4

The most striking fact to emerge from the above results is that the displacement of the neutral point from one series to another decreases with age: the shift from series I to series V was 23·5 mm at 5 to 6 years, 21·8 mm at 6 to 7 years, 18·2 mm at 7 to 8 years and 13·8 mm for adults. From series V to series I it was 27·2 mm at 5 to 6 years and 17·5 mm for adults. It can therefore be seen that subjects pay more and more attention to preceding series as they grow older and that young subjects are more influenced by elements of the series actually being judged.

The geometric mean, M_g, of all successive contributions of series I to V (namely, I to II, I to II–III, II to III, etc.) can be calculated and can be compared with the neutral points which were obtained experimentally. We find that, in ascending order, adults produced a neutral point in series IV of 90·4 mm, which corresponds to the M_g of series I to IV taken together, namely 90·5 mm; at the end of the whole series (I repeated after V), the neutral point for adults was 93·2 mm and the overall M_g for I to V was also 93·2 mm. However, the neutral point for subjects of 5 to 6 years for series III was intermediate between those of series III and II to III taken together. At series V (and after the final repetition of I) the neutral point for subjects of 5 to 6 years was equivalent to the M_g of series III to V combined (109 mm). A progressive extension of temporal effects is observed between the ages of

184

5 to 6 years and adulthood: for example, the neutral point for subjects of 7 to 8 years for series V was equivalent to the M_g of series II to V combined (101·2 mm), which indicates a superior temporal effect to that of subjects of 5 to 6 years but inferior to that of adults. (Calculations based on M_p lead, of course, to the same conclusions, with a simple displacement of the values.)

The calculations are not the same in the descending series because the two orders of succession are not mathematically symmetrical: the difference between the geometric mean of I (81·8 mm) and that of I to V combined (93·2 mm) is 11·4 mm, but the difference between the M_g of V (122·9 mm) and of I to V combined is 29·7 mm. Nevertheless, the same conclusions emerge from the descending series (V to I), but in weaker form: the adult neutral point for I (104·7 mm) approximates to the M_g for series V to II combined (101·2 mm) while the same point (I) for the children of 5 to 6 years (94·6 mm) approximates to the M_g for III to II (95·3 mm). The explanation of these shifts is, no doubt, that in the ascending series the early (short) elements produce an over-estimation of the following (larger) ones while, in the descending series, the larger elements, coming first, produce an under-estimation of the smaller ones which follow. The gradual over-estimation of the larger elements from 9 to 16 cm in ascending order has no effect on the classifications, because M_g I to V is 93·2 mm. But later elements are under-estimated in descending order (increasingly after 12 cm and progressively as temporal effects increase with age). As a result, there is an increasing disparity between the M_g and the adult subjective point: the M_g V to I of 93·2 mm no longer corresponds subjectively to an interval between elements of 9 and 10 cm but rather to a higher one.

These scalar effects demonstrate that temporal transports exist between successively presented elements of a single collection (intra-scalar effects) and that these transports are sufficiently active to give rise to neutral points that approximate to proportional or even to geometric means. Furthermore, these scalar effects prove that collections of elements act on one another in accordance with the order of temporal succession (inter-scalar effects). This is a function of development because adult temporal transports take account of the whole set while those of children of 5 to 6 years do so, of immediately preceding series only. These inter-scalar effects are, of course, of great importance in daily life: a 'small' ant, a 'small' dog and a 'small' elephant correspond to very different neutral points in each of the three classes.

These results supplement those shown in Table 79 in showing that temporal transports increase in importance with age. They go further, however, in demonstrating that these temporal transports constitute genuine perceptual activities: they consist in active processes of

185

relating, not simply in automatic associations between 'traces' which are passively conserved. The observed increase with age would be difficult to explain on the basis of simple traces which are related solely as a function of repetition and of persistence when the child's memory is more malleable (but less well organised) than the adult's. To the extent, however, that temporal transports constitute a special case of relating at increasing distances in space and time, a characteristic of perceptual activities, it can be understood why they should develop with age in the double sense of attaining a greater frequency and of encompassing greater spatio-temporal distances.

The above interpretations receive further support from all perceptual situations which involve anticipations, which are a special form of extended temporal transports. We will now examine one of many possible examples of these.

§ 7. PERCEPTUAL ANTICIPATIONS

As transports become systematised or extended in time and space, they give rise to anticipatory attitudes (Einstellung effects) or to real anticipations. When an element is transported on to another, there is no reason why any particular size relationship should be anticipated. But if earlier comparisons had been made in which $A = B = C$, or $A < B < C$, the transport of C on to D would be accompanied by an expectation that $C = D$ or that $C < D$. This expectancy is analogous to those which Tolman introduced with good reason into his theory of learning. The problem is to find out if these anticipations are activities which increase with age or if they are only residual primary effects, such as the 'after-effects' of Köhler and Wallach.[1]

A well-known example of anticipation is found in the 'size–weight' illusion in which the larger of two boxes of equal weight appears lighter when they are lifted under standard conditions. No doubt the anticipation of a proportionality between weight and volume (which, in this case, is followed by a contrast effect when the anticipation is not confirmed) is not the only factor involved in this illusion, but it does seem to be a necessary condition. For instance, imbeciles do not appear to experience the illusion, no doubt because of the absence of any previsions concerning the relation between weight and volume. Rey has also shown[2] that the size–weight illusion increases with age up to about 11 to 12 years, and thereafter declines slightly.

Usnadze[3] created a visual equivalent to the illusion in order to study the factor of anticipation without involving muscular effects.

[1] Köhler, W., and Wallach, H., *Proc. Amer. Philos. Soc.*, 1944, **88**, 269–357.
[2] Rey, A., *Arch. Psychol.*, 19, **22**, 285.
[3] Usnadze, D., *Psychol. Forsch.*, 1930, **14**, 366.

The subject was shown a pair of unequal circles a large number of times, in a tachistoscope. The two circles always occupied the same relative positions. This was followed by the presentation of a pair of equal circles, intermediate in size between the first pair and again in the same relative positions. The subject saw these circles as unequal, the one occupying the position of the previously larger circle being seen as smaller.

We made a comparison of these anticipatory effects in children and adults, with Lambercier. The inducing figures were two circles, *A* and *C*, of 20 and 28 mm diameter. They were presented tachisto-scopically three times, after which a series of pairs of circles, *B*1 and *B*2, were substituted. *B*1 was of constant size, 24 mm, while *B*2, which alternately occupied the right and left position, varied between 17 and 24 mm. Subjects were required to equate *B*1 and *B*2 for apparent size. These measurements were repeated four times (*F*1 to *F*4). After *F*4, residual effects were measured by means of ten successive trials on *B*1 and *B*2 (*E*1 to *E*10) with precautions taken not to enhance or to weaken the effect. The results obtained are shown in Table 81.

TABLE 81. *Mean % error (on standard of 24 mm) with the Usnadze figure. Values in parenthesis represent the error as % of the error at Trial 4 (n = 5 to 6 years, 28 and 20; 6 to 7 years, 30 and 22; adults, 32 and 20 for F and E trials respectively)*

Rech. 5, Tables III and V

Trial	F_1	F_2	F_3	F_4	E_1	E_2	E_3
5 to 6 years	2·5 (36)	4·6 (58)	6·2 (77)	8·3 (100)	6·7 (81)	5·4 (66)	5·0 (65)
6 to 7 years	2·9 (34)	5·8 (63)	7·5 (85)	9·2 (100)	6·2 (63)	4·6 (46)	4·2 (38)
Adult	5·0 (42)	7·5 (66)	10·4 (92)	11·3 (100)	9·0 (76)	7·9 (67)	6·7 (56)

Trial	E_4	E_5	E_6	E_7	E_8	E_9	E_{10}
5 to 6 years	5·0 (63)	4·6 (64)	3·9 (55)	3·7 (52)	3·9 (52)	3·7 (50)	4·2 (53)
6 to 7 years	3·7 (34)	3·3 (31)	2·9 (26)	2·5 (21)	2·1 (19)	2·1 (20)	1·7 (13)
Adult	6·2 (52)	4·6 (42)	4·2 (35)	3·3 (30)	2·5 (24)	2·3 (20)	2·1 (16)

Transfer effects were also examined as follows. Trials *F*1 to *F*4 were run as before (with three presentations of *A* and *C*) and were followed by *F*5 in which measurement was made on two squares, the standard square having sides of 24 mm; *F*6 followed with measurement on two squares rotated to stand on one corner; then *F*7, with the usual circles, and finally *F*8 with two filled-in circles. Results of this investigation are set out in Table 82.

TABLE 82. *Mean % error transferred to squares and to inked-in circles. Values in parenthesis represent transferred error as % of the error at Trial F4*

Rech. 82, Table VIII

Trial	F4	F5	F6	F7	F8
5 to 6 years (n = 8)	1·9 ⎫	1·4 ⎫	1·3 ⎫	2·1 ⎫	1·8 ⎫
6 to 7 years (n = 8)	1·7 ⎬ (100)	1·1 ⎬ (60)	1·6 ⎬ (64)	2·2 ⎬ (100)	1·7 ⎬ (81)
Adult (n = 12)	2·6 (100)	1·4 (54)	1·9 (73)	2·6 (100)	2·14 (82)

Two important facts stand out: (1) the effects of anticipation increased more rapidly in adults than in children, and achieved a higher level at $F4$, as did the effects of transfer; (2) in children, however, the effects lasted longer, so that the child exhibited a greater error than the adult between trials $E7$ and $E10$. These findings, both individually and taken together, are very characteristic of an activity having a double aspect of reinforcement with age and of increasing regulation with age, in the sense of a damping or a gradual extinction when the anticipation is not confirmed (in this case by the presentation of equal circles). The fact that anticipation correlates with transfer and that transfer varied with the figure used (it was strongest for filled-in circles, intermediate for squares standing on one corner and weakest for squares standing on one side), suggests the same interpretation.

These facts might, of course, be interpreted in terms of Köhler's figural after-effects, that is, by explaining apparent distances in terms of electrical resistances in brain tissue and of changes in those resistances brought about by satiation. As it is claimed by Köhler that the child exhibits a weak permanent satiation and that his less efficient fixations (self-satiation) give rise to a more widely spread area of weak satiation, his theory would be able to explain the weakness of the illusion at 5 to 6 years. Furthermore, as satiation due to the inspection of a figure is only a momentary and local increase in permanent satiation, the recovery of equilibrium (marked by the duration of the extinction of the effect) would be a homeostatic process which would be more rapid in the adult because of his higher level of permanent satiation. The theory would thus explain both the differences with age in the extent of the Usnadze illusion, and in the rate of its extinction. We would have no objection to raise to this account (leaving aside the theory's special neurological difficulties such as the problem of the relation between areas of satiation in the two occipital lobes, etc.) except that Köhler denies the effects of practice or of activity on the level of satiation. If, however, his theory could be completed by the addition of a functional dimension, through the notion of self-satiation (dependent on centration), it would no longer contradict the main results of Tables 81 and 82. These results show that the tendency to relate successive figures more rapidly and more strongly is followed by a more efficient recovery (damping by extinction). All these tendencies develop with age. Whether this anticipatory activity, whose accompanying regulatory mechanism tends towards reversibility, does or does not rest on the homeostatic properties of permanent satiation is a problem for psycho-physiology and one on which we do not need to offer an opinion: the relational characteristics of these anticipations and regulations are adequate for the purpose of drawing comparisons between these effects and other aspects of perceptual activities.

§ 8. DEFORMING AND COMPENSATORY SCHEMATISATIONS

Nearly all the perceptual activities so far considered, explorations, referrals, transports and transpositions (either simple or with changes in direction), consist in genuine sensory-motor activities, that is to say, entail the intervention of motor activity over and above the organisation of the sense data. All repeatable sensory-motor activities give rise to schematisation in the sense that whenever actions are repeated, a generalisation occurs on the basis of common structures or schemes to which new situations are assimilated in so far as they are equivalent to those which gave rise to the schemes. It is to be expected, therefore, that perceptual activities entailing motor activity will also give rise to the formation of perceptual schemes. Even perceptual activities which do not necessarily entail eye-movements (such as the temporal transports or anticipations which have just been discussed) involve links between earlier and later perceptions and this in itself is also conducive to the formation of perceptual schemes. Furthermore, as Francès[1] has shown, the perception of sounds and of music implies the intervention of a whole series of perceptual activities (including decentring, relating, transporting, transposing, etc.), in the absence of any exploratory movements of the ear comparable to those of functional significance in visual perceptual activity. This implies that the operational concepts which we employ, from centration to schematisation, should receive a 'central' neurological interpretation. This interpretation, according to the modality involved, would be either self-sufficient or would require to be completed by the description of peripheral concomitants.

With the above in mind, the facts of perceptual schematisation can be divided into four classes in a double-entry table, the divisions being between empirical and geometric schemes on the one hand and deforming or compensatory schemes on the other. An example of an empirical scheme would be Brunswik's 'empirical Gestalt'; and while it is true that all geometric good forms need not constitute schemes at all ages (because they can arise in primary field effects) it will be claimed (in II below) that they do give rise to genuine schemes as development progresses. The same schemes, whether empirical or geometrical, may be either deforming or compensatory. They may contain deforming aspects because all perceptual activities, whether they give rise to stable schematisations or not, can also have secondary illusory consequences. Perceptual schemes can also be compensatory because their laws of organisation or of equilibrium tend to

[1] In his thesis: *La Perception de la Musique*, Paris, 1960, Vrin.

compensate deformations, as in the case of secondary or schematised good forms. This can also apply in the case of certain empirical schemes when their properties, imposed by experience, involve certain geometric aspects, such as equivalent symmetries in animal and vegetable forms.

I. We have not investigated empirical schemes specifically, but some investigations do exist and may be related to the notions just advanced. In a well-known experiment, Brunswik presented, tachistoscopically, a form which was intermediate between an open hand, with fingers spread, and a sort of fan, or bundle of rays, with five spokes geometrically and stiffly spread. He asked his adult subjects to choose between these possibilities in identifying what they had seen. About 50% indicated each form, which demonstrates the existence of two sorts of pregnancies, one tending to modify the data towards a geometric form and the other towards a familiar, but not symmetrical, form.

The role of empirical schemes, with their pregnancies founded on previous experience, is of prime importance in every-day perception. When Bruner[1] maintains that perception is above all the identification of the object as a member of a class ('this is an orange'), and when he describes this act as one of categorisation, he is, of course, forced to introduce among others, a 'temporal scheme' between the indices which the subject has registered ('input') and the class to which the perceived object is finally attributed. The essential function of this temporal scheme is the organisation of the indices. As the class as such is not perceptible, and as it cannot intervene in the mechanism of perception, it has to be admitted that some form of generalisation intervenes, after perception, between the perceived object and its conceptual interpretation. This element of generalisation is distinct from the class because it has to do only with those properties available to perceptual activity (as opposed to abstraction, quantification as 'all' and 'some', etc.). This element is constituted by what may be called a scheme which results exclusively from the actions of earlier perceptions on later ones. The choice of object for perception is, of course, influenced by a conceptual framework.[2]

In other words, empirical perceptual schemes are first and foremost products of temporal transports and of transpositions which are analogous to those we saw at work in scalar effects (§ 6, II) and which terminate in relations whose associations or pregnancies are, in part, a function of the number of objects previously perceived.

[1] Bruner, J. S., Bresson, F., Morf, A. et Piaget, J., *Logique et Perception*, Etudes d'Epistémologie Génétique, **6**, Paris, 1958, P.U.F.
[2] See Bresson, F., in Bruner, J. S., *et al., Logique et Perception, op. cit.*

For example, the head of a Negro with an aquiline nose would not be striking unless a previous number of experiences had established the association 'flat nose + black skin', but the lack of trueness of an even slightly misshapen square is immediately apparent. However, the number of previous perceptions, by itself, is far from decisive, because temporal transpositions are not just automatic events but are activities which depend on the subject's interests, etc., and on his ability to co-ordinate. For example, the present author can still, after a break of forty years in the practice of zoology, immediately distinguish between two forms of terrestial mollusc at a distance of 2 to 3 m, but would need to apply a much more attentive and close examination to distinguish between two garden flowers. On the other hand, since transpositions give rise to schemes on the basis of similarities, it follows that their effects will also depend on the facility with which a person can co-ordinate properties of objects into coherent wholes.

Thus described, empirical perceptual schemes are not concepts or classes, even if the choice of the objects to which transpositions are to be applied is itself directed by the subject's activity as a whole, particularly by his notional systems which provide a framework for the perceptual schemes. We have introduced the notion of the activity of schematisation because temporal transports and transpositions which give rise to perceptual schemes entail, *pari passu* with their construction, a new activity which is comparable to a form of implication in the large sense, or of 'pre-implication'. For instance, if the characteristics of an object are taken to be a, b and c, c will be anticipated if a and b are perceived: for example, 'black skin' and 'crinkly hair' leading to the anticipation of 'flat nose'.[1] The anticipation in question remains perceptual of course, and is not a form of a conceptual judgement or mental image, but simply a recognition of the overall form when veridical, or of surprise when not. Perceptual pre-inferences to which we shall return later (Chapter VII, § 4) are made possible by these pre-implications.

II. Geometric perceptual schemes exhibit the same properties as empirical schemes except that the relations between the characteristics of perceived objects consist of simple proportions, with a predominance of equivalences and symmetries. Two distinctions need to be made. The first is between what one might, with Gestalt theory, call primary good forms and what we consider to be secondary schemes. The second is between deforming and compensating geometric schematisations.

[1] In regard to musical perception, Francès speaks in this connection of 'condensation' (alluding to the chemical sense of the word) to describe the way in which a theme is recognised on the basis of a restricted number of initial notes.

We will start with the second distinction, already alluded to at the beginning of this section. A geometric scheme is usually compensatory in the sense that the equivalences and symmetries that characterise it give rise to an homogenisation of encounters and couplings and consequently to a compensation of momentary errors which result from effects of centration. But in some cases geometric schematisations can be sources of systematic deformation. For example, as perceptual co-ordinates progressively give rise to a schematisation, so does an increasing conflict between verticals and horizontals give rise to a consolidation of the polarisation analysed in § 3 (which explains the remarkable difference in error between adults and young children when the vertical is being judged tachistoscopically with fixation on the horizontal). But there is no reason why a scheme of co-ordinates that deforms dimensions in this way should not have a compensatory effect when judgements of direction are involved.

With this in mind, and without saying anything yet about the genetic filiation between primary effects and perceptual activities, including schematisations, it is clear that a geometric good form can correspond to primary effects: a square standing on one side and presented tachistoscopically gives rise immediately to a specific perception which is dominated by the equality of the sides and by the perpendicularity of adjacent sides, or by the fact that opposite sides are parallel. But the problem remains of whether these primary effects, which give rise to a quasi-instantaneous compensation of errors of centration, reappear at another level of schematisation and are responsible for events which we are about to examine.

Firstly, a subject can recognise a familiar geometric form in the same way that he recognises a hand or a bird. Secondly, recognising it, he will bring pre-implications and anticipations into play (detectable as soon as the duration of exposure of the figure is long enough): for instance, it would be very difficult to know if a subject had distinctly perceived the equality of the angles of a square or if the equality had been perceived only by implication from the immediately recognised global form. Thirdly, and above all, his explorations and transports will be guided by these implications when the perception is equivocal, for example, when the squareness of a figure is found to be in conflict with other factors. It is this systematic exploration which, by its presence or absence, will suggest the existence of a secondary scheme superimposed on the primary good form.

This hypothesis was tested, with Maire and Privat[1] in the following experiment which was inspired by a posthumous article by Rubin[2] on the conflict between good forms and deforming factors. We presented subjects with squares whose upper and lower sides were em-

[1] *Rech.* 18.   [2] Rubin, E., *Acta Psychol.*, 1950, 7, 365–87.

bellished with the inward facing and outward facing barbs of the Müller–Lyer figure, as depicted in Fig. 48 A. Subjects were asked to compare the sides when the upper one measured 5 cm and the lower

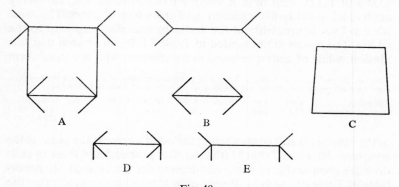

Fig. 48.

one varied from 4·4 to 8 cm. This illusion, to be called the Rubin effect, *Ru* in Table 83, was compared with the following illusions:

Mu C: a simple Müller–Lyer figure of the same dimensions as the square, with the vertical sides omitted.

Mu G: the same Müller–Lyer figure but with three vertical separations (5, 10 and 20 cm, the first being identical with *MuC*).

C: the Rubin figure matched with independent squares and trapezia drawn by the experimenter.

The order of presentation was MuC_1, $MuG5$, $MuG10$, $MuG20$, Ru_1, C, Ru_2, MuC_2. The results are set out in Table 83.

TABLE 83. *Mean % error on the figures indicated as a function of age*

Rech. 18, Table 2

Figure	MuC_1	MuC_2	MuG_5	MuG_{10}	MuG_{20}	Ru_1	C	Ru_2
4 to 6 years ($n = 36$)*	40·8	39·2	38·4	36·0	34·2	16·6	5·6	13·4
7 to 8 years ($n = 30$)	30·8	25·8	26·4	25·6	25·6	7·4	4·3	6·4
9 to 10 years ($n = 29$)	22·6	19·4	20·4	21·4	23·6	6·2	3·8	5·4
Adult ($n = 25$)	21·8	17·2	17·8	22·2	23·2	3·2	2·0	2·6

* Four of 4 years, 17 of 5 years, 15 of 6 years.

It can be seen that measurements made on the sides of the square (Ru_1 and Ru_2, and C) indicate a much weaker illusion at all ages than that obtained with the Müller–Lyer figure, but with some variations to which we shall return. However, before accepting the idea that the reduction in the illusion was due to the influence of the good form, we should mention a possible objection which was not discussed in the original publication. Our colleague Jonckheere pointed out that the reduction in the illusion might be due rather to the lines of reference which are perpendicular to the lines to be judged. To meet this objection, we presented, with the assistance of Mme Vinh-Bang, Figs. 48D and E ($D = 50$ mm, E varying from 50 to 80 mm) to twenty adults and to thirty-five children aged from 6 to 12 years. The same Müller–Lyer figure, without the verticals, was also presented to the adults. The results are presented in Table 84. It can be seen that this illusion, while of course reduced in comparison with the usual form

TABLE 84. *Mean % error with figures D and E (Fig. 48) as a function of age. Values in parenthesis represent adult errors with the classical Müller–Lyer figure (n = 20 adults and 35 children)*

Age group	6 yrs	7 yrs	8 yrs	9 yrs	10 yrs	11 yrs	12 yrs	Adult
Mean % error	22·1	18·8	22·2	22·2	23·2	23·0	22·2	17·2±3·7 (28·6±7·2)

of the illusion, is still considerable: the adult's error is the same as for condition $Mu\ C_2$ of Table 83 (that is, after practice) and those of children are comparable to those obtained under the various Mu conditions of Table 83 for 9- to 10-year-olds. It thus becomes clear that the reduction in illusion from conditions Ru_1 to Ru_2 of Table 83, in comparison to the level of the illusion in its usual form (Mu), is due to the good form of the square, of which the perpendiculars are only one aspect.

If adults and children are compared in respect of the Rubin effect (Ru_1 and Ru_2) and the Müller–Lyer effect ($MuC + MuG$), the values set out in Table 85 are obtained.

TABLE 85. *Ratio of child to adult mean error with the Rubin figure (for n see Table 83)*

Rech. 18, Table 8

Figure	Ru_1	Ru_2	$Ru_{1+2}/2$	$MuC + MuG/2$
4 to 6 years/adult	5·10	5·10	5·10	1·78
7 to 8 years/adult	2·31	2·46	2·38	1·28
9 to 10 years/adult	1·93	2·07	2·00	1·03

It can be seen that the Rubin effect is four times stronger in children of 4 to 6 years than it is in adults, while the ratio for the Müller–Lyer illusion is 1·78, which indicates that the resistance of the square increases considerably with age and that a secondary factor of schematisation comes to the aid of the primary good form. To establish this interesting fact with more precision, an attempt has been made to determine the quantitative value of this resistance.

The relative Rubin effect, RuR, as opposed to the absolute Rubin effect, RuA, will be defined as $RuA : MuC$. RuR is 0·39 at 4 to 6 years, 0·25 at 7 to 10 years, 0·13 at adulthood, that is, three times as great at 4 to 6 years as at adulthood. The resistance of the good form, RF, will be defined as the inverse ratio $MuC : RuA$. This was calculated separately for the values of $MuC_1 : Ru_1$; $MuG_5 : Ru_1$; etc. and $MuC : Ru_2$, etc., and the results are set out in Table 86.

TABLE 86. *Mean % resistance of the square to deformation and the adult/child ratio for that resistance* (*for n see Table* 83)

Rech. 18, Tables 10 and 11

	Mean % resistance			Adult/child
	Ru_1	Ru_2	$Ru_{1+2}/2$	ratio
4 to 6 years	2·25	2·72	2·47	2·98
7 to 8 years	3·60	4·25	3·92	1·88
9 to 10 years	3·50	4·00	3·75	1·96
Adult	6·60	8·15	7·37	—

Thus the resistance of the square increases by a factor of 3 from 2·47 at 4 to 6 years to 7·37 at adulthood.

An additional procedure was adopted to test the above conclusions. In this, the threshold (to be more precise, the half-threshold) was obtained for comparisons between trapezia, such as that shown in Fig. 48C, and a square (as in Condition C). There were nine trapezia of different degrees of deviation from the square. The thresholds obtained by this means are set out in Table 87.

TABLE 87. *Mean threshold* (%) *for matching a square with trapezia* (*Fig.* 48c) *as a function of age* (*for n, see Table* 83)

Rech. 18, Tables 4 (EC) and 7

Age group	4–6 yrs	7–8 yrs	9–10 yrs	Adult
Threshold	12·0	7·2	6·0	3·6
Adult/child ratio	3·33	2·00	1·66	—

Once again, it can be seen that the adult's discrimination is about three times as good as that of children of 4 to 6 years, which approximates to the value obtained for the resistance of the square.

It should be noted that the results set out in Table 87 cannot be interpreted in isolation: to say that a child sees a square when an adult sees a trapezium (even with full precautions taken against verbal misunderstandings) could mean either that the good form of a square has greater pregnance for young children or that it is more elastic. Elastic is used here in the opposite sense of having analytical mobility, elasticity being a function of the syncretism described in § 1 of this chapter, that is, of the indissociability of the parts which make up the whole. Mobility, on the other hand, is a function of their dissociation as a result of the multiple relations in which they are involved. A comparison of Tables 85 and 86 with 87 shows that the extended threshold of the child is indeed an expression of elasticity and not of the resistance of a good form which is still subordinated to primary factors. It can now be understood why the results of the measurements made under Condition *C* of Table 83 are so much better than those of measurements made under Ru_1 and Ru_2 and why they cannot be used in the calculation of the resistance, *RF*, (Table 86): the results obtained in Condition *C* simply mean that an overall square form has been attributed to Fig. 48C, without judging the upper and lower sides; and we have just seen (Table 87) how elastic this global response is!

H   195

The conclusion to be drawn from this analysis is that two levels must be distinguished in the perception of good forms. (*a*) A primary level of immediate compensation between deformations, due to the equality of the sides and to the angles of 90°. This compensation, which results from a cancellation of difference couplings, $(B-A)$ $A = 0$, is carried so far that it reduces sensitivity to real differences (Table 87) and gives rise to the feeble resistance of the square and to a syncretic elasticity. (*b*) A secondary level of schematisation which leads to explorations and systematic transports as a function of the acquired scheme (set or anticipation leading to exploration of the sides taken two at a time, of their parallelism, of the equality of angles, of their perpendicularity, and possibly of the equality of the diagonals, etc.). This ensures a greater resistance on the part of the good form. No doubt the scheme itself is directed and provided with a frame of reference by operational activities, but it nevertheless represents a new perceptual mechanism, both in its functions and in its results, by comparison with the immediate simple compensations of the primary level.

III. The above poses the fundamental problem of filiations. When only a limited sector of genetic development can be studied, as must always be the case in restricted laboratory experiments (where one cannot usually go further back than the age of 5), the first effects to be encountered are the so-called primary effects. These are followed by perceptual activities which are, in this respect, secondary. But are not the primary effects (primary within the limited context studied) themselves derivatives of anterior perceptual activities? And might not those precocious activities be essential for the structuring of figures which then give rise to primary deformations, when they can be perceived in one glance? In other words, if perceptual activities can give rise to secondary errors by some form of repercussion, why should primary errors themselves not be secondary in this sense, implying prior and precocious perceptual activities of which they are the effects or deposits?

Since new-born infants and babies of a few months cannot be submitted to the usual forms of perceptual measurement, still less to tachistoscopic techniques, all that can be done is to see if later perceptual activities, notably the schematisations we are about to discuss, are capable of producing new field effects which have the simultaneity and coerciveness of primary effects.

We think that we have discovered several such cases. We will limit ourselves for the moment to an example drawn once more from the perception of good forms. When studying, with von Albertini,[1]

[1] *Rech.* 19.

the way in which children of different ages perceived forms which were presented to them interlaced with others, truncated, outlined in broken lines, in dots, etc., we were struck by the following contrasts. Firstly, a complex figure, in which a square, a triangle, a rectangle, a parallelogram and a semicircle were interlaced, was easily separated into its constituent figures. There was 73% success at 4 years (apart from the semicircle: 66%) 89 to 93% at 5 years and 100% at 6 years. Secondly, partly obliterated forms (an omitted angle, an interrupted side, etc.) were not perceived in 75% of cases before 7 or 8 years of age. And, thirdly, single figures represented in interrupted outline (a circle of 2·1 cm diameter represented by five arcs of 6 mm; a square of 2·5 cm whose sides were represented by four angles composed of pairs of arms of 4 mm, etc.) were not perceived as overall figures until the age of 6 (see Table 88).

It seems that virtual lines which complete interrupted lines only gradually become perceptible as a result of exploratory activity, even when they form part of the outlines of good forms. In order to obtain a closer look at this construction, the following investigation was conducted. Five figures made up of two, and one of three, interlaced good forms, outlined in broken lines, were presented to 109 children, of 4 to 7 years, individually, and to 100 of 8 to 9 years, in groups, and were compared with simple figures in broken outline presented to 40 subjects (see Tables 5 and 7 of *Rech.* 19). The results are set out in Table 88.

TABLE 88. *Mean % frequency of recognition of good forms represented in broken outline (n in parenthesis)*

Rech. 19, Tables 5 and 7

Age group	3 yrs	4 yrs	5 yrs	6 yrs	7 yrs	8 yrs	9 yrs
Interlaced	—	7·7 (10)	8·4 (25)	32·4 (41)	71·5 (84)	63·4 (50)	85·4 (27)
Simple	0	38·2 (40)	41·0 (40)	100·0 (40)	—	—	—

Three stages in the evolution of virtual lines may be distinguished in a general way, with, of course, some age shift according to the complexity of the test used. During the first, the subject either perceives only an empty space or a gap; or he perceives only the drawn parts of the lines; or he fills in the gaps in his own way but with a fantasy which shows precisely that he is insensitive to virtual lines and that the overall form is as yet coercive only to the extent of demanding a length or a direction. During the second stage, the subject imagines possible virtual lines but constructs them by successive approximations, thanks to explorations, transports, transpositions and above all to anticipations which allow him, bit by bit, to build up the best form. Finally, in the third stage, the virtual line is perceived immediately and of necessity, even in the absence of any sensory support or indication that the virtual line is restricted to joining the segments actually given (cf. the amodal perceptions of Michotte).

The essential point for us is that the perception of virtual lines between the interrupted ones of a good form finally, but not initially, becomes a field effect. This field effect, although becoming mandatory in the end, becomes so only to the extent that it has been prepared by a long period of earlier perceptual activities. The force of this contention is immediately apparent: if this is the case with delayed field effects which derive from perceptual activities and whose unfolding can be followed experimentally, why should it not also be the case with more precocious primary effects? In their case, it would be as a function of simpler activities whose existence can only be inferred, during the first years, and particularly the first months, of life, from an analysis of overall behaviour.

§ 9. CONCLUSIONS: PERCEPTUAL ACTIVITIES AND FIELD EFFECTS[1]

The basic fact from which to start, in concluding this analysis of multiple perceptual activities, is that they all lead to more advanced and more objective structures of perceptual data but that they sometimes give rise to secondary or derived deformations by thus associating hitherto unrelated elements (or by associating them in a different way). Although secondary errors are secondary by derivation (being due to processes of relating which are correlates of the progress of structuring) they are always primary in regard to their intrinsic mechanism: they are products of heterogeneous centrations (incomplete couplings) unaccompanied by supplementary factors (unless deformations occur during transportation itself, a hypothesis it has not been necessary to invoke).

It is in this way that exploratory activities can both lead to simultaneously synthetic and analytic relations, which supplant initial syncretism, and to a multiplication of centrations on parts of figures which had up to then been poorly analysed (and thereby to a reinforcement of error as in the illusion of divided spaces). The activity of referral leads to the construction of perceptual co-ordinates, which mark a further advance in structuration. By making the directions mutually heterogeneous, however, the activity of referral also encourages the polarisation of centrations in the case of dimensional comparisons when changes in direction are involved (as in the error of the vertical). Spatio-temporal transports and transpositions extend the spatial field of comparisons but release fresh effects of relative centrations by relating hitherto unrelated elements. Temporal transports and anticipations lead to an improvement in successive com-

[1] Field or primary effects are those which result from the immediate interaction of elements which are simultaneously perceived in one field of centration.

198

parisons when practice and repetition are involved but, in their turn too, lead to fresh effects of relative centrations when successive inequalities are presented in serial order, or when contrasts are involved which inhibit anticipations of equivalencies (as in the Usnadze effect). Schematisations mark the attainment of certain structures but can, by repercussion, also lead to deformations, and so on.

The problem is to decide if all the primary effects studied in I and II could themselves be secondary to the active structurings which made them possible. Of course, this hypothesis does not mean that a primitive state of perceptual activities exists and is followed by a second stage during which 'primary' effects develop. This would require a revision of our terminology. It suggests only that the term 'primary' has a meaning relative to a hierarchy rather than to a temporal succession, and serves to remind us that any centration, together with its primary effects, always exists within a context of eye-movements and is therefore always subordinated to an activity. This activity, which is no doubt weak and poorly co-ordinated at first, continues to develop without interruption until adulthood (when it is channelled differently according to occupation).[1] Primary effects remain qualitatively the same at all age levels and are simply quantitatively modified by new activities which may in turn release other effects of a similar nature by introducing new relationships. The term 'primary' thus retains its meaning of 'common to all levels' and of 'relative to local effects of centration'. The only problem is to discover if primary effects are always subordinated to structuring activities. These activities would be multiple and successive, some producing effects similar to the existing primary effects, succeeding ones attenuating the primary effects only to release others in new areas opened up by new structurings.

To make our meaning more precise, the problem may be summarised as follows. Up to now we have distinguished three kinds of developmental trend, depicted in Fig. 49. Type I trend corresponds to primary illusions, which diminish progressively with age; type II trend corresponds to certain secondary illusions which seem to increase regularly until adulthood; and type III trend corresponds to other secondary illusions which increase to a certain age under the influence of one perceptual activity and then diminish under the influence of a second perceptual activity. Examples of type III are the comparison of obliques (§ 3) and the comparison of separated horizontals and verticals (§ 3): the perceptual activities provoking the illusion are those of referral and of directional transports, and the activity reducing the illusion is that of dimensional transports with changes in direction. Consequently our hypothesis is that type III is

[1] See Fraisse, P., and Vautrey, P., *op. cit.*, and Table 71 above.

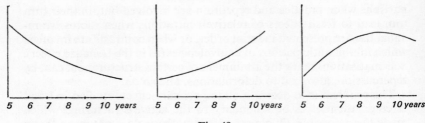

Fig. 49.

really a general form of which types I and II are particular cases, as suggested in Fig. 50. Types I and II differ from one another only in terms of the age at which the maximum appears, and in terms of the nature of the perceptual activities which lead either to a release or to a moderation of the primary effects which constitute the illusion (the primary effects always remaining similar to one another in terms of local effects of centration).

Type II might be a particular case of type III if, as Fraisse has shown (§ 4, p. 170), different professional groups respond differently to the horizontal–vertical illusion: their performances may correspond to different levels of perceptual exercise and the one developmental curve may have a variety of terminations, as shown in Fig. 50, *II*, in which *B* and *C* are of type III.

Type I, derived from studies which cannot be conducted before the age of 4 or 5 years, could also be considered to be a variant of type III, as shown in Fig. 50, *I*, if even younger subjects exhibited a weaker illusion than those of 4 or 5 years. If they did, it would not be because of weaker effects of centration, but because the dimensional

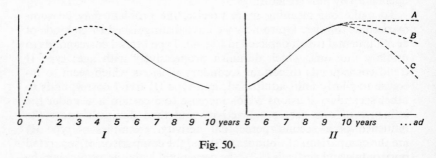

Fig. 50.

inequalities would be less striking at first glance, when the figures were less well structured and gave rise to a less heterogeneous distribution of centrations and of encounters.

In fact, there is no evidence that perception provides an immediate apprehension of Euclidean figures in the first weeks of life. On the contrary, if perception passes precociously through the same stages that later figural representations do (as evidenced by drawings, mental imagery, etc.) it is likely that it starts with a phase during which topological structures, with their relations of neighbourhood (cf. perceptual 'proximity'), of separation (cf. perceptual 'segregation'), of embedding, of being open, of closure, of boundary, etc., are dominant. In this case the relations of distance and of size would have to be constructed, instead of being given from the beginning. In fact experiments on size constancy in children during their first year of life seem to show that even the comparison of sizes (perceptions of equalities or of inequalities) is difficult before the co-ordination of vision and prehension has been achieved. Relations of parallelism and of verticality are no doubt even harder to grasp at first, etc. The result is that, before he can become sensitive to illusions such as those we have studied, the child should be well on the way to perceiving the various figures in the way that we do and, for this reason, to be structuring them on the basis of their fundamental constituent relations. But it is very doubtful if this is so at all ages, and it is probable that certain precocious perceptual activities are required for him to reach that state. These would take the form of elementary activities of fixation (because it is at first a question of learning to look at a figure from neither too far nor too close), of locating, of segregating, of noticing differences in length between neighbouring elements, of appreciating directions within the figure, etc. It is thus very likely that the initial error would be small and that it would increase as a function of elementary activities before declining under the influence of explorations of detail, etc.

It can be seen that the reduction of types I and II to type III, considered to be the most general form, would lead to an interpretation of the real development occurring between zero and 14 or 15 years as being analogous to the 'actual development' which occurs when illusions are studied as a function of exposure times (Chapter II, § 6). It was found that illusions pass through a temporal maximum because few encounters occur at very short exposures and are therefore more homogeneous (with, of course, a less good or less detailed structuring of the figure) than they are at slightly longer exposures. At still longer exposures, detailed exploration leads to more and more numerous and homogeneous encounters. The picture we are now putting forward of the succession of the three types of evolution with age will, *mutatis mutandis*, obey a similar law: there will be an initial phase of structuring, due to elementary perceptual activities, during which the illusion increases because the centrations and encounters will become more heterogeneous as the figure becomes better structured and as the dimensional or directional inequalities become clearer; then, after a temporal maximum between 9 and 12 years for type III and much earlier for type I (see Fig. 51), transports, etc., will cause the illusion to decrease. The only difference between the three types of evolution (a difference which again corresponds to those trends already found as a function of the durations of exposure)

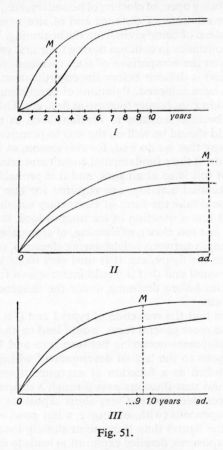

Fig. 51.

would then be the age at which the maximum error occurs, genetically precocious in I, between 9 and 12 years in III and still later in II.

There is one illusion in particular which seems to demand an explanation of this sort, that is the Sander illusion of the parallelogram. It was shown (Chapter I, § 8, Table 13), that this illusion increases from 5 to 8 years and then, following a plateau, decreases between 12 years and adulthood. This is a type III evolution. But the remarkable thing is that each of the factors contributing to the illusion give rise, by themselves, to a type I evolution: the illusion of angles (*Rech.* 10, Tables 5 and 6); the illusions of the diagonals of simple parallelograms (Table 12); and the illusion of the sides of rectangles (or the sides of parallelograms). All the component illusions are thus primary, while the complex illusion itself is secondary. This fact seems to prove that the only difference between secondary illusions (with their type II or III evolutions) and primary illusions (type I evolution) lies in the complexity of the figures, a complexity which demands an initial active structuring which establishes the connections which then give rise to the illusion before more extended explorations finally weaken it. Young subjects cannot perceive all nine parts of the figure simultaneously and therefore exhibit only a restricted illusion because of this lack of association.[1] The illusion then increases on the basis of activities which bring about a structuring of the figure. Finally, in a third phase, explorations, possibly guided by attempts at geometric construction, lead to compensations which once again moderate the error. But this final moderation is a function of different perceptual activities from those which operated before.[2]

This is no unique example. Wapner and Werner[3] studied the Titchener illusion in the form of two figures in the centre of which a circle of 16·5 mm radius was surrounded by other circles. In the first figure it was surrounded by five circles of 25 mm radius and in the second figure by nine circles of 9 mm radius. Circle 2 appears larger than circle 1. The error increases with age but its components appear to be contrast effects, which decrease with age. Here again, it is easy to see that what increases with age is only an attentional structuring of the figure: the subject sees the contrast between each of the exterior circles and the inner one more clearly as he examines each of the relations involved in the figure more closely. He then also perceives the equality of all the outer circles more clearly and this reinforces the contrast between each of them and the inner one. The causes of the increase in this illusion with age are therefore quite similar to those which explain the evolution of the Oppel–Kundt illusion except that there are, in addition, contrast effects between certain parts of the figure and not between each part and the whole. Here again, however, the increase in the illusion with age is indirectly attributable to

[1] It is known that the reversed figure gives scarcely any illusion at any age, because the two diagonals then appear as the arms of an angle which is detached from the figure and because the deforming elements of the figure are then ignored.

[2] Four repetitions reduce the error by 15 to 27% in adults.

[3] Wapner, S. and Werner, H., *Perceptual Development*, Worcester, 1957, Clark Univ. Press.

progress in structuring, the components of the illusion being primary, as they are in the Sander and in the Oppel–Kundt illusions.

But even if such facts in isolation seem to be convincing, our interpretation still remains shaky in general because its verification depends on the demonstration of what might be called a primary perceptual activity, one which must be contemporaneous with the earliest field effects. The fact that our interpretation may correspond to certain neurological models, such as those used by Hebb[1] in justification of his hypothesis of a primary form of learning, is not enough to make them necessarily correct: the correspondence only shows that they are in harmony with certain other notions that are currently widely entertained. On the other hand, if it is admitted that primary effects are part and parcel of primary perceptual activities in the same way as secondary effects are of secondary perceptual activities, field effects should increase in scope during development while decreasing in intensity. This consequence is in fact verifiable: the example of virtual lines which end up by being perceived immediately and of necessity (§ 8, III) is an illustration of it in the form of effects which are not themselves deforming; and the example of the increase with age of the error of the vertical, when tachistoscopically presented with fixation on the horizontal (Chapter II, § 6), is an illustration of it in the form of effects which are deforming.

Above all, the hypothesis of primary perceptual activities which lead to an elementary structuring of perception, finds its justification in an examination of the behaviour of an infant during his first twelve to eighteen months. This examination even leads to a further step in this functionalist and activist interpretation of perception, to a view of primary perceptual activities as subordinate to sensory-motor activity as a whole. We once studied[2] the development of an infant's reactions, exploratory activities and spatiotemporal coordinations to objects. When this is done, one cannot help but see the perceptions of the first twelve or eighteen months as being products of a continuous process of sedimentation or of successive crystallisations deriving from his sensory-motor activities: one can not identify the existence of an independent reality which directs those activities either in advance or as they develop. For example, the segregation of individual objects and of the relation between an object 'placed upon' another and the support itself (a relation studied by Szuman and by Baley before we re-examined it) are closely related to the actions of grasping and of displacing, of pulling a support to reach a distant object placed on its extremity, etc. The manipulation

---

[1] Hebb, D. O., *The Organization of Behaviour*, New York, 1949, Wiley.
[2] Piaget, J., *The Origin of Intelligence in the Child*, and *The Child's Construction of Reality*, London, 1953 and 1955, Routledge and Kegan Paul.

of an object with detailed visual and tactile explorations of its different aspects also plays a fundamental role in the construction of forms, etc.[1]

In short, the present interpretation of the relations between primary effects and perceptual activities bears on only one particular aspect of a much larger problem. This problem starts out as that of the relations between perceptual and sensory-motor activities in general, and ends up as that of the relations between perception and intelligence. An answer to these questions in their general form will be given in Part Three of this work. Before that, we must end our analysis of perceptual activities by examining what we know, from a genetic point of view, of the constancies and of perceptual causality, manifestations of compensatory perceptual activities which are relatively primitive in origin but which persist until the ages of 12 or 15. We must also examine the perception of movement, of velocity and of time.

[1] In the absence of a psycho-genetic analysis of the beginnings of perception, pathological analysis can supply many useful data. For example, in studying size comparisons in dyslexic, etc., children, Bladergroen observed that numerous subjects who could not decide, on visual grounds, which of two rods of 3 and 5 cm was the longer, succeeded by tactile means. The rarer cases of visual success and tactile failure were accompanied by difficulties in the third dimension. There is thus a level at which visual comparisons do not exist at all, and their elaboration seems to be related to action as a whole and not only to perception.

IV PERCEPTUAL CONSTANCIES
AND CAUSALITY

Perceptual activities, in their various forms and at their various levels of development, thus seem, in principle, to lead to advances in the structuring of perception (decentration) with age. However, because of the new relationships which they entail, they also lead to fresh deformations which derive from the recentrations demanded by those new relationships. It also seems that perceptual activities occur at every age (but, of course, in different forms according to the level involved) and that field effects are merely the by-products of these activities once they have become automatic (field effects having an influence on both deformations and structurings).

These interpretations are still hypothetical but will now receive further support. They have led us to consider that perceptual constancies and the perception of causality (which is a particular form of constancy involving the transfer of a motion from one moving body to another) are examples of perceptual activities, in spite of their precocious appearance and quite special importance. At any rate, this is the hypothesis which we shall try to justify in this chapter. We wish to emphasise that it is only a hypothesis and that perceptual constancies could be adopted as the model for field effects, permanent and independent of development, as Gestalt theory has maintained. A real problem therefore exists here, one which must be faced when formulating the general notion of perception which we are trying to establish. Three questions in particular require close examination.

In the first place, constancies do seem to evolve and, on the whole, to improve with age. But their relatively narrow variation requires explanation. It is also questionable whether they really exhibit, in the main, that continuous and directional change which would be a preliminary indication of the existence of a perceptual activity directed towards adaptation. An alternative hypothesis would, of course, be to consider the observed variations with age as having no significance but to be artefacts of measurement. In this connection, the objections that Burzlaff (who is a Gestaltist) raised against Brunswik and Beyrl (who are supporters of the notion of the evolution of constancies with age) will be discussed.

In the second place, constancies seem to give way, after a certain age, to secondary errors in the form of over-constancies, for example in the over-estimation of the size of a distant object or, as Pièron showed, in the over-constancy of form. These facts would support the notion that the constancies derive from perceptual activities if it could be shown how the natural extension of processes leading to a composition of the various indices present in any particular situation involving constancy led to predictable over-estimations: we have seen that such over-estimations are a general outcome of activities which are otherwise adaptive. The alternative hypothesis would assimilate over-constancies to fortuitous and negligible fluctuations, and no doubt this is the point of view of those authors who have neglected to take it into account.

In the third place, experiments on constancy have shown that, in most cases, the 'real' size or form is perceived in an immediate and coercive fashion, which is very suggestive of field effects. The question is whether this is a result of the progressive sedimentation of perceptual activities and of their secondary effects, as we have suggested, or of genetically primary field effects which result from an automatic and in some way physical equilibrium, the model with which Gestalt theory has made us familiar.

The importance of the issues at stake derives from the fact that perceptual constancies and causality are the forms of perceptual organisation which approach most closely to compositions of an operational nature. Both in the case of perceptual constancies and of the operations of intelligence, the compositions involved give rise to invariances or to conservations. In both cases, these invariances seem to be linked to the elaboration of a system of compensations. In the operational example in which a liquid is decanted from one vessel into another of different proportions, the child of 7 or 8 years discovers, after a long period of non-conservation, that the quantity of liquid remains identical. He recognises that this is because the level reached in the second container is higher while its breadth is less, and that these two variations in dimension compensate one another. Similarly, in the case of perceptual size-constancy, the subject perceives that the apparent size of the distant object diminishes and that the distance increases: it is as if these two opposed changes compensated one another and the real size of the object was derived from a multiplicative composition in the form of a ratio. It therefore becomes of great theoretical importance to establish whether this composition results from an instantaneous equilibrium, like that of field effects which derive from an immediate interaction between all those elements which are simultaneously perceived, or whether it is a product of genuine activities, such as relating to systems of reference or active readjustments, with the intervention of choice, of decision, of the selection of systems of reference, etc. The importance of this problem lies in the obvious fact that the field effects studied in Chapters I and

II are essentially deforming, while the perceptual activities analysed in Chapter III tend primarily towards adaptive structures before giving rise to secondary deforming effects as a result of the new relationships which they involve: if constancies simply arose from field effects, we should find ourselves in the very situation that Gestalt theory has been unable to avoid, of admitting the existence of primary mechanisms which sometimes give rise to systematic deformations and at others to adequately structured organisations. However, to the extent that deformations are associated with fields of centration, and adaptive structures with active decentrations, perceptual activities could lead both to adequate structures and, at the same time, in the very process of that development, to deforming recentrations; but it then becomes logically necessary to attribute the formation of the constancies to those activities and not to class them with primary field effects. The partial isomorphism between the compositions of the constancies and those of operations would then shed significant light on the nature of perceptual activities, as opposed to field effects: it would be incomprehensible under the alternative hypothesis.

§ 1. THE EVOLUTION OF SIZE CONSTANCY WITH AGE STUDIED BY THE METHOD OF PAIRED COMPARISONS

For all the above reasons it is necessary to weigh carefully the value of the arguments for and against the hypothesis we are defending. A start can be made with the question of whether or not the constancies evolve with age. Gestalt psychologists undoubtedly grasp the decisive nature of this question, because they try to demonstrate the permanence of perceptual constancies and their independence of genetic development. Köhler tried to establish the existence of size constancy in anthropoid apes, and Frank[1] in the child of 11 months. While Koffka,[2] and above all Burzlaff,[3] advanced methodological objections to the studies revealing developmental trends, reported by the Viennese researchers, Beyrl[4] and Klimpfinger[5], who were colleagues of Brunswik, Brunswik himself, with Tolman[6], re-examined the problem of size constancy from a new probabilistic point of view.

This old methodological discussion will be reviewed briefly because it inspired both our own work undertaken with Lambercier and his

[1] Frank, H., *Psychol. Forsch.*, 1928, **10**, 102–6.
[2] Koffka, K., *Principles of Gestalt Psychology*, New York, 1933, Harcourt Brace.
[3] Burzlaff, W., *Z. Psychol.*, 1931, **109**, 117–235.
[4] Beyrl, F., *Z. Psychol.*, 1926, **100**, 344–71.
[5] Klimpfinger, S., *Arch. Ges. Psychol.*, 1933, **88**, 599–628.
[6] Tolman, E. C., and Brunswik, E., *Psychol. Rev.*, 1935, **42**, 43–77.

own personal researches: it shows up very clearly the opposition between the accounts of size constancy given by the proponents of field theory and by those of theory based on the activity of the subject. The Viennese psychologists demonstrated the development of constancies in children aged from 2 to 11 years, using the method of paired comparisons. Thus Beyrl found size constancy in only 50% of subjects of 2 years, in 66% of subjects of 3 to 4 years, in 80% at 7 years and in 100% at 10 years. Koffka and Burzlaff, however, refused to interpret these results in the same way. It was not that the facts were disputed, for Burzlaff himself obtained similar results when using the same technique of measurement, but that different results were obtained with other techniques, and the discussion thus centred on the characteristics of these different situations. The contradictory facts were of two sorts. The first were obtained by Frank and seemed to show the importance of the lateral separation between the near and the distant elements: this distance was only 20 cm in Beyrl's investigation, and Frank obtained fewer errors when using 'much greater' separations. However, her experiments were certainly less precise than Beyrl's and, in fact, her results did exhibit a slight evolutionary trend during the early years. It was on this fragile basis that Koffka reinterpreted the evolutionary curves obtained by the Viennese school, which were very similar in different forms of constancy, attributing them to a simple diminution with age of the deforming effects of proximity: he claimed that, where the method of paired comparisons was used, and where the lateral separation was small, the elements would be more interdependent for younger children, and that this would give rise to the supposed evolution. The other set of contradictory facts is that put forward by Burzlaff and independently and extensively studied by Akashige.[1] By their technique the subject was required to match a distant cube with another to be chosen from an ordered series of five cubes nearer to him. With this technique, the constancies appeared to improve at all ages, providing the elements were arranged in serial order: when so arranged they form part of an ordered collection (in which the local interdependencies are no doubt supposed to neutralise one another in contrast to what happens when the comparison is made by pairs with small lateral separations) and, adds Burzlaff, one is then nearer to the circumstances of daily life in which elements to be compared usually form part of a series which can be more or less ordered.

Such being the position of the problem when we started our studies in collaboration with Lambercier, we set ourselves four particular problems:

[1] Akashige, Y., *Mitt. J. Litt. Fak. Kuysha Univ.*, 1937, **4**, 23–118.

(*a*) To study size constancy at different ages, as a function of lateral separation, being careful to alternate the positions of the standard and of the variable, a precaution neglected by all but Akashige.

(*b*) To study size constancy at different ages when the elements were serially arranged in the fronto-parallel plane or when intermediate elements were ranged between the near and distant elements.

(*c*) To compare real size judgements (constancy) at different ages with estimates of projective size to see if a better estimate of apparent size accompanied any under-constancy that might be found with younger subjects.

(*d*) Finally, to correlate size constancy at different ages with estimates of distance.

At this stage only problem (*a*) will be discussed, problems (*b*), studied by Lambercier himself, (*c*) studied in collaboration with us and (*d*), studied by Denis-Prinzhorn, will be discussed in later sections.

We must insist from the start that these four questions are interdependent and that, in order to demonstrate that constancy originates in perceptual activities, we must show not only that constancy increases with age in condition (*a*) and even in (*b*), but also that it becomes more exact as apparent size and distance become related during development.

Estimates of size obtained by the method of paired comparisons of elements separated by small lateral distances (3 to 5 cm) have been combined in Table 89.[1]

TABLE 89. *A summary of mean % errors (on the standard) in size comparisons (real size) made at different distances (3 and 4 m) and in different investigations, combined and expressed as a function of age (for n, see original publications)*

Age group	5–7 yrs	7–8 yrs	8–10 yrs	10–12 yrs	12–14 yrs	Adult
A. *Standard Nearer*						
Rech. 12 (Table 1)	—	−2·0[1]	3·0	6·0	9·0	10·0
Rech. 3 (Table 2 (3))	−6·87	−2·15	—	—	—	2·50
B. *Standard Further*						
Rech. 3 (Table 2 (4))	4·35	0·0	—	— ⌒ —		11·95
Rech. 29 (Table 1)	—	4·0	18·0	16·0		24·0

It will be noticed (exceptions apart) that the distant elements were perceived to be larger when they served as standard than when they served as variable. The error of the standard here interacts with depth effects, cumulatively in situation *B* and subtractively in situation *A*. It is therefore all the more significant to find that the same law of

[1] See also *Rech.* 29. Table 4. The results presented in Table 89 were originally reported in *Rech.* 3, 12 and 29.

[2] A negative error represents an under-estimation of the distant element and a positive error its over-estimation.

evolution applies in both situations, with, in general, a mean under-constancy at 5 to 7 years (or an over-constancy due to the error of the standard) giving way to an increasing mean over-constancy from 8 to 10 years to adulthood, with an overall mean zero error at 7 to 8 years.

But while the position of the variable and of the standard thus seems to play an important role when paired comparisons in depth are involved, we failed, with Lambercier, to confirm the importance that Frank, Koffka, *et al.*, wished to attach to the factor of lateral separation. Indeed, a comparison of the overall results obtained with children of 5 to 8 years, as well as with adults, in the above situation involving a lateral separation of 3 to 5 cm, with those obtained with a lateral objective separation of 3 m indicates that this factor has little effect on children and scarcely more (relatively) on adults who, however, show more over-constancy at small separations.

TABLE 90. *The effect of lateral separation on size comparisons obtained by paired comparisons at various distances. —ve values indicate under-constancy*

Rech. 3, Table II

	Standard nearer		Variable nearer	
Separation	3 m	3–5 cm	3 m	3–5 cm
5 to 8 years	−5·60[1]	−5·30	−4·55	−2·90
Adult	1·25	2·50	6·15	11·95

Thus the factor of lateral separation can in no way explain the evolution of constancy with age, because, at both separations and with the standard near or far, the same developmental trend occurs: from an initial under-constancy (strengthened or weakened by the error of the standard) towards a progressive over-constancy.

Leaving aside the results of condition (*b*), with the elements in serial order (which, as we shall see in § 2, in no way contradict the present conclusions), two facts may be underlined, both of which seem to contradict the theory of constancy as a permanent field effect which is independent of development. The first is that of under-constancy in children of under 7 years of age. This has been noted by all authors who have used the method of paired comparisons and reappears in the present case at the greater lateral separation of 3 m (the negative error when the standard was the closer being always a little greater than the positive error when the variable was the closer). The second fact seems to be even more significant and sheds further light on the first: the stage of relative equilibrium to which this evolution of size constancy gives rise is not one of exact constancy (as one would expect on the basis of the assumption of an equilibrium of the field comparable to a physical equilibrium) but on the contrary, of an over-constancy which becomes apparent from the age of 8 to 10 years. It achieves, in the adult, an extent of from 2·5 to 10 % with the standard close and 9 to 24 % (on the average!) with the variable close.

[1] A negative error represents under-constancy.

211

The existence of this general over-constancy is particularly revealing from the point of view of perceptual activities. There are really only two ways of explaining it and they probably come to the same thing. The first is to suppose that regulations intervene (such as those which can be presumed to exist in the co-ordinations of apparent size and distance): once initiated, these lead to forms of over-compensation. The second is to presume that some form of unconscious 'decision' (similar to the inductive inferences described in decision theory) intervenes in the process: by its means the subject chooses that course which he concludes, on the basis of some assessment of the possible gains and losses of information, will minimise his error (using Bayes', or even the *minimax*, criterion). But, in both cases, co-ordinations or precautions must be involved (it being of little immediate consequence if they result from a hyper-regulation or from a decision) and it becomes very difficult to consider these co-ordinations as being other than 'active' as opposed to automatic (as in a physical equilibrium), particularly when they exceed the point of objective equilibrium.

This recourse to perceptual activities, which seems to be forced on us by the observed hyper-regulations, does not of course exclude the crystallisation, automatisation or sedimentation (according to the preferred figure of speech) of such activities into field effects, as when estimates of size at a distance become immediate and without apparent detours.[1] This receives support from the fact that size constancy is unaffected in the adult at very short exposures, of the order of 0·1 second (whereas that of form is profoundly affected and that of colour improved!).[2] But this may not be so with children and, even if previous perceptual activities are changed into immediate effects at each level, the complexity of the process of their formation genetic studies reveal.

§ 2. THE EVOLUTION OF SIZE CONSTANCY WITH SERIALLY ORDERED OBJECTS

As the method of paired comparisons indicated the presence of an evolution with age, which was very suggestive of the intervention of perceptual activities, Lambercier undertook an examination of what happens with serially ordered objects, which Burzlaff and Koffka regarded as typical of 'natural' comparisons. In this study Lamber-

[1] A well-known American psychologist who was visiting our laboratory, and who doubted the existence of these over-constancies, took part in the current experiment: he equated, without demur, a rod of 6·5 cm with a standard of 10 cm which represents an over-constancy of 35%!

[2] Leibowitz, H., Chinetti, P., and Sidowski, J., *Science*, 1956, **123**, 668.

cier ordered the distant elements in the fronto-parallel plane (I)[1] and arranged a set of elements either serially or in random order between the near standard and the distant variable (II)[2]. We have already jointly offered an interpretation of his results in the light of those of another experiment on the relation between perceptual transposition and operational transitivity[3] (see also Chapter VII, § 4 below).

I. With an arrangement of vertical rods placed in serial order in the fronto-parallel plane, Lambercier obtained results which seem to decide the Beyrl–Burzlaff controversy and other issues: a marked improvement in constancy occurred at almost all ages when the standard was equal to the middle member of the series (although there was still a slight under-constancy at 5 to 6 years); but when the standard was equal to some other member of the series, constancy was less good than with paired comparisons. The results are presented in Table 91.

TABLE 91. *Comparison of a standard of 10 cm with a series of 15 variables as a function of the median of the series (n = 12 for each age group of children, 16 adults)*

			Rech. 6, Table 22			
Median (cm)	7	8	10	11	13	16
Range cm	3·5–10·5	4·5–11·5	6·5–13·5	7·5–14·5	9·5–16·5	12·5–19·5
5 to 6 years	8·5 cm	9·5	10·5	11·0	12·4	13·7
6 to 7 years	8·3	9·0	10·0	10·3	12·2	13·4
7 to 8 years	8·4	8·9	9·8	10·1	11·1	13·0
Adult	8·6	9·3	10·2	10·4	10·9	12·7

It can be seen that the 5- to 6-year-olds equated the standard (10 cm) with a variable of 10·5 cm when the median of the series was 10 cm. When the median of the series was 11 cm they chose this as equal to the standard and the median had to be 9 cm before they chose a variable which was physically equal to the standard.[4] Thus there was still some under-constancy in the 5- to 6-year-old child even when the elements were arranged in serial order.

This interesting exception apart, it can be seen that, for other age groups, constancy was exact only when the median was equal to the standard; there appeared to be over-constancy at all ages when the median was smaller than the standard and an apparent under-constancy at all ages when the median was larger than the standard! Although comparisons made with the variables in serial order are said to be more 'natural' than those made in pairs, the former in fact lead to a more or less artificial median effect. The apparent constancy which occurred when the standard was equal to the middle member of the series is no doubt an example of this.

[1] *Rech.* 6.   [2] *Rech.* 7.   [3] *Rech.* 8.
[4] See *Rech.* 6, p. 214, and Fig. 3, p. 176.

We will first try to explain the deterioration in constancy which occurred when the standard was not equal to the median of the series. We identify the major factor as being that of relative centrations, which would lead to a devaluation of elements shorter than the median, in proportion to their lengths, and to a proportional exaggeration of those greater than the median. The second factor which we identify is that of transpositions of differences, which will tend to keep the differences between each element of the series and its neighbouring elements equal. It is to be noted, firstly, that the second factor is one which increases in importance with age and which plays only a restricted role in young children (as will be confirmed subsequently). Secondly, although it may counteract the effects of the first factor, it does not cancel it, and a compromise becomes possible. This takes the form of the perception of equal differences which are both a little greater than the objective differences and a little less than they would be if centrations alone were at work. That being so, when the median is shorter than the standard, a point of subjective equality is sought among those elements which are longer than the median: but, as they are over-estimated by contrast effects (relative centrations), an element shorter than the standard can appear equal to it, whence apparent over-constancy at all ages. When, on the contrary, the median of the series is longer than the standard, the point of equality is sought among those elements which are shorter than the median; but, as they are devalued, one longer than the standard is chosen, whence apparent under-constancy at all ages.

When the median is equal to the standard, however, the median presents a size exactly balanced by the contrary effects of relative centrations (an equal number of elements being greater and lesser than it) and of transposition (as many equal differences on the one side as on the other). Because of its symmetrical position within the series, the median will be more resistant than the other elements to effects of under-estimation or of over-estimation in depth: it is only at 5 to 6 years that under-estimation in depth prevails over this serial support, whereas from 6 to 7 years the median is veridically perceived appropriately. On the other hand, the question may be asked why the slight mean under-estimation of the distant elements by subjects of 6 to 7 years, and, above all, their increasing over-estimation from 8 to 10 years, do not produce a subjective modification of the whole series such as to keep the effects of centration in check. The answer would be that the observed changes in constancy (in over-constancy as in under-constancy) are also due to effects of centration but in this case related to estimates of apparent size and distance. We shall try, in § 5, to describe the mechanisms by which these effects are co-ordinated. In the present case, the arrangement in series carries with it the possibility of compensations, precisely because when one element is fixated the others are not, but all remain interdependent under the effect of transpositions, which increase with age: the serial consolidation of the median ensures a privileged situation for it when it is equal to the standard, and, as a result, there is no generalised over-constancy.

In summary, serial effects, which had been cited in justification of the thesis of the permanence of constancy at all ages, only intervene in this form in the very special and quite artificial (not, as Burzlaff supposed, natural) circumstances in which the median of the series is equal to the standard. In fact, these serial effects, far from suppressing under-constancy at all ages (5 to 6 years excepted), tend to reduce over-constancy in older subjects. It remains to be shown that transpositions of differences, whose stabilising role we have just claimed, do indeed increase in importance with age.

This can be established indirectly by an examination of what Lambercier has called 'refusals', or the impossibility a subject experiences of finding an element in the series that appears equal to the standard. These secondary effects, which are additional to any so far described, clearly increase with age and with the asymmetry of the series in relation to the standard, the more so when the median is smaller: for example, compare 7 with 13 in Table 92.

TABLE 92. *Percentage of 'refusals' in the comparisons involved in Table 91*
Rech. 6, Table 18

Median (cm)	7	8	10	11	13	16
5 to 6 years	33	8	0	0	0	25
6 to 7 years	25	0	0	0	8	25
7 to 8 years	25	8	0	0	17	58
Adult	56	12	0	6	19	88

These refusals are, of course, related to effects of transposition and are opposite in effect to relative centrations, which tend to devalue smaller elements and to exaggerate larger ones. When the median is smaller than the standard, the set of elements smaller than the standard (the majority) engenders, by transposition, a general devaluation of the elements of the whole series; when the median is larger than the standard, elements larger than the standard (again the majority) engender a general enlarging of the elements of the whole series. Thus, in both cases, the subject may find it impossible to select an element apparently equal to the standard. It is possible in these cases that the difference between one element and the next is devalued in comparison with the difference between the median and the standard, and that this devalued difference is generalised by transposition (except, of course, in series 16 in which the refusals are objectively encouraged). Be that as it may, the role of transposition is undeniable, and the increment of refusals with age indicates the

215

growing importance of transpositions of differences in the course of development.

II. Lambercier studied the effects of interpolating elements between a near standard and distant variables. He used a standard rod of 10 cm at 1 m from the subject and, as variables, rods of 3·5 to 21 cm, presented by the concentric method. He used four conditions: (A) variables in linear order, without elements interposed between the standard and the variable (this condition was repeated four times, A_1 to A_4, interspersed between conditions B and D); (B) binary comparisons made when four rulers of equal length were placed in the right half of the field. They were placed horizontally and transversely and at intervals of 60 cm, between 1·60 and 3·40 m, from the subject; (C) binary comparisons made with an arrangement, also in the right half of the field (in order not to disturb the main comparison) of four vertical rods of 12, 14, 10 and 13 cm placed as above at intervals of 60 cm; (D) four vertical rods of 10 cm, equal to the standard, placed as above. The results obtained are shown in Table 93.

TABLE 93. *Mean error[1] (mm on a standard of 100 mm) in binary comparisons, as a function of the stimulus situation (see text; n = 8 for each age group of children and 17 adults)*

Rech. 7, Table I

Situation (in order used)	A_1	B	A_2	C	A_3	D	A_4
5 to 6 years	−14·7	−12·5	−14·7	−14·1	−13·7	−14·1	−14·1
6 to 7 years	−14·4	−12·8	−10·3	−9·7	−10·0	−10·3	−11·2
7 to 8 years	−6·9	−6·7	−6·9	−6·2	−6·2	−7·8	−8·1
Adult	1·2	−1·3	−0·7	−1·6	−1·7	1·2	0·7

It is also interesting to examine the improvement occurring in situations B, C and D over A in regard to the arithmetical, or crude errors. This is set out in Table 94.

TABLE 94. *Mean % improvement in situations B to D*

Rech. 7, Table II

Age group Situation	5–6 yrs	6–7 yrs	7–8 yrs	5–8 yrs combined	Adult
B	15·0	−0·1	−11·5	*3·3*	5·4
C	4·7	−0·1	3·6	*1·6*	34·3
D	−4·8	15·3	7·1	*8·9*	61·9

The following conclusions may be drawn from these facts:

(1) Rods arranged as in B tend to improve estimates of distance, and the question is whether this possible improvement modifies size constancy. The obtained improvements indicate that there is a slight effect in children (3·3%) and in adults (5·4%), an interpretation of which cannot be attempted until a systematic re-examination of the general problem of the role of distance has been undertaken (see § 4 below).

---

[1] The negative error corresponds to an under-constancy.

(2) Situation C (interpolation of unequal rods) produces almost no effect in children but leads to a clear improvement (34·3%) in adults, with, on the average, a suppression of over-constancy (but without tempering of error of the standard, which is here antagonistic to it). This quite considerable difference (which is even clearer in situation D) is obviously due to the fact that the adult's perceptual activity is influenced by some form of operational transitivity, lacking in the child of less than 7 to 8 years and to a discussion of which we shall return. But the question remains of how these unequal elements could serve as useful references. No doubt the answer is that the interpolated references encourage compensations between errors by multiplying the number of distances and sizes, and thereby of relations, between them. This possibility is supported by a comparison of the mean adult (algebraic) error of $-1·6$ mm (practically no error) with the (arithmetic) gain of 34·3%.

(3) Situation D finally demonstrates the role of the transposition of equalities: the interpolated rods were all equal to the standard and thus allowed a step by step transposition to be made of the height of the standard to the distant variables. But why, in this case, was the arithmetic mean error of children of 5 to 8 years improved by only 8·9%, whereas that of adults was improved by 61·9%? There is only one possible explanation for this: that the activity of transposition is differently oriented or directed in the two cases and that this change in orientation with age is due to some mechanism of a higher order than perception. Lambercier refers, in this connection, to 'detours',[1] which would be difficult for the child and easy for the adult. These detours no doubt originate in intelligence which would, in this case, direct the perceptual activities. It seems to us that detours, involving a passage from one element, E_1 (the standard), to a second element, E_6 (the variable), through the mediation of elements E_2 $(= E_1) = E_3 = E_4 = E_5$, also exhibit some of the characteristics of operational transitivity (and therefore of 'associativity', the operational equivalent of the detour) which raises the question of the relation between operational transitivity and perceptual transposition. It was for this reason that a special investigation was devoted to this question, with the assistance of Lambercier;[2] this will be described in § 4 of Chapter VII.

§ 3. OBJECTIVE CONSTANCY AND PROJECTIVE SIZE

We have seen that size constancy evolves with age. The extent of this evolution is admittedly not very great but tends to be unduly underestimated if adult over-constancy is not taken into consideration.

---

[1] See *Rech.* 7, p. 314.   [2] *Rech.* 8.

Table 89, for example, shows differences ranging between 7·6 and 20%, with a mean of 12%, between the ages of 5 to 7 or 7 to 8 years and adulthood while constancy begins at 5 to 6 months. These changes with age are not contradicted by the studies involving serial comparisons, and when taken in conjunction with the hyper-compensatory regulations suggested by adult over-constancy, lead to the conclusion that constancies derive from perceptual activities and not only from automatic field effects. The time has now come to examine the nature of such activities.

The current theory, which we shall adopt, interprets size constancy as the product of a co-ordination of the apparent size of the distant object with its distance: the two factors are considered to be inseparable and to compensate one another approximately. Their evolution with age, and their relation to the changes occurring in constancy itself, must now be examined.

In opening this analysis, it would be advisable to forestall a possible misunderstanding. If an operational composition between the apparent size, As, and the distance, Di, is in question, the product of which furnishes the real size, Rs, in the form $As \times Di = Rs$, it is obvious that the values of the components As and Di should remain unchanged whether they are considered as isolated components or as part and parcel of the composition itself: the inverse transformations $Rs: Di = As$, or $Rs: As = Di$, would then hold. On the other hand, a perceptual composition may be involved, one whose nature is in fact in question and about which nothing is yet known. If it is, the most probable situation is that Rs, As and Di will not keep the same values when they are considered as part and parcel of the subject's composition of Rs as they will when considered as dimensions which the subject has to distinguish. This is the most probable situation by analogy with all the other perceptual compositions so far considered and does not require that Rs, As and Di should be perceived other than simultaneously (even if differences in emphasis may occur as the attention shifts from one to the other). In other words, it must always be considered possible, or even most probable, that the composition in question is not reversible, and that when As and Di are dissociated, a deformation P (or a non-compensated transformation) may emerge. Whence:[1]

$$(44) \qquad As = (As Di : Di) + P(Rs)$$

As a result, if we try to measure estimates of projective size or distance, in adults or in children, the values obtained are very unlikely to be equal to those obtained when the same dimensions are

[1] See Piaget, J., and Morf, A., in Bruner, J. S., *et al. Logique et Perception, op. cit.*

218

involved in the compositions underlying estimates of real size. This is no reason for abandoning the analysis, of course, but it is a decisive reason for only attaching to it a significance relative to the conditions of the dissociation of *As* and *Di*, and to the probable general irreversibility of perceptual compositions.

With this in mind, we tried, with Lambercier, to measure estimates of apparent (i.e. projective, not objective or 'real') size in depth, both with adults and with children. The procedure involved the comparison of vertical rods placed respectively at 1 m and at 4 m from the subject. In one technique, *A*,[1] the nearer rod served as standard (10 cm) and the subject was required to equate its apparent size with that of the distant variable, which, in the event of an exact projective judgement, would measure 40 cm. In another technique, *B*,[2] the standard of 40 cm was the more distant and the subject was required to equate its apparent size with that of a nearer variable which, for a perfect match, should measure 10 cm.

The details of procedure may be found in the original publications, with special reference to the difficulties which had to be overcome to make the question comprehensible for children[3] (it was found to be impossible below the age of 6 or 7). Briefly, the projective comparisons were made in three stages: (I) after a preliminary explanation of the problem; (II) after practice, in which the sizes of cut-out dolls placed at various distances had been matched by tracing the projections of their outlines on a vertical sheet of glass; (III) after further practice involving the matching of the projective sizes of the rods themselves against lines of various lengths drawn, equally spaced, on a sheet of glass.

When Error *A* (with the standard nearer) was calculated as $1 - x/40$ and Error *B* (with the standard distant) as $1 - 10/y$ (where x and y represent the variables chosen by the subject), the results for situations *A* and *B* and measurements I to III set out in Table 95 were obtained.

TABLE 95. *Mean % error for projective comparisons with the standard nearer (A) and farther (B) under three conditions (see text and original publication)*

Rech. 29, Table 2

Condition	I		II		III	
	A	B	A	B	A	B
6 to 8 years	0·45	0·51	0·36	0·48	0·26	0·38
8 to 10 years	0·58	0·52	0·57	0·47	0·46	0·34
10 to 14 years	0·68	0·60	0·63	0·51	0·47	0·34
Adult	0·60	0·55	0·54	0·50	0·30	0·30

The important fact which emerges from these results is that without practice (I) the errors are much smaller at 6 to 8 years than they

[1] *Rech.* 12.   [2] *Rech.* 29.

[3] Difficulties of a notional (comprehension of the verbal instruction) not perceptual kind, as may be seen from the results.

are at 10 to 14 years, or even at adulthood. It is revealing, in this respect, to examine the detailed results thus obtained. They are shown, in terms of the actual settings, in Table 96.

TABLE 96. *Mean size and range (cm) of variables chosen under condition I. Correct match would have been 40·0 cm for A and 10·0 cm for B*

A from *Rech*. 12, Table 1, B from *Rech*. 29 Table 1

Age group	6–8 yrs		8–10 yrs		10–12 yrs		12–14 yrs		Adult	
Condition	A	B	A	B	A	B	A	B	A	B
Mean range	22·0	19·5	16·8	20·6	12·5	—	13·5	25·1	16·0	22·2
Maximum range	40·5	25·0	31·5	30·5	17·0	—	24·0	29·0	26·5	31·5
Minimum range	11·0	14·0	10·5	13·5	9·0	—	8·7	22·0	9·0	12·0

It can be seen that subjects of 6 to 8 years, on the average, selected a variable of 22 cm (but with a maximum of 40·5 cm) instead of the predicted 40 cm, while subjects between 10 to 12 years and adulthood selected one of only 12·5 cm (with maxima of only 17 to 26 cm). Reciprocally, in situation B (at 1 m), the chosen variable, which should have measured 10 cm, was 19·5 cm for subjects of 6 to 8 years and 25·7 to 22·2 cm for subjects between 12 years and adulthood. The projective error therefore increases from 6 to 8 years to 10 to 12 years and then decreases slightly. The fact of fundamental importance is that projective estimates are more accurate in the youngest subjects who can be used than they are during subsequent development.

Before trying to bring out the significance of this evidence, it should be noted that situations A and B are not psychologically equivalent. In the first place, the task of adjusting the projective size of a standard to a variable is not the same when the standard is nearer as it is when it is more distant. The second situation, B, is more difficult for children to understand. Secondly, the gap between the top of the standard and the bottom of the variables remains constant in A but the equivalent gap fluctuates in B, thus complicating the comparison. The measurements taken in A are therefore more trustworthy than those taken in B.

Note should also be taken of the part played by practice, a part which generally increased with age. Its importance is obvious when one considers that only objective size is of any use in making estimates of size at a distance in everyday life, projective size being of practically no use except to those who make perspective drawings: only two of our adult subjects were practised in landscape painting and they made minimal errors.

This evolution of projective estimates with age suggests the following conclusions:

(1) At all ages (remembering that the difficulty of understanding the instructions prevented us from going below the age of 7 or, exceptionally, 6 years), but particularly in older children and adults, there is a systematic resistance to dissociating projective size from

'real' or objective size. The 'apparent size' indicated by the subject consists, in fact, in a compromise between the two kinds of size, a compromise which lies nearer to the real than to the projective size.

(2) The error increases with age to about 10 to 12 years, and then decreases a little. The age at which this change occurs coincides, curiously enough, with that at which notional and elementary operational co-ordinations of perspective are achieved. It is as if projective notions were formed (between 7 to 10 years) *pari passu* with the deterioration in projective perception, and as if operations, once achieved and co-ordinated, contributed to an improvement, but only a secondary one, in perception. We shall return to the particular case of the relations between perceptions and notions in Chapter VII, § 4.

(3) Without advancing a hypothesis on this question for the moment, it seems obvious at least that the relatively good estimates of 6 to 8 years (relatively, since the error is already nearly 50%) are different in nature from the improved estimates of the adult which follow the phase of the maximum error at 10 to 12 years. In the adult, no doubt, some secondary perceptual activities of transportation intervene, based on the learned significance of lines of perspective associated with receding or approaching objects (which may or may not be aided by orienting operational processes). In the relatively better estimates of 6 to 8 years, on the other hand, one gains the impression of a more direct perception, more akin to a response based on 'immediate' information furnished by a perception which has not necessarily been corrected by an estimate of the distance involved.

(4) This impression is strengthened by an examination of the graph (Fig. 52) of the developmental curve, which suggests, with a certain probability, an extrapolation in the direction of even better estimates below the age of 7 to 8 years.

On the whole, it can be maintained that when size constancy is least good, projective estimates will be at their best. This suggests that constancy must result from a composition of the more or less 'immediate' projective data with an estimation of the distance. If, as we stressed at the beginning of this section, it is admitted that the dissociation of real and projective sizes must always remain incomplete in the absence of reversibility, it of course becomes inadmissible to measure projective judgements and distance judgements in the one subject (even at 6 to 8 years) and to deduce, by an operational calculation, a prediction of his estimates of real size. As it is difficult for the subject to dissociate real and projective sizes, any correlation obtained between them will be of doubtful validity. However, as the estimation of distance is more easily dissociated, the investigation of a correlation between it and constancy will involve less risk. This

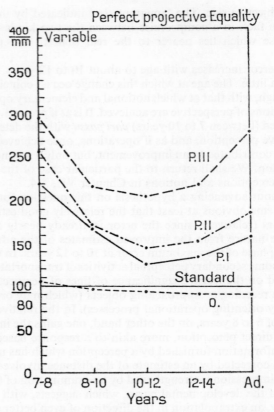

Fig. 52. (See *Rich.* 12, p. 91. P = projective size
judgement; O = objective size judgement)

question must therefore be examined before an attempt is made to
develop the suggested explanation: if the facts concerning the evolution of the perception of distance with age and its correlation with the
development of constancy should turn out to be informative, the
present findings concerning the genetic development of projective
estimates would thereby confirm our proposed hypothesis.

§ 4. SIZE CONSTANCY AND ESTIMATIONS OF DISTANCE

At our request, Denis-Prinzhorn[1] undertook to study estimates of
distance as a function of age, and their relation to the development
of constancy.

[1] *Rech.* 39.

The most efficient method for studying the first problem proved to be a simple subjective bisection of a distance in depth. It is assumed that the over- or under-estimation of the distance between a near element, *A*, and a distant element, *B*, will be a function of the distance involved. It follows that if a third element, *V*, is placed midway between *A* and *B*, the distance *VB* will be under-estimated relative to the distance *AV* when there is a general under-estimation of the distance *AB*, and will be over-estimated relative to *AV* when there is a general over-estimation of the distance *AB*. The apparatus consisted of a large table top (every precaution being taken concerning eye level, the extent of the field, the absence of references, etc.) on which three horizontal 20-cm rods (or three small lead shot) were placed. The positions of *A* and *B* were fixed, at a separation of 240 cm, and the position of *V*, by which the subjective value of *AV* = *BV* was estimated, was variable. No significant difference was found between the techniques employing the rods or the shot.

The experiment was carried out in two parts, with centration demanded on the distant interval, *BV*, or on the closer interval, *AV*. It is interesting that where centration was not so constrained, the experimenter noticed that adults seemed to look mostly at *VB* and children at *AV*. If this fact is confirmed, it needs to be considered in relation to the first important result of this research, that subjects of 5 to 7 years, on the average, under-estimated the overall distance (accepting a setting of *VB* > *AV*), while adults, on the average, over-estimated it (*VB* < *AV*) and that there was a gradual change with age. These results are set out in Table 97.

TABLE 97. *Range and mean % error for the bisection of a distance of* 240 *cm as a function of centration.*

Rech. 39, Table 10

Centration	AV			VB		
	Mean	Min.	Max.	Mean	Min.	Max.
5 to 7 years (*n* = 45 and 31)	−12·0*	−31·0	8·5	−5·2	−24·0	16·0
9 to 10 years (*n* = 30 and 30)	−6·3	−24·0	14·5	−3·0	−19·5	16·5
Adult (*n* = 30 and 30)	3·0	−26·0	28·5	8·5	−24·5	42·5

* −ve errors represent under-constancy.

It can be seen that the evolution of estimates of distance obeys a very similar law to that of the development of size constancy itself. It would be interesting, therefore, to examine the correlation between the two tasks. Denis-Prinzhorn had already measured size constancy in some of the above subjects. In that investigation she used either vertical rods (separated in depth by 376 cm and laterally by 7 cm, the chosen rod being 65 cm from the subject) or with horizontal rods as above. The results of that investigation are set out in Table 98.

Apart from a few variations, the results obtained with vertical rods are similar to those described in § 1, while with horizontal rods (not examined in the preceding sections) constancy became more nearly perfect in adults with a symmetrical distribution of errors around a mean zero error. This interesting result no doubt indicates the use of lines of perspective which would be much easier for the subject to imagine in the horizontal than in the sagittal plane.

TABLE 98. *Range and mean % error on the standard as a measure of size constancy under the conditions described*

Rech. 39, Table 15

Rod position	Vertical			Horizontal		
	Mean	Min.	Max.	Mean	Min.	Max.
5 to 7 years (n = 54 and 36)	−8·2	−36·0	26·0	−13·9	−46·5	27·0
9 to 10 years (n = 41)	−3·2	−29·0	34·0	—	—	—
Adult (n = 20 and 20)	16·7	−7·5	41·0	0·8	−22·0	25·0

The correlations obtained between the two tasks, for subjects performing both, are set out in Table 99.

TABLE 99. *Correlations between estimates of distance and of size*

Rech. 39, Table 18

	Centrations on AV						Centrations on VB					
Rods	Vertical			Horizontal			Vertical			Horizontal		
	r	n	p*	r	n	p	r	n	p	r	n	p
5 to 7 years	0·49	34	**	0·46	17	*	−0·20	20	ns	−0·25	19	ns
9 to 10 years	0·10	19	ns	—	—	—	0·27	20	ns	—	—	—
Adult	0·10	20	ns	−0·06	20	ns	0·32	20	ns	−0·17	20	ns

* Levels of significance: ns = not significant at 5% level; * = significant at 5% level; ** = significant at 1% level.

In summary, the correlations exhibit the following characteristics:

(1) For the 5- to 7-year group:

(*a*) With centration on AV, positive and significant with both vertical and horizontal displays.

(*b*) With centration on VB, negative but insignificant with both displays.

(2) For the 9- to 10-year and adult groups:

(*a*) With centration on AV, insignificant for both displays.

(*b*) With centration on VB, elevated in the positive direction but still insignificant for the vertical display, negative but almost zero for the horizontal display.

The role that centration plays in these events will be understood if it is recalled that, when centration is not constrained, the child of 5 to 7 years seems to concentrate on the closer sector, AV, and the adult on the distant sector, VB. It is consequently possible that the highest positive correlations occurred when the required centration coincided with these natural preferences, and that the correlations were reduced when the experimental restraints ran counter to these tendencies. In order to demonstrate this, Denis-Prinzhorn examined an additional twenty-two subjects of 5 to 7 years and thirty adults under conditions in which centration was unconstrained and vertical rods were used. The correlations were $+ 0.52$ at 5 to 7 years (significant at the 1 % level) and $+ 0.21$ for the adults.

Whatever the role of centration may be, the principal fact which emerges is that the correlation decreases with age. On the one hand, the highest adult correlations are much lower than those of the 5- to 7-year groups, and on the other hand, a comparison of the correlations in children reveals a decrease (with centration on AV) from $+ 0.60$ (vert.) and $+ 0.49$ (horiz.) at 5 to 6 years, to $+ 0.31$ (vert.) and $+ 0.02$ (horiz.) at 6 to 7 years.

From the theoretical point of view, the significant correlations occurring at 5 to 6 years, the age at which there is a clear under-constancy but at which estimates of projective size are obviously more accurate than in the adult, are of some interest: they of course support the hypothesis of a composition between projective size and distance, the resultant of which is the estimated real size. No less instructive is the fact that this correlation occurs during the formative years and weakens progressively with age. At first glance, one might have expected the opposite result: incoherence during development, and correlation once the structures were complete. To understand this apparent contradiction, it is necessary to recall the two assumptions which all our earlier findings forced on us: firstly, that perceptual activities and their compositions tend to become automatic in the form of field effects; secondly, that the more advanced a perceptual composition becomes, the more difficult it is for the subject to reverse the process and to reduce it to its component parts (see the beginning of § 3 and the fact that adults find it much more difficult than children to dissociate projective size from objective or real size). If these assumptions are justified, it follows that the role of estimated distance in the composition of real size (constancy) will be more common and effective during the years when constancy is developing and that, once perceptual habits have taken shape, the reduction of the composition (into its component parts) will be more difficult. These two reasons taken together seem to us to be sufficient to account for the weakening of the apparent correlation with age. The presence or absence of a correlation is, of course, only apparent because the relation between the resultant of a composition (constancy) and one of its components (distance) is being measured when it is uncertain that the component is really dissociated from the whole (from the resultant). Indeed, serious reasons exist for thinking that estimates of distance, measured in isolation, are not identical with the same estimates made within a constancy situation, that is, when judgements of real size are being measured.

§ 5. SIZE CONSTANCY: CONCLUSIONS

The comparisons made between estimates both of real and of projective size and of distance indicate the existence of a relation between these three categories of perceptual response. The nature of this relation must now be stated with a view to its bearing on possible forms of composition.

There is no *a priori* reason for assuming that there is only one type of composition, in which the real size is the resultant and projective size and distance only its components. For example, it often happens that when judging distances in the mountains, one searches for an object of known size (a tree or a house) and derives an estimate of its distance by comparing its apparent size with its known real size. Even if such an inference is of a representational nature, analogies can be found on the perceptual plane. Similarly, an object's projective or apparent size could be arrived at by combining its real size with its distance. The correlations examined in § 4 might be due to the adult being led by his over-estimation of distance to a correlated over-constancy; or it might be the over-constancy which exaggerates the distance. Again, an under-estimation of distance might lead to under-constancy at 5 to 7 years (where the correlation is highly significant); or inversely.

In fact, however, these questions of the direction or order of compositions are quite different in operational and perceptual compositions. In the first case, an operation is given with its inverse and, if one has $x \times y = z$ one will have, *ipso facto*, $x = z : y$, etc., so that it is simple to distinguish between the forward and the inverse direction followed in a given argument. In perceptual compositions, however, there is no inverse, and once the composition is under way, the components can be isolated only with difficulty; whence the difficulty of distinguishing between processes corresponding to the type $x \times y = z$ and those which correspond to $z : y = x$ because, perceptually, the event x will incorporate certain characteristics of y and of z, and reciprocally.

There is, however, one way of discovering the general formative direction of such a composition, and that is by the genetic method by means of which the separate evolutions of its three components can be studied. A first and most important observation achieved by this method is that under-estimations both of distance and of real size and the precision of projective size judgements are inversely related to age. It is therefore already reasonable to assume that the estimation of projective size does not depend on those of distance and of real size, that it is therefore not a resultant of their interaction, but is itself a possible component. In regard to the relation between the two other variables, it is difficult to imagine that size constancy could exist (even approximately) without reference to distance; but it is perfectly possible to consider relative distances without reference to size, for example, between points on a plane or between lines extending transversely across the whole plane, when differences in size do not apply. Above all, we have observed striking similarities between children and adults in response to changes in binocular fusion with disparity, in a stereoscopic situation:[1] these suggest quite primitive or even innate mechanisms of depth perception (but do not exclude the possibility that experience undergone during development plays some part in estimations of depth). As against this, the findings of Brunswik and Cruikshank, and of Akashige's colleagues, seem to indicate that the beginnings of size constancy do not appear before the age of 5 to 6 months. While this does not exclude a possible role for maturation, it is significant that the advent of constancy is placed after and not before the achievement of the co-ordination between vision and grasping (at $4\frac{1}{2}$ months on the average). The significance lies in the fact that this co-ordination must entail much experience in the estimation of depth and of changes in projective or apparent size.

The situation, then, is as follows. Genetically, the estimation of size and of distance improves slowly, passing from under-constancy through to over-constancy, while the estimation of projective size deteriorates. It must be either that these three evolving processes are independent, that two of them are interdependent and the third independent, or that they are all three related. The hypothesis of general independence is fairly unlikely in face of the correlation between estimates of distance and of constancy. In this case, only projective size could be independent, but it would then be difficult to understand why it deteriorates with the improvement of constancy, or, above all, how estimates of distance and of constancy could be related except through the mediation of projective size: while simultaneously perceiving the real size of a receding object and its distance, one inevitably also perceives its apparent shrinkage. Interaction between the three thus being indicated, it remains to be decided whether simple reciprocal relations are involved or whether composition occurs: as one of the changes involved is regressive and the other two progressive, the notion of a composition must be favoured. And as projective size and distance are easier to estimate independently than is real size, it is likely, for the reasons given, that the first two are components of the composition and that real size its resultant.

[1] Studied in collaboration with Lambercier; to be described in a forthcoming publication.

If this is admitted, and presuming that constancy is a product of apparent size and distance, why are the two not sufficient by themselves? How can there be perceptual constancy when the subject perceives objects to shrink as they recede and to expand as they approach and when his corrections are made by continuous *notional interpretations*, and without genuine perceptual composition? The situation described is not really absurd, but actually occurs beyond certain distances: everyone knows how perceptual size constancy breaks down for objects beyond 1,000 or 2,000 m distance. Seen from a mountain or from an aeroplane, houses are perceived as small dolls' houses and trees as miniature toys, but this does not prevent one from attributing to them, this time by representation and not by perception, something approaching their real sizes. Why does this not apply in nearby space? And if there is no constancy at birth (with considerable under-estimation of distances if there is, indeed, any depth perception at that age), how does perception itself correct the sensorial data in such a precocious manner that the onset of constancy in prehensile space can be detected from the age of 5 or 6 months?

In this connection, first of all, let us recall the close connection that exists between action and the estimation of size. The estimation of projective size has no relevance in action and is very poor in adults (except draughtsmen, who practise it). Objective size, however, is constantly involved in action because action has constantly to reassess the invariant characteristics of the object as it manipulates it. If we passed our lives fixed to a solid object, as do oysters to a rock, and were deprived of movement and manipulations, our projective estimates would no doubt be excellent, but size constancy would probably not develop. Secondly, note that the perceptual (and not only the notional) significance of configurations or of figural elements is modifiable on the basis of action, as will be seen in § 4 of Chapter VII when we describe how, at a certain level of development, reference lines impose the perception of equal numerosity on two series of elements (Figure 57, p. 338). Thirdly, let us note the role of perceptual assimilation between the visual and the tactilo-kinesthetic systems, whose importance we shall shortly confirm in the case of perceptual causality (§ 6 below). Finally, recall the spectacular way in which the connection between visual perception and action has been demonstrated by experiments with distorting spectacles (by Erismann, Ivo Kohler, Papert), where, for example, there is a correction of the visual scene after an induced inversion of 180°. This can only be due to the continuous influence (by reafferences, etc.) of action and of tactilo-kinesthetic impressions on visual perception.

Bearing this in mind, there is no need to go beyond perception to find an explanation for the precocious origins of size constancy. It

228

can be found in two trivial but fundamental facts: (1) that an object changes in apparent size whenever the distance between it and the subject changes, whichever of them it is that moves; and (2) that, in either event, the change does not alter the tactilo-kinesthetic size of the object: from the first co-ordinations of vision and prehension, a baby of 4 to 5 months is in a position to notice that an object held in his hand changes in apparent size when he moves it from close to his eyes to arm's length, but that its tactilo-kinesthetic size does not also change (this applies equally well whether the object moves of its own accord, whether the child moves his head towards or away from the motionless object, or whether he manipulates it while displacing it with his hand). The very exercise of manipulation, which is at first restricted within the spatial limits of prehension but later extends farther and farther into the space of locomotion, imposes a growing co-ordination between distance and apparent size while at the same time repeatedly confirming the permanence of tactilo-kinesthetic size. Under these conditions the child learns to see what he touches and to touch what he sees, and establishes an increasing correspondence, or a reciprocal assimilation, between the visual and the tactilo-kinesthetic systems. On the one hand, a need is created for a constant visual size to correspond to the permanence of tactilo-kinesthetic size (which will have to be satisfied by some appropriate construction), and on the other, the necessity for visual distance to be perceived in terms of a space to be traversed (by the object or by the subject): that is to say, for an object seen at a distance to be perceived as situated at an interval which can be crossed. Consequently a special kind of visual transport in depth will be required. This will not simply carry one unaltered object across to another, as in visual transports in the fronto-parallel plane, but will have to carry a distant object up to a near one with which it is to be compared (or simply to bring it nearer to the subject). It will have to accompany this displacement with an appropriate change in the object's apparent size as it is brought closer or made to recede. In other words, to the extent that distance is perceived as space to be traversed, the transport in depth must make it possible for one to perceive the distant object as if it were close (without, of course, the need to decide if it was the object which approached or whether the subject (or the nearer standard) moved towards it).

Size constancy is thus the simplest outcome of the co-ordination of these various activities, or the most economical satisfaction of these needs. There is no reason, in principle, why a visual perception should not exist which depends only on variable apparent sizes and on distances. But these transformations of the object would then depend not only on its own displacements but also on those of the subject. Furthermore, this form of visual perception would no longer correspond to tactilo-kinesthetic perception, either statically or from the point of view of those visual transports in depth which have to provide virtual equivalents of manual transports: the result would be a double complication. On the other hand, the co-ordination of the visual and the tactilo-kinesthetic systems, or the construction of perceptual schemes common to both, lead to a composition by which apparent size is corrected in terms of distance, the result being a relatively invariant product, the constant size. Moreover, as changes in projective size are no longer attributed to the object, only the distance between it and the subject counts and the conflict between the visual information and the tactilo-kinesthetic input is suppressed.

To understand this process, the nature of centration and of transports in depth must first be specified, because neither the one nor the other provides unequivocal estimates of distance or of size. In regard to centration in depth, we claimed in *Rech.* 3 (pp. 298–303), and Rey confirmed by means of an elegant technique,[1] that an element which is momentarily centred is seen to be both larger and closer than another momentarily peripheral one: both apparent size and distance thus vary with centration and decisions has to be made, during decentration, in attributing values to them. By transports in depth, a distant element is compared with a nearer one by a movement of the gaze: it is equivalent either to virtually juxtaposing the two elements, as if they moved within the framework of the lines of perspective, or to visually following those lines while conserving the real size throughout. It seems very probable, therefore, that the precision of such a transport must depend on experience gained during actual displacements of objects in depth (excluding a determination by geometric representation) and that, once again, the evaluations must be made with a certain degree of approximation.

It thus becomes easy to understand how the perception of size can be corrected as a function of perceived distances because, from the nature of centrations and *a fortiori* of transports, estimates of distance can be expected to fluctuate and to be subject to corrections. Everyone has observed how an abrupt change in the perception of distance alters his estimations of size: a bird which appeared to be small and close by in the mist, suddenly appears to be larger when some reference point indicates that it is really farther away, etc.

The following conclusions concerning the evolution of constancies with age may therefore be acceptable, given that a distinction is made between the values attributed to projective size (*As*) and distance (*Di*) during composition (*Asc* and *Dic* respectively) and the values

---

[1] *Rech.* 23, in which a block composed of sheets of glass was used. A parallel line was drawn on each of two sheets which could be separated by a variable number of blank sheets.

attributed to them during the process of dissociation (*Asd* and *Did*).

(1) There is no reason why the projective size, *Asc*, should not, on the average, be estimated accurately by the very young child, since the dissociated estimation of *As* (*Asd*) is more accurate the younger the child. On the other hand, there are good reasons why he should under-estimate the distance, *Dic*, if the estimation of distances depends on practice, practice which starts with prehension and continues with displacements. The composition *Asc* × *Dic* would then result in too low a value for *Rs*, or in under-constancy.

(2) During development, and above all in the adult, estimates of distances, *Dic*, fluctuate with shifts in centration and during transports, and the factor of decision becomes more important in estimates in depth than in the fronto-parallel plane;[1] consequently distances will tend to be over-estimated. This tendency to over-estimate is not due only to the avoidance of devaluations as an outcome of experience, but also to a safety measure: when two apparent distances are given alternately by centrations in depth, that one is chosen which involves the least risk of under-estimation. If apparent size, *Asc*, equals that of the child, the over-estimation of *Dic* must lead to over-constancy and *a fortiori* if *Asc* is over-estimated.

(3) If an attempt is now made to break down such compositions, namely to measure apparent size, *Asd*, independently of real size, *Rs*, or distance, *Did*, independently of size, the situation changes somewhat. This is because the difficulty of achieving this dissociation varies with age, being no doubt proportional to the stability of the compositions or, above all, to the degree to which they have sedimented into field effects. This analysis is difficult because we are not really sure whether *Asc* and *Dic* are formed before *Rs* or whether the composition *Asc* × *Dic* = *Rs* originates early in the piece; or whether *Asc* precedes *Dic* and *Rs*, which develop together, etc. What we know experimentally reduces to the evolutionary curves of *Asd*, *Did* and *Rs* and to the existence of a correlation between *Did* and *Rs* at 5 to 7 years which then becomes weaker. All the possibilities must therefore be considered before a sufficiently probable conclusion can be reached.

(*a*) The only information we have on the stability of the composition is derived from the variability of the thresholds. These are usually slight (whatever the constant error may be) and suggest a stable composition. With paired comparisons, the extent of the threshold

---

[1] When making comparisons in the fronto-parallel plane the centred element is over-estimated but usually without the subject's awareness. When the two lines in depth drawn on Rey's block of glass are alternately centred, the contrast between the over-estimation and approach of the centred element and the under-estimation and recession of the peripheral element becomes very apparent.

was 7·4% at 5 to 8 years and 2·9% for adults (*Rech.* 3, Table I, p. 268). They became narrower with age in serial comparisons (*Rech.* 6, Figs. 5 to 7, p. 195) and were always narrower when the standard was equal to the median of the variable series. The thresholds for projective sizes, *Asd*, and for estimated distances, *Did*, seem to obey the same evolutionary law.[1]

(*b*) In order to explain the better projective judgements of the child and the higher correlations at 5 to 7 years than later between estimates of distance and size constancy, it might be claimed that the composition, $Asc \times Dic = Rs$, is more easily dissociated in the child because it is less stable. This would mean that the values *Asd* and *Did* would be closer to the values *Asc* and *Dic* and the result would be a smaller projective error and a better correlation between *Did* and *Rs*. For the adult, however, a dissociation of the more stable composition would be more difficult and the values *Asd* and *Did* would differ more from those of *Asc* and *Dic*: the result would be a greater projective error and a weaker correlation between *Did* and *Rs*.

(*c*) One could also entertain the hypothesis, which at first seems to contradict the preceding ones, that the estimations *As*, *Di* and *Rs* are relatively undifferentiated in the child but become more and more independent with age. The existence of this growing independence between *Did* and *Rs* would be supported by the absence of correlation between them. The relative independence of *Asd* would be supported both by the effects of learning (in artists, etc., and in measurements II and III in Table 95) and by the fact that the projective error becomes less from 10 years on because of undoubtedly new, and therefore probably independent, factors. In the child, on the contrary, distance and real size would be little differentiated, the two estimations almost always occurring together in everyday life, whence the positive correlation at 5 to 7 years. Moreover, error is far from absent in the child's estimation of projective size, and is even considerable, which also lends support to a relative lack of differentiation between projective and real size.

(*d*) But these two hypotheses only appear to be contradictory, for it is one thing to break down the composition $Asc \times Dic = Rs$ into its components in order to establish that $Asd = Asc$ and $Did = Dic$, but quite another to combine *Rs* with components *Asc* and *Dic* which are at first entirely differentiated or relatively undifferentiated. Hypothesis (*b*) simply affirms that, in dissociating *Rs*, one finds neither $Asd = Asc$ nor $Did = Dic$ when the composition is strong or stable but may find this when the composition is less stable. Hypothesis

---

[1] Distance thresholds were not obtained but the separation of the three medians passes from 7·1 (children) to 5·8 (adults), with centration on *AV*, and from 5·6 (children) to 4·6 (adults), with centration on *VB*.

(c) affirms, first, that *Asd* and *Did* (as distinct from *Asc* and *Dic*) are subject to effects of learning relatively independently of *Rs*, which in no way contradicts hypothesis (b) but even forms quite a natural complement to it. Hypothesis (c) then affirms that *Asc* and *Dic* may be relatively undifferentiated from *Rs* (or that this applies to *Dic* and *Rs* with a greater differentiation from *Asc*, which reduces to saying that *Dic* and *Rs* are constructed concurrently on the basis of estimations of *Asc* which are dominant at first). This does not contradict hypothesis (b): on the contrary, a composition can be unstable precisely because it is based on components which are scarcely differentiated, whereas their later differentiation would increase their complementarity and thus stabilise the composition.

(e) All things considered, we shall retain both hypotheses (b) and (c). The initial (unknown) stage could well be characterised by the primacy of apparent or projective size with an absence of distance or real size estimations, *Asc* and *Dic*, or with a feeble beginning of depth estimations at very small distances. Estimations of distance would then develop and gradually become differentiated (that is, either from zero and solely under the influence of prehensile displacements, etc., or from a weak visual ability which is later strengthened and practised in movements and in prehensions). The composition of real size would be the product of the combination of *Asc* and *Dic*, dating either from the first differentiations of *Dic*, arising in exercise, or a little later, and this composition would remain fairly unstable for a long time and would depend on scarcely differentiated components (*Asc* in relation to *Rs* and also *Dic* in relation to *Rs*). Finally, by the very achievement of stability, the dissociation of the composition would become more difficult, whence an increasing difference between *Asd* or *Did*, when dissociated, and *Asc* or *Dic* when integrated. This would open the way to a relative independence of *Asd* or *Did* and to the influences of new experiences, etc.

In summary, the data assembled in §§ 1 to 4, and the interpretations they led us to propose in § 5, support the hypothesis that size constancy is neither an innate, built-in mechanism (even if it has innate components, which can never be excluded) nor an automatic equilibration similar to a physical one. It suggests, rather, that size constancy derives from precocious perceptual activities and from their composition in the form of compensations between apparent sizes and distances. These activities and compositions continue throughout development and only gradually sediment into field effects. Size constancy thus appears as a perceptual scheme of conservation, with its approximate compensations and the beginnings of very approximate reversibility in so far as the process which initiates the composition consists in the relating of changes in

233

projective size to the accompanying variations in depth. It is very likely that some link exists between this perceptual composition of constancy and the construction of the sensory-motor scheme of the permanent object which comes into effect at the same period of development, but with a slight temporal shift. This scheme of the permanent object also rests on a practical 'group' of displacements, but a more general group, not simply to do with linear displacements or distances, but with any displacements, particularly displacements and positions which extend beyond the bounds of the perceptual field. The problem remains, therefore, of the nature of the relations that exist between these two constructions. This will be discussed in § 2 of Chapter VI.

§ 6. VISUAL AND TACTILO-KINESTHETIC PERCEPTUAL CAUSALITY

Perceptual impressions of causality, discovered by Duncker and by Metzger, and then studied in great detail by Michotte, seem to us to fall into the category of perceptual constancies. A perceptual constancy has three identifying characteristics: the conservation of a perceived property in spite of transformations of other properties of the object or figure; 'phenomenal double-reference' which makes the simultaneous perception of the conserved and of the transformed properties possible; and a compensation which preserves the constancy by inverse transformations of the non-constant properties. These three characteristics can be identified in the perception of causality.

The conservation of one property of an object when others are transformed is the hallmark of all constancies: the real size of an object continues to be perceived in spite of apparent changes in its projective size; the real shape of an object continues to be perceived in spite of transformations of its apparent form (form constancy with changes in perspective); the real colour of an object continues to impose itself in spite of changes in the apparent colour of the illumination, etc. Similarly, in perceptual causality, it is no longer the property of a single object that is conserved but a property which is transmitted from one object, *A*, to another, *B*, for example, a movement passing from *A* to *B*. This conservation is clearly perceived, even when other properties change, and is based on the fact that a change always occurs in the movement of *B*, and, in most cases, in that of *A* also.

Secondly, a phenomenal double-reference occurs in size constancy when the real size of the object and its apparent shrinkage are perceived simultaneously (which does not mean that one can estimate them both simultaneously because that would require their relative dissociation, cf. §§ 3 and 5, but means that they are perceived together globally); in form constancy, the real and the apparent (perspective) forms are perceived simultaneously; in colour constancy, the real and the apparent (illumination) colours are perceived simultaneously, etc. Similarly, in perceptual causality, Michotte has shown clearly that the movement of the passive object, *B*, is perceived both as a displacement of *B* and as an extension of the movement of the agent, *A*.

Thirdly, the constancies depend on compensations. We have tried to demonstrate (§§ 3 to 5) that the apparent shrinkage of a receding object is compensated for, in size constancy, by a change in its distance, which is equivalent to re-establishing the real size of the object by virtually reducing its distance. Similarly one could demonstrate in form constancy that an apparent deformation is corrected by a virtual re-establishment of the object's normal position. No doubt colour constancy also results from a compensatory composition between the apparent colour and the illumination,[1] etc. In perceptual causality, Michotte did not introduce the notion of compensation at all, but that of the 'ampliation of the movement': in virtue of a sort of kinematic Gestalt, the movement of the agent, *A*, is perceived to prolong itself in that of *B* when certain spatial (same direction, and spatial priority of *A*), temporal (temporal priority of the movement of *A* and absence of too long a pause between the two movements) and kinematic (velocity of *A* equal to or greater than that of *B*) conditions are met. We, however, have taken the notion of ampliation to be a good description rather than an explanation, and have tried to take the properly causal aspect of this kind of perceptual impression into account by invoking a model based on compensation.[2]

The model of ampliation, without the addition of a notion of compensation, seems to possess two difficulties. The first is that it is difficult to understand how the impression of 'production' that characterises the perception of causality, and which Michotte has analysed in detail, is produced by combinations of movements and velocities only: movements apart, only a compensatory mechanism involving impressions of resistance added to those of thrust, already described by Michotte, could explain the causal character of kinematic sequences.

[1] No doubt colour constancy owes its improvement in the tachistoscope (Leibowitz, Chinetti and Sidowski, *op. cit.*) to the fact that there is insufficient time to perceive either the colour of the illumination or the apparent colour of the object; form constancy no doubt suffers from a lack of time to effect the angular correction; size constancy does not change because both the distance and the apparent size are perceived simultaneously in very brief presentations.

[2] *Rech.* 33. See §§ 11 to 13, etc.

In the second place, there are certain exceptions to ampliation in the strict sense (with homogeneity of direction): with Lambercier, we obtained causal impressions in the absence of impetus and with apparent movements of A perpendicular to those of B.[1] Gruber has also produced a good causal effect on film, when the support on which a plank (or the plate of a drawbridge) rests is removed and the apparent collapse of the object that it supported occurs. Ampliation could be invoked in these cases, but only in the broader sense of a transmission of movement: but the perception of this transmission of movement can only be explained in terms of a model of compensations between movements, thrusts and resistance; and the Gruber effect, in particular, demonstrates this impression of resistance (in this case, it is the removal of the resistance rather than the removal of the agent which seems to bring about the collapse of the supported object).

In view of this, we propose the following model based on compensations. The first three factors to be invoked are the same as those which Michotte has emphasised, while the fourth (resistance) is added by us. It will be justified by experimental evidence.

(1) The first factor is the loss of velocity which occurs in the agent, A, following the impact. If A_1 is the velocity of A before impact, and A_2 its velocity after impact, the first factor can be written as $A_1 - A_2$.

(2) The second factor, the impression of thrust, F, exerted by A, may depend on the perception of contact, T, between A and B, of shock, C, between A and B, or may even arise in the absence of both shock and contact and depend simply on the velocity of A, etc. This second factor will be written as $F(T, C)$ in which T and C may be zero.

(3) The third factor expresses the essential fact, the complement of (1), that the passive object, B, modified by the impact, generally gains in velocity after the velocity of A has decreased. If B_1 is the velocity of B before impact, and B_2 its velocity after impact, we will have $B_2 - B_1 = $ a gain in velocity of B after impact.

(4) But this gain does not always compensate for the loss suffered by A, and one would still be unable to express the perceptual causality as an equation,[2] even with the addition of the factor F. It therefore becomes essential, if the existence of a mechanism of compensation is to be preserved, to invoke a fourth factor, R, the impression of a more or less pronounced resistance on the part of the passive object. This will be defined (without any reference to the exact physical notion of resistance) as the impression that B is put in motion 'more or less easily' by A. This factor may depend, like F (of which it is the

[1] *Rech.* 33, §§ 5 and 17.
[2] For example, when $B_2 < A_1$, then *a fortiori* $B_2 < (A_2 + F)$.

reciprocal) on shock, C, and on contact, T, or be independent of both.

The general equation for perceptual causality will then express the following compensation between the terms of the first and those of the second members:

(45) $\quad (A_1 - A_2) + F(T, C) = (B_2 - B_1) + R(T, C)$

It is easy to establish that this equation covers all the particular cases of causal impression described by Michotte, Gruber and others, or discovered by us in our genetic study with Lambercier.

First, in the case of 'entraining'[1] (A contacts the motionless B and carries it along without losing velocity) one has:

(46) $\quad\quad\quad\quad O + F(T) = B_2 + O$

Or, if B itself was in motion:

$$O + F(T) = (B_2 - B_1) + O$$

In the case of 'launching' (A stops on impact and B, motionless till then, sets off at the same or at a lesser velocity) one has:

(47) $\quad\quad\quad\quad A_1 + F(T, C) = B_2 + R(T, C)$

If $B_2 < A_1$, a stronger causal impression is experienced, because B seems to resist more.

In the case of 'triggering' (B motionless until impact, sets off at a velocity greater than that of A) one has:[2]

(48) $\quad\quad\quad\quad A_1 + F[(T, C) > 0] < B_2 + 0$

The inequality, $<$, indicates that the triggering is no longer a strict form of causality which would imply conservation of the velocity and consequently an exact compensation. The same qualification applies to the perceptual impression produced when A stops against a motionless B, which, for most adults, is not a properly causal impression:

(49) $\quad\quad\quad\quad A_1 + F(T, C) > 0 + R(T, C)$

Here the inequality, $>$, expresses the fact that the loss of velocity by A is greater than the gain (0) by B, whereas in triggering, the inverse applies.

[1] *Translator's note:* In the translation of Michotte's book: *La Perception de la Causalité*, Louvain, 1946, by Miles, T. R., and Elaine (London, 1963, Methuen), the terms 'entraînement' and 'déclenchement' were translated as 'entrainment' and 'triggering'. The present translator would have preferred 'shunting' and 'releasing', but has retained the original forms in the interests of consistency.
[2] In which the sign $\rightarrow$ means 'tends towards', indicating little expenditure of $F(T, C)$.

For the Gruber effect, one would have, if A is the support which is removed and B the supported object:

$$(50) \qquad A_2 - R = B_2 - F$$

where A_2 is the movement of the base, $-R$ is the removal of its resistance, B_2 the fall of B and $-F$ the release of its pressure on A. If B is considered to be the support and A the supported object, one has, reciprocally: $A_2 - F = B_2 - R$.

Thus all the known situations[1] can be described by the same equation (45) or its transformations. We have yet to establish, however, that the resistance, R, is not introduced into this notion of compensation for theoretical reasons only but that the subject really does gain the impression that the passive object, B, is 'more or less easily displaced'. Although the introduction of R appears to be demanded by the Gruber effect, we verified it in two ways. In the first place, we changed the apparent velocity of element B in a causal sequence (or of a single moving body, without causal sequence) simply by concealing its stopping point with a movable shutter. Subjects were asked whether the apparent weight of B (or of the single object) was also thereby changed. It emerged (see Table 100) that there is a very significant correlation between an apparent increase in velocity and an apparent loss in weight.

TABLE 100. *Relation between changes in apparent velocity and changes in apparent weight expressed as % frequency of judgements. Figures in parenthesis represent the number of judgements involved*

Rech. 33, Table X

Apparent velocity change	Apparent weight change					
	Children (n = 26)			Adults (n = 10)		
	+	=	−	+	=	−
+	48·6 (34)	1·4 (1)	20 (14)	43·6 (17)	17·8 (5)	0
=	1·4 (1)	21·5 (15)	0	12·5 (5)	25·5 (5)	5·1 (2)
−	4·2 (3)	0	2·9 (2)	0	0	0

But the question is, of course, whether these two impressions are independent, that is, whether the decrease in weight has been deduced (at the notional level) from the increase in velocity or whether there really are two correlated perceptual impressions. The question becomes all the more complex if, as is very probable, previously acquired perceptual schemes intervene: because of their internal connections the subject may pass from the apparent increase in velocity to that of lightness by a perceptual pre-inference and not only by notional inference. Whatever the case may be, it is still true, and this is the essential point, that our subjects recognised the existence of a perceptual impression of lightness (or of least resistance) as well as those of thrust, shock, etc. Even if they did not always report this spontaneously (which, however, they sometimes did), this would have

[1] Including the 'paradoxical' situations: see *Rech.* 33, p. 154, Props. 6 and 7.

been because subjects typically do not report all their impressions: for example, the apparent solidity of the moving bodies, which is very closely related to resistance, was not stressed by anyone but is readily identifiable by everyone.

Our second verification was more decisive. A comparison was made between causal sequences in the horizontal and in the vertical and, in the latter, between the two directions of movement, upward and downward. Almost all subjects (at least nine out of ten) perceived a difference between the horizontal and vertical presentations and between the two directions in the vertical. In the case of launching with contact, the dominant impression was of a greater activity on the part of the passive object, *B*, when the movement was upward (as of a lift) and of a greater passivity when the movement was downward (as if *B* was slowed down by something in the surroundings). The same thing happened in the case of entraining, etc. In short, the impressions of weight and of resistance are easily made explicit, which should make us more cautious about factors which may remain implicit but which may yet intervene in the usual horizontal forms of presentation.

Accepting our explanation of perceptual causality by compensation, the question of the ampliation of movement, in the broad sense in which we have agreed to consider it, still remains to be dealt with. In the case of simple constancies (concerning the conservation of a property of a single object and not the conservation of a movement transmitted from one object to another) the problem is to establish whether the compensation which engenders the causal link is the product of an automatic field effect or of perceptual activities accompanied by compensatory regulations. Three considerations seem to be decisive in this connection. The first is that, in fact, the conservation of movement, its transmission from the agent to the recipient, never gives rise to a direct sensory registration of the passage of this movement between *A* and *B* but is always translated into the perception of a *resultant*. In concrete terms, this means that one never 'sees' anything 'pass' from *A* to *B* (a *flux*, a wave, a *phi* movement, etc.): one only sees that something 'has happened', which is quite different. In other words again, underlying the perceptual impression of causality there is no 'perceptible transmission' between the causal movement and the resultant movement. One does not *see* the movement itself pass from *A* to *B* (contrary to Duncker's and Metzger's theory, which Michotte rightly refuted): what is given perceptually is only an immediately reconstituted transmission, an impression of a transmission, which is the resultant or the product of a composition. If this is so, it becomes clear that this composition cannot correspond to a simple visual Gestalt, such as a figural field effect, but that

239

it derives from more complex activities, belonging to that class of compensatory regulations whose presence we detected in size constancy.

Secondly, it is possible to suggest a fairly simple model of these perceptual activities and of the compensatory mechanism which they use. By this model, the observer follows the movement (A_1) of A with his eyes, thus indulging in a real transport (Tp) of A from its initial to its final position; he then does the same for B. But to the extent that the movement of B follows that of A (by simple spatio-temporal extension, or because there has been contact, etc.), and that the encounter between A and B modifies their movements or positions, then the real transport of A up to the point of impact is extended by a virtual transport, Tpv. This completes the movement that A would have continued but for its encounter with B. The real transport of B which follows the impact is accompanied by an estimation of the interval which it would not have traversed but for the arrival of A. In the cases of launching and of triggering, it is the difference $TpvA - TpB$, and, in the case of unequal velocities, $A_1 > B_2$, it is the slowing of the virtual transport, $TpvA$, extending TpA, which initiates the dynamic visual impressions (visual impressions of resistance following consecutively on those of thrust, etc., which are produced at the impact). In the case of entraining, the real transport of A is conserved without entailing any virtual transport, but the transport of B is accompanied by a virtual transport, $TpvB$, if B was already moving before the impact and at a lesser velocity. Once again we would have a difference $TpB - TpvB$, with assimilation of TpB to TpA; when B is motionless before the impact, its real transport will continue to be dominated by this initial immobility (by a $TpvB = 0$, which is a kind of reminiscence of the previous immobility) and will thus be assimilated to that of A. Thus, in every case, the mechanism of the real and the virtual transports seem to explain why the transport of B is subordinated to that of A (which simply reduces to Michotte's ampliation of movement). It also explains why changes in velocities make the scheme of compensations necessary, objective decelerations being translated into resistances which prevent the virtual transports from equalling the real transports, and accelerations, or settings in motion, being translated into the direct action of one transport on the following one. In short, the conservation of the movement of A in the movement of B, and the compensation of the apparent modifications in terms of slowing and of acceleration, can be explained on the basis of transports.

It has yet to be explained why the subject perceives these various effects as objective thrusts and resistances, as external material causality rather than simply as oculo-motor causality (resistances, etc.,

240

perceived by proprioceptive means).[1] It is at this point that a third reason for supposing perceptual causality to be due to complex activities and not to simple field effects becomes apparent: schemes must exist which are common to visual and to tactilo-kinesthetic perceptual causality, schemes which allow tactilo-kinesthetic impressions to be translated into, or set into correspondence with, visual impressions, and reciprocally. Tactilo-kinesthetic perceptual causality does exist (and is no doubt genetically prior to visual causality) and it exhibits all the elements of a compensatory scheme: a movement of the agent *A*, a push on *B*, and then movement of *B* but with a resistance which is directly and explicitly perceived (weight, etc.). It is also obvious that, from the achievement of the co-ordinations of vision and prehension (whose role in size constancy has already been described), the child of $5\frac{1}{2}$ to 18 months and beyond is led, throughout his apprenticeship in imitation, constantly to establish reciprocal correspondences between tactilo-kinesthetic and visual impressions, and consequently to construct common schemes which allow them to be mutually assimilated. Our claim is that the dynamism attributed to objective kinematic sequences by visual perceptual causality (impressions of shock, thrusts and various resistances) is only the expression of a translation into visual impressions of corresponding tactilo-kinesthetic impressions, a translation made possible both by the action of schemes common to both domains and by the dynamics of the properly visual transports (the visual transports always being assimilated to the schemes).

Two sets of facts support such a theory. The first depend on the evolution with age of visual causality. We never found, with Lambercier, any great differences between age groups (leaving aside the fact that causality in the child is a little broader and includes, for example, certain arresting actions, etc. It is also less exact and its compensations are therefore more approximate). The only noticeable difference, thereby the more instructive, is that children, while exhibiting a much wider threshold for the perception of contact, generally denied any causal impression in the absence of contact. Adults, however, as Yela[2] showed, quite generally perceived the generation of motion at a distance, which must derive specifically from visual transports. This requirement of contact by young subjects is surely an indication that visual perceptual causality is much closer to its tactilo-kinesthetic dynamic sources in them than it is in older subjects. It also suggests that launching in the absence of

[1] This does happen sometimes: one of our subjects, when observing the horizontal presentations, claimed actually to feel the impressions of thrust, etc., within his own body.
[2] Yela, M., *Quart. J. Exp. Psychol.*, 1952, **4**, 139–54.

contact, while emanating from simple visual transports, is frequently assimilated by adults, and sometimes by children (when the suggestion is made by pointing to the possibility of displacing a piece of paper at a distance by blowing at it), to an empirical scheme of compression. Examples of responses obtained with launching effects (relative speeds of 6 : 1 and 3 : 1 for *A* and *B*) and triggering effects (relative speeds of 1 : 6 and 1 : 3) at variable distances, are presented in Table 101.

TABLE 101. *Frequencies of reported pushes (P), contacts (T) and compressions (Pc) under two conditions of relative velocity. Results for two ratios of velocity combined*

Rech. 33, Table IV

Velocities	Launching 6:1 and 3:1			Triggering 1:6 and 1:3		
	P	T	Pc	P	T	Pc
6 to 8 years (*n* = 16)	134	92	38	110	99	23
Adult (*n* = 12)	190	36	38	96	32	76

It can be seen that, whereas children perceived many more contacts (had a wider threshold, either because perceived contacts gave rise to causal impressions, or because causal impressions led to apparent contact, or, more probably, because of an interaction between the two effects), they exhibited far fewer causal impressions in the absence of contact than adults did. The only exception was where compression was perceived, which happened when suggestions favouring the acceptance of causality at a distance were made pre-experimentally.

This initial insistence on contact (when one would really have expected the child to accept anything), must derive from a correspondence with tactilo-kinesthetic causality. We can also add a second group of facts in support of the tactile origins of effects of thrust and of resistance. They concern experimentally provoked exchanges between visual and tactilo-kinesthetic causal impressions. The perceived location of impact in tactilo-kinesthetic causality was studied with Maroun[1] in this connection. It is well known that if the ground is touched with the end of a stick or, better still, with a plumb suspended on a flexible string, the impact is localised at the point of contact between the stick or the plumb and the ground, and not at the hand. Authors generally attribute this to effects of vision on the tactilo-kinesthetic senses, which would seem to confirm Stratton's classic experiments. We wondered if this delegation of impressions of impact and of resistance would transfer from one object to another. A row of boxes of different weights was spaced out along a slide and was pushed by the subject with a form of rake. We wanted to know if the delegation proceeded from the rake to the first box and then from box to box as they came into contact with each other. This was examined under conditions in which the subject had his eyes open

---

[1] *Rech.* 34.

and under conditions in which he had his eyes closed. The results obtained are shown in Table 102.

TABLE 102. *Frequency (%) of delegation of causality to the boxes (D), to the end of the rake (R), to the handle of the rake (B) and to the arm or hand (M) under two conditions, EO = eyes open and EC = eyes closed, and two orders of experience (n = 36 adults and 16 children)*

Rech. 34, Table 1

Order								
Condition		EC				EO		
	D	*R*	*B*	*M*	*D*	*R*	*B*	*M*
			Group 1	*EC . . . EO*				
6 to 7 years	16·6	57·2	19·8	6·4	19·4	44·9	21·9	13·8
Adult	28·4	56·8	9·1	5·7	47·2	45·4	3·8	3·6
			Group 2	*EO . . . EC*				
6 to 7 years	42·4	25·6	15·2	16·8	34·9	31·2	8·9	25·0
Adult	53·2	37·0	4·5	5·3	48·5	38·4	7·9	5·2

Three interesting facts thus emerge. The first is that reports of delegation (and also the effects of *D* + *R*, because *R* is also a kind of delegation) increased in frequency with age, which seems to exclude simple imagination. The second is that effect *D* was appreciably stronger with the eyes initially open (Group II) than with the eyes initially closed (Group I), which confirms the role of vision. The third fact is the most instructive. Subjects of Group II, who continued the experiment with the eyes closed, exhibited a stronger *D* effect than they did with the eyes open and to an appreciably greater extent than subjects of Group I, who continued the experiment with the eyes open: the effect of vision on tactilo-kinesthetic impressions is conserved, and even somewhat strengthened, when the eyes are closed.

Influences of visual causality on tactilo-kinesthetic causality are thus shown to exist, which makes the reciprocal influence during development quite as probable (without mentioning the general effects of tactilo-kinesthetic associations on visual associations demonstrated by Ivo Kohler in his experiments with distorting spectacles). It is therefore legitimate to attribute the dynamic factors of visual perceptual causality (thrust and resistance) to the establishment of a correspondence with the data of tactilo-kinesthetic causality through the mediation of schemes common to both systems. The implications of this interpretation for the problem of the relation between perceptual causality and the notion of cause will be taken up in § 2 of Chapter VII.

V PERCEPTIONS OF MOVEMENT, OF VELOCITY AND OF TIME

Our discussions of perceptual activities have yet to be completed by a summary and a discussion of the few experiments we have been able to carry out or to direct on the perception of movement (investigations of perceived changes and stabilities in the forms of moving bodies and of stroboscopic movement), of velocity and of time.

§ 1. THE PERCEPTION OF MOVING BODIES: SQUARES IN CIRCUMDUCTION (THE AUERSPERG AND BUHRMESTER EFFECT)

The perception of moving bodies raises two general problems. The first was posed by von Weizsäcker and his successors Auersperg and Buhrmester: why does a body activated by rapid and continuous movement, for example, the square in circumduction studied by Auersperg and Buhrmester,[1] retain its perceived form until it reaches a certain speed, instead of either giving way at once to a fused image corresponding to the retinal image, or to a succession of motionless or discontinuous squares, or even to a diffuse square, with or without a blurred after-trace? According to the above authors, motor activity must be involved, not only to keep the moving body in central vision but also to allow its form to be discerned or restructured; moreover, they say, this motor activity takes the form of an ability to anticipate, or of *prolepsis*, which is essential to the continuous reconstruction of the form, a reconstruction on which the perception of the moving body at any given moment depends. We therefore undertook, with Lambercier, to discover if motor activity is necessarily involved in the actual structuring of the square in circumduction and whether it always includes a factor of anticipation.

The second general problem is a genetic one: as the perception of the moving form requires a complex structuring, with readjustments of mobile centrations and a co-ordination of eye-movements in pursuit of the object, it may be wondered if the resulting perceptions are qualitatively and quantitatively the same at all ages. An attempt was

[1] Auersperg, Prinz A., and Buhrmester, H. C., *Zeitschr. f. Sinnesphysiol.*, *1936*, **66**, 274–309.

made to answer this, with the help of Lambercier[1] and in collaboration with Beggert, Aebli and Gantenbein.

Present indications are that the problem is of particular importance in regard to the way in which figures are generally structured by children. Eye-movement and tachistoscopic studies of centration and of explorations of forms have already shown that a child has difficulty in fixating the essential parts of a figure and in encompassing its various constituent elements in one enveloping centration (Chapter II, § 6, and Chapter III, § 1). We were also led, through the theoretical study of the development of illusions and through the tachistoscopic analysis of their temporal maxima (Chapter III, § 9), to the theory that developmental trends exhibiting maxima constitute the normal case. We concluded that every figure is subject to a phase of structuring, due to perceptual activities, before field effects which derive from those activities become stabilised and illusion decreases. It would therefore be particularly interesting to examine the case of the perception of moving bodies (in which the role of perceptual structuring activities is apparent) to see if the form is differently structured at different ages and to find out if an active structuring really does develop with age to allow the recognition of such simple forms as the square to occur.

In our investigations we used Auersperg's and Buhrmester's apparatus, the figure being a square of 25 mm (with lines 2 mm thick) with a radius of circumduction of 17·5 mm and rates of rotation varying between 2 and 400 a minute. Subjects were children between the ages of 5 and 12 years, and adults.

Auersperg and Buhrmester showed that perceived changes accompanying increases in rates of rotation exhibit three phases and two inter-phases, determined by the way in which the elements of the square in its successive positions are related in perception (for these positions, see Fig. 53).

Phase I: the square can be seen in clear and constant form.

Inter-phase I–II: the square becomes confused, corners interlace (as in Fig. 53) and off-centre and asymmetrical crosses appear.

Phase II: a single cross appears in the centre of the figure, inscribed inside a large 'square' with rounded corners. This large square was already visible in the preceding inter-phase but now contracts to a smaller surface (2 × 25 = 50 mm diameter) than that of the circumduction (60 mm diameter for the outer extremity of the square).

Inter-phase II–III: the single cross broadens out and more or less abruptly changes into a double cross.

Phase III (fused image): a double, motionless but flickering cross

[1] *Rech.* 13.

appears, inscribed in a large square frame (25 + 35 = 60 mm) with rounded corners.

We measured the number of rotations per minute required for the appearance of the single and of the double crosses. The rate required for the appearance of the single cross would depend on the resistance of the rotating figure to destruction and would thus constitute a measure of the strength of its structure. Distances between figure and subject, illumination of the figure and the length of the presentation were also varied. To make a closer analysis of the possible effect of anticipation, we compared the results obtained with increasing and with decreasing rates of rotation (the subjects in the latter group (decreasing rate) would not therefore have known that the figure was a square as they started with a fused image). Finally,

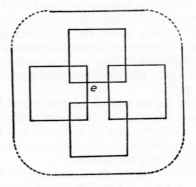

Fig. 53.

in order to establish the role of motor activity, we made a certain number of observations on ourselves in which we either fixated a white patch placed at the centre of the rotation or followed the moving square. [Results are set out in Table 103.]

It can be seen that the rate corresponding to the onset of Phases I and II increased very regularly with age, which implies that the figure persisted for longer and longer as a square (Phase I) and then as a single cross (Phase II), as a function of age. The extents of the interphases were not measured, as it would have been very difficult for measurements to be made with children, but they can be accepted as being either constant or proportional to those of the preceding phases and as not increasing with age beyond those proportions. These first results give some indication of the improvement in structuring which occurs with age.

246

TABLE 103. *Mean and range of critical rpm for the appearance of single and double crosses as a function of age and of viewing distance with medium illumination (n for age groups varied between 10 and 12)*

Rech. 13, Tables 1 and 3

Age groups	5–6 yrs		7–8 yrs		10–12 yrs		Adult	
Distance	1 m	3 m	1 m	3 m	1 m	3 m	1 m	3 m
Group I			Single Cross					
Mean	141		155		172		186	
Maximum	154		174		188		210	
Minimum	122		138		152		168	
			Double Cross					
Mean	225		230		232		264	
Maximum	280		260		260		320	
Minimum	194		196		194		210	
Group II			Single Cross					
Mean	148	160	153	164	172	184	184	193
Maximum	154	182	174	178	190	202	210	210
Minimum	140	148	144	146	152	164	170	178
			Double Cross					
Mean	216	220	228	232	225	245	274	296
Maximum	250	236	250	260	260	280	350	390
Minimum	190	200	202	206	170	204	204	214

It can also be seen that structuring improved with viewing distance. This establishes the role of motor activity because an increase in distance, while decreasing the sharpness of the image, at the same time diminishes its visual angle, thus facilitating visual pursuit by reducing the amplitude of the required eye-movements. Reciprocally, it was also shown (the figures, which need not be shown here, can be seen in Table 2 of *Rech*. 13) that, with distance constant (1 m), structuring deteriorated with reduction in illumination, the sharpness of the image being thus reduced.

A comparison of the thresholds obtained with increasing and decreasing rates of rotation are also instructive and are presented in Table 104.

TABLE 104. *Comparison of mean critical rpm for the appearance of the simple cross (Phase II) as a function of the direction of the change of rpm*

Rech. 13, Table 4

	Increasing rpm	Decreasing rpm	Mean
5 to 6 years (*n* = 10)	170	163	166
6 to 7 years (*n* = 10)	174	176	175
7 to 8 years (*n* = 10)	177	179	178
Adult (*n* = 25)	211	220	216

It can be seen that structuring seemed to be better with decreasing than with increasing rates in the adult while the opposite was the case at 5 to 6 years (which is particularly interesting), while the two orders gave equal results at intermediate ages. It may seem paradoxical that (for adults) a square should be structured at higher rates of rotation when the rate is decreasing (the subjects had not been shown first that the figure was a square) than when the rate is increasing (when all they had to do was to continue to see it). However, the paradox can be cleared up by examining the effects of presenting the displays for different durations. In summary, the results show that, at rates of rotation of 200 to 400 per minute, adults passed through Phases I, II and III as the time of presentation increased from 0·5 to 1, 2, 5 and 10 seconds. This is obviously because the visual pursuit mechanisms become fatigued when the subject tries to follow the same circular trajectory for a continuous period, or rather that the pursuit movement takes on a more and more attenuated circular or elliptical course. This, as we shall see, would explain the changes to Phases II and III. No doubt this is why the structuring seems to have been less good with increasing than with decreasing rates of rotation (the time of presentation was not limited): a restructuring is facilitated with a decreasing rate because the attention is aroused by an unfamiliar sight. That this did not occur for children of 5 to 6 years certainly indicates, when combined with the results for this age group shown in Table 103, that younger children experience a greater difficulty in structuring: in spite of the fact that the square is the best 'good form' after the circle, they have difficulty in adjusting their shifting centrations, in maintaining a regular and appropriate movement of the gaze, etc.

Observations made on ourselves revealed that fixation on the patch at the centre of rotation at rates appropriate to Phase I caused the square to become diffused and simply to lose its pure white colour. If the square itself was fixated again, it regained its distinctive form and colour but now the patch took on a relative motion of circumduction. When trying to fixate between the two, the gaze was irresistibly attracted to the moving figure, because of the well-known orientation reflex. In Phase I the role of motor activity is thus beyond question. During Phase II events were similar, although the single cross appeared motionless: when fixating the patch, the cross became double, as in Phase III, and the apparent secondary circumduction circles reached their maximum (35 mm), which again indicates the involvement of motor activity. The same thing happened when the figure was passively regarded (while thinking about something else). But it is clear that eye-movements describe only circles or ellipsoids of reduced diameter during Phase II: although still real and active, they are progressively outdistanced by the movement of the square.

We will now try to interpret the facts and what they tell us about children's structurings. We can no doubt do without the notion of *prolepsis* in Phase I, while fully recognising that a problem does exist from the mere fact that a single identical moving object is perceived rather than a succession of juxtaposed objects. We must also recognise that the movement as such cannot be reduced to a succession of snapshots but forms a continuum, linking a past which imperceptibly extends the present into an immediate future which is already linked to that present. But just as an ocular movement can transport a length or a form, or a difference, on to another to bring about their comparison, so a continuous transport of the square in position *n* on to the square in succeeding positions will make its identification possible (identity being a perceptible relation like equality or difference). While we would agree that this identity presumes an active schematisation and something more than a mere registration, it is still unnecessary to introduce the notion of anticipation because, in Phase I, the speed of the transportation is equal to, or could be greater than, that of the circumduction itself.

Phase II, on the other hand, raises a more complex problem, because it corresponds neither to the perception of a square, nor to the fused retinal image, but to the construction of an original figure (the single cross with a general contraction of the frame) whose properties need to be explained. Auersperg and Buhrmester talk about a 45° lag in *prolepsis* in this case, which would explain the appearance of a cross. But this explanation involves the difficult notion of a lag in anticipation, a lag fixed at 45° in spite of variations in rates of circumduction. It also requires that the ocular movements should maintain a constant amplitude. A simpler explanation is available and consists in admitting, firstly, that the transportation, being ill-equipped to follow the square in its complete trajectory beyond certain speeds which vary with age, describes an approximately circular movement of increasingly restricted amplitude. It follows immediately that the circumscribed space, *e* of Fig. 53, and the reference space in general, are progressively under-estimated when they can no longer be prescribed by localising the internal side of the square in the course of its circumduction. Reciprocally, those spaces can no longer be used in the localisation of the internal side. This, being unlocated, tends to fuse in its successive positions, as a function of the reduced amplitude of eye-movements. Finally a single cross (formed by the fusion of the internal side of the square as it is seen successively in its optimal positions) and the general contraction of the figure emerge simultaneously.

Phase III presents no problems, merely resulting from the progressive abandonment of ocular-motor transports.

This contraction of the referential and circumscribed spaces with the delocalisation of the internal sides of the square is not just a piece of imagination. Not only is such a contraction found in stroboscopic movements (see § 2) and in the perception of velocity in general (§ 3), but it is also demonstrated in the present case in the following way.

When a single vertical line is placed in circumduction, with its extremities masked by a screen, its circular orbit is not seen but it appears as a line lying alternately to the right and to the left of the point of rotation (see Fig. 54). Under these circumstances there is no shrinking of the space *e* during Phase I but a perceptible shrinking of it during Phase II which, however, disappears immediately if one tries to measure it, simply because the presence of the comparison line steadies the gaze.

In a general way, the phenomenon can be explained as follows. In normal conditions, a distance is judged by means of stationary reference points which mark its limits, this being mediated, no doubt, by a certain number of encounters (cf. Chapter II, § 2) on the empty space, either by direct centration on that space, or by centrations on its boundaries (its extremities).[1] If the reference points are moving slowly, their positions will have to be determined on the basis of distances judged within the reference space or background; but these distances themselves are estimated in terms of the successive positions of the moving reference points: whence a circle from which the subject can only escape if the encounters provided by the mobile centrations allow a distinction to be made between the moving reference points and the stationary reference space. With an increase in velocity, however, the only remaining distances are the intervals between the moving parts, intervals which are themselves mobile and susceptible to under- or over-estimations, for example, by the effect of a preceding one on the next succeeding one (as will be described in § 3).

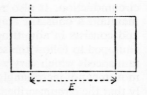

Fig. 54.

In the particular case of the square in circumduction (Fig. 55), no deformation can occur in the perception of the internal intervals between the sides of the square because the interval is constant and the sides are always perceived simultaneously. On the other hand, the intervals *AD*, between the extreme outside positions (the left side of the square when it is at the left and its right side when it is at the right), and *BC*, between the adjacent positions (the right side when the square is at the left and the left side when it is at the right), are

---

[1] As we already know, an unfilled space demarcated by two horizontals equal in length to it is devalued by them (Chapter II, § 2, *Concluding remarks*); this seems to show that estimates of length do not depend simply on retinal locus but also on the number of encounters which occur between the object and the receptors, encounters which are more numerous in the case of filled than of unfilled spaces. It follows that the more numerous are the moving objects (e.g. the sides of a rapidly moving square) which cross an unfilled reference space, the less probable will be the occurrence of encounters on that space.

intervals between successive positions: at low rates of rotation (Phase I), with a moving centration on the square itself, these positions are still located in relation to the reference space. At the greater rates of Phase II, however, when the gaze follows a circular path of decreasing amplitude and the mobile centrations no longer attach to the middle or even perhaps to the inside of the square but gradually approach the centre of the total figure, the subject must watch, in very rapid succession, both the extreme positions of the sides of the square (*A* and *D*) and their adjacent positions (*B* and *C*). This presupposes a play of centrations which are at once moving and enveloping, distributing the encounters at four points which are almost simultaneously present and the most important of which are the outer ones. In this case, *AB* and *CD* are the most likely intervals to be conserved, being constant distances and marked by simultaneously present lines. The whole interval *AD* (between immediately succeeding traces) will be devalued both because the reference space is no longer perceptible and because the positions *A* and *D* are the most widely separated from the mobile centrations and give rise to successive encounters at the greatest distances from the moving fovea. There would then be no reason for the interval *BC* (the intervening space) to remain perceptible: if the positions *A* and *D* are seen peripherally, and if the reference space is not perceptible, there would be no means of locating points *B* and *C* in relation to each other and they could be fused without losing sight of the distances *AB* and *CD*. As these events occur both in the vertical and in the horizontal directions, the result is a single cross and the general contraction of the figure. Both of these are brought about by a loss of localisation due to the nature of the centrations: they become increasingly enveloping, as they become more mobile, but at the same time follow a path of decreasing amplitude.

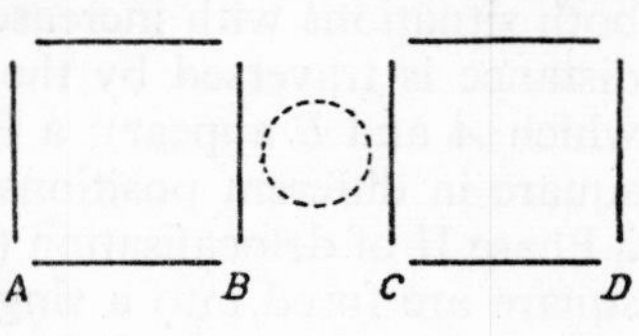

Fig. 55.

This analysis allows us to extract matters of genetic interest from Tables 103 and 104. Tachistoscopic studies have already shown that the child's centrations are less enveloping than those of the adult (Chapter II, § 6) and that, with a motionless figure, the child experiences more difficulty than the adult in adjusting his centrations and in organising his explorations and transportations (Chapter III, § 1). We now see that the child is more quickly defeated by the task when a moving object has to be followed by the gaze, and when transports have to be co-ordinated with moving and enveloping centrations (Table 103). At decreasing rates of rotation (Table 104), the child of 5 to 6 years cannot, on the average, recognise the parts of the square

251

at rates exceeding 163 rpm, compared to the 220 rpm of the adult (this refers to the beginning of Inter-phase I–II, the recognition of the square itself taking place only at an even lower rate). These various but converging results demonstrate, in a general way, the difficulties of structuring which already exist at the youngest age at which it is possible to experiment. But the age of 5 to 6 already represents a considerable perceptual experience, and one might well ask how even simple motionless perceptual forms, and, *a fortiori* moving figures which also occur in the perceptual experience of the infant, would be structured during the first months of existence. It is for this reason that these results are of some interest for a theory which posits the need for primary perceptual activities in the establishment of field effects.

§ 2. STROBOSCOPIC MOVEMENT

The obvious analogy between the results just described and the well-known phenomena of apparent or stroboscopic movements will have been noticed. The difference in the two situations is, presumably, that the square of Auersperg and Buhrmester actually moves and alternately occupies two extreme positions, x and y, whereas in stroboscopic experiments a motionless object, A, appears at x and, when it disappears, a second motionless object, B, appears at y and reciprocally. At a certain rate of alternation (velocity in the sense of frequency), objects A and B appear as one object oscillating between x and y. This essential difference apart, the same three phases occur in both situations with increases in velocity (the speed with which the distance is traversed by the square or the frequency-velocity with which A and B appear): a Phase I of distinct perception (the same square in different positions, or two objects in separate positions), a Phase II of delocalisation (the interior positions of the sides of the square are fused into a single cross, or the apparent movement of $AC = B$ between x and y) and the final Phase III of fusion (a double cross in the case of the square or two simultaneously present, motionless and separate objects). Moreover, in the same way as the child reaches Phase II of the previous experiment (single cross) at fewer revolutions per minute than the adult, so Meili and Tobler (see p. 257 below) found that a child attains the perception of stroboscopic movement (also at Phase II) at much lower frequency-velocities than the adult. It occurred to us that the account given of the Auersperg and Buhrmester effects might be applicable to the case of apparent movements. This would support the analogy often said to exist between the perception of stroboscopic movement and the perception of real movement, and would perhaps thereby shed some light on the controversial and complex question of apparent movements.

252

We therefore asked Gantenbein to compare children and adults in different stroboscopic situations. Her results[1] will now be discussed.

I. Without attempting to summarise the large amount of work, representing very different points of view, devoted to the study of apparent movements, and without trying to establish how the proposed account conflicts with well-known theses, or agrees with universally accepted ones, we will confine ourselves to outlining the hypotheses suggested by the above analogies. This will help us to understand how Gantenbein set about verifying them. It must be stressed that the account is a relational and not a causal one, and makes no reference to underlying physiological mechanisms which might be suggested in other contexts and to which most other theories refer.

The two essential relations to be considered are the identities and the locations of objects A and B. When A and B have the same form, colour and size, their identities can only be established on the basis of their locations: delocalisation can lead to their fusion into a single object. When A and B have different forms (for example, a straight line and the arc of a circle) an apparent movement then consists in seeing the line bend and the arc straighten out, with a consequent loss of the independent identities of A and B. The same thing happens when rapid succession is involved: a dot followed by lines of increasing length seems to lose its identity and progressively to lengthen out as if it were a single object which was changing in size, etc.

In regard to localisation, it will be remembered that when the gaze moves over a stable background composed of objects lying in the one plane, the objects appear to remain motionless in spite of the movement of their images relative to the retina. If, however, they are not lying in the same plane, those in the foreground appear to move in relation to those in the background and an object placed very close to the eyes seems to move a great deal as the gaze shifts. The same thing happens even with a neutral surface (a large sheet of cardboard) whose edges are invisible but whose texture can be made out: no doubt this occurs because the surface, being closer to the eyes than a background usually is, appears as an object in relation to a motionless but invisible background situated behind it (previous experience seeming to play a role in this case). In short, localisation, with objects seen as moving or as stationary reference points, depends on the organisation of planes in depth, and particularly on the relating of objects to a background which is taken, by an arbitrary perceptual decision, to be motionless. This breaks down as soon as the situation

[1] *Rech.* 14.

becomes unusual as, for example, when the eyeball is moved involuntarily by finger pressure.

A second important characteristic of localisation is that the sudden appearance of even a single motionless object among other objects in the background gives rise to an apparent movement which seems to bring it to the place at which it appears. The impression may be, for example, that it comes from behind and follows a short path perpendicular to the plane of the background. Similarly, an unseen peripheral object (generally lying at the extreme limit of the field and when the subject's gaze is motionless or almost so) appears to move on being noticed. For example, one may perceive a small movement in an object which is then taken to be an animal or a human; but it is later recognised as a motionless pebble or tree trunk when the gaze has been adjusted. These facts show that apparent movement may be associated with the identification and with the localisation of a single object and is not dependent on the successive appearance of objectively distinct objects.

It now becomes easy to interpret stroboscopic movement in terms of loss of identity and of location, relating the objective succession of *A* and *B* to the subject's perceptual activities, as was done for the rate of circumduction of the square to the speed of transports or to the positions of the mobile and overlapping centrations. Of particular importance is the fact that photographic analyses of ocular movements in a stroboscopic situation, made by Guilford and Helson,[1] and by Hulin and Katz,[2] have shown that, while there is normally a shift of the gaze from *A* to *B* and back during Phase I (the apparent successive appearance of two adequately located and motionless objects), there is, in general, no ocular movement during Phase II (of apparent movement), or at least no ocular movement correlated with the apparent movement of a supposed single object. This absence of complete oculo-motor transportation during Phase II will be used as evidence, and we have no intention whatever of explaining apparent movements in terms of ocular movements, as Fischer[3] or Higginson[4] did. On the other hand, it must be made clear that the absence of effective and complete oculo-motor transports in no way excludes the very probable intervention of incipient transports, started but not realised: for example, an initiated motor movement that is inhibited at some level or stage. Nor, above all, does it exclude the inevitable extension of the initial field of centration on *A*, which will then tend to envelop *B* as it appears (as a result of peripheral encounters which

[1] Guilford, J. P., and Helson, H., *Amer. J. Psychol.*, 1929, **41**, 595–606.
[2] Hulin, W. S., and Katz, D., *Amer. J. Psychol.*, 1934, **46**, 332–4.
[3] Fischer, O., *Phil. Stud.*, 1886, **3**, 128–50.
[4] Higginson, G. D., *Amer. J. Psychol.*, 1926, **37**, 408–13.

occur because centration on *A* becomes enveloping and relates the already perceived *A* to the newly appearing *B*).

The tendency to relate *A* to *B*, when *A* disappears physically (but with a perceptual lag) and *B* appears, will be referred to as 'an internal or incomplete transport (*Tpi*)' of *A* onto *B*, but without guessing at the possible physiological concomitants. We mean to imply that *Tpi* remains internal or incomplete precisely because an act of transportation, *Tp*, cannot be effected (because of insufficiently rapid eye-movements, etc.).

Phase I (two distinct and successive appearances) is then explained by the fact that a real transport, *Tp*, is possible and requires a time shorter than, or equal to, the time, *t*(*A*, *B*), which elapses between the perceived disappearance of *A* and the perceived appearance of *B* (the perceived disappearance corresponds to the real disappearance plus the duration of the extinction of the percept, and the perceived appearance corresponds to the real appearance plus the time for the 'arousal' of the excitation). Transports being possible, the referential space, *E*, between *A* and *B*, does not bring about a devaluation and the objects *A* and *B* are adequately located in relation to their motionless background.

When the time *t*(*A*, *B*) is shortened, or the frequency-velocity of the successions *ABAB* . . . is increased, there comes a moment when *A* tends still to be perceived but to be in the process of disappearing while *B* is appearing at a distance from it. Consequently, a complete transport from *A* to *B* is no longer possible and an internal or incomplete transport occurs when centration bears on *A* and on its neighbourhood but *B* attracts encounters and provokes an extension of the field of centration which then envelops it. If *t*(*Tp*) is the time required for the real transport, and *t*(*Tpc*) the time for the internal transport, one will have:

(51) $t(A, B) > t(Tp)$ and $t(A, B) \leqslant t(Tpi)$

But the lack of time also prevents a demarcation of the referential space, *E*, which is therefore under-estimated; at the same time the elements *A* and *B* can no longer be located during the course of the internal transport because of this absence of demarcation. The problem is then to understand why *A* and *B* are identified (with apparent movement from *A* to *B*) rather than simply seen as close together but distinct.

Before examining this, it must be remembered that nearly all investigators report the presence of inter-phases, or of intermediate situations, between Phases I and II (as between II and III). These take the form of the succession of two lines with movements associated with their appearances and disappearances; or of the movements of a single line with apparent variations in intensity (van der Waals and Roelops, etc., see p. 259 below); or even (Wertheimer, but not confirmed by everyone) of pure movements without material supports or real moving objects (*phi* movements). In addition, a fundamental experiment by Pièron[1] has shown that stroboscopic movements can be obtained by projecting images onto the eyes separately and in such a way as to involve different cerebral hemispheres and to exclude physiological explanations based on close proximity (ocular or cerebral short-circuits).

To keep to the perceived relations only (identity and localisation), and to the analysis of the conditions under which they occur (which alone makes them explanatory) it must be pointed out that during Phase II, and in virtue of Prop. 51, the existence of a non-identity between A and B and the existence of distinct localisations become perceptually indeterminate. Two elements having the same form, colour and size are perceptually non-identical if they are perceived simultaneously in different places; if they are perceived to be in the one place successively (or simultaneously), it is impossible to know if one is masking the other or if they have fused; if they are perceived successively in different places, it is impossible to know if there are two of them or if it is one that has changed its position. But when A disappears (subjectively), and B appears, they cannot be located accurately and appear to be closer together because of the devaluation of E. Is it easier, then, for the subject to identify them or to distinguish between them? The answer is that it is easier to identify them because the internal transports create a link between them and suggest their apparent identity, which only a double localisation could exclude, a double localisation which is itself impossible because of the absence of a complete transport. Similarly, in regard to the perception of a movement, the disappearance of A and the appearance of B already constitute movements. Such changes tend to be seen as movements and this is reinforced by the failure of the incomplete transport to demarcate the space E. It only remains to understand how such partial movements are compounded into an overall impression of movement, which is no greater a mystery than to understand why a succession of discontinuous segments is perceived as a whole, or how the perception of several individual letters becomes the perception of a whole word. Here again, it is a question of probabilities and of decisions, and of the operation of a principle of parsimony (of costs and gains): is it easier to perceive two almost indistinguishable objects which exhibit the beginnings of movements near positions x and y, or to see a single object move from x to y? The subject might hesitate to give an opinion if he were

[1] Pièron, H., *Année Psychol.*, 1944, 34, 245–8.

motionless, or inactive, and if he limited himself to registering the information without bias; but he is always active, and his action influences the decision in one direction or the other according to his age and, of course, according to the situation.

In the adult, the effort at the moment of decision is towards the realisation of a real or complete transport. This tends to retain the separate identities and approximate localisations and results in the late onset of Phase II. The child, in whom the speed and adjustment of real transports are no doubt less well developed (see § 1) and in whom the enveloping centrations are less precise, etc., finds it easier to abandon complete transports: he tends to be satisfied with incomplete transports. This inclines the decision towards movement only, as much because of the lack of criteria for localisation and identification, as because the internal transport alone suggests the perceptual possibility of the movement of A at x towards B at y. This also happens in the adult when the real transport is superseded, as happens, at greater velocities than in the child, in Phase II of the Auersperg effect (the perception of a single cross) to be made.

Phase III (simultaneity) poses no problem because both elements are perceived at the one time, which excludes a loss of identity and allows their correct localisation to be made.

II. Gantenbein tried to examine these hypotheses by means of a series of measurements directed at the various factors known to play a part in stroboscopic movement, notably the distance between the lines, the duration of exposure, the temporal interval, the illumination and the points of fixation, the whole being considered from the point of view of age differences.

II (1). In every situation, Gantenbein verified the law already established by Meili and Tobler,[1] according to which the attainment of apparent movement and simultaneity are inversely related to age (attained at lower frequency-velocities in children). But she also established another law (and the two results should be taken together) according to which repetition (or practice) reinforces the attainment of apparent movement and simultaneity, and this to a far greater extent in subjects of 9 to 12 years and in adults than in children of 5 to 6 years (see Table 21 of *Rech.* 14). This paradoxical finding is most instructive. In the various researches so far carried out (Chapter III, § 2), we have found, in general, that the effects of practice tend in the same direction as those of development with age: the illusions of Müller–Lyer and of the lozenge decrease with age and with practice, while the illusion of Oppel–Kundt in-

---

[1] Meili, R., and Tobler, E., *Arch. Psychol.*, 1931, **23**, 131–56.

creases in both cases, and that of the square gives equally variable results in both cases. The fact that stroboscopic movement is less readily achieved with age but improves with practice (especially in adults) thus raises a problem and seems to indicate the intervention of a double activity, the one developing with age, the other with practice. In fact, the preceding considerations demonstrate just this. On the one hand, as apparent movement results from the impossibility of achieving complete transports when the elements succeed one another too rapidly (which prevents the conservation of their distinct identities and their localisation), the improvement of transportation with age will, of course, tend to hold the achievement of stroboscopic movement more and more in check. But, on the other hand, an incomplete transport alone is not sufficient to guarantee the production of apparent movement: it provides the necessary conditions (of difficulties of identification and of localisation) but not the sufficient ones. This is because the movements associated with the appearances and disappearances of A and of B have yet to be built up into an overall movement which carries A (identified with B) from position x to position y and back again. But this generalisation of partial movements into an overall movement also implies an activity of structuring which can well be understood to develop with practice: once perceived, the striking effects of apparent movement can only reinforce further structuring in the same direction. Even if transports improve with practice, and then act against the production of apparent movement, the capacity for combining partial movements into whole movements will develop even more rapidly. Consequently it can be understood how, in this particular and perhaps unique case, the effects of development with age and those of training or practice work in opposite directions.

II (2). A second question of theoretical interest studied by Gantenbein, again in the wake of many other authors, was the role of the point of fixation. It is known that Cermak and Koffka[1] thought that they had established that the peripheral presentation of stimuli militates against *optimum* movement and favours the perception of succession (which would support the short-circuit theory). However, another Gestaltist, Galli,[2] disproved this assertion by showing that fixation on a point midway between and at a height corresponding to, the mid-points of the lines produced less apparent movement than fixation at a distance from the stimulus objects. Galli explained this result by the fact that the lines then fall on the periphery of the retina, where sensitivity to movement increases and resolution diminishes.

[1] Cermak, P., and Koffka, K., *Psychol. Forsch.*, 1921, **1**, 66–129.
[2] Galli, A., *Contributi del Labor d. psicol. dell. Univ. Cattol. d.S. Cuore*, 1926, **1**, Fasc. 4, 201–44.

This proposal is consistent with the results of Basler[1] and of Hartmann.[2] Similarly Hillebrand[3] found that fixation on the same point as used by Galli made the perception of continuous movement impossible but allowed the perception of partial movements only. Van der Waals and Roelops[4] obtained similar results and added that, while the point of fixation plays almost no role at short distances, at greater distances fixation on the first element favours apparent movement more than does fixation on the second. Scholz[5] also confirmed that peripheral vision strengthens apparent movement and concurrently reinforces the under-estimation of the intervening space traversed by the movement.

Taking up the same problems with children between 6 and 13 years and with adults, Gantenbein obtained the same three results at all ages: (*a*) the *optimum* situation is the absence of constrained fixation, no doubt because the subject spontaneously first centres on the first line (a situation which favours apparent movement), then occasionally on the second, then on the first again and so on, and with transports constantly lagging behind apparent movement; (*b*) peripheral vision also favours stroboscopic movement, but less so than the absence of fixation; (*c*) the most unfavourable situation (not entirely prohibitive in the adult) is with fixation midway between and at a height corresponding to the mid-point of the two lines (Galli's fixation point).

It can be seen that these results, which agree with those of the great majority of authors (with some details added, notably genetic ones), but which are contrary to those of Cermak and Koffka, are easily explained on the basis of the hypotheses being advanced (cf. I): fixation midway between the lines discourages apparent movement because it favours the retention of identities, of correct localisations and of complete transports; peripheral vision, or fixation on the first line (or on each alternately), leads to the opposite results.

II (3). The third question studied is more difficult, and concerns the role of the distance between the lines. Almost all authors, except Korte,[6] have maintained that apparent movement is inversely related to this distance. Korte, although a Gestaltist, obtained optimum movements with an increase in this distance when temporal intervals increased concomitantly. Gantenbein, working under the constant

[1] Basler, A., *Pflugers Archiv*, 1906, **115**, 583–601; 1908, **124**, 313–35.
[2] Hartmann, G. W., *Psychol. Forsch.*, 1923, **3**, 19.
[3] Hillebrand, F., *Zeitschr. f. Psychol.*, 1922, **89**, 209–272; **90**, 1–66.
[4] Van der Waals, H. G., and Roelops, C. O., *Zeitschr. f. Psychol.*, 1930, **114**, 241–88; **115**, 91–193; 1933, **128**, 314–54.
[5] Scholz, D. A., *Psychol. Forsch.*, 1924, **5**, 219–72.
[6] Korte, A., *Zeitschr. f. Psychol.*, 1915, **72**, 193–296.

conditions provided by the apparatus of van der Waals and Roelops, with a temporal interval of 60 ms, and exposure time of 60 ms for both elements, illumination of 65 *lux*, but with the least favourable point of fixation (midway between the lines and at half their height),[1] obtained the results shown in Table 105. The figures represent the intervals (ms) between the presentations of the two elements at which Phase I (succession) gave way to Phase II (apparent movement) at the given separations (cm) between the elements.

TABLE 105. *Mean critical intervals (ms) between the exposure of successive elements for the appearance of apparent movement as a function of age and of the separation of the elements (n = 10 for each age group)*

Rech. 14, Table 5

Age group	5 yrs	6 yrs	7 yrs	8 yrs	9 yrs	10 yrs	11 yrs	12 yrs	13 yrs	Adult
Separation (cm)										
10	1,137	1,078	1,083	994	903	765	659	601	590	209
50	1,261	1,240	1,210	1,137	1,050	855	795	708	663	271
80	1,288	1,287	1,265	1,205	1,150	936	870	786	710	383

There is obviously a very regular progression with age in the threshold for apparent movement (cf. II, 1) but, more importantly, the perception of apparent movement becomes more likely at all ages as the separation between elements increases (which was also found for the transition from the movements of Phase II to the simultaneities of Phase III). This result is altogether too consistent with the interpretation by incomplete transports (it is obvious that transports are less likely to be complete as separations increase), and, to tell the truth, we were somewhat worried about it. However, while we have not yet come across reports which confirm these findings, several visiting colleagues have told us that they too have observed similar events which contradict current opinion. The regularity of the curves is, moreover, striking, and a contradiction having appeared between the results at 10 cm and at 20 cm in other experiments which she had conducted, Gantenbein was able to establish that this was due to the effects of training: responses at 10 cm and at 20 cm, when order effects are controlled, obey the same law.

While we do not claim that this is a general law, because the opposite has usually been found, we do maintain (until more fully informed by results obtained with further variations of the factors involved) that the unusual distributions of Table 105 are due in fact to the presence of the unfavourable point of fixation. The contradiction between our results and those of most authors is only apparent and is of the same order as the equally apparent contradiction observed between the curves of development and of practice.

[1] This point of fixation was chosen in order to slow down the child's too facile perception of movement, to allow for a better comparison with adults. The durations were measured by the angle of the rotation of the disc of the apparatus, for a description of which, see *Rech.* 14.

As we have already said, two factors play a major part in the production of stroboscopic effects. These are usually interdependent, because of the subordination of the second to the first, but can be partially dissociated when a particular situation favours one over the other. These two factors are: (*a*) the incomplete character of the transports, which disrupts localisation and favours the loss of the respective identities of the two lines; and (*b*) the fusing of the movements associated with the appearances and disappearances of the objects into an overall movement. Now, in principle, short distances between the elements will favour factor (*b*) and militate against (*a*), while greater distances will favour (*a*). In the usual run of experiments on adults, where the authors probably chose the most propitious conditions of fixation (objects in peripheral vision, or an absence of constrained fixation), the fixation conditions tended to make transports incomplete (thus strengthening factor (*a*)) with the result that apparent movement was more readily obtained at shorter distances, which favour factor (*b*). In Gantenbein's experiments, fixation on the midpoint held the effects of factor (*a*) in check at small distances: under these circumstances, an increase in distance will make transports incomplete (thus strengthening factor (*a*)) and allow overall movements to be perceived (factor (*b*)) as a remedy for the loss of localisation which has been induced. In short, if the point of fixation chosen should favour factor (*a*), the shorter the distance the more probable will seen movement be, because factor (*b*) will then be strengthened; if, on the contrary, the point of fixation discourages factor (*a*), then factor (*b*), which is subordinate to it, will not be sufficient to produce a strong effect: an increase in distance will then strengthen factor (*a*) and, by doing so, the effect of factor (*b*) also, but this time to the extent that factor (*b*) is facilitated by the incomplete nature of the transports (and in so far as it is subordinate to factor (*a*)).

II (4). Gantenbein also confirmed that a reduction of the temporal interval favours the perception of apparent movement, and then of simultaneity, whereas a reduction of the time of exposure militates against it, as does an increase in illumination. It is unnecessary to dwell on these well-known facts. On the other hand, it is interesting to point out that she confirmed the findings of Scholz[1] that the space between the lines is devalued (there is a slight over-estimation when the distance is small, followed by a progressive under-estimation), which corresponds to the contraction of the frame of the single cross in the Auersperg and Buhrmester experiment (see § 1 and commentary on Figs. 54 and 55). For example, of twenty adults, fourteen

[1] *Loc. cit.*

noticed a contraction of the space of 80 cm, six noticed no change and none noticed an expansion.[1]

It may therefore be admitted that, on the whole, the explanatory scheme advanced to account for the effects produced by the square in circumduction (§ 1) applies equally well to, and establishes the relations by which, stroboscopic movement may be explained.

§ 3. THE PERCEPTION OF VELOCITY

Considered from the point of view of developed intellectual operations, velocity appears as a relation between the distance traversed and the duration of movement, or $v = d : t$. This would suggest that distance and duration are elementary components and velocity a product of their composition. Some authors have tried to describe the perception of velocity in this way: Brown, for example,[2] supposes that phenomenal velocity corresponds to a relation between phenomenal duration and perceived distance. However, even at the level of notions, resultant velocity ($v = d : t$) makes a late appearance (towards 8 to 9 years) and is preceded by an ordinal concept based on an intuitive interpretation of passing: a moving body which is first seen behind a second one and then in front of it, is judged to be moving faster in virtue of the simple successive spatial and temporal relations, but without reference to the distance traversed or to the duration of the movement. Moreover, it is difficult to imagine that distances traversed and durations are the elementary perceptual components of which perceived velocity is the product (in the same way, for example, as a constant size might be the product of apparent size and distance). In fact, the perception of velocity is at least as elementary as that of duration (if not more so), because the velocities of moving bodies crossing a motionless visual field can be perceived. Similarly, the perception of movement, *qua* displacement, depends entirely on changes in order: everything that we saw in §§ 1 and 2 concerning the perception of moving objects, or of apparent movements, is explicable in terms of ordinal correspondences. In this case the correspondences are between the movements of objects (or the discontinuous successions) and the movements of the gaze which are required for transportations, whether these succeed in following the moving objects (correspondence of spatio-temporal positions) or are outstripped by them (non-correspondence, which thus prevents the occurrence of the deformations

[1] These results were obtained in the experiments reported above with fixation on the mid-point, a situation which would lead to an over-estimation of this space but for the intervention of the apparent movement.
[2] Brown, J. F., *Psychol. Forsch.*, 1931, **14**, 199.

studied). It is therefore legitimate to entertain, as a working hypothesis, the possibility of accounting for the perception of velocity in
terms either of purely ordinal, or of semi-ordinal and semi-metric
('metric ordinals' in Coombs' sense, or 'hyper-ordinals' in Suppes'
sense) considerations; that is, in terms of estimates of spatial intervals but not of durations.

An attempt was made to verify this interpretation with the help of
Feller and McNear.[1] The hypothesis is that there is no absolute perceptual velocity (no estimate of the velocity of a single moving body),
but that one velocity is always estimated in relation to another: when
a single moving body crosses the visual field, its velocity will be perceived in relation either to that of the ocular movements (in the case
of a moving visual field) or in relation to inverse velocities (whose
nature must be specified in the case of motionless visual fields).

I. We will first examine the case of two simultaneously perceived
moving objects. In this case the velocity of each body is estimated in
relation to that of the other, and if the movements are synchronous,
it is only necessary to judge the distance between them at successive
moments to arrive at their relative velocities. Thus, if the movements
are in the same direction, the rear-most object (relative to the direction of movement) will be perceived to be travelling faster than the
one in front if the distance between them progressively decreases, is
eliminated and then increases progressively in the opposite sense.
Where the paths cross, or diverge but in the same general direction,
an immediate organisation of the symmetries allows the same kind
of estimate to be made. In the case of random directions, there is a
tendency to transport one of the paths on to the other in order to
achieve the same kind of estimate. But this comparison of intervals
makes no reference either to duration or even to distances traversed:
the perception of duration would be useless because the movements
are simultaneous, and simultaneity is a relation of order (neither
before nor after). An estimate of the interval between the objects is
involved, however, and implies a hyper-ordinal estimation (a 'greater
or lesser' interval), but not an estimation of the distance traversed by
each body from its point of departure (which would involve an appeal
to extra-perceptual levels); rather, the successive intervals are more
and more accurately estimated by means of a simple perception of
their increase, decrease or invariance.

If these interpretations are well founded, it would be expected that
passing, and even overhauling, would give rise to particular perceptual events brought about by a progressive under- or over-estimation
of the decreasing or increasing intervals. It would also be expected

---

[1] *Rech.* 36.

that the apparent positions of moving objects would be perceived in terms of the intervals (constant or variable) which separated them, rather than in terms of the total distances they had traversed.

In connection with the first of these two points, we were fortunate enough to find a systematic error associated with passing. In the experiment, moving objects were presented, by film, under the following four conditions:

1. *A* and *B*, separated vertically by 6 cm, leave the same point at unequal velocities (*A*, 17 cm/sec, *B*, 11 cm/sec). Both stop simultaneously when *B* has traversed 65 cm. After an interval of 1·5 seconds, *B* continues alone (referred to as *B'*) for a further 65 cm in the same direction.

2. As above, but with reversed roles.

3. *A* and *B* start in succession and *A* overtakes *B*. Both continue for 150 cm, when *A* is 30 cm ahead, and both stop simultaneously.

4. As for 3, but both stop simultaneously at 65 cm. After 1·5 seconds, *B'* continues as in 1.

Subjects were asked to report on the perceived relative velocities, accelerations and decelerations of *A* and of *B* (the *AB* effect) when they were both moving, and of *B* and of *B'* (the *BB'* effect) when *B* moved on alone. Reports were in terms of no effect (*nil*); acceleration of the overtaking object (*AcOv*); deceleration of the overtaken object (*DcOt*); and the inverse of these, (*DcOv*) and (*AcOt*). These are shown in Table 106.

TABLE 106. *Subjects* (%) *reporting the relative velocities indicated under AB and BB' conditions* (*n* = 21 *adults*)

Rech. 36, Tables 17 and 18

Sequence (see text)	1	2	3	4
Judgement		Condition *AB*		
Nil	0	19	20	25
AcOv	24	29	30	10
DcOt	26	42	50	50
AcOv + *DcOt*	100	71	80	60
AcOt	0	5	0	10
DcOv	0	5	0	5
AcOt + *DcOv*	0	10	0	15
		Condition *BB'*		
Nil	29	38	—	45
B' > *B*	42	38	—	30
B' < *B*	29	24	—	25
Ot > *Ov*	42	24	—	30
Ot < *Ov*	29	38	—	25

It can be seen that the effect *AB* was very strong on the average, especially in the form of a progressive slowing of the overtaken object, which was therefore perceived to have a negative acceleration. An apparent acceleration of the overtaking object also occurred, but less often. These effects could hardly be due to the relations between the distances covered nor to the relations between the durations of movement. They are much more simply attributable to a progressive over-estimation of the interval between *A* and *B* as a result of its objective enlargement. This supposes a transportation of the movement of *A* on to that of *B*, and reciprocally, or, more simply, a continuous transposition of momentary intervals on to succeeding ones. When the subject is asked to compare *B* and *B'* (the two successive movements of *B*), he neglects *A* and perceives the movement of *B* as constant, with the result that no systematic *BB'* effect occurs (apart, perhaps, from the fact that the velocity attributed to *B'* is often a sort of compromise between those of *A* and of *B*).

Conditions 1 and 2 of the experiment were repeated with sixteen children of 5 to 7 years (the *BB'* comparison, which supposes successive comparisons, being omitted) and produced analogous but attenuated results for Condition 1 (82% *AcOv* + *DcOt*) and an insignificant effect in Condition 2.

In other experiments, overhauling (when *A* starts after or behind *B*) gave rise to qualitatively similar but quantitatively weaker results (50 to 60% of *AcOv* + *DcOt* against 5 to 25% opposite effects and 20 to 38% zero effects). With intersecting paths, the proportions of accelerations and decelerations and of zero effects were approximately the same, especially when equal velocities were used. It is thus clear that the important determinants of the effects are not the intervals as such, but rather the mechanisms whereby the transportation or the transposition of preceding intervals on to succeeding ones is more or less easily made (it becomes more difficult in the case of intersections).

The second point to be examined was the apparent positions of moving bodies as a function of the interval separating them. Our findings, while commonplace, may be worth discussing. The experiment took the form of having *A* and *B* move at the same velocity but with *B*, the lower object, leading *A* by 20 cm in one condition and by 30 cm in the other. During their trajectory, *B* stops, and then resumes its course and velocity when *A* is as far ahead of it as it was first ahead of *A*. It is observed that *B* appears to move backward when it stops. The results are set out in Table 107.

TABLE 107. *Frequency (%) of reports of various movements of A and of B under the conditions described in the text (n = 15 adults)*

Rech. 36, Table 16

Separation	B reverses	A accelerates	A decelerates	A stops
20 cm	87	33	6	6
30 cm	50	25	0	8

The effect was considerable with an interval of 20 cm, but was reported on only 50% of occasions at 30 cm. In addition, the apparent backward movement increased if *B* was fixated, but decreased, and the velocity of *A* increased slightly, when *A* was fixated. It is clear that in the absence of a motionless background, the localisation of a moving body is made, not in terms of the distance it has traversed, but in terms of the interval which separates it from another moving body. If the interval does not remain constant, it ceases to be perceived in the way that the length of a motionless line is perceived, but takes on the appearance of a variable distance between two points whose positions are constantly changing. The required determination of the location of each point can thus be achieved only in terms of the determination of the position of the other, whence the appearance of a relative movement which is perceived with the same clarity as a real movement. The existence of these relative movements is fundamental to what follows.

II. The second group of problems concerns the perception of the velocity of a single moving body when fixation is not constrained. In this case, if the velocity of an object is indeed always perceived in relation to that of another, the only other moving object available would be the subject's eye. We therefore set out to verify that relative movements in the form of changes in apparent velocity of the moving object could be produced by eye-movements. Two forms of verification were undertaken: the first, IIA, in which eye-movements were varied; and the second, IIB, in which the effects are generally supposed to be due to changes in the field (in the fixed background) but which we explain in terms of eye-movements.

IIA. Earlier writers, such as von Fleischl,[1] and Aubert,[2] have already pointed out the following paradox: when fixation is demanded, a moving body crossing the centre of the unmoving visual field appears to move more rapidly than when crossing the periphery of the field; but a moving body followed by the gaze (when its image will be in the foveal area for most of the time) seems to move more slowly than it does when fixation is maintained on the mid-point of its trajectory (when its image will be in the periphery for most of the time). However, this is no longer paradoxical if the relative movements of the moving object and of the eyes are taken into account: with fixation, the moving object naturally appears to move more swiftly, but when followed by the gaze, a compromise is established between the relative velocities involved (a relative velocity which is generally zero) and the combined absolute velocities of the moving object and of the eyes.

To test this interpretation of the paradox, an apparatus was set up which could be used either in normal illumination or in the dark. In the former condition, a series of small beads, and in the latter a series

[1] von Fleischl, *Sitzungsbericht der kaiserlichen Akademie der Wissenschaften in Wien, math.-nat. Classe*, 1882, **86**; 1883, **87**.
[2] Aubert, H., *Physiologie der Netzhaut*, Breslau, 1865.

of small phosphorescent dots, was mounted on a thread which was driven by an electric motor over a distance of 120 cm. Thirty-two adults and eighteen children from 5 to 7 years were tested in normal illumination, and a further twenty-three and eighteen respectively in the dark. In both situations all adults noticed an acceleration when fixation was constrained to the middle of the trajectory; this compares with 100% of children in the dark and 72% in normal illumination (22% did not notice a difference, and 6% noticed a deceleration).

The track was next divided into two, and the number of moving objects reduced to one. The adults were asked to compare the apparent velocities in the two half-trajectories when they fixated the centre of one but followed the object across the other with their eyes. They were also asked to say if the two trajectories were of the same length and if the two movements occupied the same amount of time. This was done to see if there was any agreement between these spatio-temporal and kinematic estimates. The results are set out in Table 108.

TABLE 108. *Judgements (%) on changes in apparent velocities, distances and durations in the sector of the trajectory fixated, as a function of illumination*

Rech. 36, Table 9

	Normal illumination (n = 14 adults)			In the dark (n = 15 adults)		
	Increase	Decrease	No effect	Increase	Decrease	No effect
Velocity	65	28	7	88	6	6
Distance	21	58	21	47	33	20
Duration	36	21	43	33	33	33

An analysis of individual results reveals an agreement in 7% of cases (27% in the dark), between the judgements and the relation $v = d : t$, no agreement in 57% of cases (21% in the dark) and equivocality in 36% of cases (52% in the dark). It is clear that with fixation on the middle of the track, the apparent acceleration of the moving body cannot be explained by the establishment of a relation between distance and time, which seems to support an interpretation in terms of an ordinal composition between eye-movements and the movements of the stimulus object.

If our interpretation is correct, it clearly should be possible to obtain reports of relative movements, not only under the above two conditions of fixation and of following, but also when the path of the eye-movement crosses that of the stimulus object (as, for example, when the velocity of a train seems to increase when one crosses it). We had some difficulty in carrying out the experiment because there are several ways of fixing one's attention, it is difficult to cross the track of a moving object with one's gaze moving at a relatively constant velocity, and, in normal illumination, the motionless background has a disturbing influence. However, in the course of trying to establish, for each subject, the optimum length of the stimulus object's movement and (with the help of a metronome) the velocity of eye-movement which would produce the maximum effect (to see if this agreed with prediction), we obtained the results set out in Table 109.

TABLE 109. *Judgements (%) on changes in apparent velocity when eye-movements intersect the object's path. Viewed in the dark (n = 17 adults)*

Rech. 36, Table 12

Increase	Decrease	No effect
82	12	6

As the stimulus object is much less centred in the case of these intersecting movements than it is in the case of pursuit movements, the resulting apparent acceleration could only be interpreted as the outcome of some movement relative to the visual field.

IIB. If the movements of the gaze seem to play a role in the estimation of velocities in this way, a role which is independent of the relation $v = d : t$ but which has to do with ordinal or hyper-ordinal considerations, it must also be possible to interpret many well-known effects in the same way. These are effects which are usually attributed to field effects (such as the structure of the stable field) and which Brown explains in terms of the phenomenal relation $v = d : t$. For example, the apparent acceleration of an object at the moment when it enters the field of vision (observed by the majority of adults but by fewer children) is explained quite simply by the two facts (*a*) that the gaze is fixed on the point where the object will appear and begins to follow with a slight delay, which results in a momentary movement relative to the motionless visual field; and (*b*) that, as there is a short delay before the gaze catches up, the stimulus object seems to accelerate in relation to the gaze as it outdistances it.

The effects are less clear when the object disappears (only half as numerous, and with acceleration perceived in the proportion of 4 to 1 against 18 to 1 when the object appears). This is because the point of disappearance provides a point of possible centration ahead of and not behind the moving object: the gaze may oscillate between the advancing stimulus object and the point at which it is going to disappear, whence the mixed results.

It has been pointed out that a multiplication of reference points in the field generally produces an apparent acceleration of the moving object. We examined this phenomenon in order to choose between the ordinal interpretation based on the role of eye-movements and the metric interpretation of the type $v = d : t$. The field was divided into two equal parts, the first of which was embellished with nine vertical bars behind which the stimulus object passed (this had the advantage of providing a divided space which, in terms of the Oppel–

Kundt illusion, is supposed to lead to an over-estimation of the length of that part of the field).

The bars were arranged in three ways:

I. In the first half-field.
II. In the second half-field.
III. Between the quarter- and the three-quarter way points.

Subjects were asked to judge the relative velocities of the stimulus object in the various sectors, to estimate the relative lengths of the sectors and to estimate the relative times taken to cross them. The results are set out in Table 110.

TABLE 110. *Frequency (%) of judgements on changes in apparent velocities, durations and distances of the transit of an object across spaces divided as described (I − III) compared with estimates of lengths of divided spaces.* + = *increase,* − = *decrease and* 0 = *no change (n: adults, I* = 38, *II* = 43, *III* = 20; *children* = 17)

Rech. 36, Table 2

	Adults			Children		
	+	−	0	+	−	0
I ⎧ Velocity	84	11	5	65	30	5
I ⎨ Duration	32	55	13	53	47	0
I ⎩ Distance	26	45	29	29	47	24
II Velocity	63	17	20	41	35	24
III Velocity	70	15	15	71	18	11

It can be seen that although the effects are not very great, perceived velocity increased in the presence of the bars (except for children in Condition II). On the other hand, the divided space was generally under-estimated, as is generally the case when a space is traversed by a fast-moving object (an under-estimation which is no doubt due to a failure to centre on the motionless background). The relation $v = d : t$ agreed with the observation of only 45% of the adults and of 24% of the children, and was contradicted by 39% and 65% respectively, the remainder being doubtful cases.

Since this effect of acceleration is not due to the composition $v = d : t$, a much simpler interpretation can be offered: each bar attracts the gaze and forms an obstacle to the regularity of the pursuit movement, which results in an apparent acceleration of the moving body in relation to the movement of the gaze. Moreover, each time a bar is momentarily fixated, an effect of acceleration due to centration is produced, similar to what happens when the object first appears, so that we can envisage the succession of bars as giving rise to a sort of succession of appearance effects. The proof is that subjects now, as during the appearance effect, often report the presence of trace or trail attached to the stimulus object when it is in the vicinity of the bars. This is no doubt due to retinal persistence, which only occurs with fixation and not with pursuit movements.

The same effects occur when, instead of nine equally spaced bars, from one to four are placed at different points along the route: in particular, a single bar placed 6 cm from the terminal point of the path led to reports of acceleration in 78% of adults and to no reports of deceleration. The preceding explanation is, *a fortiori*, valid in such cases.

The effect studied by Brown, in which an apparent acceleration occurs when the width of the field of the trajectory is reduced, was subjected to study by comparing apparent velocities in a half-field of 59 × 6 cm with those in one of 59 × 24 cm. The effect was found to occur if the contracted space formed the first half of the field; if it formed the second half, the effect was found only in children.

TABLE 111. *Frequency (%) of judgements on changes in apparent velocities, durations and distances of the transit of an object across spaces, as a function of reduction in the vertical dimension of the first half (I) and of the second half (II) of the track (n as for Table* 110)

Rech. 36, Table 5

	Adults			Children		
	+	−	0	+	−	0
I ⎰ Velocity	86	5	5	57	43	0
I ⎨ Duration	9	73	18	—	—	—
I ⎱ Distance	23	50	27	—	—	—
II Velocity	24	62	14	53	27	20

Sixty per cent of adults, but only 23% of the children, perceived an acceleration in the first half of the field independently of its width. No doubt this is due to an appearance effect, which would work against a tendency for a deceleration to be apparent in the narrower pathway. This deceleration would be expected to the extent that the narrower path favours the pursuit movement. In the case of children, however, the restricted field would prove to be a hindrance to pursuit movements because of their poorly adapted ocular movements (which lead to a weaker appearance effect than in adults). As a result, there is an apparent acceleration of the stimulus object independently of appearance effects.

Thus the perception of velocity in a single moving object in a moving visual field also is due to ordinal or hyper-ordinal compositions and not to the relation $v = d : t$, nor to the perception of the duration itself of the movement.

III. It only remains for us to discuss the perception of the velocity of a single moving object crossing a stationary visual field. There is a perfectly clear perception of velocity in this case, but the problem is to identify the second moving object with which the movement of the stimulus object is compared. An observation frequently made by our subjects put us on to its track. They often pointed out that the length of the trail left behind by the moving object was proportional to its speed, and that this trail extended back towards the point of fixation. Thus, in the dark, a line of moving phosphorescent points (one at every 5 or 10 cm) appeared as a series of lines; with fixation half-way along the track, these lines appeared to be longer the closer they were to the fixation point, presumably because of the well-known fact that retinal persistence is greater in the foveal region than in the periphery. Therefore two velocities are still involved when a moving body crosses the motionless visual field: (*a*) the trace of the onset of excitation; and (*b*) the trace of the termination of excitation (itself a function of the rate of extinction). In this case, if the moving body appears to accelerate, the interval between the events (*a*) and (*b*) will increase, and if it appears to decelerate, it will decrease. Because the retinal cells are more densely packed in the foveal than in the peripheral zones, as our colleague Fraisse pointed out on reading the first manuscript on this subject, the apparent velocity of the object will be a function of the number of cells included within the length of the train of excitations included between (*a*) and (*b*). Thus, even in this situation, the perception of velocity can be explained in terms of purely ordinal or hyper-ordinal considerations (the extent to which trace (*b*) exceeds trace (*a*) together with a consideration of the interval between them, or of the length of the train of excitations). Here again, there is no need to invoke the relation $v = d : t$. The kinship between this interpretation and the hypothesis of encounters can also be seen, because, with fixation, the apparent velocity of the stimulus object will, in the final count, be a function of a certain class of 'successively simultaneous' encounters.

In conclusion, the above analyses seem to establish that the perception of the velocity of movement is independent of that of duration but that it is directly related to the perception of movement itself.

IV. Apart from these spatial velocities, one can still use the term velocity in the sense of frequency: the number of repetitions of a single event during an interval of time. This subject cannot be taken up in detail here, but we would like to show that, in spite of its purely metric appearance, frequency-velocity gives rise to perceptual responses of an ordinal character which parallel those applying in the case of one moving body passing another.

The experiment, carried out with Feller, consisted of comparing two unequal auditory frequencies (provided by metronomes beating at different rates) to see whether an impression of acceleration or of deceleration was produced as the metronomes moved into and out of phase. By way of control, a single metronome was used to find out if the subject perceived accelerations or decelerations in its beat. The parallel with the experiment reported on p. 264 and in Table 106 was retained by designating the effect when the two metronomes were beating together as *AB*, and the comparison between the perceived

271

frequency of B beating with A and beating alone as BB'. When subjects were asked to report on the relative frequencies of the beats under the various conditions shown, the results set out in Table 112 were obtained.

TABLE 112. *Subjects (%) reporting the relative velocities indicated under AB and BB' conditions at the beat frequencies shown. Abbreviations as in Table 106, add Ir = irregular (n as in Table 106)*

Metronome	1	1	2	1	2
Frequency	100	100	104	100	96
Judgement		Condition AB			
Nil	90	0	10		
AcOv	0	5	10		
DcOt	0	81	54		
AcOv+DcOt	0	86	64		
AcOt	0	0	0		
DcOv	0	5	26		
AcOt+DcOv	0	5	26		
Ir	10	5	0		

				1	2	1	2
		Condition BB'		100	108	100	92
Nil	—	23	17	—	—
B' > B	—	39	75	—	83
B' < B	—	23	0	38	—
Ot > Ov	—	39	0	—	—
Ot < Ov	—	23	75	38	83

It can be seen that the AB effects were remarkably similar to those of movement-velocity obtained with two simultaneously moving objects (Table 106): at the moment of what here may also be called passing, the slower metronome seemed to slow down. Most subjects reported that the slowing increased as the beats moved out of phase (cf. the increasing interval in movement-velocity!), then abruptly decreased and gave way to an acceleration or to a return to the initial value when the beats were again in phase. The curve of these periodic effects is thus sinusoidal. All subjects reported that the effect was weakest with beat frequencies of 100 and 96 per minute.

The BB' effects were further examined with slightly greater frequency differences (100–108 and 100–92; even greater differences produced no effects) as shown in Table 112. Certain transitory effects were noticed when Phase B commenced.

An obvious kinship can be seen to exist between the perception of frequency-velocity and that of movement-velocity, and is of some interest for the study of the relations between the perception of time and the perception of velocity.

§ 4. THE PERCEPTION OF TIME

This is a complex and delicate problem of which others have made a close study, notably Fraisse with his admirable work on rhythm. We have so far carried out only a little work in this area and still have some research in progress. We shall not, therefore, try to give a complete picture of the whole problem, but would like to give a small place to it in this account in order to indicate two points at which it appears to have important consequences for what is already known about the perception of movement and of velocity. Firstly, there is the question of the relation between the ordinal structure of temporal perceptions (order of succession and simultaneity) and their quantitative or metric structure (intervals or durations); and secondly, there is the question of the relation between the perception of duration and of velocity.

I. On the first point, Fraisse[1] (the only authority we shall consult on this point) has shown clearly, as much by his review of the numerous publications covering a whole century of studies as by his own results on the perception of rhythm, that duration is only 'one of the characteristics of the organisation of succession' (Fraisse, II, p. 78).

In other words, where the organisation of events in terms of order of succession is not sufficiently pregnant, duration is hardly perceived. For example, 'two adjacent temporal intervals delimited by two sounds and an interposed flash (i.e. sound–light–sound) are compared with much less precision than are two intervals demarcated by three identical sounds, because the latter constitute a perceptual unity' (Fraisse, II, p. 76). In a similar way, when certain groups of constant rhythm are listened to, subjects can reproduce the intrinsic repetitive intervals very accurately, but do not spontaneously notice the durations of the intervals which occur between the rhythmic groups (Fraisse, I, p. 74). It is true that the rhythm is no longer perceived if the interval between the sounds exceeds about 2 seconds (Fraisse, I, pp. 13 and 41), and, reciprocally, there is a variable threshold for the minimum interval required for sounds to be perceived as successive rather than simultaneous (various perceptual events occurring in that region: apparent movements, etc.). These facts thus establish that the perception of succession is itself influenced by duration in the form of intervals between successive events. But it is one thing to be influenced by these durations (just as the spatial effect of a bigger element on a smaller one depends on the distance between them not being too great) and another to perceive them. The essential point is that the perception of duration always implies the perception of an order between the points which delimit its extent, whereas there can be a perception of order without the perception of the size of the interval, as when an interval is simply perceived and no adequate estimate is made of its duration.

Fraisse divides intervals into three categories (Fraisse, II, pp. 117–18): (1) shorter intervals of about 0·5 second: the ordered limits

[1] Fraisse, P., I. *Les structures rythmiques*, Paris, 1956, Erasme II. *Psychologie du temps*, Paris, 1957, P.U.F.

rather than the interval itself are perceived; (2) intervals between about 0·5 second and 1 second: the duration of the interval and the order of the limiting points form a unity; (3) intervals of more than 1 second: the perception of an interval between events predominates, and the relating of the limits of each event into a single perceptual act requires an effort.

We thought it necessary to begin by emphasising this primacy of order of succession over duration, because it is a fundamental fact which has to be related to the whole body of facts of kinematic perception. Firstly, the perception of displacement reduces to that of a change in order. Velocities, as we have tried to show, can be perceived independently of the perception of temporal intervals or of duration, being derived simply from the order of temporal succession, the order of spatial positions and from a hyper-ordinal estimation of the spatial intervals between moving bodies. We now see that the perception of time itself presumes, above all, an ordinal framework on the basis of which the perception of intervals or durations is organised. If this law is so general, might it not be applied equally well to space (it is strikingly so in the pre-operational representations of the child up to 6 to 7 years)? In this case, however, there would be a considerable genetic advance and it would have to be examined during the first months of life because the perception of spatial intervals and distances occurs so much earlier and more widely than that of temporal intervals. In the meantime, these considerations bring us back to velocity.

II. The problem of the relation between the perception of time and of velocity can be presented as follows. We have seen (§ 3) that the perception of velocity does not seem to conform to the relation $v = d : t$, but exhibits an autonomous structure of an ordinal and hyper-ordinal nature involving the intervention of spatial order, of spatial intervals, and of the order of temporal successions but not of durations. Three possible solutions can be entertained regarding the perception of duration: either (1) it is based on the perception of velocities (one would then have $t = d : v$, in which the terms would, of course, have only phenomenal or subjective meaning); or (2) it is derived from an autonomous source but is subject to the influence of variations in velocity; or (3) it is both autonomous and independent of any kinematic influence.

To decide between these possible solutions, we carried out the following investigations with Feller.[1] Subjects observed the passage, for 5 seconds, of the small beads (separated by 10 cm) previously used in the investigation of the perception of velocities. The sound of

[1] Piaget, J., Feller, Yvonne, and Bovet, Magali, *Arch. Psychol.*, 1962, **38**, No. 151.

274

the driving motor was masked by a constant background noise and the velocity of movement was varied. Subjects were required to judge the relative durations of exposure when the objects moved at the different velocities, the order of presentations of velocities being counterbalanced. Control measures were also taken on intervals with equal velocities, to discover if there was an order effect. The results are set out in Table 113.

TABLE 113. *Subjects (%) reporting the relative durations shown when viewing two successive movements (T_1 and T_2) of equal velocity and duration ($n = 20$ adults)*

Arch. 1962, 151, Table 4

Velocity (cm/sec)	$T_1 = T_2$	$T_1 > T_2$	$T_1 < T_2$
50	42	10	48
65	40	10	50
90	37	10	53

A tendency for subjects to under-estimate the second duration in relation to the first at all three velocities can be seen.

Comparisons made with unequal velocities produced relatively large effects, particularly with greater inequalities, as shown in Table 114.

TABLE 114. *The same judgement with unequal velocities*

Arch. 1962, 151, Table 5

Velocity (cm/sec) T_1	T_2	$T_1 = T_2$	$T_1 > T_2$	$T_1 < T_2$
50	65	25	15	60
65	50	20	65	15
50	90	10	0	90
90	50	5	95	0

Perceived duration therefore increases with the velocity of movement and as a function of the extent of the differences in velocity.

To be able to use these results, two possible variables must first be eliminated. We first investigated the possible influence of the sound of the motor. When the sound of the motor was present without the masking noise and without the visual display, the duration of the second run, at all motor speeds, was over-estimated on 66% of occasions. It was judged to be equal to the first on 17% of occasions, which should be compared with the opposite tendency in visual displays (Table 113). When the pitch of the motor's sound was low (at low speeds), the duration of the second run was over-estimated on 17% of occasions whereas the same subjects had over-estimated the durations of *rapidly* moving visual displays (Table 114). The factor of motor noise can therefore be ignored.

The second possibility was that the greater duration attributed to the faster procession of moving objects resulted from their greater number rather than from their velocity. Fraisse, we know, attributes subjective estimates of duration to the number of changes noticed by the subject, and it would be quite plausible to consider the number of moving objects seen as a factor contributing to our results. To test this, a single moving object could be used, but duration would then be interpreted as a function of the space traversed (as occurs in the pre-operational representations of the child). We therefore attempted the following counter-proof. As our apparatus has two tracks, we placed two beads on one and four on the other, and gave them velocities of 80 and 40 cm/sec respectively, which, with an exposure of 7 seconds, ensured that subjects saw four objects on each track, the beads on the first track coming round twice.

The number of changes is now equal, but two difficulties arise. The first is not serious because it appears that subjects do not take account of it: on the 80 cm/sec track only one object is seen at a time, two being seen at a time on the other track. However, results indicate that perceived duration continues to be a function of velocity and therefore the presence of two objects, as opposed to one, plays no part in the subjective lengthening of the duration. The second difficulty is that the spatial interval between the more rapidly moving objects is greater, as two of our twenty subjects pointed out. However, the inconvenience of this supplementary factor is minor, because, on the one hand, Table 114 shows that the velocity or the number of changes is the decisive factor, the intervals themselves being equal, and, on the other, we are now involved in testing the role of the number of changes, not of the spatial intervals.

Subjects were asked to report both on the apparent relative durations at the two velocities and (without prior warning) on the relative number of objects that they thought they had seen. The results are set out in Table 115.

TABLE 115. *I. Frequency distribution (%) for perceived relative durations of two displays of equal duration (7 seconds, separated by 2 seconds) and of unequal velocities ($T_1 = 80$, $T_2 = 40$ cm/sec). II. Frequency distribution (%) of perceived densities of the displays as a function of those perceived durations (n = 20 adults)*

Arch. 1962, 151, Table 6

	$T_1 > T_2$	$T_1 < T_2$	$T_1 = T_2$
I Judged duration	90	10	0
II Judged density			
$N_1 > N_2$	18	5	—
$N_1 < N_2$	53	—	—
$N_1 = N_2$	18	5	—

Two conclusions can be drawn from these results: (*a*) with an equal number of changes, subjective durations are a function of velocity; (*b*) subjects who demonstrate this temporal illusion tend to see more moving bodies in the slower display (when the duration was judged to be shorter). Those subjects who experienced the opposite temporal illusion (only two in twenty) saw, on the contrary, either an equal number of objects in both displays or a greater number in the faster display.

Of course, this experiment was not designed to invalidate Fraisse's theory, which we believe to be correct in most cases, but rather to show its limitations in a case where the number of changes is in conflict with the movement-velocity. Where the number of changes do seem to play a part, however, we have two remarks to make. The first is that it is very difficult to find a general definition of the change noticed by the subject, which complicates the attempted verifications. The second is that, objectively speaking, the number of changes presented in a unit of time is still a velocity, but simply derived from frequency-velocity and no longer from movement-velocity. We think, therefore, that the most general law should be that of the relation between duration and velocity, and not between duration and the number of changes, even if the latter do intervene effectively in the particular cases where frequencies are manipulated.

III. We have yet to find out whether a simple influence of perceived velocities on an otherwise autonomous perception is involved, or whether in perception, as in representational thought, velocities are constitutive of time. This would be in the sense that time is based on a co-ordination of velocities in the same way as space is based on a co-ordination of displacements. Two problems arise. The first is to discover if the velocities involved pertain to the stimulus objects or to the subject's actions (which, for example, might be combined with his 'work' in the form of 'power' in the physical meaning of the term). Our second problem is raised by the following considerations: duration is inversely related to velocity, in that a rapidly moving object takes less time to traverse a given space than does one that is moving more slowly; but this is frequently inverted in the pre-operational representations of the child, in the sense that faster = more time; one also knows that, in adults, a duration which seems very short while it occurs, may seem long in retrospect if it was well filled. We therefore need to discover to what extent the perception of duration is subject to the error faster = more time and to what extent it thus upsets the physical relations.

A second experiment involving the estimation of time in relation to velocity was accordingly undertaken. The subject, who was required either to fixate (*TC*) the middle of the track along which the stimulus objects moved, or to follow the objects with his gaze (*TM*), was asked to judge under which condition the duration of movement was longest. Results are set out in Table 116.

Of the eighteen subjects who over-estimated the duration of *TC* when the order was *TM* − *TC*, sixteen also reported that *TC* was longer when the order was *TC* − *TM*, but, of these, six in a weakened form.

277

TABLE 116. *Frequency distribution* (%) *of judgements of the durations of two equal displays* (7 *seconds*) *as a function of centration. TC = centred on the mid-point of the track, TM = object followed by the gaze*

Arch. 1962, 151, Table 7

Order	TC > TM	TC < TM	TC = TM
TM−TC	90	10	0
TC−TM	80	10	10

Eleven subjects were further tested with exposures of 7·5 and 10 seconds: seven of these over-estimated *TC* at all three durations of exposure and two of the remainder reported no effect at 10 seconds.

We can now compare the results shown in Table 114 with those shown in Table 116. They have two characteristics in common. The first concerns the perceived velocities of a moving object: although the velocities were objectively unequal in Table 114 and equal in Table 116, subjects reported greater velocities in both cases when fixation was required; it can therefore be said that 'faster = more time' in both cases. However, there is no proof that this factor is general, and it was not found to be constant in other experiments. The second common characteristic concerns the subject's work: he has to do more work when he has to follow the faster-moving objects (Table 114) than when he has to follow the slower ones; and undoubtedly more work is involved when he has to fixate on a point past which the objects move than when he can follow the objects with his gaze (because of the very coercive nature of the visual pursuit reflex, known as the orientation reflex, which he must resist when fixation is demanded but to which he can yield in the second case). Now, from an operational point of view, duration can be thought of either as corresponding to distance related to velocity ($t = d : v$) or as work related to power, which comes to the same thing because work is physically the displacement of force (df) and power is equal to fv. But in the first place, a child at the pre-operational level frequently estimates duration proportionally to the distance traversed or to the work expended, that is, in direct and not inverse ratio to the velocity, and with reference to the external results of the action and not to its actual development.[1] Operationally, of course, duration is inversely proportional to velocity or to power (which is why an hour of work seems long if the work is boring and short if it is interesting, for interest, as Claparède pointed out, mobilises the available forces).

Our hypothesis is, therefore, that the laws of perceptual duration are analogous to those of pre-operational representational duration. We are not yet in a position to say if these perceptions ever attain the inverse proportionality of time to velocity; we do not even know

[1] Piaget, J., *Le développement de la notion de temps chez l'enfant*, Paris, 1946, P.U.F.

how to distinguish between true perceptions of duration (those which occur around the point of indifference, in the vicinity of 0·5 to 1 second) and genuinely representational intuitions. Obviously the facts collected in Tables 114 and 116 are insufficient to confirm the hypothesis, but they do support it and this is all we could hope for in the present state of our investigations into the perception of time.

PART THREE

STRUCTURES OF PERCEPTION AND OF INTELLIGENCE

The problems which have yet to be examined must be faced sooner or later in any systematic study of perception or of intelligence.

In analysing the relations between primary perceptual effects and perceptual activities (Chapter III, p. 198), we came to the conclusion that the effects are always closely associated with perceptual activities and that perceptual activities themselves depend on sensory-motor activity in general. If this is so, it is obviously necessary to discover to what extent early perceptual activities also depend on developing intelligence, because a sensory-motor intelligence undoubtedly exists. As we saw in Chapter IV, the particular problem is to establish to what extent early perceptual constancies of size and of form develop in close association with the scheme of the permanent object.

Another problem is to discover to what extent, and in what way, operations are capable of orienting, or even of enriching, secondary perceptual activities which emerge at a later stage, contemporaneously with the earliest of these operations.

One of the fundamental problems of the study of intelligence is undoubtedly to discover if, and to what extent, general notions and operational structures derive from perception. Whatever the answer, experimental facts employed in its examination will be equally instructive for the study of perceptual structures as for the understanding of intelligence itself.

It will not, therefore, exceed the bounds of our programme for the study of perception if we first compare intelligence and perception and then examine the filiation that exists between them.

VI DIFFERENCES, SIMILARITIES AND POSSIBLE FILIATIONS BETWEEN THE STRUCTURES OF PERCEPTION AND THOSE OF INTELLIGENCE

On the basis of the known facts, the most natural genetic interpretation seems at first glance to be of a linear continuity between perception and intelligence, in which perceptual structures extend themselves and become progressively more mobile until they give rise to operational structures. For instance, unless we are mistaken, Köhler interpreted elementary sensory-motor forms of intelligence, and Wertheimer the nature of logico-mathematical structures, on the basis of some such unitary schema. An alternative interpretation would be to distinguish, at all levels of cognitive development, between an operative[1] aspect (from simple motor behaviour to intellectual operations), and a figurative aspect (perception, image, etc.). Operative structures would originate in a filiation between perception and intelligence, a continuous filiation from sensory-motor activities to operational intelligence. Figurative structures, on the other hand, would always be subordinated to operative structures. They would not develop by direct filiation between perception and intelligence but rather by a process of enrichment by operative structures and by interaction with the events of experience.

By the first interpretation, perceptual field effects would be primitive; they would extend into perceptual activities, which would themselves give rise to sensory-motor activities; these in turn would be internalised in the form of representational activities and would finally give rise to intellectual operations.

By the second interpretation, however, field effects would derive, initially from certain perceptual activities and would be enriched by further perceptual activities as they arose; perceptual activities themselves would depend, from the beginning, on sensory-motor activities and would derive their enrichment from them in the course of development; at the stages of the interiorisation of sensory-motor

---

[1] A distinction will be made between operational (*opératoire*), relating to operations in the strict sense, and operative (*opératif*), relating to actions at all developmental levels and to operations.

activities into pre-operational and then operational activities, perceptual activities would continue to be enriched by the direct or indirect repercussions of intelligence, and to sediment into new field effects; in the meantime symbolic and representational functions would be making possible the formation of other figurative structures such as images and imaginal representations.

The following method will be adopted to decide between these unitarist[1] and interactionist[2] interpretations. We will begin by making a systematic comparison of perceptual and intellectual structures, concentrating in turn on their differences and on their similarities. We will then try to decide if the observed differences can be explained away during the course of development: can the distance between the two extremes be bridged by a simple internal perceptual modification, in the sense of an increasing range and mobility, or must the transformation be explained in terms of extra-perceptual events? At this point, we will try (in Chapter VII) to provide a certain number of other facts concerning the relation between some concepts or operational structures and corresponding perceptual data. The purpose will be to discover if concepts are 'abstracted' from perception, or how concepts add new elements to perception. This analysis will allow us to choose between the alternative interpretations of the transition from perception to intelligence: by generalisation or progressive extension (the unitarist hypothesis); or by the intervention of a set of new and external factors (the interactionist hypothesis).

§ 1. FUNDAMENTAL DIFFERENCES BETWEEN PERCEPTION AND INTELLIGENCE

It would seem at first glance that a group of fundamental differences distinguish perception, in its most specific form of field effects, from the characteristic operational structures of intelligence. These differences can be grouped under two headings:

I. Those originating in the relations between subject and object;
II. Those relating to structures or to forms as such.

[1] Oléron, P., 'Perception and Intelligence' in *Proc. XVth. Int. Congr. Psychol.*, Brussels, 1957.
[2] In the sense in which the operative structures of action require information (symbolic or not) supplied by figurative structures in order to function. In return, figurative structures are constantly modified by the progress of the operative structures. Operative structures supply knowledge of transformations from one configuration to another, and figurative structures supply knowledge of the states which are linked by transformations. It follows (without prejudice to an issue which will be discussed in Chapter VIII) that a functional interaction exists between the roles of the knowledge of transformations and those of the states of knowledge, perceptual or general.

We will first enumerate them without critical discussion; we will then (§ 2) describe both the partial isomorphisms which temper the differences, and the intermediate states which exist in each case between genuine field effects and operational structures.

I. RELATIONS BETWEEN SUBJECT AND OBJECT

(1) In so far as it is always tied to a sensorial field,[1] perception is subordinated to an object of which it supplies a direct knowledge: an outlined rectangle can only be perceived as a figure whose characteristics are strictly determined by the presented data (form, absolute and relative lengths of the sides, colour, etc.). By contrast, intelligence can evoke the absent object by means of a symbolic process (imagery, verbal connotation, etc.) and, even in the object's presence, interprets it only in terms of the mediate associations which have been formed by means of conceptual frameworks: the perceived rectangle would thus be interpreted as a particular case of rectangles in general (independently of dimensions and, above all, of material aspects of the drawing, such as the thickness of the lines, colour, etc.), or even of quadrilaterals in general (independently of the equality of the angles, parallelism of pairs of sides, etc.).

(2) Perceptual field effects are not only subordinated to the presence of the object but also to limiting conditions of spatial and temporal proximity: looking at a tussock of grass in the garden, I cannot avoid perceiving neighbouring tussocks at the same time; but I cannot see a distant tree or the house behind me. On looking at the full moon, I cannot at the same time see the missing half whose image is evoked by my memory or by my intelligence. The more proximity causes simultaneously perceived elements to interact, the more numerous do possible deformations become; but intelligence, which can relate any elements, whatever their spatio-temporal separation, can, in thought, equally well dissociate neighbouring objects and reason on them in isolation.

(3) Perception is essentially egocentric from every point of view: tied to the perceiver's position in relation to the object (centration), it is strictly personal and incommunicable except through the mediation of language or of drawings, etc. This egocentricism is not only limiting but is also the source of systematic errors, as we saw in connection with centration (Chapters I and II). The essence of the operations of intelligence is, on the contrary, the achievement of knowledge, which is independent of the ego, independent of a

---

[1] At least some part of the perceived configuration corresponds to a sensory field even in the case of 'amodal' perceptions in Michotte's sense (tunnel or screen effects).

particular individual's point of view (but not of human subjects in general, i.e. of activities common to a given level). Its essence is also the achievement of communicable or universal knowledge.

(4) A fourth difference, which is not independent of, but probably more general than, the above differences, can be derived from them: 'primary' perception is phenomenal, in the sense that it is concerned with the appearance of objects. This means, firstly, that it is concerned essentially with the data (presence and proximity) relative to a particular point of view (egocentricism), which so far adds nothing to the preceding differences; but it also means that what is given in perception remains essentially a datum and does not lead on to deductive reconstructions: perceiving a closed box, I perceive it clearly as a three-dimensional object, having volume and an interior, but to decide on its content, I have to make use of mechanisms other than those of the perception itself (or of prior perceptions affecting the present one independently of memory-images, etc.). Intelligence, however, even in the presence of the given object, constantly exceeds the data with interpretive reconstructions: the contents of the box, or the internal composition of any opaque solid, are as much objects of thought as are the appearances of those objects.

(5) Every perceptual datum carries a meaning without exceeding the bounds of perception, but the 'signifiers' and 'significates' pertaining to that perceptual meaning are no more than indices and thus remain relatively undifferentiated and mutually interchangeable. This is in contrast to 'symbols' and 'signs', signifiers which are differentiated from the objects they signify and not interchangeable with them. For example, if I perceive the intertwined branches of a dead tree, I cannot tell if branch a is in front of or behind branch b until, reaching their point of intersection, I see that a passes over b and b behind a. This relation 'a over b' then acquires the role of an index which allows me immediately to structure the overall pattern of the relative positions of the other parts of the branches. But this index is itself a part, or an aspect, of the totality of what is signified. It is an interchangeable part because I could first have perceived that a was nearer to me than b and this would have led me to anticipate, in looking for the point of intersection, the overlaying of b by a; in this case, the global estimate of distances would have served as an index, or perceptual signifier, through which the position of a over b at their intersection, had it been rather difficult to see, would have been indicated and would have acquired the role of a significate. Similarly, the visible half, a, of a circle, whose other half, b, is covered by a screen, does not give the perceptual impression of a truncated circle but of a whole circle of which one half is covered; but if a is

then the signifier and *b* part of the significate, those roles could be reversed simply by displacing the screen. In short, perceptual indices are already signifiers, but are still only partial and interchangeable aspects of the signified object. But a symbol, whether it is an image or even a present object representing an absent one, and *a fortiori* a sign, are increasingly differentiated from what they signify.

(6) Finally, there is a sixth difference which is related to the preceding ones but which is not simply reducible to them: abstraction plays no part in primary perception. In the presence of an object (1), and of neighbouring elements (2) seen from a certain position (3), and considering only the phenomenal data (4), perception cannot avoid simultaneously apprehending the whole event involved, even if it does receive some initial orientation from a partial index (5). Perception cannot retain certain elements or characteristics of the object while 'setting others aside'. The essence of intelligence, on the contrary, is to select what is necessary for the solution of the intellectual problem in question; but as the data have to be exceeded in order to solve the problem, deductive reasoning and abstraction are then interdependent. It is as well to specify in this connection that, in a perceptual investigation, the subject is not asked to solve a 'problem' (deductively) and that therefore abstraction is not called for. When, for example, a subject, faced with the classical Müller–Lyer figure, is asked to compare the two horizontal lines, no deductive problem is involved because he is only asked to compare them to 'see' if they are equal. Even if he tried to perceive the shafts as perceptually isolated from the enclosing barbs (an attitude which exceeds the bounds of primary perception and which can be thwarted in tachistoscopic presentation), he would not be able to do so; but he could measure them with a foot-rule (a metric operation of some complexity which is inaccessible to the young child).

II. DIFFERENCES OF STRUCTURE

Differences (1) to (6) stem from the way in which the subject comes to know the object whether by perceiving it or by thinking about it. Certain differences in structure will, of course, also be entailed as he elaborates his perceptual or notional knowledge of the object, whatever it may be.

(7) Primary perception constitutes an indissociable totality which can be described as 'rigid' even when a displacement or a velocity is involved, while an operational totality exhibits the primary and fundamental characteristic of being mobile in the sense that the subject himself can decompose and reconstitute it at will. Of course, the perception of a form may entail explorations, thus exceeding the

bounds of primary perception, which lead to different results according to the fixations of the moment; but the overall form does not change much as a result, and when there are two possible and equivalent ways of seeing the same form, as in the case of invertable figures (wrongly called reversible), perception cannot encompass both at the same time. In contrast, an indefinite number of manipulations, both internal in the form of decompositions and rearrangements, and external in the form of generalisations, are possible in any classification or numerical system.

(8) A form is indissociable from its content in perception but can be manipulated independently of its content in the realm of operations, in which even forms devoid of content can be constructed and manipulated. Not even in the most elementary perception does the content (sensation, etc.) precede, and later become structured by, the form, but is always perceived as a function of a form, good or bad, stable or unstable: there is always a form, and even a collection of objects in disarray constitutes a kind of perceptual form). Reciprocally, one never perceives a form without content: a perceived geometrical form is still a detectable form, detachable from its ground, possessing a colour, etc. On the other hand, from the advent of what we have therefore called the stage of formal operations, logico-mathematical operations allow the construction of arrangements which are independent of content and which thus make possible the construction of pure forms which may lack concrete content and which are simply based on symbols.

(9) A related but only partly coincident difference is that while perceptual compositions are both incomplete and poorly delimited, for want of abstraction, operational compositions are both well delimited and, in the present context, complete. For example, when we try to measure an illusion such as that of the rectangle (Chapter I, § 3), we can never be sure of having exhausted all the factors involved: the quantitative relations between the long and the short side may be selected for examination, but note has also to be taken of the overall size of the figure, the thickness and colour of the lines, the dimensions of the ground, those of the margin between the contour of the figure and the edges of the paper on which it is drawn, etc. If, nevertheless, the illusion can be described by an equation (for example, Prop. 4), this will only be so because of an abstraction made by the experimenter, who reasons by approximation and makes the assumption of 'all else being equal'. But there is no abstraction on the part of the subject, who perceives the whole figure at once. However, in spite of the fact that all the factors involved are recorded, perceptual composition remains an incomplete process. It has a probability of less than 1 and lacks strict necessity because the subject never sees everything with

the same intensity at one and the same moment: he either limits himself, in the case of short exposures, to a single centration, thus dispersing his encounters heterogeneously, or else explores the figure freely, with the result that effects of succession, of polarisation, etc. intervene. The perceptual composition which results from the set of relations which have been apprehended is thus incomplete and poorly delimited. An operational construction, on the other hand, even if in no sense formal and involving, for example, the summing of three enumerated sub-collections, say $3 + 2 + 5 = 10$, is both well delimited and complete. It is well delimited because the qualities of the objects, their order, the local temperature, etc., can be ignored when making an addition. Thus delimited, the construction is complete, because $2 + 3 + 5$ give exactly 10 and not a little more or a little ess according to the context.

(10) A third difference stems from the last two but is not co-terminous with them: a perceptually good form has, at best, 'pregnance', whereas an operationally good form imposes itself of 'necessity'. It is true that Gestaltists did consider logical necessity to be a form of pregnance, but the difference is nevertheless fundamental. Pregnance is indeed dependent on causality, because a subject, faced, for instance, with a figure such as ∶∶, is obliged by a precise psychophysiological determinism to perceive a square, and is quite unable to 'see' the infinite number of figures which could be constructed by joining the four points in every imaginable way. But logical necessity gives rise to an obligation which is comparable to a moral obligation, in the sense that the subject feels himself constrained by this obligation only to the extent that he reasons 'honestly' and does not reject any particular element of the demonstration out of ill-will or personal interest, etc.; and particularly to the extent that he accepts a certain number of principles which are fundamental to the demonstration. In the case of the figure made up of four dots, there would thus be a logical necessity to recognise the existence of an infinity of possible ways of connecting the four points; but, to feel 'constrained' by this demonstration, he would have to agree to a number of initial axioms or hypotheses, the necessity of that form which is actually the most highly evolved being of a hypothetico-deductive rather than of an absolute nature.

(11) Because form is never dissociable from content in primary perception, it is to be anticipated that logical forms will not be entirely isomorphic in detail with perceptual forms, but only partially or weakly so. This is particularly so in the case of the special structure of 'classes', which can be handled by logico-mathematical operations but not by primary perception: classes are not perceived, but they can be represented and manipulated operationally. But a distinction must

289

be made in this connection between collections, which are perceptible as such, and perceptual schemes which may intervene at all levels of perception.

Collections of discontinuous elements (a line of objects, objects arranged in a square, etc.), cannot be assimilated to classes because their spatial form constitutes an integral part of their perceptual properties: classes are not involved here, because a class is independent of the spatio-temporal disposition of its elements, but 'infra-classes' are, in the sense of assemblies of elements which form a spatially or temporally indissociable whole.[1] But the laws of composition of logico-mathematical infra-classes are isomorphic with those of classes. In the finite case, in particular, they exhibit an elementary form of additive composition: the sum of the segments AB, BC, etc., of a line AE, is equal to the length of AE. But it is well known that there is no additive composition in perceptual infra-classes, which amounts to saying that perception knows only 'pre-infra-classes' (where

A ———————————————— A'

Fig. 56.

the prefix 'pre-' is relative to the level of development and where the prefix 'infra-' is used in the sense defined above, without reference to genetic considerations). In fact, in a case such as that depicted in Fig. 56 in which $B = A + A'$ and where A ($> A'$) is over-estimated under the influence of A', the segment A does not retain its identity across the situations in which it is either juxtaposed to A' or presented in isolation. One thus has:

(52) $$(A + A') - A' \neq A$$

whence:

(52b) $$A + A' \neq B$$

These two propositions thus express the characteristic non-additivity of perceptual pre-infra-classes which is found in all situations analogous to that represented in Fig. 56, namely in all illusions: even good forms are not exempt from deformations (for example, the diagonal of a square, the diameter of a circle, etc.) except in those rare cases where their composition is additive because of a compensation between opposed deformations.

In the same way, perceptual schemes cannot be assimilated to classes, because the subject does not know how to extend such

[1] For this notion, and for the development of what is here summarised under (11) and (12), see Piaget, J., and Morf, A., in Bruner, J. S., *et al. Logique et Perception. op. cit.*

schemes. Recognising a familiar form, x, the subject limits himself to assimilating its properties to those of other x's which have been perceived before, but he never perceptually assembles all x's into one class of determined extension; and if he sees a collection of x's, we are back with spatial infra-classes. The perceptual scheme is thus only a temporal scheme, involving successive assimilations which cannot be united into a simultaneous whole which would constitute a class.

(12) What we have just said about classes also applies to relations, where a fundamental difference exists between perceptions and operations: the former are deforming in the sense that the perception of a relation between two terms, A and B, generally modifies the terms themselves by the very fact of bringing them together, while operational relations conserve (in the sense of not modifying) the related terms. If, for example, objectively $A < B$ and $B < C$, B will be perceptually over-estimated when compared with A, and under-estimated when compared with C. In writing $B(A)$ to indicate that B is compared with A, one would have, perceptually:

(53) $\qquad B(A) > B$ and $B(C) < B;\ B(A) > B(C)$

while operationally one has, of course:

(53b) $\qquad B(A) = B$ and $B(C) = B;\ B(A) = B(C)$

(13) Certain inferential processes do, of course, occur in perception, but they do not exceed the level of immediate 'pre-inferences' whose composition the subject cannot control. In the case of intellectual inferences, however, he can distinguish between the data and the conclusions drawn from them. Above all, he can control the method by which the conclusions are drawn from the data (controlled composition). The presence of certain inferential processes in the mechanisms of perception results from the existence both of perceptual indices and of perceptual schemes. It results from the existence of schemes because, if a scheme includes the characteristics x, y and z of which x and y are well-defined and z ill-defined, the subject may be enabled to perceive z by perceiving x and y. The perception of z will then be due to a form of implication (in the broad sense, which we will call 'pre-implication'), existing between x, y and z rather than to a direct registration of z. But the subject will not differentiate between the characteristics x and y, which he has effectively registered, and z, which he has pre-inferred rather than registered; even less can he control the way in which he attains z through x and y. He perceives z, the resultant of the process, at the same time as he perceives x and y, and thus exercises no conscious direction over its formation.

The same may be said to apply whenever some index gives a direction to perception, because if x or y entail z, they may be considered as indices, or signifiers, and z as a significate; or, again, one may differentiate an indicative and a significative aspect within x and y themselves. Only a relative distinction can be drawn in perception between the relation of signifier (index) to significate, and of implicant to implicate, because the perceptual index constitutes only a part, or a partial aspect of the signified totality. In intellectual operations, however, the relation of signifier to significate (designation), and of implicant to implicate (implication), is clear. This is because the signifiers (symbols or signs) are differentiated from the objects they signify, and implication is only concerned with the mutual relations between significates.

(14) A last fundamental difference between perceptual and operational structures summarises, but is more general than the preceding ones (7 to 13); operations are reversible and perceptions are not. Such a statement carries three distinct and complementary implications:

(*a*) In the first place, if compositions corresponding to infraclasses and to relations are non-additive, it follows that there can be no inverse process of dissociation or of subtraction to correspond with processes of union in the positive sense. This can be expressed by saying that a non-compensated 'transformation', P, intervenes in all perceptual compositions. This is 'deformation' or 'illusion' itself. One would have:

$$(54) \qquad B = A + A' + P$$

for pre-infra-classes, and

$$(55) \qquad B(A) = B + P \text{ and } B(C) = B - P$$

for relations.

P thus constitutes a measure of perceptual irreversibility in this first sense, related to inversion.

(*b*) But perception is equally irreversible in the sense of reciprocity: perceptual estimates always depend on the order in which the comparisons are made. This can be expressed as follows:

$$(56) \qquad A(B) + B(C) + \ldots \neq \ldots C(B) + B(A)$$

when $A(B)$ signifies, as before, '*A* compared with *B*'.

(*c*) Finally, one may speak of perceptual irreversibility in an extrinsic (relative to differences 1 to 5) and not only in an intrinsic sense (differences 6 to 11). This follows from the fact that perception is always tied to the flux of irreversible external events and cannot, like thought, retrace the course of time. If, for example, a figure is modified by the addition or removal of elements, the resulting perception

292

cannot be equated to the original one by a process of perceptual transformation. Even if the original figure is recreated, the return is not exact because each new perception is affected by preceding ones. One can, of course, return to the preceding percept in memory; or reconstitute it deductively, but, in that case, perception alone is no longer involved. In the case of operations, however, all external modifications can be reversed in thought by an exercise of appropriate transformations which free deduction from the irreversibility of temporal events.

With these essential differences in mind, the problem is to discover whether, and to what extent, the gulf between the structures of primary perception and those of operations can be bridged by a simple progressive extension, or increasing mobility, of primary perception; or whether progression from one to the other extreme requires the intervention of contributions external to perception, which would exclude any direct filiation between them.

§ 2. SIMILARITIES (PARTIAL ISOMORPHISMS) AND INTERMEDIATE STATES BETWEEN PRIMARY PERCEPTUAL AND OPERATIONAL STRUCTURES

We chose to conduct the above discussion on the basis of differences between primary perceptual effects and the operational structures of intelligence, thus exaggerating the differences. In reality, neither perception nor intelligence can be reduced to such extremes: perception exhibits a multiplicity of activities and a variety of stages over and above field effects. Operational intelligence is in turn divided into distinct stages and, above all, is genetically preceded by sensory-motor intelligence and then by pre-operational forms of representational intelligence. It follows that a series of graded differences will be found to exist between the extremes compared in § 1. This gives rise to three problems, all of which impinge upon the central problem of this chapter.

(*a*) The first is whether, in spite of the differences described above and in view of the intermediate states which we are about to examine, the various cognitive structures, particularly those of primary perception and of operations, share common elements. In other words, are there partial isomorphisms between perception and intelligence? This question would be meaningless if it were not considered genetically, because, of course, partial isomorphisms can be established between any two events. It will, therefore, be fruitful to start by identifying those elements which, from a genetic point of view, are common to the two areas of behaviour under each of the above fourteen distinctions: these common elements provide the context within which the differences exist and in reference to which their filiative significance can be understood.

(*b*) The second problem is to identify the graded differences which can be inserted between the extreme forms of the fourteen differences so far considered.

(*c*) Because grades of difference and common elements may exist during development, it will have to be established, for each of the fourteen distinctions, whether progression from one rung of development to the next only involves a progressive extension from lower to higher states or whether it exhibits signs of the intervention of novel contributions in the form of influences of superior levels on lower ones.

(1) The advantages of the comparative method which we have just recommended becomes obvious in the case of the first difference which we studied (the immediate character of perception, tied to the presence of the object, and the mediate character of operational intelligence, which does not depend upon such a presence). While the immediate and the mediate, or the presence and the absence of the object, may not appear to have anything in common when the discussion is conducted in terms of the extremes, common elements become immediately apparent in a most instructive manner as soon as the continuity of the intermediate states is considered. The supposed immediate then becomes no more than a limiting case of the mediate: all knowledge of objects entails an element of elaboration or of re-elaboration, the reconstruction merely being more rapid in the presence of objects than in deduction and when relying on their symbolic representations alone.

Let us note that, on the level of perceptual activities, we can no longer speak of immediacy in the strict sense. In the exploration of a figure whose size exceeds a few centimetres, for example, estimates of the lengths of its parts change continually with changing fixation, perspectives may alter to some extent and apparent movement may also occur, requiring the observer to decide whether only his eyes moved or whether the figure itself also moved. The fact that the figure is perceived to be both immobile (which is not the case if the eyeball is displaced by finger pressure), and to retain its permanent identity (which is no doubt a more elementary form of permanence than the form constancy which accompanies physical displacements), implies the existence of some sort of subjective elaboration. This would consist in internal transpositions between successive centrations, and thereby in the construction of a momentary scheme.[1] Furthermore,

[1] In this connection see Jonckheere, A., Mandelbrot, B., and Piaget, J., *La Lecture de L'Experience*, Etudes d'Epistémologie Génétique, **5**, Paris, 1958, P.U.F., pp. 72–6.

the subject extends his perception to objects which are no longer simultaneously present in the same field of centration when he compares two elements by means of a spatial transport, or especially, by means of a temporal transport when the figures are presented successively. In these cases he has to relate fields which are spatially or temporally only neighbouring, which, of course, diminishes the immediacy of the perceptual judgement. The activity of relating objects to systems of reference removes perception even farther from pure immediacy, because, for example, judgements about horizontals, about verticals, or about the inclination of obliques, can only be made on the basis of elaborations which embrace ever wider frames of reference. Transpositions and perceptual anticipations are as much functions of an active process of relating as of immediate data. Finally, perceptual schematisation (Chapter III, § 8) provides the best proof of the intervention of mediate processes in perceptual activities, and the possibility has to be entertained that schematisation may intervene, of necessity, in the most elementary structuring of figures, in field effects themselves.

Sensory-motor functions are clearly less immediate than perception. Certainly, sensory-motor intelligence functions in a stepwise fashion and only in the presence of perceptible situations which arouse the activities of its schemes. But these schemes exceed the boundaries of the perceived event: the search for a hidden object gives evidence of a mediate permanence bordering on, but nevertheless exceeding, the boundaries of the perceptual field. The achievement of the group of displacements, and of objective causal or temporal series, also demonstrate such a capacity.

At the level of pre-operational representational intelligence, the whole system of increasingly verbalised preconcepts marks the advance of mediate processes; but all the forms of non-conservation demonstrate the limitations of pre-concepts and the persistent subordination of thought to directly perceived configurations. Concrete operations allow the child to throw off these subordinations and to achieve transformations as such, but the logico-mathematical apparatus of thought cannot finally function in the absence of 'objects' until formal operations have been achieved (when its structuring of events in the presence of 'objects' becomes more efficient as a function of the dissociation of the factors involved, etc.). If this progression from the immediate to the mediate does exist, it will be easier to identify what elements are common to all levels and to establish the degrees of filiation that exist between levels.

(*a*) The constitution of mediate frameworks (schemes, conceptual frameworks and operational structures), is only achieved step by step, and, right up to the final stage, in the presence of the object.

Only in the final stage does the process become independent of the object, and an increasingly exact interpretation of experience becomes possible because the characteristics of the object are so much better understood when located, by means of the mediate frameworks, within the system of possible comparisons and transformations.

(*b*) The relations between the mediate and the immediate can only be understood if it is realised that the adequacy of the assessment of the properties of an object, even in its presence, is proportional to the richness of the mediate frameworks which the subject has at his disposal. Immediacy, on the other hand, is as much a source of deformation as of information: the subject's deforming point of view can only be corrected by an increasing number of decentrations (perceptual and representational), and the varied properties of the object can only be apprehended as a totality by the exercise of multiple and successive comparisons.

(*c*) The result is that the presence of the object required for the most 'immediate' forms of perception is not necessarily accompanied by an exhaustive registration of even its apparent properties, and that, even in the case of primary perceptions, the effective registration can be helped by the intervention of schematisations derived from previous activities.

(*d*) It must be remembered, in examining elements common to all levels, that distinctions drawn between the immediate and the mediate, and even between the presence and the absence of the object, are matters of degree. In the first place, a perceptually present object is not, so to speak, present to the subject in its totality, but is only attained as a result of an exercise of incomplete and heterogeneous encounters. In the second place, to the extent that the couplings between those encounters originate in an activity and are open to schematisation, so is the process of mediation initiated from the beginning of even the most immediate of perceptions. If this is so, then the encounters themselves, which are subordinate to those activities during which the points of centration are chosen, can be schematised, as we saw in the tachistoscopic perception of verticals (Chapter III, § 3). Immediacy is thus only a limit which is never attained.

(*e*) In regard to filiation, if mediation begins at the level of primary perception, because of schematised activities, then it follows that primary perception must be subordinated to perceptual activities from the beginning, as was suggested in connection with the possible reduction of all evolutionary curves to that of type III (Chapter III, § 9). Moreover, since perceptual activities themselves are only varieties of sensory-motor activity, it is likely that they too are subordinated from the beginning to sensory-motor activities as a whole. For example, it is surely of significance for the visual structuring of a figure that its form does or does not correspond to objects which were or were not manipulated at the same time as they were being visually perceived.

This is only a hypothesis, of course, and will only be retained if supported by fresh data to be presented in Chapter VII. If verified, the implication will be that the transition from the relatively immediate to the mediate does not arise in a simple process of extension, but involves successive contributions from perceptual activities to field effects and from sensory-motor activities to perceptual activities.

(2) The second fundamental difference between perception and intelligence, relating to proximity, gives rise to analogous considerations. First of all, in spite of appearances, the difference is only of degree, because every perceptual field, at whatever level, involves some distances, no matter how short, between simultaneously perceived elements: 'proximity' is really a matter of very short distances. Secondly, escape from the restraints of proximity is achieved very gradually, not suddenly. Even perceptual activities lead to comparisons at increasing distances in space and time, as spatial and temporal transports, anticipations, the establishment of 'absolute' points of neutrality, systems of reference, etc., indicate. Those distances are further extended by sensory-motor activities.

The same thing applies, of course, to pre-operational representational activities, where the symbolic function consists precisely in allowing comparisons to be made independently of perceptual contact with the object. But it should be noted that this freedom remains quite relative for a long time, because the essential characteristic of pre-operational representation is that it remains subordinated to spatial configurations and consequently to certain, sometimes extended, conditions of proximity (see, for example, the differences between figural, or even non-figural, 'collections' and classes).[1] Concrete operations themselves are not entirely freed from such limitations, as can be inferred from the differences in difficulty encountered in the quantification of class inclusion when applied to classes of animals and to classes of flowers.[2] Only formal thought attains almost complete freedom in respect of distances.

From the point of view of filiation, the essential fact to be explained is not that new functions (movements, images, operations, etc.) allow the construction of connections which progressively become independent of early perceptual proximity, but rather that the perceptual field itself is extended in the sense that the influence of

---

[1] Inhelder, Bärbel, and Piaget, J., *The Growth of Logical Thinking*, London, 1964, Routledge and Kegan Paul, Introduction and Chapter 1.
[2] *Ibid.*, Chapter IV.

proximity and of immediate interactions is gradually reduced (which Meili, a Gestaltist, expressed by saying that the adult is less subservient than the young child to conditions of proximity: see Chapter III, § 1). Thus we saw in *Rech.* 2 that adults grouped the comparison rods into a composite 'figure' at distances at which children of 5 and 7 years were unable to see a figure but compared the elements in isolation. Such an extension of the field of immediate interaction, or of proximity relative to the subject, can only result from increasing practice and from the development of perceptual activities, because the number of nerve cells does not increase during growth and the extension of the field is out of proportion to the limited growth of bodily organs. If this interpretation is accurate, it provides a good example of the influence of perceptual activities on field effects themselves.

Judgement must be reserved for the moment on two other questions. The first is whether perceptual activities can be guided and modified by sensory-motor activities in general and later by representational activities. The second concerns the role played by extensions in, or by external contributions to, the relations between intelligence and perception, particularly in regard to this question of proximity.

(3) The ego-centricism of perception, as opposed to the decentration of operations, provides a third and a particularly clear example of a continuous evolution in the course of which new contributions intervene repeatedly in the absence of linear filiation between primary effects and higher forms of structure. To start with common elements, examples are found at all levels which illustrate the fundamental fact that the acquisition of knowledge, or better, of a body of knowledge (because, of course, all knowledge, including even the most elementary perception of an isolated element, forms an integral part of a system), is not a purely additive process but entails continuous reorganisations stemming from initially privileged elements or relations: a continuous series of decentrations are seen to succeed initial centrations.

The topics of perceptual centration and decentration were adequately discussed in Chapters I and II and need not be resumed. It is worth noting, however, that although these mechanisms occur in every case of perception (centration, by definition, stemming from field effects and decentration from the beginnings of perceptual activity), processes of decentration are found to occur more widely in perceptual activities where they apply to overall perceptual systems and not only to momentary perceptions. It is by this decentration that the progressive construction of perceptual co-ordinates takes place: spatial directions, which were judged initially with reference to the position of one's own body, are decentred in order to be related to wider frames of reference. In this case these processes, centration relative to one's own body and decentration focused on relations between objects, take on a global and no longer a merely local significance. It is essentially in this global sense that important advances in decentration occur during sensory-motor development. The preceding phase of systematic centrations, based on personal actions, controls the first sensory-motor schemes. These schemes include those of sensory-motor space as a whole, in the successive forms in which the universe is represented before the formation of the scheme of the permanent object, early sensory-motor causality (which we named magico-phenomenalist in contrast to the spatial and objective causality of later sensory-motor stages) and subjective temporal sequences. In contrast, the construction of a space which contains all objects (including one's own body), the scheme of the permanent object, spatial causality and objective temporal sequences, are the products of a global decentration which unfolds throughout the course of the development of sensory-motor intelligence.

There is no need to emphasise that the advance from pre-operational representation to operational structures is characterised by such a process. To take projective space as an example, it is easy to show how the development of the co-ordination of perspectives, starting with one's own earliest perspectives, constitutes a form of decentration which is analogous to those mentioned above. Systematic centrations and renewed decentrations are found at all subsequent levels. The generality of these processes, even with adults, is demonstrated by the history of all sciences and of astronomy in particular.

In regard to filiations, it is clear that higher forms of decentration are not simple extensions of local perceptual decentrations of the kind that occur in the perception of a figure. On the contrary, it is perceptual activities which are responsible for local decentrations, at the same time giving rise by generalisation to the global forms of decentration mentioned above in connection with, for example, systems of reference. Moreover, sensory-motor and representational forms of decentration could not derive in any simple way from those forms of decentration which are initiated by perceptual activities, because new connections are involved which concern action as a whole and not only perceptions corresponding to a single sensory modality. But these higher-level global decentrations might play a part in the direction of decentrations associated with later perceptual activity: we shall see in Chapter VII, § 4, how operational and notional systems of co-ordinates influence the elaboration

299

of perceptual co-ordinates through the introduction of references to which perception, by itself, would never have turned.

(4) Numerous intermediate states can also be detected between the phenomenalism of primary perception and the rational constructions of operational structures. The most striking, in regard to perceptual activities, are the constancies of size, etc. (in which 'real' sizes are substituted for apparent ones), and perceptual causality (in which various dynamic compensations are introduced into what is essentially a succession of kinematic events). The construction of the scheme of the permanent object is a good example of the overcoming of phenomenalism at the sensory-motor level. However, many forms of pre-operational non-conservation show that the victory is limited and that a considerable degree of phenomenalism still exists at this level of representation. Concrete operations, introducing the first true notions of conservation, extend the control of deduction over appearances, a control which becomes decisive only with the advent of formal operations.

But once again, from the point of view of filiation, operational conservations cannot be thought of as simple extensions of perceptual constancies (the question is to be taken up again in Chapter VII, § 3): only the intervention of a series of fresh contributions can account for the interval of some six or seven years which separates the first perceptual constancies from the first conservations. It is, on the contrary, quite possible that the scheme of the permanent object, itself inexplicable on the basis of constancies alone, reacts upon the developing constancies and plays a key role in a composite sensory-motor construction from whose existence the dawning constancies of form, size and colour will at least benefit.

(5) Numerous intermediate states exist between perceptual indices and the signifiers of intelligence, symbols and signs.

(*a*) Various levels of complexity within perceptual indices must first be distinguished. They extend from primary intra-figural indices (for example, those which, as described in Chapter III, § 8, enable 73% of children of 4 years to recognise a square embedded in a group of overlapping forms), to inter-figural indices (for example, those indicated by the perceptual activity relating to systems of reference, as when the horizontality of a line is recognised on the basis of indices provided by distant frames of reference).

(*b*) Secondly, perception is not alone in its exclusive use of indices as opposed to signifiers which are differentiated from their significates (symbols and signs): all sensory-motor activities, from simple and conditioned reflexes (in which the 'signals' of the conditioning processes are simply indices) to refined forms of sensory-motor intelligence, share this characteristic. However, the indices employed by sensory-motor intelligence are much more complex than perceptual indices in that they relate to schemes of action of an advanced level of differentiation and of an increasing complexity of co-ordination. An example would be the significance attributed to movable supports, or to strings and sticks when objects have to be attained by means of implements.

(*c*) Finally, important intermediate states are to be identified between sensory-motor indices and the first differentiated symbols. Leaving aside the beginnings of the symbolic function in anthropoids, and the dance language of bees (as described by von Frisch), it is noteworthy that the first symbolic games of childhood are based on an imitation which is gradually disengaged from its sensory-motor context of on-going adaptation, and that mental images (which are terminal forms of symbols which have been differentiated from pre-operational indices) are certainly interiorised imitations. It is imitation, therefore, which effects the transition from sensory-motor to representational behaviour.

Two conclusions emerge in respect of filiations. The first is that no filiation can be traced between perceptual indices and systems either of signs (which presuppose a social life with its established conventions) or of symbols. It is true that symbolic systems may be related to aspects of sensory-motor behaviour through imitation, but imitation does not derive from perception. Furthermore, everything that we know about mental imagery suggests that it is more than a simple extension of perception: it presupposes an active, schematising reproduction, as does imitation itself from which it derives by interiorisation.

The second conclusion is that, while higher-order signifiers do not derive from perceptual indices but involve a series of external contributions beginning with sensory-motor functions (which prepare them through imitation), perceptual indices themselves may well be influenced, during their evolution, by sensory-motor indices in general. This means that perceptual indices may often refer to activity as a whole and not only to perceptual activity. We will reconsider this point in Chapter VII, § 4, in relation to schemes which play a part in certain pre-inferences concerned with correspondences, seriations, etc.

(6) Certain explorations of an analytical nature which represent an elementary form of abstraction can be found at the level of higher perceptual activities. For example, in Dadsetan's experiment (Fig. 46, p. 174), the horizontality of a line was judged by referring it to a distant frame of reference and by attempting to 'make abstraction' of (or ignore) the nearer square or triangle. But in such cases the effort of dissociation is directed by intentions deriving from supra-percep-

tual levels (conceptual schemes, etc.). On the other hand, a filiation cannot be established between these forms of behaviour and genuine operational abstraction, because genuine abstraction is an indissociable part of generalisation and of multiple operations which imply constructions exceeding those of perception.

(7) A continuous series of intermediate states may also be detected between the rigidity of perceptual structures and the increasing mobility of those of intelligence. For example, the role of perceptual activities is precisely to introduce an increasing number of mobile relations between configurations, or between their elements, while the operational mobility of intelligence is achieved only after numerous pre-operational phases during which the thought of the young child remains attached, at many points, to relatively rigid configurations which resemble those of perception. A whole range of increments in mobility, of innumerable gradations, could be shown to exist between the extreme cases of perception and of operations. However, as with proximity (2), it is impossible to decide at this stage if the relation between the early forms of mobility found in perceptual activities and the mobility of various forms of intelligence should be attributed to a progressive extension or enrichment of perception by a sequence of contributions which have their origins in intelligence. It is clear, however, that increases in mobility which occur in field effects (the reduction of syncretism, for example: Chapter III, § 1), are due to the influence of perceptual activities.

(8) The central problem for the study of the genetic connections between intelligence and perception is that of the relations between form and content: indissociable at the level of primary effects, they become entirely dissociated at the level of formal operations.

It must first be emphasised that these two extremes have the fundamental mechanism in common that both always involve forms, whether these are separable from their content or not. On the other hand, the whole history of the development of cognitive mechanisms is of a slow and laborious liberation of these forms from their content. Even at the stage of concrete operations, operational forms are not qualified to function on no matter what content, nor are they independent of those intuitive influences which always permeate such content.

The genetic relations between the various levels must, therefore, be examined very closely, but with the following question held clearly in mind: are partially new forms constructed when the forms are liberated or dissociated from their content, or do the dissociated forms differ only in respect of the circumstances of that liberation?

To carry out this examination, we will discuss, in turn, the dissociation as such, then forms of composition (9), the nature of necessity

(10), classes (11), relations (12) and reversibility (14), all of which are interdependent aspects of the problem. The general question is therefore: do the structures of intelligence result from a progressive extension of those of perception, or do they entail certain fresh contributions which cannot be reduced to primary perceptual activities but which do react upon the latter through the mediation of perceptual activities?

These questions can be answered in terms of one simple difference between the two situations: the forms or structures used by intelligence derive from a genuine construction which has its origins in actions and operations, while perceptual forms are discovered in the object. This discovery, once again, is achieved on the basis of actions, but, in this case, of a very restricted scope, reconstructive rather than inventive, and never achieving, or even attempting, new constructions. We therefore conclude, firstly, that forms dissociate themselves from their content to the extent that they are genuine or new constructions. And secondly, that the forms of intelligence do not derive from those of perception but do, on the contrary, react upon them by directing perceptual activities: one perceives better what can be constructed and reconstructed.

A progressive dissociation of forms from content occurs between sensory-motor intelligence and higher formal structures. Sensory-motor schemes are ill-differentiated from their contents because they consist only of general forms of action (such as pulling an object towards one by means of the support on which it stands): they cannot be evoked independently of the performance of the action itself, or symbolically, as concepts can by means of words or of combined visual and gestural images. Nevertheless, because of their propensity for generalisation, these sensory-motor schemes are more readily dissociable than those of perception. This is because schematised and generalised actions are constructions on the part of the subject and not just abstractions from the properties of the object. With the advent of pre-operational representation, forms further dissociate themselves from their content under the influence of symbolic functions, but continue to adhere to spatio-temporal configurations (figural collections leading to classifications, figural numbers, etc.). At the level of concrete operations, classes, relations and operational numbers are forms which can be manipulated in their own rights, but, as we have already remarked, these manipulations are still tied to content in that the advance is made area by area (from quantity, to weight and then to volume), with a considerable interval between the steps and without immediate or formal generalisation. Only the formal combinatorial structure finally emancipates forms from their content, generally between the ages of 12 and 15 years.

In comparison with this evolution, slow indeed but of great consequence, the dissociation of perceptual forms from their content is very limited. The two are indissociable at the level of field effects, the form being perceived as one of the characteristics, or as the essential characteristic, of the object. Dissociation first appears with transportations, and especially with transpositions and perceptual anticipations. It takes the form of a schematisation whose essential role, in the presence of the object, is to canalise exploratory and information-collecting processes in response to certain anticipated relations, such as the equality of the sides and angles of a square (cf. the changes which occur with age in the resistance to deformation of this good form, Chapter III, § 8). It is clear, however, that this early perceptual dissociation does not constitute the point of departure for that progressive dissociation of the forms of intelligence which we have just discussed. While these forms of intelligence do, of course, make use of perceptual data, they both enrich them with an entirely novel set of constructions and, to the extent that they themselves are manipulable in a dissociated manner, facilitate or even direct perceptual activities.

(9) The difference between the poorly delimited and incomplete compositions of perception, and the complete, because well delimited, compositions of intelligence, are therefore easy to understand. As the structures of intelligence are the products of genuine actions and then of operations, the limitations placed on any given composition will be simply a matter of the choice of one kind or another of action or operation according to the demands of the situation. In the perception of a form, however, no choice is available because the form is not composed at will but is discovered or reconstituted on the basis of the objective data in which all factors exert their influences concurrently. It follows that the compositions of intelligence can be complete because their delimitation is a matter of choice, while the compositions of perception, in which the freedom of choice does not exist, must be probabilistic.

The same reasoning applies to all the intermediate sensory-motor events and pre-operational representations that are to be found ranged between the two extremes. In brief, the delimited and complete compositions of superior stages cannot result from a simple extension of the incomplete and poorly delimited compositions of perception. Even if we consider that necessary deduction results from compensatory adjustments between probabilistic inductions, it is still the case, as we are about to stress, that the establishment of superior structures must involve a series of new contributions.

(10) The question can be posed initially in terms of the relations between perceptual pregnance and logical necessity, between which a certain number of transitions occur. While the hypothetico-deductive

necessity of formal operations alone meets all the requirements of logical necessity under its double aspect of internal obligation and the independence of the real and the possible (with the latter of which it is closely bound up), certain forms of necessity can already be detected in concrete operations: 'it must be', will say a child of 7 to 8 years, when justifying a transitive composition, in which $A = C$ if $A = B$ and $B = C$. At this level, however, the differentiation and co-ordination between the possible, the real and the necessary are not as complete as will be at the stage of formal operations, and it is difficult to identify anything more than momentary impressions of necessity at the level of pre-operational representations. *A fortiori*, it will be adventurous to identify traces of necessity in sensory-motor behaviour. Nevertheless, the way in which a baby of 18 months finds, without hesitation, an object hidden behind successive screens (failing to find it behind screen B, he immediately looks for it behind A, which had previously been placed behind B), seems to involve more than perceptual pregnance. But even granting a relative continuity of transition between perceptual pregnance and logical necessity, we would not go so far as to conclude that the latter derives from the former.

Psychologically speaking, necessity is only the expression of the regulated compositions of a self-contained operational structure which leaves no room for indecision. The structure must be truly operational, integrating mutually determining transformations, and cannot be reduced to a static configuration. Pregnance, on the other hand, is only a coercive effect produced, in a perceptual field, by a form whose elements, by their equivalences, succeed in compensating any deformations which are present. It is clear, therefore, that in spite of their kinship, necessity could not derive from such a pregnance unless a system of transformations itself could be drawn from such a configuration; but as the transformation is richer than the configuration, it is the configuration which would be explained by the transformation if derivation was involved. We do not mean to imply by this that pregnance derives from necessity; perception does not achieve transformations (or if it does apprehend them, it is only in the guise of states: kinetic forms, etc.), while the incorporation of configurations as a whole into a system of transformations, which both surpass and illuminate them, marks the greatest contribution, or the major achievement of, intelligence.

But while logical necessity may not be the source of perceptual pregnance, a certain indirect connection can nevertheless be presumed to exist between them. While it is likely that good forms are structured by primary perceptual activities (Chapter III, Conclusions to § 9), and that their resistance to deformation is reinforced by secondary perceptual activities (Chapter III, § 8), it is also likely that operational activities of various levels act upon and direct those perceptual activities. The logical necessity of operational activities would then indirectly reinforce (but not originate) certain pregnances, just as sensory-motor activities in general can influence primary perceptual activities.

(11) We may now consider the differences between perceptual schemes and logical classes, and between perceptual pre-infra-classes and operational infra-classes (classes of continuous elements). We are already familiar with the succession of transitional states which extend from certain sensory-motor schemes, through the 'figural collections' of the early representational stage and through non-figural collections (without regulated inclusion), to emerge finally as the diverse structures of the logic of classes. Here again, the superior structures cannot be derived from their perceptual counterparts, but it is possible to show that, because of their sensory-motor origins, higher structures can enrich perception by having an indirect effect on perceptual activities and thereby an influence on field effects.

Logical classes cannot derive from the schemes and collective forms of perception, because logical classes are part and parcel of a system of transformations and of operations which require an understanding of logical addition and multiplication and of their inverse operations. So, once again, transformations cannot be reduced to configurations which, in fact, they eventually incorporate.

But the repercussions of the development of classes upon perceptual schemes can be seen in the formation of two phenomena: 'empirical Gestalts', in which the subject's schemes are characterised by current significances rather than by geometric good form; and 'temporal schemes', by means of which Brunswik and Bruner explain the perceptual recognition of familiar objects.

(12) While perceptual relations are deforming and logical relations conserving, various operational systems which derive from action, and not from perception, are once again ranged between them: seriations and serial correspondences for asymmetrical relations, and additive compositions and multiplicative equivalences for symmetrical relations. It must be repeated, in this connection, that the existence of the series of intermediate states (including all the representational and yet deforming relations of the sensory-motor level, and all the 'pre-relations' of the operational level) in no way establishes the perceptual origin of logical operations: operational systems can only be accounted for in terms of events occurring in action as a whole, events which lie outside perception. But, here again, the development of the relations of intelligence will modify perceptual

activities and thereby new sedimentations within field effects. Some typical facts relating to this will be presented in Chapter VII, § 4: we demonstrated, with Lambercier, that the achievement of the logical transitivity of equivalences can sometimes lead, by directing the perceptual activities of transposition, to an improvement in the transpositions of equalities in size.

(13) In the case of inferences in general, it is easy to distinguish a series of intermediate states between the most elementary perceptual pre-inferences and logically governed operational inferences. However, it is equally clear that the transition is not brought about simply by an extension of the structures of lower levels, but rather by the construction of new schemes which form the basis of the inferences of higher levels.

The most elementary perceptual pre-inferences are probably those which intervene in threshold judgements, when the subject has to 'decide' or discriminate between effects due to the external stimulus and those which are due to 'noise' accompanying it.[1] In such cases, the pre-inferences consist simply in an assimilation of the perceptual elements (encounters and couplings) to a scheme of presence or absence, of equality or inequality; but an inference is involved whenever a decision is made, because a choice has to be made on the basis of supporting or negating indices. The next level is reached when perceptually available aspects of a scheme (x or y) lead to the perception of another aspect (z) which is not directly registered (see item 13 of § 1 of this chapter).[2]

Subsequent levels involve secondary perceptual activities: the pre-inferences which then occur no longer involve a direct passage from one aspect to another of the same figural scheme, but the employment of more complex forms of relation which are themselves assimilated to various schemes (of transposition, anticipation, spatial co-ordinates, etc.) which in turn bring about the resulting perception. Such processes are involved, for instance, when the estimation of a constant size, or of a perceived relation of causality, depends on several variables.

The next level is that of sensory-motor inference, which should, of course, be subdivided in detail. However, we will simply note that these sensory-motor inferences are partially under the subject's control, even if they do derive from pre-inferences whose various stages of composition are beyond his control: when a child of 12 or 18 months

---

[1] See the studies of Tanner, W. P., and Swets, J. A., *Psychol. Rev.*, 1954, **61**, 401–9, in which threshold variations are successfully interpreted in terms of the concepts of decision theory (games theory).

[2] These levels of perceptual pre-inferences are discussed by Piaget, J., and Morf, A., in Bruner, J. S., *et al. Logique et Perception, op. cit.*, Chapter II, §§ 5 and 7.

solves a problem in stages by selecting the most adequate means of attaining his goal (as, for instance, making a chain into a ball in order to insert it into an opening, or finding an object under several superposed screens), he distinguishes between, and actively controls, the passage from antecedents to consequents.

Pre-operational representational inferences also provide a whole range of transitions between types of immediate and uncontrolled pre-inferences, and mediate and controlled inferences. The pre-inferences in question might easily be taken for perceptual inferences except that they introduce elements which are clearly notional, for example, comparing the lengths of two paths by referring only to their terminal points, which is neither a perceptual nor a metric, but an ordinal, interpretation. Finally, operational or regulated inferences appear whose hallmark is the employment of compositions belonging to a closed system.

It is again clear that higher inferential structures cannot derive by simple extension from perceptual pre-inferences. Advances in mediation and in control over the steps of composition do not consist in making the implicit explicit, but in the continuous creation of new compositions as ever richer and more coherent schemes are elaborated. Conversely, the autonomous development of sensory-motor inferences could, in many cases, explain the evolution of perceptual pre-inferences, to the extent, at least, that sensory-motor schemes can influence perceptual schemes and because perceptual pre-inferences are related to secondary activities. A case will be made in support of this in § 4 of Chapter VII.

(14) We can now return to the fundamental difference between the reversibility of operations and the irreversibility of perception, and choose between the unitarist and interactionist solutions with which this chapter opened.

The unitarist solution would trace the sources of logical reversibility back to those very approximate compensations which, through perceptual activities, moderate the errors which themselves express the irreversibility of perception. These regulatory mechanisms, originating with the development of perceptual decentration and achieving a semi-reversibility, would require to be supplemented by sensory-motor and then by representational regulations, until increasing compensations gave way to complete reversibility.

The interactionist point of view, which we have defended in sections (1) to (11) of this chapter, would also suggest the existence of a filiation. This would extend, by a series of steps, from sensory-motor regulations, which would of course include an integral perceptual component, to reversible operations. But the progress of perceptual regulations towards semi-reversibility would be seen as deriving from, rather than as a cause of, the central genetic progression from actions to operations.

A choice can be made between these two interpretations if we recall that operational reversibility is bound up with the existence of inverse and reciprocal operations, and that these operations, of necessity, bear on classes, relations, numbers or propositions, in other words, on realities which cannot be reduced to perceptual forms. Reference to the many ways in which developing intelligence reacts upon perceptual activities, explains how the development of reversibility, closely associated with actions and operations, comes to influence the development of those perceptual activities. Each such repercussion leads to a refinement in perceptual regulations, in other words, to a modification towards reversibility.

CONCLUDING REMARKS

In sum, the notion of a course of development in terms of a continuous extension from perception to operational intelligence can be entertained only in the cases of proximity (2) and of mobility (7). For the rest, the analysis has indicated the intervention of contributions arising in action, contributions which then have repercussions on perception itself. As the conditions of distance (or proximity) and of mobility derive from the most general aspects of perceptual and of intellectual behaviour, as does reversibility (14), the unknown implications of the evidence provided by their evolution cannot stand in the way of our general hypotheses.

These hypotheses, which are only ideas at this stage, require verification. Two kinds of fact can be invoked to this end. The irreducibility of operational structures to those of perception will be examined by devoting the whole of Chapter VII to an analysis of the relations between certain notions, or certain operational structures, and corresponding perceptual events. This will allow us to show why notions could not be 'abstracted' from perceptual data and why our insistence on action as a source of operations is not a disguised form of reference to perception, in the form of the perception of action (because the schemes of action, principal sources of concepts, are not perceptible as such). The crucial problem of the influence of the development of actions and of intellectual operations on the development of perceptual activities, accompanied as it is by new and successive contributions to field effects, will also be taken up again in Chapter VII. A certain number of new facts to illustrate this influence will be presented in § 4. The facts to be presented will also add to what has been said in the present chapter about the immediate and the mediate, about perceptual schemes and the perceptual pre-inferences to which those schemes give rise.

VII THE PERCEPTUAL OR NON-PERCEPTUAL ORIGINS OF THE STRUCTURES OF INTELLIGENCE

As we saw in the introduction to Chapter VI, the present state of our knowledge suggests that there are two likely genetic hypotheses concerning the relations between perception and intelligence. The first is of a direct filiation from perceptual field effects to operational structures, through perceptual and sensory-motor activities and finally through perceptual representations. The second is of an autonomous development of intelligence from action (sensory-motor activities), accompanied by a continuous enrichment of perceptual structures under the influence of the development of structures of action and of intelligence. The latter would again be achieved (but in an inverse direction) through perceptual activities and would be accompanied by a progressive sedimentation of perceptual activities into field effects.

To choose between these two theories, we first (Chapter VI) analysed the differences and the similarities which exist between perceptual and intellectual structures. We established, in the case of almost every one of the differences, that the transition from the structures of perception to those of intelligence required the intervention of fresh contributions arising in actions or in operations, and that the transition could not be explained simply as an extension of, or an increased mobility in, perceptual structures. However, the analysis served only as a simple introduction to the study of these questions, and facts have yet to be produced which will demonstrate both the effects of the development of the structures of intelligence on the development of particular perceptual activities, and the sedimentation of the latter into new field effects.

We can now pose the question in its general form. If the first (unitarist) hypothesis is accepted, its least consequence would be the verification of the classical opinion that notions elaborated by intelligence are 'abstracted' from perception. Notions would thus originate in sensory data (no matter what modifications might be added by later abstractions or what generalisations accompanied or directed them). Its most extreme consequence would be the verification of the

310

idea that the operations of intelligence themselves (of which abstraction and generalisation are products) derive from the general laws of organisation already at work in perception: so Wertheimer tried to extend the concept of perceptual Gestalt to encompass the operational structures of productive thought, including logico-mathematical structures. If the other hypothesis is correct, it would follow, on the contrary, that neither the operations of intelligence nor even notions are drawn from perception.

We believe that a direct analysis of the formation of operations shows that the irreducible elements they bring to figurative organisations support the second hypothesis. However, this hypothesis receives its most decisive support from the finding that notions are never abstracted from perception in any area of knowledge in which a system of notions is accompanied by a corresponding system of perceptions (e.g. space, velocity, time, notional and perceptual causality, etc.). On the contrary, notions originate in sets of actions and of operations which begin with sensory-motor organisation, of which perceptual activities represent only a particular sector. This sector is limited by its own mode of functioning, which is concerned only with the organisation of spatially limited and temporally present data (the here and now).

We will try to demonstrate this by presenting a very schematic summary of the research we have been able to carry out or to direct in areas in which the operational development of a notion can be compared with the corresponding perceptual data. The discussion will be limited to a few special topics concerning which we have pertinent results (a general account having been attempted in Chapter VI). These results are probably varied enough to allow the reader to form his own opinion concerning the formulation to which they seem to point and which we shall try to identify in the conclusion to this chapter.

Four types of relation between notions and corresponding perceptions will be distinguished: (I) When the perceptual events corresponding to the notion in question consist of very 'primitive' field effects whose origins probably lie in primary perceptual activities, but at too elementary a level for their development to be traced. In this case, the notion entails the intervention of new organisations which have no direct relation to field effects. (II) When the perceptual events under consideration consist of relatively precocious activities and the schemes of intelligence consist of sensory-motor (pre-representational) schemes. In this case there is a fairly advanced isomorphism (cf. the 'prefiguration' discussed in (III) below) between perceptual activities and corresponding sensory-motor activities, but with reciprocal and not one-way action. (III) When the perceptual

311

events also consist of activities (in opposition to field effects) and the notion makes its appearance appreciably later. In this case it can be said, with Michotte, that perception 'prefigures' the notion, but not in the sense in which the notion is simply abstracted from perception. The implication would be, rather, that the relevant perceptual activities exhibit characteristics of composition which are partially isomorphic with the forms of operational composition at work in the construction of the notion, and that they share common filiations with early stages of sensory-motor activities. (IV) Sometimes the supposed prefiguration takes the form of an influence of notional and operational structures on the compositions of perceptual structures. At most, the observed correspondence between certain perceptual events and the notions which seem to derive from them reduces to the direction of perceptual activities by operations.

§ 1. SITUATION I: THE DIVERGENT EVOLUTION OF NOTIONS AND OF CORRESPONDING PERCEPTIONS

We have two good examples which illustrate the first of the four possibilities enumerated above: those of notions of projection and of the estimation of the length of two off-set horizontal lines.

I*A*. The study of the development of elementary projective representations indicates that its trend is opposite to that found in the corresponding perceptions. It has been shown (Chapter IV, § 3) that younger children perceive projective sizes more accurately than older children do, that the ability deteriorates between 7 to 8 and 10 to 11 years, and that it then improves a little but not to the point where the inexperienced adult equals the 6- to 7-year-old child. But in a child's spontaneous drawings, perspectives do not generally appear before 9 to 10 years; and the experiments in projective geometry mentioned above show that the representation of changes in perspective only begin at about $6\frac{1}{2}$ to 7 years and are not organised before 7 to 9 years, even in the case of a single object. A comprehension of changes in perspective associated with changes in points of view when three objects are involved (in terms of the relations left-right and in front-behind), is not acquired before 9 to 10 years. It can be claimed therefore: (*a*) that the notion, or the representational image, does not exist at the time when projective perception is at its best; (*b*) that the notion is in the process of being formed while projective perception is deteriorating; and (*c*) that at an intermediate age, when projective perception is least good, notional organisation is reaching its first equilibrated stage.

This situation is all the more paradoxical because the role played by visual perception in the elaboration of projective notions cannot be denied: historically, projective geometry was first advanced as a theory of the transformations inherent in changes of 'points of view'. So Enriquès,[1] who tried to link various forms of geometry to different sensory domains, found his simplest example in this association of projective notions and vision. But it is one thing to recognise a link between perception and projective notions and quite another to maintain, as do empiricists, that notions are simply 'abstracted' from perceptions. Our hypothesis, on the contrary, presumes that notions add an essentially new element to perceptual data, a framework within which perceptual data are interrelated and within which they are consequently incorporated and often corrected. This framework itself cannot derive from perceptual data (by simple abstraction and generalisation) because it constitutes a system of transformations, not a system of configurations.

In the case of projective notions, this framework consists in a 'co-ordination of points of view' whose laborious construction can be followed step by step between the ages of 6 to 7 and 10 to 11 years. All that projective perception can supply (with all sorts of errors) are the visual configurations which correspond to one point of view or another. It cannot supply either the correspondence itself or that system of transformations, the co-ordination of points of view, which permits changes in point of view to occur in a reversible and associative manner (in the logical sense).

There are two reasons why the correspondence between perceived configurations and points of view cannot be established on the basis of perception. Firstly, to know that one perceives an object from a certain point of view consists in distinguishing it from other possible points of view (closer or farther away, on another side, etc.). To distinguish them, one must compare them, which presumes the intervention of sensory-motor schemes at least; and, in so far as a complete comparison is involved, the intervention of representational schemes, because the points of view occur successively, not simultaneously. The second reason is that in the most elementary case, in which the subject limits himself to comparing immediately succeeding points of view (e.g. causing the apparent size of an object to vary by moving towards or away from it), the changes in perception are subordinated to a system of movements. It might be said that perception has not been exceeded in this case, because information about the movement of the body has itself been supplied proprioceptively. But can perception itself link heterogeneous perceptual systems (visual and proprioceptive), or does this depend on a supra-perceptual mechanism? In fact, the correspondence between changes in the apparent size of an object and movements of the observer is not

[1] Enriquès, F., *Encyclopédie des Sciences Mathématiques*, Paris, 1909.

established by associating (in the psychological meaning of the term) a muscular sensation with a visual perception, but by relating the perception (whose data are visual) to the change of position (whose data are proprioceptive), the relating itself being neither visual nor proprioceptive.

If the instrument of this action of relating is referred to as a 'scheme' (being repeatable in any analogous situation) we must insist (and will be led to insist more strongly later on) that while it may influence perceptions, modifying and enriching their structures, it is not itself an object of perception. This claim is particularly clear in the present case. The same scheme which relates apparent sizes and positions can assimilate three perceptually different situations: that in which the object is motionless and the observer moves; that in which the observer is motionless and the object moves; and that in which the observer, without changing his position, himself moves the object towards or away from him. In summary, the correspondence between projective perceptions and points of view presumes a reference to action as a whole. Each movement (or lack of movement), position or apparent size may be perceptible, but the sensory-motor scheme which links them cannot be perceived as such since it occurs at a level superior to that of perception.

The co-ordination of points of view, already initiated by movement from one position to another, makes even greater demands and consequently is not completed until the operational level of 9 or 10 years. It implies that an observer, perceiving an object from one position, can reconstitute or anticipate his perceptions of the same object from a different, and not merely neighbouring, position. This is no longer a question of perceived transformations, but of deduced and in some way calculated transformations, depending on a special system of operations which are precisely the operations of projective geometry. If the scheme of the action involved in perceived transformations itself exceeds the limits of perception, then the operational schemes which allow the subject to infer what he will see of a given scene when passing from one point of view to others, can have nothing in common with perceptual mechanisms. Such operational schemes form a mobile system (or a system of transformations as such), in which perceptions are included as content and in which they may play a verifying role (but remain subject to correction as a result of the co-ordinations involved).

The origins of the system itself are not to be found in perception but, inasmuch as operations are interiorised actions, in the sensory-motor schemes which co-ordinate perceptions with the subject's positions. If these schemes are not objects of perception, the argument is even stronger when applied to operations and their structures.

For these various reasons we conclude that projective notions are not abstracted from corresponding perceptions. On the contrary, the notions incorporate the perceptions into frameworks which derive from action itself, and at the same time correct them. The frameworks are superimposed on the perceptions at every stage but are not themselves derived from perception. This is why projective perceptions and notions do not exhibit any direct evolutionary connections but even seem to move in opposite directions.

I*B*. A second equally striking example of discordance in the evolution of perception and of corresponding notions was obtained in studies conducted with Taponier[1] on the estimation of the lengths of two off-set horizontals. It had been shown, in studies on ideation,[2] that a young child who judges two perceptually congruent rods to be equal in length may no longer judge them to be equal when one is off-set. He will usually state that the rod which extends beyond the other in the direction of the movement is 'longer'. We found at Geneva, that on the average only 15% of children conserved the length at the age of 5 as against 70% at 8 and 100% at 11 years. It was obvious from the protocols that the children were basing their judgements on the projection of one of the rods while neglecting the projection of the other at the other end. We nevertheless wondered if a perceptual factor might not be involved in these reactions, particularly in view of the supposed difficulty of estimating the lengths of two off-set horizontals. We therefore tried to find out if there was any correlation between non-conservation and some relevant systematic perceptual error. We found no evidence of any such correlation, but made the paradoxical discovery that young children of 5 years made better perceptual estimates than did older children while still entertaining the notion that the displaced rod became longer.

For the perceptual experiment, two black lines, 6 cm in length, were drawn so that one extended 3 cm beyond the other. Two degrees of vertical separation were used, 3 cm and 1 cm. The main results obtained are shown in Table 117.

TABLE 117. *Mean error (% of the standard) on the variable (upper of two off-set horizontal lines) as a function of their separation (n in parenthesis)*

Rech. 32, Table 1

Age group Separation	5 yrs	8 yrs	11 yrs	Adult
3 cm	−0·73 (16)	−2·69 (15)	−2·46 (16)	−2·25 (15)
1 cm	−1·32 (15)	−2·40 (15)	−0·62 (15)	−1·54 (15)

It looks as if the oblique comparison required by the displacement troubled the 5-year-olds less than children of 8 years and over (the differences being less marked with a vertical separation of 1 cm). This

---

[1] *Rech.* 32.　　[2] *The Child's Conception of Geometry, op. cit.*, Chapter IV.

can be explained (as in the case of the figures that we suggested to Würsten, Chapter III, § 4) by the fact that younger children have not yet structured their perceptual space in terms of the natural co-ordinate axes, and that the progressive achievement of this structuring with age makes the oblique direction of the comparison more obvious and therefore more difficult. But how, then, can one account for the fact that younger children do not use this facility in perceptual judgements when making conceptual judgements, but entertain the strange idea that when congruent rods are off-set, the displaced one becomes longer because it 'projects beyond' the other? The answer is that the *notion* of length used by the child of 4 to 6 years does not correspond to perceptual length but derives from a quite different structure (which may nevertheless be analogous to structures which determine perception at a much earlier age than 5 years). Given that the length of a line is determined by one of its extremities (its leading edge), by the other extremity (its trailing edge), and by the interval contained between them, we find that the child does not start, at the notional level, with a metric evaluation based on the interval, but with an ordinal estimate based on a comparison of the leading edges. One rod or path is said to be 'longer' if it reaches 'farther', no regard being paid to the trailing edges or to the intervals. It is only by a progressive evolution, comparable to that which characterises the transition from ordinal velocity (overtaking-velocity) to metric velocity ($v = d : t$), that the child comes to take account of the trailing edges and finally to be satisfied with the intervals alone.

The notion of metric or interval-length is, of course, more complex than that of ordinal length ('longer' = 'farther along') because the interval between the extremities of a line is essentially relative, being independent of the absolute positions of those points. In comparing the lengths of two lines on the basis of the intervals between the extremities of each, the four points have to be considered, whereas the judgement 'farther along' need refer only to leading edges: even at the age of 5 to 6 years, only one projecting end is involved in the notion. In perception, however, the whole configuration is encompassed (except, perhaps, during the first months of life), and both projections are apprehended at once. This does not trouble younger children, but does trouble the older ones by forcing them to make a comparison which takes note of the oblique aspect of the figure.

No doubt it will be said that an ordinal notion of length, founded on the equivalence 'longer' = 'farther along', is also abstracted from perception and simply makes use of only one of the perceived projections. To elucidate this situation, it will be compared with other analogous ones which are fairly general at these levels. Between 3 and 4 years, for example, a child will draw a square, a triangle and a circle with the same closed, approximately circular, curve. He can of course *perceive* the differences between the figures, but notionally retains only their common topological character of closure, and neglects their metric properties. Here again, as in the case of the topological character of order in the notion of ordinal length, it could be claimed that this closure also is abstracted from perception.

But it is one thing to extract a character, x, from a set of objects and to classify them together on this basis alone, a procedure which we shall refer to as 'simple' abstraction and generalisation (and which is invoked by classical empiricism), and quite another to recognise x in an object and to make use of it as an element of a different (non-perceptual) structure, a procedure which we shall refer to as 'constructive' abstraction and generalisation. In our examples, the abstraction of only one projection results in an evaluation of the length which is different from the perception of the interval, and the abstraction of closure results in a perceptual form which is different from a square or a triangle. In these particular cases, the notions (being still topological) are at a more primitive level than the perceptions (which are already metric or Euclidean), but they nevertheless result from structures which are different from those of the perceptions from which they borrow certain elements.

At later levels, notions become fully concordant with perceptions (a metric estimation of the length of off-set lines and a Euclidean treatment of the square and the triangle), and, because of this, one would, *a fortiori*, be tempted to say that notions are abstracted from perceptions. Such an interpretation would be unassailable if the preceding stages were not known (before 7 to 8 years for length, and before 4 to 5 years for Euclidean 'good forms'). But the existence of the earlier detour leading to these metric notions through topological notions (ordinals, etc.) shows that a complex construction is involved: the convergence between perceptions and notions is achieved slowly and not by a 'simple' abstraction of notions from perceptions.

Where there is this divergence between perceptual field effects and corresponding notions (divergence, but with later possible convergence), it is possible that the field effects could have derived from earlier perceptual activities. There might then be a partial isomorphism between the levels of construction of these earlier activities and the corresponding levels of notional construction, but with a considerable temporal lag (and, of course, great differences in extension and generalisation). For example, it is possible that interval-lengths, easily perceived at 5 years, mark the final stage of a perceptual evolution which also began with ordinal lengths (characteristic,

317

perhaps, of the first four or five months of life) and that the same evolution repeats itself on the notional plane, at a much slower pace, some years later and with other content. It is also possible that projective perception is inadequate from the beginning (this would be inevitable if the perception of length and size were not innately given) and that, at the perceptual level, an elementary perceptual co-ordination of points of view prefigures, in a minor way, what will eventually become the operational co-ordination of perspectives. If these hypotheses could be verified, form III correspondence between perceptions and notions, that is 'prefiguration', would be the general case and only the sedimentation of perceptual activities into field effects would entail the partially divergent forms of evolution of which two examples have just been given. But we shall see that such prefigurations, where they can be verified (which may be possible in the case of perceptual developments which occur later), in no way a 'simple' abstraction of notions from perceptions, but only imply a convergence of the laws of construction, a convergence which is brought about by the fact that notions spring from sensory-motor activities which also control the evolution of perception. We will now take a brief look at this problem with an examination of correspondences of form II.

§ 2. SITUATION II: RECIPROCAL ACTION BETWEEN PERCEPTUAL AND SENSORY-MOTOR SCHEMES

II*A*. The sensory-motor scheme of the permanent object takes shape during the second half of the first year and is characterised by the fact that the child starts to look for an object which has disappeared behind a screen. Before this, he behaves as if its perceptual disappearance was equivalent to its momentary destruction or to its provisional resorption. This scheme is naturally part and parcel of the spatial schemes of localisation and of displacement, the appearance of behaviour associated with the substantial permanence of the object coinciding with that of the 'group' of displacements. Two problems arise in connection with this formulation: does this scheme itself derive from perception? If not, what are its relations to perception?

Certain authors, like Szuman (of Cracow), have claimed that the construction of the scheme of the object can be explained in terms of its polysensorial character: the object acquires its specific consistency because it can be grasped manually at the same time as it is perceived visually. But even if these events do play an undeniable part in the concretisation of the perceptual object, they do not explain why a child searches for an object which has disappeared perceptually.

There is a level at which the infant gives up looking for a toy which has been covered by a handkerchief, or fails to look for his feeding bottle when it is hidden behind the experimenter's arm (but within the child's reach), although he is quite capable of raising the hand-kerchief or of reaching for the object behind the experimenter's arm (as he does if he sees a projecting part of the toy or of the feeding bottle). As the perceived object is already polysensorial at this level (the co-ordination of vision and prehension having been achieved by that stage), its polysensorial characteristics cannot be called upon to explain the permanence of an object which has been removed from the field of vision.

Some of Michotte's pupils (Sampayo[1] and others) have tried to explain the object's permanence on the basis of two of the effects described by him: the 'screen-effect', in the course of which an object is seen to pass 'behind' another[2] instead of simply decreasing in size in one dimension (as it should on the basis of sensorial data alone); and the 'tunnel effect' in which the moving object, emerging from behind the screen, is identified with the one which passed behind it on the other side. Its invisible journey behind the screen is per-ceived 'amodally' (no senses being involved), and an approximate speed and a continuous localisation is attributed to it (provided that the movement is uniform, and given certain restrictions concern-ing its speed).

However, while fully recognising the relevance of a comparison between the formation of the scheme of the permanent object and the 'screen' and 'tunnel' effects, both remarkable and certainly quite pre-cocious, we cannot accept the proposed interpretation for two reasons. The first is the existence of a fact which cannot be explained in terms of the screen and tunnel effects. We observed a phase in two of our children which such good observers as Kurt Lewin and Käthe Wolf have told us that they have also observed. The subject sees an object disappearing under cushion A, to his left, looks for it[3] and finds it there, under A; when the same object is then slipped under a cushion B, to his right, the child looks for it under A again, that is, where he first succeeded. The beginnings of the search for the van-ished object thus testify to a surprising failure in localisation which cannot be explained by the mechanisms of the screen and tunnel

[1] Sampayo, A. C., *Phil. Diss.*, Louvain, 1943.
[2] The screen and the moving body are distinguished by the fact that their com-mon boundary belongs to the screen and not to the moving body, following Rubin's law.
[3] This concerns the beginnings of behaviour associated with the search for van-ished objects, and follows the stage where no such search is observable: see Piaget, J., *The Child's Construction of Reality*, London, 1955, Routledge and Kegan Paul, Chapter 1, § III.

effects, if they exist at that age. Our second cause for doubt is that there is no proof that the screen and tunnel effects are congenital. If they are acquired, it is highly improbable that they would be established before the search for the vanished object made its appearance, or by the time that this search began (as just described). Far from explaining the formation of the scheme of the permanent object, the screen and tunnel effects, undeniably perceptual as they may be, are probably of later or at best of contemporaneous elaboration. There is, therefore, no reason why the sensory-motor scheme of permanence should not collaborate in the development of these perceptual effects. Nor is there any reason why there should not be reciprocal action between them: the sensory-motor scheme would constitute a necessary (but not sufficient) condition for the screen and tunnel effects, and they, once established, would facilitate the search for the vanished object and thus improve the sensory-motor scheme whose development is far from being instantaneous.

Similarly, one may suppose that the perceptual constancies of size and of form, whose beginnings in part precede the formation of the scheme of the permanent object, also collaborate in this development. But here again it is a question of knowing whether a one-way or a reciprocal action is involved. Regarding the relation between the conservation of the object and form constancy, we can quote the following observation[1] which seems to be quite informative:

> Laurent, before the age of 0;9(17) or perhaps 0;8(29), does not make a systematic search for objects which have disappeared behind a screen. From the age of 7 months exactly, however, he can hold his bottle while drinking from it. If I present it to him the wrong way round he does not know how to turn it round and sucks the wrong end (unless he catches sight of the red rubber nipple at the other end). From 0;7(4) to 0;8(24) he succeeds, over a series of twelve separated successive trials, in turning the bottle round if it is presented three-quarters or almost completely reversed, but sucks the wrong end, or refuses it (crying, etc.) if I present it completely reversed. But if the bottle is moved away from him a little and presented vertically, he runs his eyes over it attentively and centres the two ends in particular. On the other hand, from 0;9(9) and 0;9(10) he at once turns the bottle round.

Thus, before he can look for a hidden object, the child exhibits some degree of constancy: he recognises the feeding bottle and turns it round when it is presented to him almost the wrong way round. But this does not imply the existence of a complete constancy of form.

[1] Abstracted from Piaget, J., *La Construction du Réel*, Neuchâtel, 1937, Delachaux et Nièstle, obs. 34 (pp. 48–9), 78 (pp. 127–9), 92 (p. 165). Translation by present translator.

Until he possesses the scheme of the permanent object he cannot comprehend the existence of the wrong side of an object and the possibility of re-establishing its correct position by a rotation of 180°. Then, at 9 months, plus or minus a few days, he succeeds both in looking for hidden objects and in turning the feeding bottle round in order to find the completely hidden nipple. As this new behaviour undoubtedly favours (and exceeds) perceptual form constancy, we may admit the existence of a reciprocal action between the construction of the permanent object and the constancy of its form. The same can, of course, be said in regard to size constancy. But these constancies alone cannot engender the scheme of the permanent object which entails, in addition, an organisation of displacements in translation (and, as we have just seen, in rotation), on the lines of the structure of a 'group'.

In conclusion, the explanation of the formation of the scheme of the permanent object in terms of perceptual factors alone, or by mere abstraction from perception, seems to be excluded. The screen and tunnel effects could give rise to such an abstraction, but there is no doubt that they are antedated by the scheme in question. Polysensorial experience and the constancies of size and form may also contribute to its elaboration, but cannot alone give rise to it because the permanence of the object beyond the bounds of the perceptual field constitutes the invariant of a 'group', the 'group of displacements', in which action as a whole intervenes: to believe that the object continues to exist beyond the limits of the perceptual field amounts to locating it on the basis of the last of its successive displacements. It is this indissociable union between the scheme of the object and the group of displacements which confers a supra-perceptual character on the sensory-motor scheme and which is dependent on action as a whole. In addition, the schemes in question (like those discussed in § 1) are not perceptible: even if each movement and each position is perceptible, and if the object itself is perceptible in each unconcealed position, neither the group of displacements and positions as such, nor the scheme of the permanent object, are accessible to perception.

While perceptual factors certainly collaborate either in the preparation or in the completion of the scheme of the permanent object, no doubt the latter also has repercussions upon perception. This is equally likely to be the case in the elaboration or completion of the perceptual schemes of the screen and tunnel effects as in the improvement of the constancies of size and form. In regard to constancies, we saw (Chapter IV, § 5) that the development of size constancy required the co-ordination of vision and prehension and depended on the fact that the tactilo-kinesthetic object conserved its

321

dimensions wherever the hands might move it. As the permanence of the object derives from the continued organisation of manipulations once they have been structured as a group of displacements, it is very likely that this scheme will go on to favour the construction or improvement of the constancies. This process will be favoured by the fact that most of the permanent solids of the universe with which the child's action comes into contact have constant dimensions and form.

II*B*. Sensory-motor intelligence leads to the formation of other general schemes in addition to the scheme of the permanent object. These are of considerable importance for the later evolution of notions and one of the most significant of them is that of causality. Sensory-motor causality presents a remarkable evolution, the trend of which recurs, transposed and restructured in terms of representations and operations, during the whole of the succeeding period which extends approximately from 2 or 3 to 11 or 12 years. At the beginning of this sensory-motor evolution (and also at the subsequent beginning of the development of the representational scheme), causality can be said to be 'magico-phenomenalist' in the sense that a successful action (for example, shaking the toys hanging from the canopy of the cradle by pulling a cord which also hangs from it) is now applied in an entirely different situation, regardless of contacts or distances. For example, the same cord is pulled to cause the continued swinging of another object which is 2 m away, or to cause the repetition of a whistle which came from behind a screen. In the final stage of this evolution (and that of representational causality as it becomes operational) causality becomes tied to objects and spatially located, in the sense that it is transferred to the action of objects themselves and demands spatial and kinematic contacts.

The problem is the same as it was with the scheme of the permanent object: is sensory-motor, and subsequently notional, causality abstracted from perception and, if not, what are its relations with perceptual causality? The theory of the perceptual origin of the notion of cause has been supported by Michotte, who reinterpreted facts which we had previously described concerning sensory-motor causality in this way. But with due regard to Michotte's brilliance and to the intellectual generosity with which he has discussed our views, it is difficult for us to follow him in his attempt to reduce notional to perceptual causality. There are two complementary reasons for this, one of which results from our own reinterpretation of perceptual causality, and the other from the nature of the evolution which we have just outlined for sensory-motor and representational causality.

In regard to perceptual causality, we have already seen (Chapter IV, § 6) that it is necessary to assume a reciprocal assimilation between visual and tactilo-kinesthetic causality in order to explain both its formation and the system of compensations that it uses. Just as assimilations between the visual and tactilo-kinesthetic realms are demanded by the development of prehension, imitation, etc., no adequate account could be given of the dynamic impressions of thrust, shock, resistance, etc. (known through tactilo-kinesthetic experience long before the visual equivalent is achieved), nor of the dynamic character of causality itself, without reference to this progressive assimilation. Tactilo-kinesthetic causality lies at the source of perceptual causality and therefore has chronological precedence. But while visual causality bears equally on relations between external objects and relations between the observer's body and those objects, tactilo-kinesthetic causality knows only one type of cause, the causality inherent in the body itself as it acts on external objects. As it is thus interdependent with actions themselves,[1] to a far greater degree than visual causality is, tactilo-kinesthetic causality cannot be considered to be exclusively perceptual: its component perceptual schemes exhibit continuous interactions with sensory-motor schemes in general, which themselves are not simply abstracted from perceptual schemes.

On the other hand, the evolution of early forms of sensory-motor causality in general is marked by a precocious tendency for them to free themselves from limitations of contact and of distance (which is why we named them 'magico-phenomenalist'). In contrast, it is still very difficult to obtain effects of perceptual visual causality without contact or at a distance, even in a child of 5 to 7 years. This immediate extension of the field of sensory-motor causality demonstrates both a remarkable indifference to the need for contacts and the relative autonomy of sensory-motor causal schemes (and, *a fortiori*, of representational schemes) compared with perceptual schemes.

In short, sensory-motor and representational causality proceed from an assimilation of perceived sequences to the schemes of action proper, without the perception of those sequences necessarily constituting forms of perceptual causality. But as perceptual causality, in the strictly limited conditions in which it can occur, is also structured on the basis of the schemes of action proper (given its tactilo-kinesthetic origin), it follows that interaction between the schemes of perceptual causality and those of sensory-motor causality must be established very early. This is why the origins of causality are to be found in the situations of form II which we are at present examining.

The course of evolution of causality leads, however, to a further situation, III (to be examined in § 3), in which notions are prefigured

---

[1] Each one considered in its entirety (that is, in terms of its scheme which is not, as such, perceptible) and not simply as a proprioceptive signal.

by perceptual activities. As causality becomes operational, it ceases to appear as a simple assimilation of external sequences to action proper and becomes an assimilation of those sequences to the system of operations. Causes are then to be seen as producing their effects in a manner analogous to that in which operations engender their consequences as they group themselves (those operations themselves being derived from actions by a continuous process which is repeated during the development of causality).

A first result is that operational causality takes shape in association with spatio-temporal operations in general. An orientation in this direction can already be seen at the sensory-motor level when causality, originally magico-phenomenalist, takes on its objective and spatial forms. But the most important result is that operational causality takes on the form of a system of compensations: *causa aequat effectus*, or, what the cause loses, the effect gains (an idea which is already implicit in causality by assimilation to action proper, for the cost of the action is recovered in its result). It is a remarkable fact that the scheme of compensation, which thus characterises causality in its evolved forms (such as mechanical causality, the most typical form of operational causality), is found to be prefigured in perceptual causality, given the interpretation attributed to it in § 6 of Chapter IV. Michotte himself also insisted, on several occasions, on this analogy between his perceptual visual causality and mechanical causality.

But what is the significance of such a 'prefiguration'? In this particular case, and without prejudging other examples to be discussed in § 3, it simply shows that all causality tends towards certain common characteristics once an adequate level of organisation has been achieved. These characteristics, and the level of organisation, recur in perceptual, sensory-motor and operational activities. As this level occurs relatively late in sensory-motor and representational realms, it is probable that, perceptually speaking, the achieved compensations described in § 6 of Chapter IV only are relatively advanced forms of the perception of causality: we have tried elsewhere[1] to reconstruct the earlier stages, basing our attempt on the difficulties in structuring experienced by the youngest subjects and on analogies with the sensory-motor and representational stages. If the above is correct, the prefiguration of the notion in perception only demonstrates that the processes of formation are analogous, but does not establish that notions derive or are abstracted from perception. On the contrary, the fact that the same formative processes are found in perception, in sensory-motor activity and in representational or operational intelligence (no doubt with certain similarities between the suc-

[1] *Rech.* 33.

cessive stages which occur at very different chronological periods in these three areas), seems to show once more that sensory-motor organisation is the common source of perceptual and intelligent activities. Causality is seen to originate in action. The resulting sensory-motor causality both orients those perceptual activities which are destined to lead to its own recognition and, through the interiorisation of actions, itself develops into pre-operational and then into operational representational causality. If this is the case, the prefiguration of notions in perception only testifies to an indirect, or so to speak collateral, genetic relationship, the direct filiation that some writers claim to detect being due simply to a neglect of the sensory-motor domain.

§ 3. SITUATION III: THE PREFIGURATION OF NOTIONS BY PERCEPTUAL ACTIVITIES

We have seen that some form of reciprocity occurs when those perceptual activities which lead to perceptual schemes, such as those of size and form constancy, precede, by a short interval of time, the achievement of corresponding schemes of intelligence (permanence of the object): the group of displacements constituting the scheme of the permanent object is partly prefigured by the simple movements which occur in the constancies (transports in depth for size, and partial rotations for form) and the sensory-motor scheme in turn helps to improve the constancies. Situation III differs from the preceding one in that a much longer interval separates the perceptual construction from that of the corresponding notion (operational notion in this case). As a result, there is no, or scarcely any, noticeable repercussion of the notion on to the perceptual construction which prefigures it (a repercussion which will, however, be observable in situation IV). The present problem is to analyse the significance (already indicated in connection with causality) of such 'prefigurations' in general and to try to decide if they carry the implication that the notion is abstracted from perception.

III*A*. A first example, which forms an extension of the preceding ones, is the operational notion of conservation, which begins at about 7 to 8 years and which can, in certain respects, be said to be prefigured by the perceptual constancies. The scheme of the permanent object constitutes the first form of conservation, and we have just seen that it incorporates the constancies of size and form. Moreover, perceptual constancies in general are based on systems of compensation (Chapter IV) which is also true of operational forms of conservation (conservation of collections, of continuous quantities, etc., when the component parts are spatially redistributed, etc.). The analogy between the formation of perceptual constancies and of notional conservations is therefore quite striking and the separation of about 7 years between the beginnings of the constancies (5 to 6 months) and the beginnings of conservation (7 to 8 years, leaving aside the sensory-motor scheme of the permanent object) is therefore very instructive.

We will first try to account for this temporal separation, and this will help us to understand the relations which link perceptions and notions in this area. There seems to be an essential difference between notional conservations and perceptual constancies, in spite of their common mechanisms of compensation. In the constancies, there is (a) a deforming factor, which is the only objective modification of the system (for instance, changes in distance in the perception of real size, changes in perspective in the perception of the real form, or changes in illumination, etc.); (b) a deformed factor which is the subjective modification of the system (apparent size, form or colour); (c) a constant factor, the product of the compensation between (a) and (b). In notional conservations (except in the particular case of the sensory-motor scheme of the permanent object, to which we shall return in a moment), factors (a) and (b) are both objective modifications of the system and, as such, co-vary (consequently one cannot be qualified as 'deforming' and the other as 'deformed'): the constant factor, (c), then constitutes the product of the compensation between the objective variations (a) and (b): the whole system may be said to be objectively modified but according to complementary or reciprocal transformations which leave their resultant, factor (c), invariant. For example, in the case of the conservation of a collection of objects, factors (a) and (b) are the surface occupied (or the length of the row) and the density of the elements, while (c) is the number, or the logical extent, of the collection.

It may therefore be admitted that perceptual constancies are more precocious than conservations, because the object in question is not physically transformed but merely gives rise to a subjective modification: the apparent change (b) is more easily compensated by the perception of the deforming factor (a) because the latter is not, properly speaking, a property of the object itself (which has not been altered physically) but of the system relating the object to the subject (its distance, position, illumination, etc.). In notional conservations, however, the object itself is transformed and the invariant property (c) cannot be extracted from the perception alone of (a) and (b): they must be *understood* to compensate one another. This requires the intervention of a system of genuine reversible operations.

In summary, perceptual constancies require only a compensation which is accessible to perception and do not call on operational comprehension. This is because they are limited to correcting a perceptual modification (the modified or 'apparent' quality, (*b*)) by the perception of the modification of the relation between the object and the subject (the modifying quality, (*a*)), in which (*a*) and (*b*) compensate one another, not because of an understanding of their indissociability, but because the subject has experienced this unity during the exercise of the inherent schemes of action. In notional conservations, on the other hand, the objective transformations (*a*) and (*b*) exclude this experienced unity because, both being objective, the one can be represented without the other (in the same way that only one of the two modifications is 'noticed' in the early stages, although both are 'perceived' simultaneously). This compensation can therefore only be made on the basis of a genuinely conceptual comprehension which requires years of elaboration.

This interpretation receives significant support from the fact that, in the case of the scheme of the permanent object (which is related to notions of conservation, but in such a precocious way that it is completely grasped by the end of the first year), it is the position of the object but not the object itself which is transformed. Consequently, the conditions under which this scheme develops are very similar to those of the perceptual constancies (which explains its precocity) except that an element of comprehension, which goes beyond mere perception, is involved when the object passes out of the perceptual field. But the same cannot be said in the case of the conservation of the lengths of two off-set lines (7 to 8 years): it is true that, once again, only the position varies, but now it is not a question of the conservation of the object but of length; and the length is estimated by the child in terms of the relative positions of the leading edges.

It can therefore be understood in what sense both perceptual constancies 'prefigure' notional conservations without the latter being in any way abstracted from them, and how conservations introduce relations which were not previously included in the constancies.

Constancies prefigure conservations in the sense that both rest on the same functional process of compensations: in both cases variations of certain properties, *a* and *b*, compensate one another and assure the relative or absolute invariance of *c*. However, only a functional analogy is involved and both the structural mechanisms involved and the final precision of the obtained invariances are different in the two cases. In the case of the constancies, the compensation is achieved by a system of approximate re-adjustments: the resulting invariance evolves from a systematic under-constancy to a fairly systematic over-constancy which reveals characteristics of precaution

327

and of over-compensation which are peculiar to this type of re-adjustment. In the case of conservation, on the contrary, where the variations of qualities *a* and *b* are objective, the representational re-adjustments give rise to a system of genuine operations whose strict reversibility in turn engenders an equally strict invariance character-ised by its deductive necessity and not by probabilistic approxima-tions.

Conservations thus have new properties and cannot therefore be abstracted from constancies. Nevertheless an obvious genetic kinship exists between them, one which is indirect and non-linear: conserva-tions are the product of a reconstruction, on the operational plane, of sensory-motor organisations which are already tending towards a degree of reversibility (cf. the practical group of displacements). This reversibility, within its limits, gives rise to the scheme of the per-manent object; and we saw (§ 2) that certain interactions occur be-tween the establishment of this scheme and the beginnings of the constancies. Therefore the origins of the kinship which apparently exists between the constancies and conservations is to be sought in a common sensory-motor stock.

In conclusion, the analogy between the case of the constancies and of conservations and that of causality may be noted (remembering that perceptual causality demonstrates a structure which is related to that of the constancies). Causality, deriving from intelligence, occurs in two forms, one sensory-motor and the other representational. Simi-larly, in conservation, one form is sensory-motor (the scheme of the permanent object) and the other operational. In both causality and conservation, the sensory-motor form develops in interaction with perceptual structures (situation II), and the operational form is pre-figured by these perceptual structures (situation III). In neither case does this prefiguration arise from a direct genetic continuity between perception and notions, but from their common sensory-motor origins.

III*B*. Another example of the prefiguration of a notion in percep-tion is found in the concept of velocity, or, more precisely in the first of the two concepts of velocity which occur during the development of intelligence. The second concept, which attains its equilibrium at the level of formal operations (with the proportionality of space and time) is the classical notion of velocity conceived as a relation be-tween distance and time. But this notion, whose appearance is rela-tively late, is preceded by an ordinal notion based on overtaking: the faster of two moving bodies is the one which was behind at one moment and in front at the next.[1] It is interesting to note that this

[1] Piaget, J., *Les Notions de Mouvement et de Vitesse chez l'Enfant*, Paris, 1946, P.U.F.

earlier notion, which depends on spatial and temporal order only, and which refers neither to spatial intervals nor to durations, is in fact a sufficient and rational concept: Abelé and Malvaux used it in their reformulation of relativistic concepts,[1] which they undertook in order to escape from the vicious, if not ineluctable, circle of velocity and time.

Our discussion of the perception of velocity (Chapter V, § 3) demonstrated the existence of an undeniable kinship between the notion of overtaking-velocity and the corresponding perceptual structures, while no such kinship seemed to exist between perceptual structures and the notion of velocity based on space–time.

Given, on the basis of the earlier discussion, that the perception of velocities is based on an ordinal comparison (between two moving bodies, between a moving body and the movement of the eyes, or between the comparative rates of excitations and extinctions in the receptor organ), it seems clear that some sort of kinship exists between the perception of overtaking and the ordinal notion of velocity. It is particularly striking to find that subjects so often detect an apparent acceleration in the overtaking object (or an apparent slowing down in the other) at the moment of overtaking. It may also be recalled that perception need not remain attached to purely ordinal structures but can attain a 'hyperordinal' level (in Suppes' sense): increasing or decreasing intervals between moving bodies can be compared in terms of 'greater' or 'smaller'.

But this prefiguration of the elementary notions of velocity in perception neither proves nor excludes the possibility that the notion of overtaking-velocity is abstracted from perception: the prefiguration could result from a simple functional analogy, the ordinal structure being simpler than a metric one in both cases. On the other hand, this case may, like others, support the existence of a collateral kinship, the common progenitor being sensory-motor activities.

Unfortunately, nothing is known about the sensory-motor schemes of velocity, although they certainly exist (cf. the way in which, at the level of tertiary circular reactions, the baby is capable of accelerating the oscillation of a hanging object, etc.). In view of this, all we can do is to examine to what extent the observable responses to velocity are abstracted from perception.

The response to velocity (in the presence of two simultaneously perceived moving bodies) is not necessarily perceptual. It is only so if the velocities are great enough and if the field of comparison allows a direct estimate to be made; when these conditions do not exist, the perceptual response gives way to an immediate conceptual interpre-

[1] Abelé, J., and Malvaux, Ch., *Vitesse et Univers Relativiste*, Paris, 1954, Sedez.

329

tation. This might be taken to be perceptual, because of its immediate nature, did it not differ fundamentally from perceptual responses in using only some of the perceptual information: for example in judging which object does the overtaking, a child takes account only of the points of arrival and neglects the points of departure, thus confounding precedence with overtaking and possibly inverting the velocities.

The question is whether this pre-operational representational and then operational activity, which leads to the notion of overtaking-velocity and then to the notion of space–time velocity, derives from perceptual activities or not. It is obvious that the contents of these representations (positions, displacements, etc.) derive from perceptual information. But it is quite another matter to suppose that their structures, at first ordinal and then metric, are abstracted from perceptual kinematic structures (which nevertheless prefigure them). This supposition cannot be entertained in this case for what may appear to be a paradoxical reason which nevertheless has quite general implications: although perception is at first clearly in advance of representational structures, it eventually drops farther and farther behind. For example, at one level, perception is hyper-ordinal (the comparison of successive intervals between moving bodies) while representation is still scarcely ordinal (when the subject does not generalise from an understanding of overtaking in certain situations to an appreciation of the significance of partial overtaking). Later, however, representation reaches a metric level while perception remains at the hyper-ordinal level.

This initial advance and subsequent loss of ground on the part of perception, of which many other examples may be found (the perception of Euclidean good forms at a level when their representation remains topological, etc.), obviously speaks in favour of a general reconstruction on the representational and operational planes rather than of a progressive abstraction of their structures from perception. If they were drawn from perception, it would be difficult to understand why they should lag behind at first. To reply that it is more difficult to represent a structure than to perceive it, would be equivalent to accepting the other solution because, if representational comprehension is more difficult than perception, a new construction and not just an abstraction must be involved; on the other hand, it is because of this new construction that the initially lagging representation finally overtakes perception.

However, the essence of the matter is that this particular lack of synchrony is not peculiar to the relation between representation and perception but applies quite generally to the relation between representational and sensory-motor activity. For example, we saw that the permanent object was acquired by the second year at the level of action, whereas representational conservations are only acquired at, or after, 7 to 8 years. This fact is of fundamental importance because motor events do not lag behind perception in the same way. Thus all the conditions are fulfilled for sensory-motor structures to play the dual role of regulators of perceptual activities (which are particular cases of sensory-motor activities) and founders of representational and, eventually, operational activities (which derive from the interior-isation of sensory-motor structures and their structuring on the sym-bolic plane, which in turn allows them to extend into new construc-tions). We shall return to this general question at the conclusion to this chapter (in § 5).

III*C*. Certain prefigurative analogies also occur in the perception and in the notion of time. The evolution of the notion of time ex-hibits two remarkable characteristics. The first is that a preliminary ordinal framework (the notion of the order of succession of events) is necessary before intervals of duration can appear. The observed con-struction of this ordinal framework during development is analogous to the events described (§ 1, I*B*) for ordinal lengths (the order of spatial succession of points of arrival) and metric lengths (intervals). It is interesting to observe how difficult it is, even for an uneducated adult, to abstract duration (or temporal interval) from order. If a peasant in the Alps is asked how long it will take to get from his village to a neighbouring village, he almost never replies directly with 'an hour' or '20 minutes', etc., but finds it necessary to consult his watch before replying. It is as if an hour had no concrete meaning unless inserted between two ordinally determined points of time.[1] The implicit reasoning is analogous to: it is seven o'clock, you will not get there before eight, so it will take 'one hour'. The second remarkable characteristic of the formation of the notion of time is that it is bound up with that of velocity: the judgements a child makes of the simultaneity or the succession of the arrival of two mov-ing bodies and, particularly, of the durations of their journeys, depends for a long time on the equalities or inequalities of their velocities. The genesis of the notion of time thus seems to depend on a co-ordination of velocities, in the same way that space is a co-ordination of positions and of displacements, independently of velocity.

It is consequently very interesting to note that the perception of

---

[1] This is not a reference to an isolated observation but to a general fact that we have amused ourselves in verifying over a period of several years. The only notable exception occurs with old people who have no watch and who sometimes reply: 'A pipe and a half of tobacco', etc., the abstraction of the interval thus being facilitated appreciably.

time, in so far as we understand it, prefigures the notion in that there is a degree of isomorphism between the two in terms of the two characteristics described above. For example, all studies have shown the existence of a better perception of order of succession than of duration as such, and a tendency for estimates of duration to depend on those of succession.[1] Furthermore, our studies on the perception of duration, begun with Feller (Chapter V, § 4), seem to show that estimates of duration vary as a function of the velocities of the objects in question.

Once again, however, it is clear that this prefiguration is not enough to establish the perceptual origins of the notion of time. To start with, notional time rests on operations of the ordering of events and of the successive inclusions of intervals (or durations) and, finally, of measurement. These operations, like all other operations, result from a long process of construction.[2] Secondly, a sensory-motor time which is not exclusively perceptual but is linked to the various sets of schemes of actions, does exist. This is particularly clear when an order of temporal succession has to be introduced into the co-ordination of means and ends: the perceived successions are built up on the basis of successions which are established as a function of action. But successions ordered on the basis of action cannot be reduced to perceived successions for the reason already given: the scheme of an action cannot be reduced to a mosaic of perceptions because it entails a total organisation which belongs to a higher plane than that of its perceptual and motor elements.

In summary, the notion of time cannot be considered to be abstracted from perception any more than could spatial and kinematic notions, because a sensory-motor time exists which is broader than perceptual time and which is the source of the operational notions of time which develop later. It is also very difficult to determine (particularly in the case of time) if what one 'perceives' in estimating the duration of a sound or of a movement is a property of the physical events or an internal duration projected on to them. In the event, as in all analogous elementary assimilations, the two become indissociable because the border between perceptual and sensory-motor domains becomes more difficult to trace. Finally, it is difficult to imagine that notional time could be abstracted from, or could be compounded of, the very brief durations that are usually involved in perception. It is easy to understand, however, how perceptions of duration could be derived by differentiation from, or by subdivision of, sensory-motor time.

[1] Fraisse, P., *Psychologie du Temps*, Paris, 1957, P.U.F.
[2] Piaget, J., *Le Développement de la Notion du Temps chez l'Enfant*, Paris, 1946, P.U.F.

§ 4. SITUATION IV: PREFIGURATION WITH REPERCUSSIONS OF INTELLIGENCE ONTO PERCEPTUAL STRUCTURES

This situation is the same as situation III except that the repercussions of intelligence are now sometimes demonstrable whereas, in situation III, they were either non-existent or not yet known.

IV*A*. The first case, apparently a clear one, is that of perceptual co-ordinates (Chapter III, § 4). It will be remembered that the origins of estimates of the vertical and of the horizontal are to be sought in the mechanisms of Donders' law and that, as Werner and Wapner showed (in their sensory-tonic field theory), they also depend on posture. But when a vertical or a horizontal has to be assessed in a field containing other helpful or disturbing elements, a further set of relations intervenes which can be studied with profit from the point of view of perceptual activities and their relations with intelligence. These relations are automatically involved whenever the elements are sufficiently close together, but entail more and more complex activities as separations increase. The question is, therefore, to discover on what factors this spatial co-ordination depends as it progresses with age. Two sets of fact, one perceptual (analysed by Dadsetan, Würsten, *et al.* : Chapter III) and the other representational (predicting the level that water will adopt in a tilted jar, etc.),[1] are involved and are related in the following way.

In the first place, perceptual co-ordinates prefigure operational co-ordinates. This is clearly so because relating the directions of elements which are perceived together (or objects with the line of regard or with the position of the body, etc.) depends on a form of organisation which is analogous to that of later representational co-ordinates. In the second place, this kinship has become so close by the age at which children can be questioned concerning both their representational predictions and their perceptual responses, that Dadsetan obtained a high correlation between the two sets of judgement. Must we therefore attribute representational predictions (predicting the water's level) to an abstraction from perceptual responses (estimating the horizontality of a line inscribed in a tilted triangle or square by referring to the sides of the sheet of paper in order to correct the disturbing influence of the figure)? Or, rather, should we explain perceptual responses in terms of the influence of intelligence?

The solution presents no problem in this particular case. As the 'primary' perception (field effects) of the young child is limited by the classical conditions of proximity, he fails to use the external frame

---

[1] *The Child's Conception of Space, op. cit.*

333

of reference. This failure is not due to a lack of that perceptual activity which allows the child to explore and to relate objects to a system of reference, but rather to a lack of the 'idea' of such possible referrals. When he later (9 to 10 years) makes this reference, his more or less correct estimates of the horizontal can of course be attributed to the perceptual activities of relating and of referral. In this case, however, there is the fundamental difference that they are not random, but, in almost every subject at this level, are directed from the beginning by the 'idea' of finding such references. As the essential role of intelligence is to bring about comparisons at any distance in a mobile and reversible manner, and as the essential role of perceptual activity is to relate successive inter-field centrations at ever-increasing distances, it is very likely that sooner or later, depending on the domain involved, the perceptual activity will come under the direction of any representations which have already become organised in that domain. Now, the system of representational co-ordinates provides the exact model of the schemes of relating at a distance, and applies in every spatial situation of a metric nature. It would therefore be very strange if a subject who possessed such an operational scheme were to ignore it and to force himself to use a rather complex perceptual reference system. It is much more likely that he would subordinate his perceptual explorations to habits acquired elsewhere, habits which consist in at once referring to distant frameworks and economising on a succession of pointless trial and error explorations.

The origins of the operational scheme itself can be traced, step by step, in the formation of the operation of measurement as it applies first to one and then to two or three dimensions. When we do this, we see that the system of natural co-ordinates provides the keystone or the overall structure of Euclidean space, a structure which is prepared by all the operations associated with that space (conservations of distances, etc.) and which is completed at exactly the same time as the co-ordination of perspectives, or the overall structures of projective space. There is, therefore, much more to this operational system than simple abstractions from perception: it involves the general co-ordination of reversible spatial operations of a metric or Euclidean nature.

To summarise, we see (*a*) that the operational system of co-ordinates is prefigured in perceptual referrals; (*b*) that it does not simply derive from them but adds all the Euclidean operational structures to them; and (*c*) that it has repercussions on perceptual co-ordinates by directing the activities of referring to external systems. This seems to be the only way of interpreting this complex situation, because it would be incomprehensible for a structure of intelligence to intervene retroactively on perceptual activities if it had derived from them in the first place. It is much more likely that perceptual co-ordinates are influenced by sensory-motor and sensory-tonic structures from the first. As representational and operational structures are products of a development which stems from sensory-motor activities, it is likely that perceptual activities will, to some extent and at all levels, be influenced by those broader systems. It is also likely that perceptual activities will depend on them for the stage by stage elaboration of perceptual schemes, which will bear signs of their imprint.

IV*B*. A second example typical of situation IV is the relation between perceptual transpositions and operational transitivity, which we studied with Lambercier.[1] We saw, during the investigation of size constancy (Chapter IV, § 2), that interpolating elements equal to the standard between it and the variable, resulted, after a certain age, in an improvement in judgements. This was due, no doubt, to the use made by the child of the intermediate elements as middle terms in the comparisons. This would entail a recourse to logical transitivity ($S = M$, $M = V \ldots S = V$, where S is the standard, M the middle term and V the variable). But if this logical transitivity did intervene, it could only have done so, in the case in question, by directing the comparisons by means of perceptual transpositions of judged equalities. We therefore undertook, with Lambercier, to analyse the relations actually existing between this transposition and transitivity. This was done in a series of five situations:

(*a*) The standard, of 10 cm, was placed at 1 m from the subject and the variable at 4 m. The middle term was not yet in use, the comparison being made simply between S and V.

(*b*) The standard was placed at 0·60 m from the variable with a lateral displacement of 0·20 m.

(*c*) As in (*a*), the standard was placed at 1 m from the subject. A middle term was placed next to it, to allow the subject to establish their equality, $S = M$; it was then moved to a position 0·60 m from V (as was S in (*b*)). The comparison between S and V was prefaced simply by asking whether M would 'help'.

(*d*) As in (*c*), but with comparison between V and M.

(*e*) The perceptual tests being completed, the child was asked how he had proceeded, to see if he had made use of M: he was questioned to find out if he acknowledged the logical transitivity $S = V$ if $S = M$ and $M = V$.

Twelve children from 5; 2 to 6; 10, and from 7; 0 to 8; 10 years, and

---

[1] *Rech.* 8.

some between 9 and 11 years, were tested. The results obtained are set out in Table 118.

TABLE 118. *Mean % error (under-estimation) of distant variables in a size-constancy experiment involving perceptual transpositions and conditions described in the text*

	Rech. 8, Table on p. 331			
Condition	*a*	*b*	*c*	*d*
5 to 7 years	−16·0	−2·7	−12·1	−4·0
7 to 9 years	−11·0	−2·0	−5·7	−3·7
9 to 11 years	−6·6	0·0	−2·5	—

These results are quite clear. On the one hand, there is a progressive diminution in error in (*b*) and in (*d*) as a function of age, with its complete elimination by 9 to 11 years. On the other hand, the error in the crucial situation (*c*), is about equal to what it was in (*a*), for the 5 to 7 age group, is halved at 7 to 9 years and tends to be eliminated at 9 to 11 years (as it was in a few adults also examined).

But the main interest of these responses lies in their relation to the operational comprehension of transitivity. Three stages are observed. During the first (at 5 to 7 years), the children, with one or two exceptions, did not acknowledge the transitivity and therefore the middle term did not alter their perceptual responses in (*c*). During the third stage (9 to 11 years), the subjects of course acknowledged the transitivity, with the result that the error was almost completely suppressed in (*c*). But during the second stage (7 to 9 years), the curious and instructive fact was observed that the subjects, while acknowledging the transitivity, failed to eliminate the error in (*c*): these children *knew* that if $V = M$, then $V = S$, but continued to *see* V as smaller than S!

The succession of these stages leads to two conclusions. The first is that, in the case in question (as elsewhere no doubt), logical transitivity is not abstracted from perceptual transposition, since it precedes it at Stage II and ends by directing it entirely at Stage III. We here find ourselves in a situation which is analogous to that of perceptual co-ordinates (see IV*A*), but one which is much clearer because it exhibits well-defined stages in the relations between perception and operations. It must therefore be acknowledged that transitivity derives from sensory-motor processes which are more general than the perceptual processes (transfers, etc.), and that it has repercussions upon perception instead of being derived from it; but as these general sensory-motor processes of transfer, etc., themselves include perceptual transpositions as particular cases, it is natural that the transpositions should in a sense prefigure operational transitivity. But because operational transitivity reacts upon and influences the transpositions, there need be no direct filiation between them, but only a collateral kinship.

The second conclusion is that the effect of operational transitivity on perceptual transpositions is not immediate, in the sense that to 'know' that $V = M = S$ does not ensure that $V = S$ will be 'perceived', which is an example of Stage II. In this particular case, the way in which intelligence acts on perception can be discovered by an examination of the way in which the perceptual activities of children are organised during the three stages. Broadly speaking, the subject, oriented by the transitivity based on the perceptual aid afforded by the middle term, makes his comparisons in the form of a complete circuit $SMVS$ and $SVMS$, or $VSMV$ and $VMSV$. This facilitates the transposition of $S = M$ and $M = V$ onto the relation between V and S. On the other hand, the younger children of 5 to 7 years, not being guided by transitivity, restrict themselves to the direct comparisons SV or VS, without a 'detour' through M; or to separate comparisons SM, SV, VM, etc., without a complete circuit. It can thus be seen that the action of intelligence on perception does not consist of directly modifying the elaboration of the input, but simply of modifying the orientation and the organisation of the perceptual activities of exploration and of transposition. Errors are thus reduced by changing the course of the comparisons made and, particularly, by transferring perceived equalities into the overall system.

IV*C*. Although the above example illustrates the action of intelligence on perceptual activities, it still has two shortcomings. On the one hand, the repercussions of transitivity onto the transpositions which prefigured it occur only at operational levels; and secondly, the perceptual activities which are thus influenced by intelligence do not sediment into field effects (or only very momentarily). In the examples to follow (at least in IV*C* and IV*D*) we shall come across genuine sedimentations of perceptual activities into field effects and repercussions of intelligence onto perception at all levels.

Examples IV*C* to IV*E* are taken from the area of perceptual pre-inferences (Chapter VI, §§ 1 and 2, under 13 in both sections). This is an area in which representations, and even operations, are clearly being prepared in perception because pre-inferences prefigure inferences. Pre-inferences always constitute applications of schemes (or of schematised indices), which again indicates their prefigurative role because perceptual schemes prefigure concepts in spite of all the differences which distinguish them (and which separate pre-inferences themselves from representational inferences).

The fact that pre-inferences are closely linked with the properties of perceptual schemes will also allow us to present some fresh examples of those schemes at different levels. The course of their development will also be illustrated with one or two new cases of the sedimentation of perceptual activities into field effects under the influence of developing intelligence. However, a possible misunderstanding needs to be anticipated: our aim is in no way to draw the conclusion from these facts that the inferences of intelligence play a central part in perceptual mechanisms; if they did, it would be impossible to distinguish perceptual pre-inferences from immediate and unconscious representational inferences. It is because Helmholtz's 'unconscious inferences' have generally been interpreted in this way (as we did at the beginning of our work on perception) that a certain disrepute has delayed the adoption of this hypothesis for so long. The pre-inferences which we are going to cite constitute genuine perceptual processes, and if intelligence intervenes in the formation of the schemes that they use, it is only indirectly and by orienting their component perceptual activities.

The first group of facts studied from this point of view (with the assistance of Morf)[1] concerned the perception of the 'numerosity' of two collections. Numerosity is used in the sense of more, less or equally numerous, in the way in which Ponzo[2] for example, showed that a line composed of several dots seems to contain more units when it is contained within the arms of an acute angle (owing to the over-estimation of the angle) than when it is not under the influence of this angle.[3]

One hundred and forty children of 4 to 10 years were shown the three figures represented in Figure 57. The figures were presented one

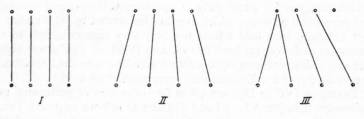

Fig. 57.

at a time with exposures appropriate to age (1 second for most groups, slightly longer for the younger subjects). Subjects were asked whether there was the same number of dots (or small discs) in the top as in the bottom line of the figures. The connecting lines could be

[1] Bruner, J. S. *et al.*, *Logique et Perception, op. cit.*
[2] Ponzo, M., *Arch. ges. psychol.*, 1928, **65**.
[3] Another example of the perception of numerosity is the fact that an Oppel–Kundt figure containing twenty thin hatchings seems, to many adults, to contain more hatchings than the same figure containing twenty thicker lines (see *Rech.* 10).

omitted, shortened or interrupted, and the number of elements in the rows varied (see the original report for fuller details).

The results obtained under the two main conditions (with and without connecting lines), and for the three figures, are presented in Table 119.

TABLE 119. *Subjects (%) claiming equality for the two series of dots arranged as shown in Fig. 57 and with or without connecting lines (n = 20 for each age group)*

Etudes,[1] 1958, Vol. 6, p. 122, Table I

Figure	I		II		III	
Lines	With	Without	With	Without	With	Without
4 years	70	100	0	20	0	20
5 years	80	100	0	65	0	65
6 years	100	100	30	85	30	70
7 years	100	100	80	100	80	40
8 years	100	100	90	100	90	35
9 years	100	100	100	100	100	45
10 years	100	100	100	100	100	90

Four stages can be identified.

Stage I (4 to 5 years). Without the connecting lines, equal numerosity is detected only where the rows of units are of the same length (Fig. *I*) but not where the rows are of unequal length (Figs. *II* and *III*). The effect of the connecting lines is still slight at 4 years (20% for Figs. *II* and *III*, those subjects thus belonging to Stage II).

Stage II (5 to 6 years). The connecting lines lead to impressions of equal numerosity in Fig. *II* (65% at 5 years), but without the lines, the collections are still estimated to be unequal. However, the false connections of Fig. *III* produce the same result as the genuine ones of Fig. *II*.

Stage III (7 to 9 years). The equalising effects of the lines is limited to Fig. *II*. The false references of Fig. *III* are recognised but still prevent the perception of equal numerosity.

Stage IV (9 to 10 years). The false connecting lines of Fig. *III* are neglected and no longer exert a disturbing influence on the perception of equal numerosity.

It can be seen that the perception of reference lines has a different significance at various ages. The problem is to know whether these changes in significance affect the notional interpretation of a situation that is perceived in the same way from the age of 4 to the age of 10, or whether they change the perception of numerosity itself. Now, during Stage I (80% of subjects of 4 years, 35% of those of 5 years and 15% of those of 6 years) the perception of the connecting lines does not change the impression of inequality in Fig. *II*, whereas at Stage II (20% at 4 years, 65% at 6 years, etc.) the perception imposes an immediate impression of equality between the two sets of units in both Figs. *II* and *III*. If the notion undergoes a transformation

[1] Refers to the series: *Etudes d'Epistémologie Génétique*, Paris, P.U.F.

between Stages I and II (implying the possibility of an equal numerosity of units attached to lines of different lengths), it would be difficult to deny that the same thing must have happened in perception, because the impression of numerosity has changed from inequality to equality. In the same way, the presence of the false connecting lines in Fig. *III* masks the equality of these groups of units for 55 to 65% of subjects between 7 and 9 years (Stage III), whereas the perception of the same figure without lines leads to an impression of equality in 80 to 100% of subjects at the same ages. Finally, at Stage IV, the false references of Fig. *III* are clearly distinguished from the true references of Fig. *II*, but no longer conceal the equal numerosity of the units. It would seem, therefore, that at the ages considered, the significance of the lines changes as a function of the child's level and that these changes modify perception as such and not only its interpretation: one could hardly claim that the figures were perceived identically when the sets of units were seen as being equal or unequal under the influence, respectively, of the facilitating or masking effects of the connecting lines.

The perceptual significance of these connecting lines can be analysed as follows. At Stage I they have no significance for Figs. *II* and *III*, because their addition does not affect the perceived inequality of the units, except in 20% of the subjects of 4 years who *ipso facto* belong to Stage II. It is true that the addition of the lines in Fig. *I* raises the perceived equality to 100%, but in this case the lines only serve to consolidate the perception of the equality of the length of the rows, whereas in Figs. *II* and *III* they do not compensate for the impression of inequality created by the different lengths of the rows. At Stage II, however, the lines become effective by linking the units in pairs, thus imposing their equality in spite of the inequality in length of their rows (65% at 5 years and 20% already at 4 years). Two comments need to be made in this connection: (*a*) after Stage I, although subjects often perceive the lines of Fig. *II* as linking pairs of units (they then reproduce the figure by means of what they call 'dumb-bells', 'two circles and a stroke'), this does not succeed in creating an impression of equality; (*b*) at Stage II, Fig. *III* is perceived globally and the false references are not distinguished from the true ones of Fig. *II*. At Stage III, the lines once more create impressions of equality, but only when the units are correctly paired: if not, they mask the equality of the units. At Stage IV, the lines no longer play any role.

With this in mind, let us recall the definition of perceptual pre-inferences and try to discover if they intervene in this situation. As all perceptual structures are characterised by a certain number of properties, we may first distinguish those which are physically given at the moment of perception (for example, that the units of the figure

340

to be estimated are linked by lines, etc.) from those which are not so given but are added by the subject on the basis of previous experience. For example, at Stage I the subject does not perceive that the upper and lower units are equal in number, but he does so at Stage II. Once he has perceived it, the fact is incorporated into the perceptual structure itself. It might then be claimed that pre-inferences are involved when those properties added by the subject are entailed by the presence of those which are physically given. But to explain how they are entailed (and differently according to the stage) requires us to distinguish the following four elements:

(*a*) Physically given properties: presence of the lines, etc.

(*b*) Additional properties signified by (*a*): for example, that the lines do or do not link the units in pairs (overall correspondence or correct analysis). This significance derives from the assimilation of properties (*a*) to a scheme which also contains properties (*b*) (b_1 or b_2, etc.).

(*c*) Properties which are resultants of (*a*) and (*b*): the lines are present and are perceived to signify a correspondence, (*b*). This entails the equality, (*c*), of the units.

(*d*) Factors of composition which ensure the passage from (*b*) to (*c*): a sort of 'pre-implication' relating the properties (*b*) and (*c*) of a single scheme. Does the relation between (*a*) and (*b*) already constitute such pre-implication? This could be claimed on the grounds that it only involves a relation of signifier to significate because (*a*), and its aspects, serves as an index which leads to the assimilation of the relation to the scheme which gives it the significance (*b*), whereas the pre-implication (*a*), relates one significate (*b*), to another, (*c*). However, we have already seen (Chapter VI, §§ 1, 5 and 13) that the relation between signifier and significate is less clearly distinguished in perception than that of implicant to implicate on the representational level. Consequently, one would only need to distinguish between the given characteristics (*a*), the implied characteristics (*b*) and (*c*), etc., and the pre-implication (*d*). There might, however, be some interest in distinguishing, in general, between the assimilation to a scheme (the activity of conferring a significance) and the pre-implication between the characteristics of that scheme.

The essential difference between perceptual pre-inferences and representational inferences is that, in the former, the subject does not dissociate (*a*), (*b*), (*c*) and (*d*), but perceives (*a*), (*b*) and (*c*) as a single whole without any conscious judgement of (*d*). In the case of representational influences, he considers (*a*), adds (*b*) as a distinct entity, and then (*c*), modified by a consideration of (*d*). We have seen that quasi immediate representational inferences, very difficult to distinguish from perceptual pre-inferences, may occur in the pre-operational thought of the child of 2 to 6 years. But, in the present experiments on correspondence, the phenomena seem, in part at least, to be of a perceptual nature. This is strongly suggested by the presence of factors facilitating or hindering judgements of equality and by the fact that the accuracy of judgements diminishes reliably as a function either of the addition of units or, especially, of a shortening of the connecting lines. The considerable variations that occur with age clearly argue against a Gestalt explanation.

As perceptual pre-inferences thus depend on the intervention of schemes, it becomes necessary to discover whether the origins of these schemes are purely perceptual or whether their perceptual origins are themselves influenced by sensory-motor activities, etc., and are thus enriched by contributions of a higher order.

That the schemes involved are dependent upon action in general, and not only on eye-movements, is shown by the fact that the significance of the lines changes with age. From being lines which touch the elements, they develop into means by which sets of units are related and by which the equality or inequality of the sets is then judged. They act in this role while sedimenting into new field effects even if their lengths are changed in various ways. It also shows that the gradually acquired habit of manually placing sets of objects into correspondence influences the perception of the configurations relating to that activity and makes a contribution to the transformation of the perceptual schemes.

These claims can be justified in the following way. Firstly, from Stage II, and especially Stage III, the connecting lines, in their role of organisers of perceived equalities, acquire the status of field effects. This is because, at these stages, the subject can perceive the equality of the sets of units at shorter and shorter presentations, directly and without explorations. As these new field effects are therefore acquired and not primitive (because they are not detectable during Stage I), only sedimentations of perceptual activities can be involved. Secondly, the appearance of these activities themselves cannot be explained by simple oculo-motor explorations because the lines themselves are perceptible at all levels; what is gained is a new significance, an advance in schematisation, which would be difficult to account for except by the establishment of multiple correspondences based on the subject's actual manipulation of objects, (drawings, constructional games, etc.) between Stages I and IV. Our whole hypothesis on this second point reduces to the following proposition: structures which the subject can otherwise construct or reconstruct are perceived differently from those which do not yet correspond to anything in his daily activities; this perceptual difference must be due to a difference in schematisation. It is in this sense, and in this sense only, that perceptual activities can be considered to be directed or influenced, firstly by sensory-motor activities, and then by representational activities in general. This takes place while they are sedimenting into new field effects in the course of becoming more automatic.

IV *D.* The same processes were examined in a second experiment in which two contiguous straight lines, whose lengths were to be compared, were placed horizontally or at an inclination of 135° to one another. The comparison was made either with or without the presence of an external index, a circle whose centre coincided with the junction of the two lines (Fig. 58). As the differences in length of the

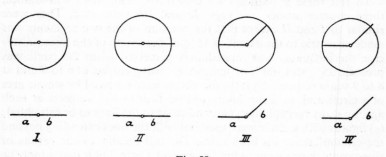

Fig. 58.

lines approximated to threshold values, the circle served as an index of their equality or inequality. The question was once more to establish whether the use made of this index, and of the pre-inferences that it might give rise to, was the same at all ages. The results obtained by Morf are presented in Table 120.

TABLE 120. *Subjects (%) judging lines to be equal under conditions illustrated in Fig. 58. Abbreviations: R, random replies; =, more than 2/5 judgements of 'equal'; ≠, more than 2/5 judgements of 'unequal' (n = 20 for each age group)*

Etudes, 1958, Vol. 6, pp. 134 and 137, Tables IV and VIII

Figure	I						II					
Circle	Present			Absent			Present			Absent		
Judgement:	R	=	≠	R	=	≠	R	=	≠	R	=	≠
4 to 5 years	90	5	5	85	5	10	80	5	15	75	5	20
6 to 7 years	95	5	0	20	75	5	80	0	20	25	5	70
8 to 9 years	90	5	5	15	75	10	80	5	15	30	0	70
Figure	III						IV					
4 to 5 years	80	5	15	80	5	15	70	10	20	85	10	5
6 to 7 years	85	10	5	70	20	10	80	10	10	75	15	10
8 to 9 years	90	0	10	40	55	5	85	5	10	40	10	50

With Figs. *I* and *II* the presence of the circle had no effect at 4 to 5 years, whereas from 6 to 7 years, it led to 75% of judgements of equality being made when the segments were equal and 70% of inequality when they were unequal. With Figs. *III* and *IV*, however, it was not until 8 to 9 years that the presence of the circle affected the estimates, in 55% of cases where there was equality and in 50% where there was inequality. This difference in response as a function of alignment seems to indicate that the circle does not have the same effect at 6 to 7 years as it does at 8 to 9 years. It may be presumed that, at 6 to 7 years, it simply serves as an indicator of extension (the line which projects beyond the circumference of the circle is judged to be the longer) but that from 8 to 9 years it intervenes as a 'secondary good form' (see Chapter III, § 8), its radii being perceived to be equal, independently of their directions.

To test these hypotheses we undertook, with Morf's assistance, three counter-proofs: (*a*) Figs. *Ib* and *IIb* were used. They were similar to *I* and *II* except that the junction of the two segments was made eccentric to the extent of 15% of the length of the lines (in this case the inequality was immediately perceived when the circle was present: 95% and 100% of judgements being correct at 6 to 7 and at 8 to 9 years respectively); (*b*) the circles were replaced by simple arcs of a circle and, in a subsidiary test on four or five subjects at each age, by short vertical lines, perpendicular to the lines to be estimated; (*c*) figures with a circle were used but with the lines extending beyond the circumference on both sides. The full details[1] of the results of these counter-proofs need not be presented here, but it may simply be noted that reliance on the scheme of extension was confirmed at 6 to 7 years (and at 5 years for the arcs of the circle) and that this gave way, from 8 to 9 years, to reliance on the index of the circle as a good geometric form. We can thus distinguish three stages of development in the responses to these various tests.

During Stage I (4 to 5 years), no use is yet made of the reference circles, either as circles or as indices of length. From 5 years, however, responses to the arcs of circles and, in part, to the eccentric arrangements, indicate that a scheme of extension is beginning to have its effect.

During Stage II (6 to 7 years) responses to the circles, to the arcs (judgements based on the side on which the line extended beyond the arc), to the eccentric arrangements (*idem*), etc., indicate that a scheme of extension is operating.

During Stage III (8 to 9 years), the circle serves as an index only in terms of the equality of its radii.

Two kinds of pre-inference may be invoked to account for these responses, the first based on the index of extension (because if this

[1] Bruner, J. S. *et al.*, *Logique et Perception, op. cit.*, pp. 134–7.

index acted independently of pre-inferences it should have its effect at all ages), and the second based on the index of the equality of the radii of a circle. Although there can be no doubt that both the ordinal scheme of extension and the metric scheme of a good form (circle) depend on perceptual activities (of relating, etc.), because they evolve with age, it has yet to be shown why these activities appear when they do and are neither more precocious nor more retarded. But we have already established, in regard to correspondences (III*C*), that there is a remarkable synchrony between this development and that of the schemes of the corresponding actions: between 5 and 7 years, pre-operational intelligence is more and more dominated by the schemes of ordering and of extension, while metric considerations first appear at about 8 years with the development of concrete operations. It must be conceded, therefore, either that the present facts have nothing to do with perception, and depend on representational inferences rather than on perceptual pre-inferences; or that the supposed perceptual activities constitute the source of the corresponding representational schemes; or, finally, that the activities (together with the perceptual schematisations that they engender, and the pre-inferences that the action of these perceptual schemes make possible) do arise in perception but are subject to direction and to enrichment by the more general schemes of intelligence, which would account for the observed synchrony. Once again, it is difficult to deny the intervention of perception (since reductions in threshold occur which are not attributable to simple reasoning) and at the same time to claim that perception explains everything (since the transformations occurring in perceptual activities remain to be explained); the third solution thus seems to be the most probable.[1]

IV*E*. This is supported by a further set of facts. Seventeen or 81 vertical rods were placed at equal intervals along a base of 40 cm. Their lengths increased either uniformly (the line formed by their summits making an inclined straight line), with acceleration (their

---

[1] It must be emphasised that the example of the effect of the 'good form' of the circle on estimates of length constitutes an example of situation IV. Firstly, the circle and other perceptual good forms do indeed prefigure corresponding operational forms. It cannot, however, be claimed that operational forms are abstracted from perceptual good forms because the operational forms derive from new constructions and good perceptual forms themselves are not necessarily elementary (despite the theory of Form), but may have been preceded by topological forms which lack regular metrics. There is simply an isomorphism between the two constructions, the first prefiguring the second without containing it in advance. Secondly, there are repercussions of intelligence on perception because, after Stage III, the circle is raised to the rank of a 'secondary good form' (see Chapter III, § 8), under the influence of operational schemes which embody the perceptual activities. It is these secondary good forms which then influence estimates of length. The effects of extension (Stage II) can be handled in a similar way.

summits forming a concave parabolic curve), or with deceleration (convex parabolic curve). The subject was asked to compare the difference in length, *a*, between two neighbouring rods with a difference, *b*, between two other neighbouring rods elsewhere in the series and at varying distances from the first pair. The purpose was to discover if the subject would make use of the line formed by the summits as a perceptual index or whether he would limit himself to making a direct comparison of *a* and *b* without first inspecting that line. The difference between this situation and those of experiments IVC and IVD was that the summits were joined by a virtual, not a drawn line: the line had to be constructed perceptually[1] before it could serve as a reference or an index. It was hoped that part, at least, of this construction would become available for inspection. A distinction would have to be made between: (*A*), pre-inferences of an inductive nature, from part to whole (from the details of the figure to the line formed by the summits because, of course, the subject does not look at each of the 81, or even of the 17, units, but proceeds by some kind of sampling accompanied by decisions and generalisations, as in all forms of induction); and (*B*), pre-inferences of a deductive nature, from whole to part (comparisons of the differences *a* and *b* through the mediation of the line formed by the summits). Added to these are (*C*), pre-inferences from part to part, when the subject, without referring to the line, considers only what he has gleaned from one difference without making an adequate assessment of the second.

The following criteria are available for the analysis of these forms of pre-inference:

(*a*) Reference to the lines formed by the summits, or a direct transportation of the difference *a* onto *b* and reciprocally.

(*b*) Changes in the subjective appearance of the line formed by the summits, which occurs as a result of exploration. The changes may consist in displacements of boundaries between segments of the curve (which may at first appear to be heterogeneous, parts being seen as rectilinear and others as concave or convex). Or they may consist in a correction of this first impression.

(*c*) The results of local comparisons of adjacent couples. These comparisons are often incoherent at first (for example, $a = b$, $b = c$ but $a < c$, etc.), but may gradually become coherent.

The main difficulty in this experiment is, of course, to distinguish perceptual pre-inferences from representational inferences. The latter are easily recognised, when they are of an operational nature, by the

[1] That is why we chose a large figure (32 × 40 cm): in a smaller figure (15 to 10 cm), the line joining the summits would have been perceived immediately.

fact that the subject starts to reason and describes the curve of the line formed by the summits in genuinely quantitative terms. A more subtle criterion is required when pre-operational representational inferences are involved because they are almost always implicit. The best way to decide whether perception is involved, or if the subject is making use of inferential and notional interpretations, is to study the changes that occur in differential thresholds during the course of the experiment.

The results obtained with the figure of 81 units are presented in Table 121 in which the abbreviations mean:

Ci = comparison between pairs contiguous of elements 1 to 41.
Cs = *idem* for elements 42 to 81.
Cd = comparisons at a distance.

TABLE 121. *Frequency distribution (%) of correct responses on the series of* 81 *elements. Figures in parenthesis represent % frequency of doubtful responses.*

Etudes, 1958, Vol. 6, pp. 145–6, Table IX

Form Judgement	Convex			Concave			Rectilinear		
	Ci	Cs	Cd	Ci	Cs	Cd	Ci	Cs	Cd
5 years (n = 20)	25 (12)	0 (0)	22 (11)	60 (20)	66 (0)	60 (30)	12 (12)	0 (0)	20 (20
6 years (n = 17)	20 (40)	12 (25)	62 (25)	54 (9)	60 (20)	65 (34)	40 (30)	20 (20)	16 (33)
7 years (n = 31)	55 (45)	35 (17)	76 (24)	28 (32)	77 (18)	88 (0)	27 (27)	38 (11)	33 (3)
8 years (n = 26)	50 (50)	13 (18)	75 (25)	25 (15)	63 (25)	46 (11)	40 (16)	50 (0)	37 (26)
9 years (n = 25)	75 (20)	4 (13)	76 (24)	36 (36)	57 (35)	85 (0)	72 (13)	54 (9)	45 (13)
10 years (n = 20)	57 (43)	36 (26)	100 (0)	—	—	—	45 (27)	66 (11)	60 (0)

A regular evolution with age occurs for comparisons at a distance (except for Cd concave at 8 years), while the fluctuations exhibited in contiguous comparisons can be attributed to the diversity of methods used by subjects (reference to the line formed by the summits, or a return to direct comparisons).

To supplement the above analysis, results obtained with 17 units are set out in Table 122 in which the abbreviations refer to the following judgements made by the subject: Pg = correct global perception

TABLE 122. *Frequency distribution (%) of classifications of responses to the series of* 17 *elements*

Etudes, 1958, Vol. 6, p. 147, Table X

Form Classification	Convex					Rectilinear			
	Pg	Ds	Ep	Pd	Co	Pg	Ds	Pd	Co
6 years	0	0	10	0	10	0	0	0	0
7 years	37	0	39	0	72	15	27	25	14
8 years	40	0	44	0	43	40	33	33	54
9 years	67	18	0	6	60	55	47	47	83
10 years	100	37	0	28	67	100	89	89	100

(initially and before an analysis of the line formed by the summits is made); Ds = correct description of the line formed by the summits (this question was put at the end of the experiment); Ep = perceptual extrapolations; Pd = inferential or pre-inferential processes, from whole to part; Co = consistency between local estimates.

The following conclusions can be drawn from these results (which exhibit a very regular evolution with age, with one exception, which is only apparent this time)[1] when they are considered in relation to those of Table 121.

Three stages can be distinguished:

During a first stage, which often extends to 6 to 7 years, no reference is made to the figure as a whole, nor are any inferences made on the basis of partial judgements. The overall figure itself remains heterogeneous (part of the parabolic line formed by the summits is judged to be rectilinear).

During Stage II (7 to 8 years), both local perceptual extrapolations (category C of the previously distinguished pre-inferences) and an increase in the coherence and the global nature of perceptions occur. These are the beginnings of pre-inferential processes of an inductive nature (category A), factors which govern the perceptual organisation of figures.

Between Stages II and III, there is some loss of coherence which can be attributed to the fact that extrapolation drops out and that the inferential processes, from whole to part (category B), are not yet well enough organised to replace them.

Finally, Stage III is characterised by type B pre-inferences (from whole to part) and by genuine inferences, both of which consist in the application of available schemes of reference. This application is more precocious with the rectilinear than with the parabolic figures, but is still delayed because of the large size of the figures.

In brief, this evolution expresses the construction, and then the application of, the scheme of reference corresponding to the overall figure and, above all, to the line formed by the summits. The delayed nature of this construction and of its application, relative as they are to the dimensions of the figures (a large figure demanding a continual exercise of transports and of explorations where a smaller figure would have given rise to immediate field effects), is very instructive in regard to the relations between perceptual schemes and intelligence. Let us recall that there is a sensory-motor form of seriation (fitting cups of decreasing size into each other, from 18 to 24 months), that operational seriation begins towards 7 to 8 years, and that, from 5 and 6 years, 55 and 73% of subjects respectively knew how to represent correctly, in a drawing, a series of ten short rods of 10 to 16 cm so that their summits appeared to lie in a straight line (only 6 and 22% of the same subjects then succeeded in operational seria-

[1] The strong consistency between local estimates at 7 years is due to the fact that most subjects of this age consider the line joining the summits to be rectilinear in those sectors involved in the judgements cited.

tion without trial and error).[1] One might, therefore, have expected the present comparison of differences to be organised immediately on the basis of the line formed by the summits, even with the large figure of 40 cm. We have found that this is not the case, that even the perception of the line presupposes a considerable preliminary elaboration (Stage II).

What interests us most in this experiment on serial configurations is not the mechanism of pre-inferences of type *B* (which makes its appearance later than in the preceding experiments and which is therefore probably mixed with representational inferences) so much as the construction itself of the scheme of the whole figure, a construction which makes use of the pre-inferences of types *C* and *A*. There can be no doubt that this construction is largely perceptual, because serial configurations are usually 'good forms' and because, in this particular case, perceptual extrapolations (Ep = type *C*) and increasing coherence (Co) do not derive from reasoning but from progressive adjustments which can be attributed to explorations and to transpositions. The striking fact is that this perceptual construction occurs so late, while perceptual activities of exploration and of transportation can function much earlier. In this case, much more so than in those of correspondence or of the reference circle (IIIC and IVD), we have, for the lack of an acceptable alternative explanation, to fall back on the trivial but no doubt fundamental remark that as soon as the restricted, habitual and coercive limits of field effects are exceeded, we 'see' only what we think of looking for. In other words, where perception requires the intervention of an actual perceptual activity (in contrast to field effects, considered in the present theory to be the products of sedimentations of previous perceptual activities), that activity has still to be directed by something other than perceptual mechanisms, which can only register what the subject has learned to perceive.

This direction can only come from the schemes of action as a whole, which amounts to saying from the schemes of intelligence at every level of its development. In the particular case of these serial configurations, children of 5 to 6 years, when asked to compare two differences between two well-separated pairs of units, simply do not have the 'idea' of using the line formed by the summits, but make a comparison by direct transportation. Children of 8 to 9 years, however, being accustomed to operational seriation, do have the 'idea'. This does not mean that they reason instead of perceiving, but that their reasoning compels them to orient their movements of exploration and of transportation in new directions, in terms of what 'must be looked at to see better'. This explains the responses at Stage III, with their passage

---

[1] *The Growth of Logical Thinking, op. cit.*

from whole to part and then inferences of a deductive type (with the perceptual pre-inferences of type *B* embodied in its perceptual activities, which are themselves directed by intelligence). But from Stage II, and before this method becomes systematic, a progressive construction of the scheme of the overall figure can be observed: the subject, although beginning with direct transportations between the differences (*a*) and (*b*), comes to relate his successive perceptual estimates to the serial configurations with which he is familiar and which, in fact, he can anticipate in drawings (in 50 to 73 % of cases from 5 to 6 years). This relating is made perceptually, but by means of perceptual activities such as transpositions which are themselves organised by intelligent purpose, which gives them direction without interfering with the detail of their mechanisms (perceptual schematisation and pre-inferences of type *C* and then *A*).

On the whole, the same two conclusions can be drawn from these few experiments, IV*C* to *E*, which verify the interpretations put forward under IV*A* and *B*. (1) Perceptual schemes, products and sources of pre-inferences, are elaborated through perceptual activities of various forms and levels. When they have been schematised and have become automatic, they are liable to sediment into new field effects. (2) These perceptual activities develop in only a partially autonomous manner. They are constantly motivated by the requirements of action and, as a result, are embodied into, and in part directed by, more general schemes than those of perception, that is, sensory-motor schemes (regulators of action), and schemes of intelligence in general (from sensory-motor to operational intelligence). Each new cognitive structure expresses the new orientations of action and thereby gives new directions to the perceptual activities which provide that action with its necessary information.

§ 5. PERCEPTION AND NOTIONS

We can now identify the common elements which can be abstracted from the four apparently very different possibilities examined in §§ 1 to 4. The differences are really of degree only and are concerned with the chronological interval which separates the perceptual and the representational facts that have been considered. There is a clear discordance between perception and action in form I situations, in which field effects were compared with representational notions of a spatial order. This comparison had to be made in the absence of information concerning the perceptual activities which give rise to the field effects and concerning the sensory-motor schemes which lie at the source of representations and of operations. In spite of this lack of direct evidence, it is very likely that perception, at quite an elementary level (which takes us back to the first months of life), begins with essentially topological structures (neighbourhood [cf. 'proximity'] and separation, continuities and discontinuities, being open or closed, embedding, order, etc.) which do not involve estimations of real or of projective sizes, which only appear with the advent of size and form constancies. If this is so, the precocious perceptual events of § 1 must be the products of even more precocious perceptual activities which would then 'prefigure' later representational activities (which advance from topological to metric and projective structures). Consequently, form I situations would in fact reduce to those of form III, the established comparisons being only partial instead of bearing on the whole of the perceptual, sensory-motor and representational developments of the area being considered. The analogies between situations II, III and IV have received sufficient attention and it is unnecessary to review them here: interaction between perceptual and sensory-motor activity when they are contemporaneous, prefiguration of representational activity in perceptual activity when there is a temporal disparity between them, and repercussions of intelligence onto perceptual activity at every level.

To claim that perceptions prefigure notions, is simply to affirm that perception is in advance of representational but not over sensory-motor intelligence. It is then only a question of establishing whether notions are abstracted from perception or from sensory-motor activity as a whole. The latter is possible because sensory-motor activity also prefigures representational intelligence while perceptual activity does not prefigure sensory-motor activity but is contemporaneous with it, and even constitutes a particular case of it.

The real significance of the prefiguration of the notion in perception is not that perception leads to a definitive construction, to which intelligence has only to apply itself to make it more general, or possibly to extend it, but rather (*a*) that knowledge is constructed or reconstructed in an analogous manner at each stage of development or of havi</u>ural hierarchy, previous constructions, being carried over, to, but then surpassed in, the next stage; and (*b*) that this prefiguration is not direct or linear, but indirect or collateral, because the principal link is between sensory-motor and representational activity.

The problem of tracing the perceptual or non-perceptual origins of notions becomes much more delicate when it is considered in terms of this perspective of continuous reconstructions than it would be if considered in terms of a concept of a stratified mental life in which stages are simply superimposed on one another.

The preliminary question is to decide whether notions are richer or poorer than corresponding perceptions. By the classical scheme of abstraction and generalisation, notions would be the poorer: being

351

general, in contradistinction to perceptions which are particular, they lose everything that is discarded when only the common characteristics of that richer source were abstracted. From the point of view of reconstructions, however, with their shifts in phase and of priority, the operational notion becomes incontestably richer than the corresponding perceptions in that it forms part and parcel of a system of transformations (or operations) which are not given in the particular configurations.

If this is admitted, the fact which seems to dominate the whole question of the relation between perception and intelligence, as previously noted (§ 3, IIIB), is that, in every area, perception starts with a clear lead over representation, is overtaken and is then left farther and farther behind. If this happened only in the case of the relations between perceptual and representational structures, it would still be interesting but would probably lend itself to a variety of explanations. The generality of the events can, however, be established because the evolution of intelligence provides us with two other examples of the same process. These two examples illustrate in a striking way what appears to be one of the most general laws of development, that knowledge of a given object is reconstructed at every stage by means of new, richer and more comprehensive structures. The first example is that knowledge acquired on the plane of action (sensory-motor activity) is subsequently reconstructed and surpassed by knowledge at the level of concrete operations and of representations; the second is that that knowledge is in turn reconstructed and surpassed by formal or hypothetico-deductive thought. Being aware of this, we are forced to find out what is and what is not prefigured in perception, and to establish the limits of any prefiguration that may exist.

If we take space as an example, we find that the space of sensory-motor activity reaches the threshold of reversible operations with the group of displacements which is acquired in a practical way by the age of about 1; 6 to 2 years. But it is one thing to put displacements into effect and quite another to represent them, and it is not until the level of concrete operations (7 to 11 years) that the group of displacements is reconstructed on the representational plane and is completed by a system of co-ordinates, etc. Finally, as verbal hypothetico-deductive reasoning is again quite different from deduction based on concrete manipulations, it is not until the level of formal operations (12 to 15 years) that children can be taught classical geometry.

Having refreshed our memories about these stage by stage reconstructions, the question is to discover where the systems of operational transformations (classifications, seriations, spatial and kinematic transformations, etc.) come from, and from what their elements are abstracted. As we have often emphasised elsewhere, there are two types of abstraction or of experience: abstraction based on perceived objects, which characterises material or physical experience, and abstraction based on actions on objects, which characterises logico-mathematical experience. It should be remembered, moreover, that if a logical or purely mathematical knowledge exists (at an advanced level of development), physical or material knowledge is always integrated within logico-mathematical frameworks. The reason for this is that we learn to know objects only to the extent that we act upon them and because this action then gives rise to logico-mathematical (classification, order, etc.), as well as to material, abstraction. It thus becomes obvious that the operational aspects of notions, what they add to perception, can derive only from a mechanism which is tied to action itself.

It is at this point that our real problem becomes apparent. The analyses made in Chapters I to V have all tended to underline the active character of perception and the subordination of field effects to perceptual activities. It might be thought that an interpretation would be preferred which reconciled the operational nature of notions, and the irreducible originality of the systems of transformation on which they are based, with their perceptual origins. This interpretation would abandon the idea that notions derive from sense data organised into field effects, as classical empiricism believed, and would substitute for it the idea that notions derive from perceptual activities, from what is already active in perception.

However, this solution cannot be adopted for two important reasons drawn from §§ 1 to 4 above. The first is that perceptual activity is never self-sufficient, particularly in those cases where a reasonably detailed analysis is possible (cf. the constancies, co-ordinates, etc.). Perceptual activity only functions when integrated with, and directed by, action as a whole, which means by sensory-motor or even, from a certain level of development, by representational intelligence.

The second is that the operational systems of transformation, which constitute elaborated notions, are abstracted from action as a whole, and above all from its co-ordinations. This means that operations or systems of transformation are not abstracted from any particular action but from the schematisation which relates those actions and gives them their unity: to speak of action 'as a whole' is to refer to a mode of organisation which is hierarchically superior to the perceptual mode, and which is the scheme by means of which actions can be repeated, generalised and assimilated to a variety of situations.

The fundamental fact concerning the origins of both perception and of notions is that, although the schemes of action direct perceptual activities at every level, they are not themselves perceptible. It could not, therefore, be maintained that the influence of actions on the perception of external objects is only that of compounding the perceptions of objects with those of actions. In fact, it is not the particular action involved at the moment which influences the perception of an object, but rather the general scheme of the action. The particular *action* is perceptible, but the scheme is not. For example, when a subject is adapting to Ivo Kohler's inverting spectacles, it is not the action executed at the moment of correction, nor above all the perception of this action (for example, standing a bottle on its base rather than on its cork), which explains the correction: it is the general scheme of the action, that is, the habitual sensory-motor organisation which embodies both the motor characteristics of the action and the proprio- and exteroceptive perceptions which relate to it. Indeed, without this scheme, the particular action would have no significance and could not provide the means of effecting the correction.

It becomes clear, therefore, that the source of notions must be looked for in those sensory-motor schemes or in the schemes of actions in general, but not in perception alone even if those schemes do coincidentally contribute to its organisation. The reason that perception seems to prefigure the notion, or in one sense does prefigure it, is, as we have repeatedly seen, that it is itself influenced by the schemes which lie at the source of the notion.

The examination of the relations between certain notions and corresponding perceptions thus seems to confirm, at every point, the analyses made in Chapter VI: intelligence does not develop out of perception by simple extension or by the introduction of an increasing mobility, because the operational factor in the system of transformations is not reducible to figurative structures, even if these also derive from genuine activities, but, in this case, ones which, like perceptual activities, are oriented towards figuration. Consider, for instance, the simplest of the 'groups' of transformations, the one that leads from a state A to a state B, with possible return from B to A. Perception can provide knowledge of states A and B as configurations, or of the change of A into B, or of B into A, as movements, that is, as configurations again (because Gestalt theory has rightly insisted on the figural nature of the perception of movement). But none of these perceptions, nor all of them together, is equivalent to the system constituted by this 'group', however elementary it may be. This is because the group presumes the comprehension of the fact that the change from B to A is only the inverse of the change from A to B, and presumes the subordination of the states A and B to the transformations as such. This system thus constitutes a new totality of a supra-perceptual order, one which is no longer perceptible as a system. That is why, although perception may begin at birth, we have to wait seven or eight years for the achievement of operational reversibility, upon which the elaboration of rational notions is always conditional.

VIII CONCLUSION:
THE EPISTEMOLOGY OF
PERCEPTION

What, then, is the role played by perception in knowledge? This question can now be examined, and should be, because our rejection of the idea that notions derive from perception alone has raised the problem of the significance of perception in the act of knowing.

§ 1. FIGURATIVE AND OPERATIVE ASPECTS OF KNOWLEDGE

All knowledge has to do with structures, while effective life provides the energetics, or more precisely, the economics of action.[1] These structures may be figurative, for example, perceptions and mental images, or operative, for example, the structures of action or of operations (in this connection we shall speak of 'operational structures' in the proper or restrained sense,[2] while 'operative' will be used to refer to all external or interiorised actions which precede operations and to actions which attain the operational level). Our problem is to identify the roles played by these figurative and operative structures, and to discover how they are related to one another.

To know is to construct or to reconstruct the object of knowledge in such a way as to capture the mechanism of that construction. If those expressions against which positivism has constantly but vainly levelled its criticism are preferred, this is equivalent to saying that to know is to produce something in thought in such a way as to reconstitute the 'way in which phenomena are produced'. This definition corresponds to the way in which scientists generally think (in spite of the prohibitions of positivism), and, if accepted, it follows that operative structures must play the leading role in knowledge. The indisputable primacy of logico-mathematical explanations then follows.

The role of figurative structures, particularly of perceptual structures, would then have to be explained. We are not yet in a position to deal with figurative structures in general, because we have not yet completed our researches into the role of the image in the developing

[1] Economics in Janet's sense of the regulation of forces.
[2] An operation is an action which can be interiorised and reversed and which, with others of a like kind, constitutes a structure characterised by laws of totality which incorporate one or other form of reversibility.

thought of the child, and we will therefore limit ourselves in this connection to what is widely accepted.

It might be objected that the proposed definition of knowledge is too narrow because discussions of configuration have an important place in some scientific disciplines, including even mathematics in which geometry was at first essentially figurative. This example is particularly instructive for perception because a distinction has long been maintained between 'pure' mathematics (theory of number and analysis) and those mathematics considered to be applied, such as geometry which is based on 'intuition', or, in other words, on perception. But the recent evolution of geometry demonstrates the fragility of a concept in which figurative structures are kept isolated from, but on the same plane as, operative structures. Indeed, and particularly since the famous 'Erlangen Programme', in which Klein proposed to reduce each variety of geometry to a fundamental group of transformations, geometry has become clearly operative and has thereby achieved its legitimate place in pure mathematics: not only can each form of space be engendered by the operations which constitute its fundamental 'group', but it is possible to pass from one geometry to another by means of the rules under which a 'sub-group' is subordinated to a group. Thus the primacy of transformations over configurations is established in geometry as elsewhere.

It would be vain, therefore, to try to distinguish two types of knowledge, one operative and the other figurative, according to the objects or domains to be explored, and some other mode of relating these two aspects of cognition must be sought.

One might begin by saying that an operative system of transformations consists in reciprocal changes between states and that these states can only be characterised as configurations: thus the figurative aspect of knowledge would indicate the existence of, or represent, the perceived states of objects or events, while the operative aspect would have to do with their transformations. Both aspects would be mutually indispensable at the level where their unity became inevitable, but on the basis of a subordination of configurations to transformations: if the figurative aspect were left to itself and had to rely on its own capacities, it would give rise to all sorts of systematic illusions, being centred on the states of objects and lacking the corrective decentrations of transformations; whence the errors of perception (leaving aside the deficiencies found in imagery at sub-operational levels).

But this account, even if true, is quite inadequate, because the operative nature of knowledge in general, and the operative nature of intelligence in particular, leads, if its full meaning is brought out, to the antipodes of intellectualism. Intellectualism (which some call

357

idealism) dissociates subject from object and supposes, from the single fact of the existence of a 'pure' logic and mathematic, that the whole universe could be known and deduced by simple achievements of thought. But, in fact, the object imposes itself on the subject through interactions which must be dependent on experience,[1] even if it is necessary for the subject to act on the object and to reconstruct it in order to know it (this reconstruction attaining the object perhaps only to the extent to which, in mathematics, one tends towards a 'limit'). The essence of the operational concept of intelligence is to negate the existence of any radical dualism between experience and deduction. It considers experience to be a progressive structuring rather than a simple recording, and deduction to be a co-ordination of operations rather than simply an exercise in logic: since experience consists in acting on objects, and deductive operations consist of interiorised and co-ordinated actions, there is only a difference in degree (functionally speaking) between the structures of experience and deductive constructions. This difference results from the fact that in purely deductive constructions everything is either constructed or postulated, while in experimental constructions a certain amount of more or less important additional information has to be extracted from the facts. Furthermore, in a purely deductive construction, a configuration is only one of the states situated between, but strictly homogeneous with, two transformations. In experimental constructions, on the other hand, a configuration is not simply transformable as such, but provides factual knowledge which cannot be integrated completely with deduction, but only tends to become so. A number of fundamental consequences therefore emerge for the respective roles of figurative and operative aspects of knowledge (or of configurational and of transformational structures).

To understand these roles, we must again insist on the fact that logico-mathematical knowledge does not detach us from reality or from the world of objects, but only enlarges that world by incorporating it into the set of all possible events. Nevertheless, a remarkable concordance does exist between these possible frameworks, or some of them, and the data of experience, so that one can always construct a logico-mathematical theory of the physical phenomenon after the event and sometimes even predict it in advance. But it requires experience to decide which of the possible frameworks is the appropriate one, and even then mathematical deduction can only be applied approximately or statistically because the individual facts of experience will be resistant to such mathematical treatment. This resistance

[1] Even to a certain level of the formation of logico-mathematical operations, because a form of logico-mathematical experience, based on abstraction from action, exists over and beyond physical experience.

will be greater if the fact cannot be located within a previously made analysis of the factors involved, or if it forms part of a general flux of events, or if it is a chance event; these limitations illustrate the characteristic individual and irreversible originality of each particular event and considerably reinforce the obstacles to the integral deducibility of experience.

It is this partly-deducible, partly-nondeducible character of experience which explains the ambiguity of figural aspects of knowledge: they tend to take the form of organisations of configurations when they, the figural aspects, represent states of deducible transformations, but provide the only possible source of knowledge when they represent states, and transformations of states, which are not, or are not yet, deducible. This dual character of experience also explains the problems of filiation discussed in Chapter VI and VII: the figural structures of perception do not lie at the source of systems of operational transformations, but prefigure them indirectly (or by collateral kinship) in so far as they have already been structured by the operative structures involved in the relevant sensory-motor activity. We will not return to these questions of filiation but will restrict ourselves, in this conclusion, to those of knowledge.

Whenever the imbrications of the data of experience are such that the deductive construction of a particular experience cannot be completed, the significance of the figurative aspect of knowledge resides in the dual role it plays in the hindrance of that construction: (1) it provides indices (in the broad meaning of indices for perception) which tip the balance in favour of one rather than another of the possible deducible frameworks within which the experience could be interpreted; (2) it provides an approximate, and necessarily symbolic (in the broad sense of symbols for images), sketch of the given experience when the immediate nature of that experience, being mixed and fortuitously contingent, prevents its deduction in detail.

In other words, while operations elaborate general frameworks and tend to reduce the real to structures of deducible transformations, perception is of the *here and now* and serves the function of fitting each object or particular event into its available assimilative frameworks. Perception is not therefore the source of knowledge, because knowledge derives from the operative schemes of action as a whole. Perceptions function as connectors which establish constant and local contacts between actions or operations on the one hand, and objects or events on the other. Perceptual messages are transmitted in a figurative form, which is the only form available, and are decoded by being integrated, as far as possible, into the system of transformations.

The double nature or bipolarity of perceptions, and even of figural structures in general, thus becomes clear: they are polarised either towards the subject or towards the object, the distinction being less precise the more primitive they are.

In regard to its polarisation towards the object, the figurative aspect of knowledge is tied to the *here and now* and consequently does not allow comparisons to be made at sufficiently great spatio-temporal distances for the transformations to be structured. It is therefore limited to the construction of approximations to objective configurations, approximations which are based on sampling (centration and encounters) and whose means of co-ordination are restricted (incomplete couplings). The result is that, in regard to the object, perception is neither the source of knowledge (information provided by it acquiring significance only when assimilated to sensory-motor schemes), nor a reliable connector (information provided by it having to be completed and corrected before it can lead to assimilation).

At the subjective pole, however, perceptual activities themselves are already susceptible to some extent to these processes of elaboration and of correction. They are also susceptible (even while sedimenting into field effects) to early forms of assimilation and of schematisation under the influence of sensory-motor and then of representational activities. The figural aspect of knowledge tends, therefore, to be organised by the subject, through perceptual activities, into configurations which are homogeneous with the transformations. In other words, they can be used as links between two determinate transformations of a coherent system, and perception thus provides the connective service expected of it. A result is the apparent prefiguration of operational notions in perception and, thanks to a succession of contributions from higher levels, a reflection of the intelligible which is sufficiently consistent for sensualists and empiricists of every age to have been encouraged to attribute to it the origins of our knowledge.

Figural structures thus play a necessary part in knowledge, but a subordinate part on two counts. The first is that, once operational structures have been completed, figural structures correspond only to 'states' between which transformations are effected; the second is that, while the composite configurations to which figural structures give rise at pre- and at sub-operational levels then prefigure operational structures (to the extent that they have already been enriched by contributions from higher levels), they themselves continue to be subject to deformation (to the extent that they are not yet benefiting from the decentred perspective which is characteristic of systems of transformation).

§ 2. EMPIRICISM, APRIORISM AND INTERACTION BETWEEN THE SUBJECT AND THE OBJECT

The epistemological problem of perception occurs at two levels. The first concerns the classical problem raised by sensualists and empiricists: given that perception provides us with adequate knowledge of the object, to what extent does all knowledge derive from perception? The second concerns the same question at a more elementary level: to what extent, if at all, does perception provide us with adequate knowledge of the object?

I. There is no need to discuss the first problem again, our preferred solution having been explained in Chapters VI and VII. This solution rejects the idea that everything that is involved in intelligence has passed through the senses: '*Nisi ipse intellectus*' as Leibniz remarked profoundly, but it is still necessary to reach agreement on what is meant by *intellectus*. If it means the sensory-motor schemes and all the logic of action, then one can only agree with Leibniz. But if its meaning is restricted to the system of the operations of representational thought, then it would be wrong to concede to empiricism that the entire content of intelligence derives from the senses, because the schematisation of action contributes to that content (each succeeding structure providing a content for higher structures and a form for lower structures) even if the schemes as such are not perceptible. In other words, it is impossible simply to divide cognitive functions into perception ('the senses') and reason, because action as a whole is both the point of departure for reason and a continuous source of organisation and of reorganisation for perception.

However, the most telling reply to empiricism does not lie in this Leibnizian rationalism but rather in the reversal of positions effected by Kant in regard both to perception and to intelligence. Kant raised an insurmountable problem for the empiricist position when he pointed out that if space and time are *a priori* forms of 'sensibility', then an organisation of perceptual forms can originate within the subject himself. No doubt Kant was referring to a transcendental subject rather than to actual perceptual activities and real constructions. No doubt, too, he continued to be influenced by the traditional water-tight compartments of sensibility on one side and understanding on the other. But if we keep to the spirit of his pronouncement rather than to the letter, Kant was undoubtedly right in claiming that perception is organised from the outset, that it does not proceed from an association between isolated sensations, and that the

361

same subjective[1] sources which underly the categories of understanding underlie perceptual organisation. An analogous solution to the problem of the prefiguration of notions in perception (in its second aspect) was adopted in Chapters VI and VII. By adopting Michotte's formulation, it was stressed that prefiguration does not consist in an abstraction of notions from perception but rather in the fact that perceptions are structured in the same way as notions because they share sensory-motor roots.

II. But carrying epistemological questions right into the heart of perception raises the second problem concerning the relations between the subject and the object during the development of perceptual processes.

It is interesting to note that, as early as 1912, Gestalt theorists had transferred the original question of the relation between 'the senses' and 'reason' to their discussion of the relation between sensation and perception. *Nil est in perceptione quid non fuerit in sensu*, as G. E. Müller could have said to Köhler during their controversy. The latter could have replied: *nisi ipsa perceptio*, which is an indirect way of saying that there must be more in perception than the elementary recordings of sensation, because perception is farther removed from the object than sensation is. This raises two questions. To what extent is perception a 'copy', or at least a faithful translation, of the object, and to what extent does it make additions (such as transpositions and co-ordinations or, in brief, assimilations) to structures which derive from the activity of the subject? An examination of the positions adopted by various authors and schools shows that it is quite easy, on this exclusively perceptual level, to identify the principal epistemological positions adopted.

First of all, we have the classical union of associationism and empiricism. When Müller opposed the notion of Gestalt with that of 'an associative complex' achieved by automatic associations between elementary sensations, he provided a concept of perception which contained all that was necessary for the justification of the empiricist's theory of the knowledge-copy, the copy being perception itself. Pièron also was not far from such an explanatory model of perception, but corrected its possible epistemological interpretation at the end of his work 'La Sensation, Guide de Vie' by making the fundamental remark that sensation itself is only symbolic and provides a less accurate image of the object than mathematical equa-

[1] It is this same Kantian notion of the activity of the subject which no doubt inspired Karl Marx to one of his celebrated theses against Feuerback, in which he opposes 'sensibility as a practical activity on the part of man's senses' to 'sensible perception'.

tions do. The 'copy' has thus become an approximate translation, and Ampère was already making remarks of the same kind about the symbolic character of sensations.

There is no need to remind the reader that we base our principal objections to empiricism on the considerable contributions made to perceptual processes by the activities of the subject, and on the role played by choice or decision in those activities. The subject does not submit himself to the constraints of the object but directs his perceptual activities as if he were solving a problem: he explores, first choosing the points of centration, then relates objects to their contexts, transports, anticipates and so on. What is most remarkable is the number of steps involved in making even the most elementary estimation, such as of size: far from remaining simply receptive, the subject proceeds by a method of sampling, selecting the most profitable point of centration, hoping thereby to multiply encounters and to co-ordinate them by an exercise of couplings. It will be remembered that this distinction between the mechanisms of sampling and of coupling had to be introduced in connection with the law of temporal maxima to give expression to this more or less 'active' co-ordination which has to supplement the mere collection of information. When it becomes a question of the 'identification' of objects, even more complex activities are required, as the models of Bruner and of Bresson suggest when they introduce such concepts as 'filtering', temporal schemes, 'theories', 'decisions', etc. All of this argues against the notions of associationism.

Apriorist notions of perception are found in certain trends of the Gestalt school. We once made this identification, and Koffka reproached us for it, claiming that it was untenable. But even if the inspiration which guided Wertheimer, Köhler and Koffka is clearly phenomenological, it is still true that authors like Metzger interpret the most general geometric 'Gestalts' in an authentically Kantian sense[1] when they claim to discern in them those 'conditions of organisation which are preliminary to all experience'. We have already pointed out (§ 2, I) that the idea of perceptual schematisation, whose importance the present work has underlined, is subject to a similar inspiration, but in the sense of a genetic and not a transcendental construction. For this reason we could not follow Metzger in his properly called apriorism, because the perceptual conditions which are supposed to be preliminary to experience are not necessarily *anterior* to it: it may rather be a question of processes of equilibrium which intervene after, but not before, the subject's first contacts with the object. These processes would then govern that experience from

[1] Metzger publicly confirmed this at a meeting of La Société suisse de Psychologie.

the beginning by supplying the immanent (but not transcendental) conditions of its structuring.

This recourse to laws of equilibrium and to the assumption of a fundamental interaction between subject and object are characteristic of phenomenological aspects of the Gestalt position, and the role that we attribute to these two general notions has been seen in the present work. However, our concept of equilibrium is not identical with that of the Gestaltists. This is particularly so because our view of the interaction between subject and object appears to be quite different from that which the founders of Gestalt theory borrowed from phenomenology. The notion of perceptual equilibrium suggested by the facts is not that of a physical field with an exact and automatic balance of the forces present, but rather of an active compensation brought about by the subject, one which tends to moderate external disturbances. This active compensation is particularly noticeable in those over-compensations which appear as over-constancies (Chapter IV): they suggest precautions against error rather than a mechanical equilibrium.

In general, the interaction between subject and object is not brought about by a form of organisation which is independent of development and which has no genesis. On the contrary, the interaction is due to an endless construction of new schemes by the subject during his development, schemes to which he assimilates the perceived objects and in which there are no definable boundaries between the properties of the assimilated object and the structures of the assimilating subject. As we have already said in the Introduction, it is necessary to oppose the geneticism without structure of empiricism and the structuralism without genesis of Gestalt phenomenology with a genetic structuralism in which each structure is the product of a genesis and each genesis merely the passage from a less evolved structure to a more complex one. It is in this context of an active structuring that the exchanges between subject and object take place.

What, then, is the nature of such exchanges, and to what extent do they allow us to think of perception as being adequate to the object? The same conclusions apply to perception as to all knowledge: (1) objectivity is constructed on the basis of, and in proportion to, the activities of the subject; (2) the initial state of each process does not provide the properties of the object but an undifferentiated mixture of the contributions of the subject and of the object; (3) it is by decentring himself from these initial states that the subject succeeds in gaining control over his structures, by co-ordinating them, and in simultaneously attaining the specific characteristics of the object by correcting deformations produced by his initial centrations.

(1) Objectivity is constructed in perception, as in other domains,

on the basis of the activity of the subject because, while the most immediate contact with the object is provided by field effects, these also produce the greatest deformations. These deformations are in principle then corrected by perceptual activities (during which the role of the subject is certainly greater) which lead to a more adequate representation of the object. It is true that these activities also produce secondary errors, because of the recentrations to which they give rise, but these secondary errors obey the same laws as primary effects, and are, in their turn, moderated by new perceptual activities from higher levels.

(2) However adequate the representation of the object achieved by these perceptual activities may be, the initial state from which each process of the achievement of objectivity starts (for example, the initial centrations from which attempts to explore or to relate the object to a context originate) is even less 'objective'. It will consist of a mixture of information about the object and of relations provided by the subject, both of which contain certain factors which contribute to, and others which detract from, the adequacy of the representation.

While the object does, of course, bring certain of its properties to the situation, various factors hinder its adequate attainment. For example, it may not be immediately perceptible as a whole because it is too big, too complex, or because its context is too complicated; or the duration of its exposure may be so short that it has to be represented by only a few encounters; or, if it does arouse several centrations, later ones may override the earlier ones, etc.

Similarly, although the subject does seek out certain objective relations as soon as his co-ordinating activities are put into operation, he is, nevertheless, himself a source of deformation. This is because what he perceives is always relative to his perspective, which is both private and initially unco-ordinated (for example, the effects of centration).

(3) In the end, the relative adequacy of any perception to any object depends on a constructive process and not on an immediate contact. During this constructive process the subject tries to make use of whatever information he has, incomplete, deformed or false as it may be, and to build it into a system which corresponds as nearly as possible to the properties of the object. He can only do this by a method which is both cumulative and corrective, and which, in perception, is based on decentration or on a consideration of successive centrations which correct one another's deformations. It is of great interest to find this event of decentration occurring even at the perceptual level, because it appears in one form or another as a necessary condition for cognitive adaptation at all levels of the elaboration of knowledge. It is only by decentring himself from himself that the subject manages

to escape from factors which are called 'subjective' because they are deforming, and to adopt activities which are also called 'subjective' (but in quite another sense) because they are co-ordinating, and which allow him to achieve objectivity.

Thus, the dual nature of perception recurs throughout this work. Source of systematic errors on the one hand, but mirror and indirect prefiguration of intelligence on the other, perception enjoys no special privileges in the conquest of the object. To the extent that it attains the object *here and now*, which is its original function, it runs the constant risk of deforming it, as in the effects of centration; to the extent that it grasps the object with a relative adequacy, it takes its place in the general current of cognitive structures which, from sensory-motor to operational levels, obey common functional conditions, one of the most remarkable of which is that of decentration.

APPENDIX

The *Concentric and Clinical Method* of measuring thresholds used in the situations described in this book originated in the author's laboratory. The brief description of it given below was abstracted and translated from a longer description written by B. Matalon (lately of the University of Geneva) and dated 26th December 1957. Unless otherwise stated, it may be assumed that this method was used in each of the experiments described and when that experiment was conducted in the author's laboratory.

I. The concentric and clinical method is a quick way of measuring geometrical illusions. It embodies two principles:

1. The alternate presentation of variables perceived by the subject to be larger or smaller than the standard, while closing in on the point of subjective equality (*P.S.E.*).

2. The presentation of variables in an order determined by the responses of the subject so that they are distributed symmetrically around his *P.S.E.* and follow any shifts of this *P.S.E.*

II. An initial series of variables is presented in a more or less random fashion to find the subject's approximate *P.S.E.*

On the basis of this approximation, a series of variables is chosen which includes the tentative *P.S.E.* value. This group of variables (or series) is presented concentrically, beginning with the variables farthest from the *P.S.E.*

When the whole series has been given, it can be decided from the subject's judgements whether it is necessary to use other variables in order to keep the *P.S.E.* in the centre of the series. If not, the same series is given again, but with the order reversed. For example, if the first series (not presented in the order shown) gives the following result:

$$1\ \ 2\ \ 3\ \ 4\ \ 5\ \ 6\ \ 7\ \ 8\ \ 9 \quad \text{Variables}$$
$$-\ -\ +\ -\ +\ -\ +\ +\ + \quad \text{Judgements}$$

it may be assumed that the variables, 3, 4, 5 and 6 include the *P.S.E.*: the series is then presented again, perhaps, in the order: 1 8 2 7 3 6 4 5, 9 being omitted. Suppose the judgements are then:

$$1\ \ 2\ \ 3\ \ 4\ \ 5\ \ 6\ \ 7\ \ 8$$
$$-\ -\ -\ -\ -\ +\ +\ +$$

the assumption is made that the *P.S.E.* lies between 5 and 6, and

367

the next variables taken will be 3 to 9 in the order: 9 3 4 8 4 7 5 6. This time the result may be:

$$3 \quad 4 \quad 5 \quad 6 \quad 7 \quad 8 \quad 9$$
$$- \quad - \quad - \quad + \quad + \quad + \quad +$$

This seems to confirm that the *P.S.E.* lies between 5 and 6. Variable 9 can now be omitted and the series 3 to 8 can be given in the order: 8 3 7 4 6 5. If the *P.S.E.* has not shifted, the same series can be given in the order: 3 8 4 7 5 6.

The inversion of the order has two advantages:

1. It breaks the alternation of the judgements 'larger' and 'smaller' without involving the use of traps (variables outside the series) whose arbitrary inclusion might affect succeeding judgements.

2. The critical variables (in this case 5 and 6) are presented sometimes after larger, sometimes after smaller variables, which tends to balance out contrast effects.

Judgements are tracked in this way until enough information seems to have been collected.

III. The *P.S.E.* may be calculated in various but widely understood ways, which need not be reviewed here.

IV. The concentric method has various advantages and disadvantages.

1. It has the advantage of being quick, since it reduces to a minimum the presentations of variables which are distant from the *P.S.E.* and which provide no information.

2. The alternation of variables which are larger and smaller than the standard to some extent balances out contrast effects without the need for the large number of variables and presentations which a random method requires.

3. By letting the subject, in a sense, choose for himself the part of the scale which he will be shown, no information is given to him about the limits of the scale which might lead to false responses in terms of anchoring effects, etc.

4. Since different subjects are experiencing variables around their own *P.S.Es*, their experiences are comparable.

5. The concentric method reveals and permits examination of systematic temporal variations.

On the other hand:

1. The method of defining the *P.S.E.* is not unique. However, this disadvantage is shared by most psycho-physical methods.

2. Systematising the order of the presentations could itself bring about systematic effects.

3. It leaves a certain amount to the subjective judgement of the experimenter.

V. In conclusion, the concentric and clinical method seems a good solution when a quick experiment is required (which is often essential with children), when the maximum information is required on contrast effects and when it is considered desirable to adapt the procedure to each individual subject.

LIST OF *RECHERCHES*

Recherches sur le Développement des Perceptions originally published in *Archives de Psychologie* are listed below showing the title, author's name, date, volume and page numbers. In the original publications serial and volume numbers are given in Roman numerals.

1. *Introduction à l'étude des perceptions chez l'enfant et analyse d'une illusion relative à la perception visuelle de cercles concentriques (Delbœuf)*, J. Piaget, M. Lambercier, E. Bœsch, and Barbara von Albertini, 1942, **29**, 1–107.
2. *La comparaison visuelle des hauteurs à distances variables dans le plan fronto-parallèle*, J. Piaget, and M. Lambercier, 1943, **29**, 173–253.
3. *Le problème de la comparaison visuelle en profondeur (constance des grandeurs) et l'erreur systématique de l'étalon*, J. Piaget, and M. Lambercier, 1943, **29**, 255–308.
4. *Essai d'interprétation probabiliste de la loi de Weber et de celle des centrations relatives*, J. Piaget, 1945, **30**, 95–138.
5. *Essai sur un effet d''Einstellung' survenant au cours de perceptions visuelles successives (effet Usnadze)*, J. Piaget, and M. Lambercier, 1945, **30**, 139–96
6. *La constance des grandeurs en comparaisons sériales*, M. Lambercier, 1946, **31**, 82–282.
7. *La configuration en profondeur dans la constance des grandeurs*, M. Lambercier, 1946, **31**, 287–325.
8. *Transpositions perceptives et transitivité opératoire dans les comparaisons en profondeur*, J. Piaget, and M. Lambercier, 1946, **31**, 325–68.
9. *L'évolution des comparaisons de longueurs de l'enfant à l'adulte*, H. Würsten, 1947, **32**, 1–144.
10. *Les illusions relatives aux angles et à la longueur de leurs côtés*, J. Piaget, H. Würsten, and L. Johannot, 1949, **32**, 281–307.
11. *L'illusion de Müller–Lyer*, J. Piaget, and Barbara von Albertini, 1950, **33**, 1–48.
12. *La comparaison des grandeurs projectives chez l'enfant et chez l'adulte*, J. Piaget, and M. Lambercier, 1951, **33**, 81–130.
13. *La perception d'un carré animé d'un mouvement de circumduction (effet Auersperg et Buhrmester)*, J. Piaget, and M. Lambercier, 1951, **33**, 131–95.
14. *Recherche sur le développement de la perception du mouvement avec l'âge (mouvement apparent, dit stroboscopique)*, Maria-Martha Gantenbein, 1952, **33**, 197–294.
15. *La comparaison des différences de hauteur dans le plan fronto-parallèle*, J. Piaget, and M. Lambercier, 1953, **34**, 73–107.
16. *L'estimation perceptive des côtés du rectangle*, J. Piaget, and Marianne Denis-Prinzhorn, 1953, **34**, 109–31.
17. *L'évolution de l'illusion d'Oppel–Kundt en fonction de l'âge*, J. Piaget, and P. A. Osterreith, 1953, **34**, 1–38.
18. *La résistance des bonnes formes à l'illusion de Müller–Lyer*, J. Piaget, F. Maire, and F. Privat, 1954, **34**, 155–202.
19. *Observations sur la perception des bonnes formes chez l'enfant par actualisation des lignes virtuelles*, J. Piaget, and Barbara Stettler-von Albertini, 1954, **34**, 203–42.
20. *L'action des facteurs spatiaux et temporels de centration dans l'estimation visuelle des longueurs*, J. Piaget, and A. Morf, 1954, **34**, 243–88.

INDEX

Note: Where appropriate, page references to principal definitions have been given (marked 'df.').

In the case of other central topics, page numbers have been given in two forms: major references in bold type, minor references in normal type.

In a few cases, the words given may not be found on the page listed but the topic to which they refer will. This has been made necessary by the author's and the translator's frequent use of paraphrase and synonym.

INDEX OF CONTENTS

INDEX OF AUTHORS

383